The Cambridge Companion to Contempora

In the last fifty years Irish poets have produced some of the most etry in contemporary literature, writing about love and sexuality, violence and history, country and city. This book provides a unique introduction to major figures such as Seamus Heaney, but also introduces the reader to significant precursors like, Louis MacNeice or Patrick Kavanagh, and vital contemporaries and successors: among others, Thomas Kinsella, Nuala Ní Dhomhnaill and Paul Muldoon. Readers will find discussions of Irish poetry from the traditional to the modernist, written in Irish as well as English, from both North and South. This *Companion* provides cultural and historical background to contemporary Irish poetry in the contexts of modern Ireland but also in the broad currents of modern world literature. It includes a chronology and guide to further reading and will prove invaluable to students and teachers alike.

THE CAMBRIDGE
COMPANION TO

CONTEMPORARY IRISH POETRY

EDITED BY

MATTHEW CAMPBELL

CAMBRIDGE
UNIVERSITY PRESS

PUBLISHED BY THE PRESS SYNDICATE OF THE UNIVERSITY OF CAMBRIDGE
The Pitt Building, Trumpington Street, Cambridge CB2 1RP, United Kingdom

CAMBRIDGE UNIVERSITY PRESS
The Edinburgh Building, Cambridge, CB2 2RU, UK
40 West 20th Street, New York, NY 10011–4211, USA
477 Williamstown Road, Port Melbourne, VIC 3207, Australia
Ruiz de Alarcón 13, 28014 Madrid, Spain
Dock House, The Waterfront, Cape Town 8001, South Africa

http://www.cambridge.org

© Cambridge University Press 2003

First published 2003

Printed in the United Kingdom at the University Press, Cambridge

Typeface Sabon 10/13 pt.   *System* LATEX 2$_\varepsilon$ [TB]

A catalogue record for this book is available from the British Library

ISBN 0 521 81301 8 hardback
ISBN 0 521 01245 7 paperback

CONTENTS

CONTRIBUTORS

JONATHAN ALLISON is Associate Professor of English at the University of Kentucky, and Director of the Yeats Summer School, Sligo. His publications include *Yeats's Political Identities* (1996), *Patrick Kavanagh: A Reference Guide* (1996), *Poetry and Contemporary Culture*, edited with Andrew Roberts (2002) and *Poetry for Young People: William Butler Yeats* (2002).

GUINN BATTEN is Associate Professor of English at Washington University in St Louis. The author of *The Orphaned Imagination: Melancholy and Commodity Culture in English Romanticism* (1998) and a co-editor of *Romantic Generations: Essays in Honor of Robert F. Gleckner*, she is currently completing *The Muse of the Minus: Ideology and Alterity in Recent Irish Poetry*.

FRAN BREARTON is lecturer in English at Queen's University Belfast. She is the author of *The Great War in Irish Poetry: W.B. Yeats to Michael Longley* (2001) and co-editor of *Last before America: Irish and American Writing* (2001).

TERENCE BROWN is Professor of Anglo-Irish literature at Trinity College, Dublin. He is also a Fellow of the College and a member of the Royal Irish Academy and of Academia Europaea. He has published and lectured widely on Irish writing in English and on Irish cultural history. His most recent book is *The Life of W.B. Yeats: A Critical Biography* (1999, 2001). He was awarded an honorary CMG in the New Year's Honours List in 2002 for his contribution to Anglo-Irish relations.

MATTHEW CAMPBELL is Senior Lecturer in English Literature at the University of Sheffield. He is the author of *Rhythm and Will in Victorian Poetry* (1999) and editor of books on Victorian, modern and contemporary literature. He has published a number of articles on English and Irish poetry.

LUCY COLLINS was educated at Trinity College Dublin and at Harvard University. She has published on twentieth-century Irish poetry, especially on contemporary women poets and has an additional research interest in American poetry of the 1950s and 1960s. She is currently a lecturer in English at St Martin's College, Carlisle.

ALEX DAVIS is Senior Lecturer in English at University College, Cork. He is the author of *A Broken Line: Denis Devlin and Irish Poetic Modernism* (2000) and co-editor of two collections of essays, *Modernism and Ireland: The Poetry of the 1930s* (1995) and *Locations of Literary Modernism: Region and Nation in British and American Modernist Poetry* (2000).

ROBERT FAGGEN is Professor of Literature at Claremont McKenna College and the author of *Robert Frost and the Challenge of Darwin* and editor of *The Cambridge Companion to Robert Frost, Early Poems of Robert Frost, Selected Poems of E.A. Robinson* and *Striving Towards Being: The Letters of Thomas Merton and Czeslaw Milosz.*

JOHN GOODBY is a Senior Lecturer in the Department of English, University of Wales Swansea. He has published widely on Irish and British poetry and his recent publications include *Irish Poetry Since 1950: From Stillness Into History* (2000) and *Under the Spelling Wall: The Critical Fates of Dylan Thomas* (2003). He is the co-editor of *Colonies of Belief: Ireland's Modernists* (Angel Exhaust 17, 1999), *Dylan Thomas: A New Casebook* (2001) and *Irish Studies: the Essential Glossary* (2003). A collection of poetry, *A Birmingham Yank*, was published by Arc in 1998.

DILLON JOHNSTON has published two editions of *Irish Poetry after Joyce* (1985 and 1997) and *The Poetic Economies of England and Ireland* (2001) and many essays, mostly about Irish and British poetry. He was founder and director of Wake Forest University Press. He currently directs the Creative Writing Program in Washington University in St Louis.

PETER McDONALD is Christopher Tower Student and Tutor in Poetry in the English Language at Christ Church, Oxford. His published poetry includes *Biting the Wax* (1989), *Adam's Dream* (1996) and *As If* (2001). He is the author of *Louis MacNeice: The poet in his contexts* (1991), *Mistaken Identities: Poetry and Northern Ireland* (1997) and *Serious Poetry: Form and Authority from Yeats to Hill* (2002). He co-edited *Selected Plays of Louis MacNeice* (1993) and is the editor of the forthcoming edition of *The Collected Poems of Louis MacNeice.*

SHANE MURPHY is a lecturer at the School of English and Film Studies, University of Aberdeen. He has published articles on Seamus Heaney, Brian

Friel, Paul Muldoon and Medbh McGuckian, and works on intertextuality in contemporary Irish writing and the visual arts.

FRANK SEWELL is Lecturer in Creative Writing and Irish Literature at the University of Ulster. He is the author of *Modern Irish Poetry: A New Alhambra* (2000) and translator of Cathal Ó Searcaigh's *Out in the Open* (1997).

DAVID WHEATLEY lectures in English at the University of Hull. He is the author of two collections of poetry, *Thirst* (1997) and *Misery Hill* (2000) and co-editor with Justin Quinn of *Metre* magazine. He writes on poetry for many publications, including *The Times Literary Supplement*, *The Guardian* and *The London Review of Books*. He is currently writing a book on contemporary British poetry for Cambridge University Press.

PREFACE

Much has happened to Irish poetry since October 1916, when Yeats wrote about the nine-and-fifty swans that he saw at Coole Park:

> Unwearied still, lover by lover
> They paddle in the cold
> Companionable streams or climb the air;
> Their hearts have not grown old;
> Passion or conquest, wander where they will,
> Attend upon them still.
>
> ('The Wild Swans at Coole')

We might expect 'Passion or conquest', love and war, from the Irish poem. Indeed such epic material must 'attend' Yeats's wandering swans, servile to the history which follows them. The reader, too, Yeats seems to demand, must 'Attend upon them still', to concentrate on hard stuff: mysticism, history, poetry. These lines, though, are about more than coldness and power. Swans may be imperious in flight, but on the water they 'paddle', and it is hard to disconnect this word from the bathos of tentative human paddling or the comic duck. While the poem imagines immortality, and a long history of power and desire, it also has time for what the swans might say for us, more grounded, creatures. These are love birds, and their paddling is in 'cold / Companionable streams': the swans are companionable with the cold water and one another. They are also, adapting Coleridge, 'companionable forms', the chance discovery of something fluttering, paddling or soaring in nature which is analogous to the passion or conquest which preoccupies poet and reader. The swans provide the company of symbol for Yeats, as his symbol may do in turn for his readers.

Yeats's swans are 'brilliant creatures', and this Companion looks at the continuation of the 'brilliant creatures' of the generations of Irish poets which followed. Yeats shadows some of the following pages, but one of the stories they tell is of a sense of confidence and cultural achievement no longer dependent on cultivating heroic indifference or intellectual disdain. The companionable streams of this book are those occupied by a poetry finding its feet among the traumatic times of the divided island of Ireland in the latter half of the twentieth century. Yeats might have recognised the rural and parochial concerns of much of the writing, even if he might not have approved of the ambivalence of its attitude to its own pastoralism. He might also have recognised the meditation on historic events, local or international. But this meditation may speak less of passion or conquest, and more in the voice of the 'Lost people of Treblinka or Pompeii' in Derek Mahon's great poem of 1975, 'A Disused Shed in County Wexford'. They cry: ' "Let the God not abandon us / Who have come so far in darkness or in pain / We too had our lives to live." '

It is hoped that this book will be companionable for those who seek to understand the history and development of Irish poetry in the second half of the twentieth century. Its chapters focus on individual figures, groups of poets or important movements and sub-periods within the broadly 'contemporary'. The usual dates for what this word might mean in Irish literary history vex many commentators. Frequently its threshold is placed around the deaths of Yeats and James Joyce, in 1939 and 1941 respectively. Others though, like Mahon along with Peter Fallon in their Penguin selection of contemporary Irish verse, would rather that the 'contemporary' referred to those who are still writing. This book opts for a middle way: the example of Yeats, say, may be taken as given, but the work of Patrick Kavanagh or Louis MacNeice or Seán Ó Ríordáin still reverberates for living Irish poets, some of whom still work within or against their differing examples.

No less contentious is the notion of what constitutes 'Irish' verse, since Irish literature continues to be written in the UK, Europe or the US. It is also written in two languages, English and Irish (when speaking in English, the 'Gaelic' poet would nowadays say that he or she speaks and writes in 'Irish'). Ireland as well, might ostensibly be said to be two places, the twenty-six counties of the Republic of Ireland and the six counties of Northern Ireland, a state which is still part of the United Kingdom. This book offers no solutions to these questions, but attempts to be a companion to those who would wish to encounter the range of poetry written by Irish men and women, parochial and international, Irish and English, North and South.

The chapters in this Companion also suggest the breadth of the practice of Irish poetry in its local and international contexts and the range of its forms, giving some sense of the characteristic imagery, metric and aesthetic scruple of the Irish poem, while allowing a grasp of both continuity and tradition and the innovatory and the new. The 'relevance' of the Irish poem is not just to Irish history or politics, important and pressing as that must always be. It is also to many of the reasons why we read poems, looking to answer questions relating to passion – love and sexuality, longing and loss – as well as conquest. The American critic and publisher Dillon Johnston here describes the current brilliant generation of Irish poets as likely to be remembered for their quality along with other great literary generations, the Elizabethan, Jacobean and Romantic English poets and those American poets who followed the Depression. This book seeks to be companionable with those brilliant creatures and the place from which they have come.

Ray Ryan at Cambridge University Press set this book in motion and has watched it with vigilant enthusiasm throughout its preparation. Initial planning is indebted to the comments of four anonymous readers at the Press and the contributions of David Ford and Kevin Taylor. Thanks are due to Martin Fanning of Four Courts Press and David Crone for the cover illustration. The editor would also like to acknowledge the contributions and advice of Alex Arnison, Brian Campbell, Claire Connolly, Valerie Cotter, Alex Houen, Dillon Johnston and Neil Roberts.

CHRONOLOGY

1939   January, death of W.B. Yeats. September, 1939, outbreak of war: Ireland neutral. Louis MacNeice, *Autumn Journal.*

1941   January, death of James Joyce.

1942   Patrick Kavanagh, *The Great Hunger.*

1945   End of Second World War. Labour landslide in United Kingdom.

1946   Denis Devlin, *Lough Derg.*

1949   Republic of Ireland declared and Republic leaves the British Commonwealth. Ireland Act passed by Westminster Parliament, guaranteeing status of Northern Ireland within UK.

1950   Death of George Bernard Shaw.

1951   Noel Browne's 'Mother and Child' scheme fails in the Republic.

1952   Seán Ó Ríordáin, *Eireaball Spideoige.*

1955   Austin Clarke, *Ancient Lights.*

1957   Máirtín Ó Direáin, *Ó Mórna agus Dánta Eile.*

1958   John Montague, *Forms of Exile.* Thomas Kinsella, *Another September.*

1959   Eamon De Valera becomes President and Sean Lemass becomes Taoiseach.

1960   Patrick Kavanagh, *Come Dance with Kitty Stobling and Other Poems.* Derek Mahon and Michael Longley begin publishing in *Icarus* magazine in Dublin.

1961   Radio Telefís Eireann (RTE) begins broadcasting.

1962   Thomas Kinsella, *Downstream.*

1963   Death of Louis MacNeice. Philip Hobsbaum arrives at Queen's University, Belfast and forms 'The Group'. Richard Murphy, *Sailing to an Island.* Máirtín Ó Direáin, *Ar Ré Dheoróil.*

1964   Patrick Kavanagh, *Collected Poems.* Seán Ó Ríordáin, *Brosna.*

1966   Celebrations for Fiftieth Anniversary of 1916 Easter Rising. Austin Clarke, *Mnemosyne Lay in the Dust.* Seamus Heaney, *Death of a Naturalist.*

1967   January, Civil Rights Association formed in Northern Ireland.
        Death of Patrick Kavanagh. Eavan Boland, *New Territory*. Thomas
        Kinsella, *Nightwalker*.

1968   October, Clashes between police and civil rights marchers in Derry.
        The Honest Ulsterman founded in Belfast by James Simmons.
        Richard Murphy, *The Battle of Aughrim*. Derek Mahon, *Night
        Crossing*.

1969   January, Civil rights marchers attacked at Burntollet Bridge, outside
        Derry. Riots in Derry. British troops arrive August. Samuel Beckett
        wins Nobel Prize. Michael Longley, *No Continuing City*. Thomas
        Kinsella, *The Táin*.

1970   Establishment of Provisional IRA. *Innti* founded in Cork with
        Michael Davitt as editor.

1971   August, British government introduce internment without trial.

1972   Death toll of 496 in political violence. January, thirteen shot dead
        by British troops at Bloody Sunday in Derry; April, Widgery Report
        exonerates army. Thomas Kinsella, *Butcher's Dozen*. Suspension of
        Northern Ireland parliament and Direct Rule from Westminster
        introduced in North. July, nine killed and 130 wounded by
        twenty-one IRA bombs on Bloody Friday in Belfast. Seamus
        Heaney, *Wintering Out*. Derek Mahon, *Lives*. John Montague,
        The Rough Field.

1973   Republic enters European Economic Community. Michael Longley,
        An Exploded View. Paul Muldoon, *New Weather*. Thomas
        Kinsella, *New Poems*.

1974   Birmingham bomb (IRA) kills twenty-one. Dublin bombs (UVF) kill
        twenty-five. Death of Austin Clarke.

1977   Eiléan Ní Chuilleanáin, *The Second Voyage*.

1975   Michael Hartnett, *A Farewell to English*. Seamus Heaney, *North*.
        Derek Mahon, *The Snow Party*.

1979   August, Murder of Lord Mountbatten and eighteen British soldiers
        at Warrenpoint on same day. Seamus Heaney, *Field Work*.

1980   October, beginning of first hunger strike by Republican prisoners in
        the Maze Prison. Tom Paulin, *The Strange Museum*.

1981   May, death of Bobby Sands on hunger strike; by October, nine more
        prisoners had died. Nuala Ní Dhomhnaill, *An Dealg Droighin*. Seán
        Ó Tuama and Thomas Kinsella, *An Duanaire, 1600–1900: Poems
        of the Dispossessed*. Medbh McGuckian, *The Flower Master*.

1982   Derek Mahon, *The Hunt By Night*.

1983   Abortion referendum in Republic. Gerry Adams elected
        Westminster MP. Brendan Kennelly, *Cromwell*. Paul Muldoon,
        Quoof. Tom Paulin, *Liberty Tree*.

1984   British Prime Minister Margaret Thatcher survives Brighton bomb
        attack. Seamus Heaney, *Station Island*.

1985   October, signing of Anglo-Irish (Hillsborough) Agreement between
        British and Irish governments. 'Ulster Says No' campaign. Paul
        Durcan, *The Berlin Wall Café*.

1986   Republic votes against divorce in referendum.

1987   November, eleven killed in Remembrance Day bomb at Enniskillen.
        Ciaran Carson, *The Irish for No*. Seamus Heaney, *The Haw
        Lantern*.

1989   Death of Samuel Beckett.

1990   Election of Mary Robinson as President. Eavan Boland, *Outside
        History*. Nuala Ní Dhomhnaill, *Pharoah's Daughter*.

1991   Michael Longley, *Gorse Fires*. Eiléan Ní Chuilleanáin, *The Brazen
        Serpent*. Publication of *Field Day Anthology of Irish Writing*.

1993   Downing Street declaration of no British 'strategic interest' in
        Northern Ireland. Cathal Ó Searcaigh, *Homecoming / An Bealach
        'na Bhaile*.

1994   IRA ceasefire.

1995   Divorce referendum passed in Republic. First Drumcree
        confrontation in Northern Ireland. Seamus Heaney receives Nobel
        Prize. Eavan Boland, *Collected Poems*.

1996   Renewal of IRA violence in England. Seamus Heaney, *The Spirit
        Level*.

1997   New IRA ceasefire. Mary McAleese elected President.

1998   Good Friday Agreement; May, joint referenda accepting it North
        and South. August, Omagh bomb planted by dissident Republicans,
        twenty-nine die. John Hume and David Trimble receive Nobel
        Peace Prize. Seamus Heaney, *Opened Ground*.

1999   Northern Ireland Assembly meets, briefly, in Belfast for first time.
        Flood committee hearings begin to investigate political corruption
        in South. Derek Mahon, *Collected Poems*.

2000   Assembly revived, with nationalist and unionist ministers in cabinet.

2001   Thomas Kinsella, *Collected Poems*. Paul Muldoon, *Poems
        1968–1998*. Seamus Heaney, *Electric Light*.

2002   Publication of *The Field Day Anthology of Irish Writing: The
        Women's Tradition*.

I

MATTHEW CAMPBELL

Ireland in poetry: 1999, 1949, 1969

I

Ireland in 1999 appeared to be ending its trouble-strewn twentieth century as a remarkably prosperous, culturally confident and optimistic place. The Good Friday agreement of the previous year had moved the Northern Irish Peace Process further towards the cessation of the thirty years of violence that since 1969 had cost more than 3,500 lives. The new Northern Ireland Assembly met, briefly, for the first time. Capitalising on the benefits of a highly-educated workforce, the Irish embraced an increasingly globalised market. The Irish phenomenon of rapid growth based on foreign investment in new technologies mirrored the achievements of Asia, and the Irish economy became known as the 'Celtic Tiger'. To the world, though, Ireland still had the glamour of its ancient traditions, music and poetry. It represented a mix of authenticity and the intellectual and spiritual integrity of a cultural development which the popular stage hit of the 1990s, *Riverdance*, pictured stretching forwards from pre-history.

Irish literature was widely represented in the bookshops and campuses of the anglophone world, and new Irish poetry shared in that world's appetite for Irish music, cinema and art. Translated into many languages, the poet Seamus Heaney had received the Nobel Prize in 1995 and was a Harvard and Oxford Professor. The President of the United States, Bill Clinton, was so taken by the miracles of justice envisaged in a chorus from Heaney's 1990 version of Sophocles' *Philoctetes*, *The Cure at Troy*, that he hung a copy of it on the wall of his study in the White House. Heaney's chorus desired that 'hope and history might rhyme', and Clinton couldn't resist yoking it to his hometown of Hope, Arkansas in the title of his 1996 campaign manifesto, *Between Hope and History*.[1] Yet Heaney's international success had followed those of his fellow poets, Thomas Kinsella and John Montague, who had both held prestigious posts at American universities. Eavan Boland, Nuala Ní Dhomhnaill and Derek Mahon were to follow. Paul

Muldoon was Professor in Princeton, and soon to be Oxford Professor of Poetry.

Irish poetry appeared to be thriving, in Ireland and further afield, as writing from a small country on the Atlantic seaboard of Europe assumed central importance for readers of contemporary literature in Ireland, Britain and the USA. In the years around 1999 a succession of prestigious collected or selected editions of Irish poets appeared, along with substantial and internationally-read anthologies. The 1990s had begun with the publication of the monumental *Field Day Anthology of Irish Writing*, and its three volumes represented over a thousand years of writing in Latin, Irish and English. The anthology had its detractors, particularly those who felt it laid too much emphasis on the politics of Irish literature, or those who felt that it downplayed writing by Irish women. The literary history of the 1990s, though, tells of a renaissance of women's writing, for the stage and in fiction, as well as by poets. By 2000, an influential US-published anthology, *The Wake Forest Book of Irish Women's Poetry* portrayed a wide-ranging and diverse canon of writing. In 2002, two further volumes of the *Field Day* anthology appeared, a massive act of collaborative scholarship dedicated to the women's tradition in Irish writing.

Significant collections of Irish poetry, by men and women, in English and Irish, were also published by English, American and Irish presses throughout the 1990s. In 1999 the Irish-based Gallery Press published Derek Mahon's *Collected Poems*, and further substantial collections appeared from Richard Murphy and Pearse Hutchinson in 2000 and 2002. The British publishers Faber and Faber, and the American press Farrar Straus and Giroux, had long supported Irish poetry, and they published Seamus Heaney's *Opened Ground: Poems 1966–1996* in 1998. In 2001, Paul Muldoon's *Collected Poems, 1968–1998* also gathered together thirty prolific years of writing. Thomas Kinsella produced his second collected volume within ten years, from the British press Carcanet in 2001. Carcanet published Eavan Boland's *Collected Poems* in 1995, and she was also published by Norton in the United States. The work of Irish language poets, Nuala Ní Dhomhnaill and Cathal Ó Searcaigh, appeared in handsome collaborative volumes, translated by leading Irish poets of the day. Irish poetry readings filled auditoria, with Ní Dhomhnaill, Brendan Kennelly and Paul Durcan popular performers of their poems and satiric commentators on the public realm. Durcan's 1999 volume, *Greetings from our Friends in Brazil* contained a long elegy written for the twenty-nine people who had died in the Omagh bombing of the previous year, but it also contained poems about the years in which Mary Robinson had been the first woman President of Ireland. Supporter of the arts, dedicatee of volumes by Durcan and Boland, she was one of the great liberalising influences on a changing Ireland. She was later to serve as a United Nations High Commissioner.

However, the investigations begun in 1999 by the Flood Tribunal in the Republic of Ireland, were the most prominent reminder of the corruption that had long attended southern Irish public life. Neither was optimism encouraged by the atrocity at Omagh nor the difficulties that the new Northern Ireland Assembly experienced in its early meetings. Nonetheless, constitutional and social change had come. In Northern Ireland, the devolved powers granted to the Northern Ireland Assembly matched those the Labour government of the United Kingdom had granted to similar assemblies in Scotland and Wales. From the 1980s onwards, not only politicians, but also historians, novelists, poets, critics and journalists, had shared new ways of thinking about the culture and history of Ireland, in relation to Britain, Europe and beyond. This being Ireland, controversy attended every part of this new thinking, but it centred around assumptions about its history as a colonised and now postcolonial country, and of the challenge of its new status as an important part of the European Union in a global market. There was still the continuing fact of the partition of the island, and other divisions existed, social and economic as well as sectarian and political. But these began to take new forms.

Emigration, for instance, has long been a fact of Irish life, and much Irish writing still took place outside Ireland. The enormous popular success of Irish-American writer Frank McCourt's *Angela's Ashes* (1996) perpetuated the view that exile was the only antidote to poverty, repression and endless rain. But in a shrinking world, the poetry still told of the sense of place, voice and community, even from displaced locations. The poets Matthew Sweeney and Bernard O'Donoghue wrote Irish verse from London or Oxford. Eamon Grennan pursued a successful critical and poetic career in the USA. A younger poet like Justin Quinn could move to Prague and still co-edit the influential magazine of the younger Irish poets, *Metre*, exploring connections between the Irish experience and the no-less historic changes of the Eastern Europe of the 1990s.

Exile and change, however, did engage the Irish poet and his or her characteristic mode of elegy, still preoccupied with the sense that change may also mean loss, the loss of the traditions and certainties of a recognisable national identity. As the Irish poem was written in a world facing environmental as well as economic and social change, so it adapted its traditional concerns with elegy or nature, to these new conditions. Paul Muldoon's 1994 volume *The Annals of Chile* was written from the United States, and contained two great elegies, 'Incantata' for a former lover, and 'Yarrow' for his mother. They are concerned with the failing of the human body and the eradication of the rural past. Both poems end, grief-stricken and barely articulate before the facts of death from cancer, as they also watch a fast-disappearing pastoral world, in which even the singing birds – corncrake, bittern – face extinction.

The paradox may be that such writing about loss – personal, environmental or social – can come together in work such as Muldoon's, major poetry written with confidence for an increasingly international audience. That sense of its own confidence meant that Irish poetry could pursue its assimilation not just of the English, American or Irish language traditions, but also various world literatures, Eastern European, Hispanic, Modern Greek. Seemingly assured of modern classic status, in the 1990s Irish poetry also sounded an older classical note. As the poets tiptoed through the possible peace of the 1990s and into the twenty-first century, Michael Longley, Seamus Heaney, Eavan Boland and Muldoon all turned to the eclogue or the pastoral elegy. The models were Homeric or Virgilian, and their recurrent note was of exhaustion after war. Written from an old world, they faced the unknown world of the future in poems of homecoming or retreat. But they knew that peace was the first pre-requisite. In his sonnet 'Ceasefire', first published in 1994, Longley re-imagines a conversation from the Trojan wars, between Achilles and Priam. It reminds its reader of the difficulty of a necessary forgiveness, as it is allowed to conclude with the full rhyme of the concluding couplet of the English sonnet: 'I get down on my knees and do what must be done / And kiss Achilles' hand, the killer of my son'.[2]

II

Fifty years previously, around 1949, such confidence was hard to find. In the cinema, popular perceptions of Irish culture and politics veered between those in the English film-maker Carol Reed's dark tale of a wounded gunman on the run in Belfast in his 1947 *Odd Man Out* and the Irish-American director John Ford's piece of 1952 west-of-Ireland paddywhackery, *The Quiet Man*. Yet in 1949, Ireland had made a constitutional assertion of its independence. On a state visit to Canada the previous September, the Irish Taoiseach (Prime Minister), John Aloysius Costello, announced that he was going to declare Ireland a Republic. Since 1921, twenty-six of the thirty-two counties of the island of Ireland had been self-governing while remaining within what was left of the British Empire, the Commonwealth. In 1937, the previous Taoiseach, Eamon de Valera, had framed a Constitution for the new state which allowed it effective independence from Britain. The aim was to further the establishment of the institutions of an Ireland which was rural in population, agricultural in economy, Roman Catholic in religion and Gaelic in culture. Irish was to join English as the official dual language of the state. Ireland also sought to be non-aligned in foreign allegiance. Neutrality was to follow through the 1939–45 'Emergency', as the Irish referred to the period of war in which much of the rest of the world was to participate. The further break-up of the British Empire followed the war, with the British granting independence to India, Pakistan, Ceylon and Burma, and the establishment of the state of Israel in 1948 on former British territories in Palestine. In 1949, Ireland and India declared themselves Republics. Unlike India, Ireland also left the Commonwealth.[3]

Surely now, Ireland was free and confident, self-sufficient in politics and culture? Given that it had secured its independent status, could it not also continue to contribute to the growing artistic culture of international modernity for which its writers had been so important? In the early years of the century, the establishment of the Irish Literary Theatre had proved a significant example to national theatrical movements across the world. In 1922, James Joyce had published a novel set entirely in one day in Dublin, *Ulysses*, from which world fiction has yet to recover. In 1923, William Butler Yeats won the Nobel Prize for Literature, and in 1925, George Bernard Shaw was to receive the same accolade. All of these achievements had been gained in writing in the English language, a language which the Irish had used to establish a powerful national culture with an international readership. However, Yeats and Joyce died in 1939 and 1941 respectively. Joyce had lived across Europe, and Shaw had lived in London. The writer who was to be Ireland's next Nobel Laureate (1969), Samuel Beckett, had left the safety of Dublin to return to Paris in 1940, deciding that it was better to lend resistance to the occupied French during the war than maintain the neutrality that his Irish citizenship gave him. 'You simply couldn't stand by with your arms folded',[4] Beckett later said, in marked distinction from the policy of the Irish government. After the war, he decided to write in French.

Politically, the April 1949 declaration of the Republic of Ireland was followed in June of that year by a reminder of one reason why the constitutional future of the new Republic might not be entirely settled. The recently-elected British Labour government retaliated with the Ireland Act, confirming the status of the six counties of Northern Ireland within the United Kingdom as long as a majority within that state voted to remain British. While it was to benefit greatly from the post-war health and educational reforms of the nascent British Welfare State, the culture and government of Northern Ireland was still remarkably conservative. The example of the poets Louis MacNeice and John Hewitt was to be important for a later generation of Ulster writers, but it was received with ambivalence in mid-century Ulster. The son of a Church of Ireland bishop, MacNeice was educated at an English public school and at Oxford, and had lived through, and participated in, the highly politicised movements of British 1930s writing. He was closely involved with a leftwing set that included W.H. Auden and the Soviet spy Anthony Blunt. While MacNeice was ambivalent to the politic commitment of his friends, he had directed a diatribe towards Ireland in the sixteenth section of his 1939 *Autumn Journal*. It contained a swingeing attack on factionalised Ulster and Irish politics. 'Kathaleen Ni Houlihan!' MacNeice had exclaimed, 'Why must a country, like a ship or a car, be always female / Mother or sweetheart?' 'Yet we love her forever and hate our neighbour', he continued, 'And each one in his will / Binds his heirs to continuance of hatred'.[5] While MacNeice worked for the BBC in London for most of his life, Ireland exercised a strong pull even on this self-consciously deracinated intellectual. He was to write his best poetry just before he died in the early 1960s, but this uncertainty of identity – an Ulster protestant Irish poet writing at the heart of the English Establishment – and the uneven quality of his work in the late 1940s and 1950s, meant that his influence was not as great then as it has become for those, like Derek Mahon or Michael Longley, who have paid tribute to his sceptical intelligence.

Hewitt was an Ulster Protestant of Scottish descent, and his work emphasised regional identities within the United Kingdom. He could still describe himself, though, in the title of a 1945 poem, as 'Once Alien Here'. The poet movingly sought to speak with an 'easy voice', while aware that his British or southern neighbours possessed 'the graver English, lyric Irish tongue'.[6] A socialist in a state run by a Unionist party still dominated by the landed interest, his career as a museum curator was balked and in 1957 he had to leave for a job in Coventry, in England. There he helped in the cultural rebuilding of a city destroyed by war. It would take a particularly unusual imagination to find succour in the climate of the unreconstructed Belfast Hewitt left behind, like that of the English poet Philip Larkin, who travelled the other way. Coventry-born, he arrived to a job in Belfast in 1950. Belfast taught him, in the title of one of his poems, 'The Importance of Elsewhere' (1955). His strangeness in that part of the United Kingdom kept him 'in touch' with his characteristic sense of social 'difference'.[7]

As Ireland faced the second half of the twentieth century the poetic mood was one of estrangement, division, cynicism and aftermath. The best writing continued to take place in exile, and both parts of Ireland appeared to be turning their backs on the great changes which were about to beset a postwar world. In the South, the poets were, in the main, dissenting voices. With a few exceptions – Beckett's friends the poet and curator Thomas McGreevy and the diplomat-poet Denis Devlin, or the Irish-language poet Máirtín Ó Direáin – they were attuned neither to world movements in modern art nor the isolationist project of the new Republic. The farmer-poet Patrick Kavanagh's 1942 *The Great Hunger* had shown the pastoral ideal of the new nation suffering from spiritual and sexual famine. Alluding in his title to the potato famine of a century previously, in which a million Irish had died and after which many more had emigrated, Kavanagh had presented the actualities of toil and cultural repression in a rural world in which the future might only be viewed with cynicism and despair. His elders and contemporaries, the poets Austin Clarke, Padraic Fallon or Sean Ó' Ríordáin, the novelists and story-writers, Flann O'Brien, Seán O'Faoilain and Frank O'Connor, and the playwright Brendan Behan, made for a conspicuously disaffected group when they could be conceived of as a group at all. Memoirs of late 1940s and 1950s Dublin, such as the poet Anthony Cronin's *Dead As Doornails*, tell of begrudgery and anti-modern inwardness in the environs of Dublin's Palace Bar.[8]

The great danger, according to Kavanagh, was a settling down into provincialism. While Hewitt emphasised regionalism, Kavanagh contrasted the provincial with the parochial, since the parish was the basis of 'all great civilisations . . . Greek Israelite, English'. An embrace of the parish would then enable Irish poetry to return to international relevance, since, 'Parochialism is universal: it deals with the fundamentals'.[9] A signal moment thus occurs in the sonnet 'Epic' (1951), where he compares a dispute over a field boundary to the 1938 Hitler-Chamberlain agreement over Czechoslovakia. 'Which / Was more important?' he asks, and is answered by the ghost of Homer: 'I made the Iliad from such / A local row. Gods make their own importance'.[10] Epic may be made out of the 'local row' of a parochial poetry and politics, and Kavanagh shows it gaining expression in the small-scale sonnet form. The poet Eavan Boland recalls meeting with the older Kavanagh in the 1960s. She remembers that for all of her distinctness from him, not least that of gender, she found in work such as this 'an example of dissidence . . . someone who had used the occasion of his life to rebuff the expectations and preconceptions of the Irish poem'.[11]

Emphasising the small-scale and the parochial as he did, and then turning to satirise the provincial culture around him, Kavanagh's example was to be great for the generation that began to publish in the years following his death in 1967. Just as pastoral or anti-pastoral had given way to satire in Kavanagh's post-1949 work, so even established poets like Austin Clarke felt bound to mark their distinctness from the burgeoning institutions of the new Republic. Under the influence of the Catholic Church, censorship had been prolific throughout the period of the Free State, and even the spiritually-inclined came to find themselves satirically removed from the growing cultural and sexual repression of Church and State. Kavanagh's great hunger had been in one sense that of frustrated male sexual desire. Padraic Fallon's love poems from this period, too, tell of the fantasies of the Irishman. Fallon's goddesses, nuns or whores are placed in modern surroundings, influenced by Freud or anthropology. As in the poem 'Women', however, they still remain uncertain of how to move beyond an imagery inherited from Yeats:

> But a woman is a lie
> And I have a tower to climb, the tower of me,
> And a quarrel to settle with the sky
> But 'rest' says the woman. 'O lean back more:
> I am a wife and a mother's knee,
> I am the end of every tower.'[12]

There is ambivalence here: the poem either rejects Yeatsian self-sufficiency in the embrace of domesticity and marriage or it reiterates the auto-erotic's ultimate fantasy. But it does tell of an adaptation of the Irish poem to changing conceptions of sexuality, no matter how awkwardly male that new form initially was.

In 'The Siege of Mullingar, 1963', a poet of the next generation, John Montague, viewed with delight the frank sexuality of the youth at that year's Fleadh Cheoil (music festival). The poem's refrain parodies Yeats, before taking a dig at his dissident elders (his emphasis): *'Puritan Ireland's dead and gone / A myth of O'Connor and O'Faolain'*.[13] Maybe the conflation of political and personal dissidence with the sexual repression of Church and State was passing, but one important poem remained to be published from these dry years, Clarke's 1966 *Mnemosyne Lay in the Dust*. His long career had suffered in conditions of personal breakdown, religious crisis and political trauma, and the attention that his early work gave to instilling the rhythms of Irish-language poetry within the English poem had given way in the 1950s to satire and frequent polemic. Clarke's breakdown occurred in 1919, a year of revolutionary insurgence, and the poem tells of personal crisis against a background of initial political upheaval and liberation, written through conditions of reaction and repression. The poem of alienation and recovery was not to appear until the year of the celebrations of the fiftieth anniversary of the 1916 Easter Rising.

One of those executed after that rising, the poet and critic Thomas Mac-Donagh, had taught Clarke much at University College Dublin. But Clarke's later style was to show ambivalence towards what MacDonagh called the 'the Irish Mode', the mixing of the accents of Irish language poetry with the metric of the English poem. In these revisionary conditions, though, the Irish language poem continued to thrive. The leader of the Rising, after all, was an Irish language poet, Padraic Pearse. The Irish poetry of the 1950s is marked by innovation and an openness to experiment that is rare in the corresponding English-language poem. Seán Ó Ríordáin, Máirtín Ó Direáin and Máire Mhac an tSaoi produced poetry influenced by American and English modernist models. Ó Ríordáin's 1952 *Eireaball Spideoige* introduced a poet influenced alike by James Joyce and the Catholic theology with which Joyce quarrelled for so long. The poet Nuala Ní Dhomhnaill has complained that accounts of Irish poetry around mid-century ignore these poets.[14] Yet the audience that spoke and read Irish was small and dwindling. An Aran Islands writer like Ó Direáin knew that the western rural areas in which Irish survived was suffering waves of emigration which rivalled those of the nineteenth century.

The new beginning of 1949 was not matched with a new beginning in Irish culture. In the two decades that followed, the continuing partition of the island, the conservative political majorities associated with the dominance of non-conformist Protestantism in the North and Roman Catholicism in the South, and the struggle between that conservatism and attempts to modernise the Irish economy, seemed to be returning Ireland to a provincial backwater, unnoticed by the world. Yet as Montague's 'Siege of Mullingar' suggests, even this Ireland couldn't ignore the 1960s. The growing affluence of western economies did not leave Ireland alone. And the struggles for Civil Rights in the American South and the student risings of 1968 in the US and France were not unnoticed by the Irish of 1969.

III

After a decade of economic modernisation, the Ireland of the late 1960s was lambasted by Thomas Kinsella, in his long modernist poem *Nightwalker* (1967). Kinsella had served in the office of T.K. Whitaker, the Irish Secretary for Finance. Working with the Taoiseach, Sean Lemass, Whitaker suggested that one reason for Ireland's economic problems was the country's isolationist approach to economic, and by association foreign, policy. He recommended that the Irish economy expand, and that it open itself up to increased foreign investment. Kinsella, for one, saw danger in what such changes might mean for an Ireland which had recently left the Commonwealth but would soon exchange it for the Common Market (in 1972, the Republic voted to join the European Economic Community). In *Nightwalker*, the disillusioned civil servant Kinsella described an Ireland suffering from the odd mix of residual Republicanism, Catholic conservatism and a freed entrepreneurial business class, sponsored by a new class of politician, often less than scrupulous in its dealings. Rather than be faced with a statue of liberty, say, or even Kathaleen Ni Houlihan at the mouth of Dublin harbour, the Irish are greeted by another female allegorical figure, 'Robed in spattered iron . . . Productive Investment'. She asks of the nation that would treat with her: 'Lend me your wealth, your cunning and your drive, / Your arrogant refuse'.[15] Kinsella is ambiguous on the subject of the dissenting poet: whether this means that the arrogant who refuse are mere refuse, rubbish, to Productive Investment, or whether Ireland's refuse be allowed the arrogance of a wasteful modern economy is not clear. What is clear is the poem's turn to elegy for the loss of the Gaelic culture which was supposedly supported in the constitution of the greedily modernising state. The third section ends with Irish silent across irrecoverable time: 'A dying language echoes / across a century's silence'.[16]

Kinsella's concerns in *Nightwalker* were primarily with the South, with language, and the unaccommodated self of the modern poet. They were not, explicitly at least, with the unsettled 'national question' of how to accommodate a divided island. But events in Northern Ireland were soon to affect the whole island, and the United Kingdom as well. In January 1967, the Northern Ireland Civil Rights Association had been formed, pledged to restore the equal electoral representation of Catholic and Protestant, primarily within the increasingly segregated and ghettoised cities of Northern Ireland. Poet and critic Seamus Deane's 1996 memoir-novel of the 1950s and 1960s, *Reading in the Dark* presents a grim picture of the poverty and repression suffered by working-class Catholics in the city in which he was born.[17] To its majority Catholic and nationalist population the city was called Derry. Its Unionist City Council – guaranteed a majority by electoral divisions which were engineered or 'gerrymandered' according to religion – insisted on its seventeenth century colonial title, Londonderry. Divided by class and religion, Northern Ireland was unable even to agree on the names of places. For the Civil Rights protestors, Northern Ireland was like the southern US states, a divided part of a supposedly liberal modern democracy.

The initial years of protest for civil rights were non-violent, but the ruling Unionist party was slow to grant the legitimacy of the claims of the minority. After all, they could point to the religious intolerance and corruption of the new Ireland south of the Border as a warning against conceding too much to those who wished to rejoin their co-religionists. A subsequent escalation of violence followed, through rioting and the heavy-handed response of the police. In August 1969, increasing civil disorder meant the arrival of British troops on to the streets of Derry and Belfast. By November 1969, eventual electoral reform righted the civil wrongs which had led to this state of affairs. Instead of peace and political settlement, however, the violence was to get worse. The Irish Republican Army (IRA) was conspicuously absent from these early 'troubles', but the actions of armed police and troops quickly led to increased support. In January 1970, the Provisional IRA was born, committed to an 'armed struggle' in the cause of the expulsion of the British and the reunification of Ireland. In 1969, eighteen people died in political violence in Northern Ireland, ten of them killed by the army or police. But only three years later, in 1972, the worst year of the troubles, 496 were to die, 234 killed by the IRA. Political terror became an everyday occurrence in Northern Ireland, and in April 1972 the British suspended the Northern Irish parliament and assumed Direct Rule.

It is tempting to find consolation for historical trauma in imaginative rennaissance. Coincident with the upsurge of political violence in Ireland around 1969 was the extraordinary increase in the volume and quality of Irish poetry. However, while historical events may have provided the conditions in which this poetry was written, they cannot entirely account for its causes.[18] Landmark collections from both North and South appeared at the end of the 1960s and early 1970s. Kinsella's *Nightwalker* volume contained his great poem of illness and rebirth 'Phoenix Park', and paved the way for the experimental poetry of his subsequent career. Richard Murphy had also viewed the divisions of Irish history in his inventive long sequence of 1968, *The Battle of Aughrim*. The poem mixed lyric, epic, ballad and history in an account of the final defeat of Gaelic Ireland in 1691, and the subsequent flight of the Wild Geese. The internationalist, anti-clerical and libertarian poems in Pearse Hutchinson's 1969 *Expansions* would have been recognised across much of the more peacefully dissenting late 1960s Europe and America. Imaginative and political energies were released in many countries across the world, liberalised by pop music, cinema and a briefly-politicised youth culture, and Ireland shared in this great upsurge of creativity.

Poetic energy did not come only from the powerful subject matter that local events now suggested. The 1960s had seen the development of a newly thriving poetry scene in Belfast, famously gathering around the poet and critic Philip Hobsbaum. A product of the universities of Cambridge (F.R. Leavis) and Sheffield (William Empson), and friend of English poets Ted Hughes and Peter Redgrove, Hobsbaum had arrived to teach in Queen's University Belfast in 1963. He subsequently established a writer's seminar, 'The Group', and was to find that young talent of the calibre of Seamus Heaney, Michael Longley or James Simmons joined in its famously combative discussions. In 1966, Heaney's first book, *Death of a Naturalist*, appeared from the English publishers Faber and Faber. Rural in subject matter, romantic in outlook, highly formal in execution, the book showed the influence of Kavanagh, Gerard Manley Hopkins and Robert Frost. It was already demonstrating the range of this new poetry in its appeal to Irish, English and American literary traditions. Simmons founded a poetry journal, *The Honest Ulsterman* in 1968, and in the same year Oxford University Press published Derek

Mahon's *Night Crossing*. Longley's *No Continuing City* was to come out from Macmillan in 1969. The poets were talking, performing and publishing well before the outbreak of violence in 1969.

Derek Mahon had maintained his distance from the Hobsbaum coterie, allowing the influence of French literature and Samuel Beckett to develop his characteristic tone of social and philosophical estrangement. But very early after the events of 1969, he made one of the most telling statements about these poets' relation to the history unfolding around them. In a piece from 1970 called 'Poetry in Northern Ireland', Mahon was careful to distinguish between the traditions of Protestant poets like himself, Longley and Simmons and those of the Catholic poets, Heaney and John Montague. The voices of the latter could remain 'true to the ancient intonations' of Ireland. They could thus 'assimilate to the traditional aesthetics which are their birthright some of (to risk pretentiousness) the cultural fragmentation of our time'. Speaking of Longley and Simmons, but implicitly about himself, Mahon makes the contrast: 'ironic heirs of a threadbare colonialism, [they] have as their birthright that very fragmentation'. The difference may seem small, but it relates not only to the greater cultural fragmentation of modernity, but the smaller-scale local rows of Irish religion and politics.

Mahon ends with a vision of the function of poetry within these competing local and international fragmentations:

> Battles have been lost, but a war remains to be won. The war I mean is not, of course, between Protestant and Catholic but between the fluidity of a possible life (poetry is a great lubricant) and the *rigor mortis* of archaic postures, political and cultural. The poets themselves have taken no part in political events, but they have contributed to that possible life, or to the possibility of that possible life; for the act of writing is itself political in the fullest sense. A good poem is a paradigm of good politics – of people talking to each other, with honest subtlety, at a profound level. It is a light to lighten the darkness; and we have had darkness enough, God knows, for a long time.[19]

The darkness was to continue for nearly three decades, but Mahon's lubricant, his good poem which is the paradigm of good politics, focused the debate on the political responsibilities of the poet in the violent decades ahead.

The poets did feel a need to respond, touched as many were by atrocity. How, then, can we learn from the way the Irish poem treated these events? Writing in 1999 about the Belfast artist David Crone, Michael Longley says that Crone's attitude to the Troubles in his work is that of 'the Ulster poets . . . an oblique approach'. Crone, he says, 'prefers us to view his concerned expression out of the corner of his eye'.[20] Taking its title from a poem of Mahon, Frank Ormsby's anthology of poetry about the Troubles, *A Rage for Order*, contains oblique and direct treatments of the history and politics of the period. One event, though, in January 1972, when British soldiers shot dead thirteen civil rights protesters on 'Bloody Sunday', produced expressions which were varied in their approach to the obliqueness and concern appropriate for the poem in the circumstances. Ormsby gives a small selection of Bloody Sunday poems, by poets North and South: Thomas McCarthy, Seamus Deane and Seamus Heaney.[21] The responses range from invective to elegy. Heaney also wrote ballad verses on the subject and sent them to Luke Kelly of The Dubliners folk group to sing. Kelly never took up the offer, and Heaney waited twenty-five years before he consented to the publication of the ballad in a 1997 commemorative issue of the *Derry Journal*.[22] The ballad, 'The Road to Derry', courts what is rare for Heaney, the risk of direct rather than oblique political comment: 'And in the dirt lay justice like an acorn in the winter / Till its oak would sprout in Derry where the thirteen men lay dead'.

The ballad measure was also adopted by Thomas Kinsella, in what is the most outspoken of poetic responses to the event, his 1972 *Butchers Dozen*. Kinsella's anger was provoked by the findings of the official inquiry, the Widgery Report, in which the British Lord Chief Justice exonerated those responsible for the killing. Like Heaney's ballad, it recounts a visit to the city:

> I went with Anger at my heel
> Through Bogside of the bitter zeal
> –Jesus pity! – on a day
> Of cold and drizzle and decay.

Mixing testimony from the ghosts of the dead in the manner of an eighteenth century Irish vision poem, or *aisling*, *Butcher's Dozen* reaches for the tone of *saeva indignatio* of the satirising classical poet, a bitterness which is quite deliberately removed from Mahon's 'people talking to each other, with honest subtlety, at a profound level'.

It is a poet of the succeeding generation to these poets, Paul Muldoon, who brings together these seemingly conflicting tonal approaches to the fact of atrocity in a heightened political climate. Muldoon's 1973 debut *New Weather* ended with a long poem which he subsequently said was a 'direct response' to Bloody Sunday, 'The Year of the Sloes, for Ishi'.[23] The poem tells of the last member of a tribe of Californian Indians. His death will mean the eventual extinction of his people, in conditions that imply genocide. The conceit of the conclusion to the poem is chilling, as it envisages the dead lying side by side across the land:

> I realised that if his brothers
> Could be persuaded to lie still,
> One beside the other
> Right across the Great Plains,
> Then perhaps something of this original
> Beauty would be retained.[24]

This is not just a play with the picturesque, or the chill of seeking to make aesthetic the facts of atrocity or death through the recreation of 'original / Beauty'. Muldoon's environmentalism also grieves the loss to nature of the tribes who subsisted across the Great Plains, those who were for centuries its indigenous people. But in its evocation of a story of colonialism and the destruction of a natural and social order, 'The Year of the Sloes' brings itself obliquely back to the matter of the Ireland from which it was written in 1972. Its politics may indeed appear to be a direct response, given the narrative of genocide that they tell in the context of the bloody events of January 1972. It is the form, though, which expresses elegiac concern out of the corner of its eye: the poet doesn't so much take sides as construct colonialism and atrocity in allegorical or parabolic terms, as Emily Dickinson might say, telling the truth slant.

It would be a mistake to think that all Irish poems from this period were preoccupied with violence or atrocity. While elegy might be a characteristic mode of Irish poetry, it is one which can be private as well as public. The still-dominant Irish pastoral or even anti-pastoral mode showed an Irish culture still substantially agricultural in economy and rural in preoccupation, continuously engaged with the natural and the environment. Formally too, Irish poetry sought to find its shape in both of the languages of Ireland, aware that it was written from within a dual or divided linguistic tradition. After the innovations of Murphy's narrative of the defeat of Gaelic Ireland in *The Battle of Aughrim*, Irish poets played with a mixing of genres and language. Kinsella conflated his *Butchers Dozen* with elegies for John F. Kennedy and the Irish composer Seán O Riada, thus linking the historical and the personal. The year 1969 had seen the publication of his great translation of Irish myth, the Cúchulainn cycle of *The Táin*. Yet Kinsella's *New Poems* of 1973 returned to the matter of family and memory as he embraced the longer evolutionary histories of Darwin, while attending to myth read through the Jungian archetype.

The Táin appeared from Liam Miller's innovative Dolmen Press, with striking illustrations by Louis le Brocquy. Dolmen also published John

Montague's *The Rough Field* in 1972. The loss of Irish also haunts a number of its lyrics, which Montague had brought together from many of his
poems of the 1960s. The new sequence of the poems then told of the history
of the divided mid-Ulster townland from which Montague came, attending
to Kavanagh's prescriptive parochialism. But it is the volume's innovative
physical sense of itself which is most striking, influenced as it was by experiments with the concrete poem in the American modernist tradition, by
Ezra Pound or Charles Olsen. The book's mixture of lyric, narrative and
newspaper report was matched by its appearance with illustrations from
sixteenth-century woodcuts, and the sequence was performed and recorded
with the musicians who were later to become The Chieftains.

Montague's sequence brought together pastoral concern and modernist
invention, but it was still ambivalent in its grief for the loss of the continuity
of tradition and in its concern for what Mahon terms the 'cultural fragmentation' of the new. In the words of poet and critic Dennis O'Driscoll,
speaking about the international significance of Montague's 'global regionalism', 'The global village casts light on the deserted village'.[25] A similar
engagement with the politics of pastoral – land, ownership and sovereignty –
may have been inherent in this new global regionalism, but it also meant
that Irish poets sought equivalences outside the violent confines of parish,
province or nation. Seamus Heaney's *North* (1975) received the greatest
international acclaim (and local controversy) in these years. Its inventive-
ness was parabolic or allegorical, seeking historic or archetypal equivalences
across Northern Europe and in classical myth for seemingly unbearable local
events. It ended, though, in an internal exile of a sort, with 'Exposure', written from County Wicklow in the Republic. As Heaney says in that poem, he
had now 'escaped from the massacre'. Other poets were to follow.

IV

How was Irish poetry to change between the late 1960s and early 1970s
and the last years of the twentieth century? The answer, in part, lies as much
in the matter of the typical allegorical or parabolic approach to history in
these poems, as in any sense of historical change. The objection initially
came from those who had been cast as images in the allegories of the Irish
tradition, and not as poets: 'An é go n-iompaíonn baineann fireann / Nuair
a iompaíonn bean ina file?' (Is it that the feminine turns masculine / when a
woman turns into a poet?) Seán'Ó Ríordáin had asked in 'Banfhile' ('Woman
Poet'). 'Ní file ach filíocht an bhean.' (A woman is not a poet, but poetry.)[26]
Montague's *Rough Field* and Heaney's *North* had both taken a common
trope from the aisling poems of Irish literary tradition, that of the figure

of the nation as a woman, sometimes beautiful, sometimes aged, frequently evanescent, usually violated. Then, through the 1980s and 1990s, the writing of Irish women poets such as Eavan Boland, Eiléan Ní Chuilleanáin, Medbh McGuckian and Nuala Ní Dhomhnaill, began to engage in debate about their position as metaphor in the history of Irish poetry, and the whole question of the oblique approach implicit in metaphor itself. This, after all, was writing taking place after the other great changes wrought on literature in the late 1960s, and new thinking in feminism, psychoanalysis, linguistics or philosophy.

Boland was a major critical as well as poetic figure in this new turn of Irish poetry towards a critique of its traditionally-gendered forms. In the essay 'Outside History', in *Object Lessons* (1995), she discusses a ballad elegy by Francis Ledwidge for the executed leaders of the 1916 rising, which relates the keen of a 'Poor Old Woman' mourning the loss of her blackbirds. The poem revives old figures and forms as it faces a new political situation, adapting tradition for the purposes of sounding grief at the failure of a present insurgency. Boland fastens on the figure of the woman, who disappears out of the poem as soon as the meaning becomes clear:

> The woman, on the other hand, is a diagram. By the time the poem is over, she has become a dehumanized ornament. When her speaking part finishes, she goes out of the piece and out of our memory. At best she has been the engine of the action, a convenient frame for the proposition.[27]

The mourning nation is represented by a female figure in Ledwidge's poem which is merely one example of an Irish poetic tradition in which women appear as mere diagram or ornament. In Ó Ríordáin's terms, they are poetry not poet.

Boland's sequence 'Outside History' (1990) ends kneeling at a roadside beside the dead of the Troubles, bemoaning that she has come along 'Too late'. In the third poem in the sequence, 'The Making of an Irish Goddess', the myth of the sudden loss of the goddess of the harvest, Ceres, is used to represent the Famine, that great historical trauma of the nineteenth century to which Kavanagh had alluded in the title of his *Great Hunger*. The poet uses her own scarred menopausal body as an image for the infertility of the land and the scar in the national memory. She points to her concealment of 'the stitched, healed blemish of a scar' and says that it 'must be // an accurate inscription / of that agony' of Famine.[28] Moving all the way from her own body to the horrors of famine and cannibalism, Boland attempts to figure the national trauma through the metonym of her own Irish woman poet's bodily history. That 'must be' doubly reinforces the traditional figure, describing a

reaching after significance ('ah, that must be it!') and an unavoidable necessity, as if there is nothing she can do to avoid the use of the body as an
inscription for what it must be.

Generations of Irish poets after 1999 may not feel bound to this determination to represent the body of the nation. Certainly Boland's poem ends
with a vision of her daughter, 'her back turned to me', and thus hopes for
the future. For Irish, too, there is hope, although the Irish language poet
Nuala Ní Dhomhnaill has found some horror in the responsibilities of her
success. In 'Cailleach'/'Hag' she dreams that she herself has become the Kerry
landscape and consequently allows her typically whimsical reaction to this
fantasy give way to horror, as she sees the dangers of binding her daughter
to this tradition. Walking along a beach, she is surprised by the daughter's
crying: ' "Cad tá ort?" "Ó, a Mhaim, táim sceimhlithe. / Tuigeadh dom go
raibh na conic ag bogadaíl, / gur fathach mná a bhí ag luascadh a cíocha, / is
go n-éireodh sí aniar agus mise d'íosfadh" '. (' "What's wrong?" "O, Mam,
I'm scared stiff, / I thought I saw the mountains heaving / like a giantess, with
her breasts swaying, / about to loom over, and gobble me up" '.)[29] This is a
gothic note, in which the fantasy figure becomes real, terrifying those who
might object to the continuance of such repression. But Ní Dhomhnaill's
poetry is also a welcome reminder to the reader that sometimes visions of
women in Irish poems may not inevitably be symbolic of the national fantasy.
Irish love poetry has its earthy, material tradition too.

Younger Irish poets thus strive to express not only the nightmare of the
dead generations but the need to get away from their deathly influence.
This younger generation may be less than patient with the traditions of their
parents. Caitríona O'Reilly's poem 'Fragment', in *The Nowhere Birds* (2001)
takes the daughter's position and watches a mother suffering dreams of an
animated land – and seascape. She views with dread the creatures from the
past emerging from the sea of nightmare or memory.

> I see them, those obsessive dead –
> their watery features sea-blurred, merged, evasive.
> I hold my breath above her sinking head,
> dreading their opaque past and fossil histories,
> inky and indistinct as night water.[30]

The danger is of being dragged not into 'an accurate inscription' but the
oblique allegorical tradition which prizes the 'merged' forms of the hybrid,
or the 'evasive' positions of the colonised. For O'Reilly, like Boland's and Ní
Dhomhnaill's daughters, the alternative to embracing the new thing that has
happened is the continuation of the family nightmare.

As Ireland and the world contemplated the future of a new millennium, the 1990s brought a number of significant commemorations to a land still obsessed with memories of its violent past. These might have been of recent events (the 1997 25th anniversary of Bloody Sunday, for which Heaney had released his ballad), those earlier in the century (the 75th anniversary celebrations of the Easter Rising were notably muted), or those from a longer past (commemorations for the 150th anniversary of the Famine continued throughout the decade and 1998 brought celebrations for the bicentenary of the Rising of 1798.) In millennial circumstances, though, memory might have given way to thoughts about the future, and thoughts about the role that poetry might play in its shaping.

In 1998, Ciaran Carson gave his version of the Irish tradition of imagining lands beyond the known. These places might only exist in an impossible time, the *Twelfth of Never*, to adapt the title of his sonnet sequence. Nonetheless, they are the lands that poetry might be within its responsibilities to imagine. In the sestet of 'Tib's Eve', he says,

> This is the land of the green rose and the lion lily,
> Ruled by Zeno's eternal tortoises and hares,
> Where everything is metaphor and simile:
>
> Somnambulists, we stumble through this paradise
> From time to time, like words repeated in our prayers,
> Or storytellers who convince themselves that truths are lies.[31]

From the reminder of more than three hundred years celebrating the Battle of the Boyne every Twelfth of July, through Zeno's paradox of the immeasurable instant at which one object overtakes another, to the paradox of a time outside time, the twelfth of never, Carson imagines an allegorical place which exists in metaphor and simile and cannot distinguish between truth and lie. This is one virtual world of poetry and even if it may never have existed, it is a place where Irish poems and their readers in a new century must figure out their responsibilities. As seen in Carson and the other poets discussed in this book, the means of figuring out an approach both to history and a changing contemporary society has led to a writing which is by turns oblique, metaphoric, allegorical and opaque. The reader of such poetry must recognise metaphor and simile but not make the Platonic mistake that in fictional worlds truths might as well be lies.

NOTES

1 Seamus Heaney, *The Cure at Troy* (London: Faber and Faber, 1990), pp. 77–8.
2 Michael Longley, 'Ceasefire', in *The Ghost Orchid* (London: Cape, 1995), p. 39.

3 For further historical background on these and other events related here, see Terence Brown, *Ireland: a Social and Cultural History, 1922–1985* 2nd edn. (London: Fontana, 1985); R.F. Foster, *Modern Ireland, 1600–1972* (Harmondsworth: Penguin, 1989); J.J. Lee, *Ireland, 1912–1985: Politics and Society* (Cambridge University Press, 1989).

4 Samuel Beckett to Alec Reid, quoted in James Knowlson, *Damned to Fame: The Life of Samuel Beckett* (London: Bloomsbury, 1996), pp. 304 and 763.

5 Louis MacNeice, *Collected Poems* (London: Faber and Faber, 1966), p. 132.

6 John Hewitt, 'Once Alien Here' in *The Collected Poems of John Hewitt* ed. Frank Ormsby (Belfast: Blackstaff, 1991), p. 20.

7 Philip Larkin, *Collected Poems*, ed. Anthony Thwaite (London: Faber and Faber, 1988), p. 104.

8 Anthony Cronin, *Dead as Doornails: Bohemian Dublin in the Fifties and Sixties* (Oxford University Press, 1976).

9 Patrick Kavanagh, 'The Parish and the Universe', *Collected Pruse* (London: MacGibbon and Kee, 1967), pp. 282–3.

10 Patrick Kavanagh, *Collected Poems* (London: MacGibbon and Kee, 1964), p. 136.

11 Eavan Boland, *Object Lessons: The Life of the Woman and the Poet in Our Time* (Manchester: Carcanet), pp. 99–100.

12 Padraic Fallon, *Collected Poems* (Manchester: Carcanet, 1990), p. 71.

13 John Montague, *Selected Poems* (Winston Salem: Wake Forest University Press, 1982), p. 62. The allusion is to Yeats's 'September 1913': 'Romantic Ireland's dead and gone / It's with O'Leary in the grave'.

14 See Nuala Ní Dhomhnaill, 'Why I Choose to Write in Irish', *The New York Times Book Review*, January 8, 1995, p. 27.

15 Thomas Kinsella, *Collected Poems* (Manchester: Carcanet, 2001), p. 78.

16 Kinsella, *Collected Poems*, p. 82.

17 Seamus Deane, *Reading in the Dark* (London: Jonathan Cape, 1996).

18 I am adapting a remark from Louis MacNeice, in *The Poetry of W.B. Yeats* (1941) (London: Faber and Faber, 1967), p. 23: 'Critics often tend to write as if a condition were the same thing as a cause'.

19 Derek Mahon, 'Poetry in Northern Ireland', *Twentieth Century Studies* 4 (Nov. 1970), pp. 92–3.

20 Michael Longley, 'The Fire in the Window: A Response to the Paintings of David Crone', in *David Crone: Paintings 1963–1999*, ed. S.B. Kennedy (Dublin: Four Courts Press, 1999), p. 7.

21 Frank Ormsby, ed., *A Rage for Order: Poetry of the Northern Ireland Troubles* (Belfast: Blackstaff, 1992), pp. 112–16. The poems are 'Counting the Dead on the Radio, 1972' (McCarthy), 'After Derry, 30 January 1972' (Deane), 'Casualty' (Heaney). See also the poem that leads in to this selection, Eamon Grennan's powerful 'Soul Music: The Derry Air.'

22 *Derry Journal* (Bloody Sunday Commemorative Issue, 1 Feb. 1997).

23 Muldoon is quoted by Clair Wills, in *Reading Paul Muldoon* (Newcastle: Bloodaxe, 1998), p. 38.

24 Paul Muldoon, *New Weather*, 2nd edn. (London: Faber and Faber, 1994), p. 47.

25 Dennis O'Driscoll, 'Foreign Relations: Irish and International Poetry', *Troubled Thoughts, Majestic Dreams: Selected Prose Writings* (Loughcrew: Gallery, 2001), p. 84.

26 Seán Ó Ríordáin, 'Banfhile' ('Woman Poet'), *Tar Éis Mo Bháis*, p. 45.
27 Eavan Boland, 'Outside History' in *Object Lessons: The Life of the Poet and the Woman in Our Time* (Manchester: Carcanet, 1995), p. 143.
28 Eavan Boland, *Collected Poems* (Manchester: Carcanet, 1995), p. 151.
29 Nuala Ní Dhomhnaill, *Pharaoh's Daughter* (Loughcrew: Gallery, 1990), pp. 134–5; trans. John Montague.
30 Caitriona O'Reilly, *The Nowhere Birds* (Newcastle: Bloodaxe, 2001), p. 12.
31 Carson, *The Twelfth of Never* (Loughcrew: Gallery, 1998), p. 13.

2

JOHN GOODBY

From Irish mode to modernisation: the poetry of Austin Clarke

I

It is almost a truism of Irish literary history that the work of Austin Clarke (1896–1973), one of the Irish poets of the greatest range and achievement since Yeats, has yet to receive the attention it deserves. Somehow it still hovers both in and out of the canon, frequently more honoured in the breach of oversight than in the observance of university syllabuses, summer schools, anthologies and bookshop poetry sections. Clarke was excluded by Yeats from his *Faber Book of Modern Verse* in 1936; but while he was restored in most anthologies between *The Oxford Book of Irish Verse* in 1958 and Patrick Crotty's *Modern Irish Poetry* of 1995, it was still possible for Yeats's snub to be repeated half a century later in (or out of) Paul Muldoon's *Faber Book of Modern Irish Poetry* (1986). Clarke remains in print, yet precariously; a *Selected Poems* edited by Hugh Maxton, which was published in 1991, is still available, but the only *Collected* is the 1974 edition prepared by Liam Miller of Dolmen Press with the poet himself.[1] The contrast with, say, Patrick Kavanagh (for whom complete and selected poems are currently, and recently, in print), is marked.

In critical terms the story is similar. In the 1950s, it took an English critic, Donald Davie, then teaching at Trinity College Dublin, to alert the Irish literary world to the importance of the poetry Clarke had begun publishing in 1955, after a seventeen-year silence. The seconding of Davie's judgement was soon followed by Clarke's brief elevation following *Flight to Africa* (1963), his most varied single collection, and the remarkable late masterpiece, *Mnemosyne Lay in Dust* (1966). But the 1960s were to be the highpoint of Clarke's reputation. Although critical attention traditionally wanes after a poet's death, before reviving, there is still little sign of it picking up again in Clarke's case. He is dutifully accorded his place in literary histories, and some critics – W.J. McCormack, Terence Brown and Neil Corcoran – have written very finely about him indeed, in essay form.[2] But although Susan Halpern

(1974), Craig Tapping (1981) and Maurice Harmon (1989) have all offered book-length studies of the *oeuvre*, all are currently out of print. Nor has there as yet been a biography, or any study of Clarke informed by contemporary developments in literary criticism. Most revealing of all, several notable Irish critics of modern poetry, Declan Kiberd, Seamus Deane and Edna Longley among them, have avoided discussing Clarke in any but a cursory manner.[3] Admittedly, Clarke has been named as an important forebear by Thomas Kinsella who, like Maxton, has edited his poetry. But such a claim is almost unique, and the general impression is of a writer's writer; skilful, prolific, of occasional power, but patchy and narrowly parochial, a poet whose crabbed style and not-so-lightly-worn learning make him something of a mid-century curio.

As I have argued elsewhere, Clarke's reputation has suffered from the po-larisation of Irish culture which set in in earnest around the time of his death and is only now starting to weaken.[4] Thus, Clarke's critique of the 'Ill-fare state' and resolutely demythologising tendency has rankled with, or seemed irrelevant to, those nationalist-inclined critics and poets who spent the 1970s and 1980s agonising over myth and Irish identity. Conversely, the prospect of upsetting this group was not sufficiently tempting for those of an opposed persuasion to overcome their dislike of Clarke's penchant for foreground-ing the constructedness of the poem as literary artefact.[5] Unconscriptable, he was ignored by both camps. Moreover, his anomalous place in literary history had made such a critical failure relatively easy. Refusing to acknowl-edge modernism until late in his career, the radical elements of Clarke's poetic and ideology were for long occluded. As a result he had been cast by Samuel Beckett in 1934 as one of those offering 'segment after segment of cut-and-dried sanctity and loveliness',[6] the whipping-boy-in-chief of the cosmopoli-tan strain of Irish modernism.[7] Yet his dense and highly-wrought style always seemed artificial and laboured when set against the realist vernacular style championed by Kavanagh and more or less dominant in Irish poetry since the 1960s. Ironically, as Crotty and Maxton have noted, Clarke is best regarded as an Irish example of a neglected strain of modernism, that which attached itself to a specific region or nation, which in Britain included Basil Bunting and Hugh MacDiarmid, and in the USA William Carlos Williams; a hy-brid writing which articulated the tensions between modernism and realism, region (or nation) and the transnational space of the revolution of the word.

II

Austin Clarke was born in Dublin in 1896, of a lower-middle-class family. After a conventional Roman Catholic upbringing and schooling, he went to study at University College Dublin (UCD) in 1913. Here he encountered the force which, together with religion, was to shape him most strongly, that of the Literary Revival. UCD was home to many of the intellectuals behind the Revival, among them Douglas Hyde, Thomas MacDonagh and George Sigerson, and Clarke soon came under their influence. The activity of some of these figures was, famously, not confined to a purely cultural nationalism. In 1916, the year Clarke graduated, the Easter Rising took place, with MacDonagh as one of its leaders. Thus it came about that the man who was to have supervised Clarke's MA was executed by the British Army just two weeks later, on 6 May 1916, and Clarke appointed to take his place, as an assistant lecturer in English, in 1917. Yet despite his own Republicanism, Clarke played no part in the events of 1916–22, and his ambivalence, even guilt, at the outcome of the Rising may be imagined. In the year of his appointment, however, his first book, *The Vengeance of Fionn*, had appeared to considerable acclaim. A literary career beckoned, and *Fionn* was followed at no great distance by two more long poems, *The Fires of Baal* (1921) and *The Sword of the West* (1923).

These three early works were in the epic mythological manner of Samuel Ferguson, Herbert Trench and the early W.B. Yeats, and they established Clarke's reputation as one of the leading writers of the newly-independent Free State. Together with F.R. Higgins, Padraic Fallon and other poets of his own generation, Clarke was in the 1920s busily forging a national po-etry which owed much to what MacDonagh in *Literature in Ireland* (1916) had dubbed the 'Irish mode', a means by which Irish poets might avoid be-coming 'John Bull's Other Rhymers'.[8] Technically, this meant devising ways by which the unique particularity of traditional Gaelic Irish verse patterns and Hiberno-Irish speech could be foregrounded in English verse by Irish poets. Yet from its inception this project rested on a contradiction; that, given the identification of language with national essence, and the lack of first language fluency in Irish among the intelligentsia, the 'Irish mode' was a compromise. Given the climate of national self-definition, even purification, after Independence, the ideological presuppositions of the project were well summed up in Daniel Corkery's prescriptions, offered in *Synge and Anglo-Irish Literature* (1931), for a new Irish literature. Extending the ideas of MacDonagh, Corkery laid down a literary litmus test according to which the true Irishness of Irish literature should be judged according to the degree to which it reflected '(1) The Religious Consciousness of the People; (2) Irish Nationalism; and (3) The Land'.[9] Corkery's prescriptions were shaped by the conservative nature of the new state, even as they acted to shape its policies, which included approved literary representations. In this sense neo-Revivalist poets were not merely influenced by official ideology; the official ideology *was* a form of poetry, an aestheticised mode of the anti-British struggle based on an inversion of colonial discourses, one which tended to mirror the concerns of its Other. To outsiders, the idealisation of the rural and the peasantry by the neo-Revivalists seems similar to, if not indistinguishable, from, that of older Revivalists; yet the similarity was glossed over by opposing what was deemed to be a 'masculine' Gaelic 'hardness' to their predecessors' effeminate Celtic 'softness'. Pre-eminent among these was W.B. Yeats, whose newly plain and rugged style had to be overlooked for the argument to make sense.

This revamped ruralist ideal, suitably Catholicised and purged of its English and continental taints, played a large role in the process of state formation, for it offered 'essentially a literary trope' as 'a cornerstone for cultural and economic policy', and it swiftly became complicit with the essentialist ideologies used by the Catholic-Nationalist middle-classes to dominate the post-Partition State.[10] In this way, the 'Irish mode', an interim tactic for asserting literary-cultural identity, became a long-term strategy which embodied literary-cultural schism (between Anglo-Irish Protestant and Catholic authors, and between monoglot English and bilingual Gaelic/English speakers). Whereas Revival poetry had previously trafficked and toyed with the innovations of international modernism, from the early 1920s it would be bound to conservative forms and themes; and its lachrymose, shamrock-tinted Georgianism was precisely what Kavanagh would react against so violently in *The Great Hunger* (1941). Ironically for an early form of cultural decolonisation, the 'Irish mode' was wedded to a State and a Church whose illiberalism, by the late 1920s, was to be emblematised in the flight abroad of many of its leading writers.

In this fraught atmosphere, Clarke's contribution to the cultural reconstruction project was both considerable and remarkably undogmatic. He soon abandoned his early epic pretensions, and in *The Cattledrive of Connaught* (1925) and *Pilgrimage and Other Poems* (1929) displayed an expressively complex lyric style. Admittedly, the verse largely celebrated a revamped version of the Irish West beloved of the first phase Revival writers, as well as his fellow neo-Revivalists; in it, a congeries of green islands, grey skies and fiery sunsets are set to a tin-whistle soundtrack, its landscapes populated by obliging peasant girls, hard-drinking fishermen, merry cattle-drovers and sage turf-cutters. It is poetry at once mildly risqué and hopelessly in thrall to 'buckleppery', to use the term with which Kavanagh dismissed F.R. Higgins. Nevertheless, Clarke's work in this manner was always a cut above that of his contemporaries, technically impressive in the way it manages to replicate in English the complex assonantal and consonantal alliteration and rhyme schemes of Irish verse. As Clarke put it in his note to *Pilgrimage*:

Assonance, more elaborate in Gaelic than in Spanish poetry, takes the clapper from the bell of rhyme. In simple patterns, the tonic word at the end of the line is supported by a vowel-rhyme in the middle of the next line. Unfortunately the internal patterns of assonance and consonance are so intricate that they can only be suggested in another language.

The natural lack of double rhymes in English leads to an avoidance of words of more than one syllable at the end of the lyric line, except in blank alternation with rhyme. A movement constant in Continental languages is absent. But by cross-rhymes or vowel-rhyming, separately, one or more syllables of longer words, on or off accent, the difficulty may be turned: lovely and neglected words are advanced to the tonic place and divide their echoes.

(*Collected Poems*, 547 n.)

Internal rhymes and advancement to the 'tonic place' (*deibhde* rhyme) feature, for example, in 'The Scholar'.

> Summer delights the scholar
> With knowledge and reason.
> Who is happy in hedgerow
> Or meadow as he is?
>
> Paying no dues to the parish,
> He argues in logic
> And has no care of cattle
> But a satchel and stick. [. . .]
>
> But in winter by the big fires,
> The ignorant hear his fiddle,
> And he battles on the chessboard
> As the land lord bids him.

Here, to deal with the internal rhymes first, the short 'o' sound of 'scholar' in line 1 raises that of 'knowledge' in line 2, which becomes the long 'ow' in 'hedgerow' in line 3 (a word which also reverses the 'ow' and 'edge' phonemes of 'knowledge'). 'Reason', in the 'tonic place' at the end of line 2, also looks ahead to a sight rhyme with the 'ea' of 'meadow' in line 4, although by that point assonantal double rhyme has been achieved between 'hedgerow' and 'meadow'. The end-rhyming of the 'o' of 'scholar' with the 'ow' sound of 'hedgerow' and the 'eas' sound of 'reason' with 'is' in the tonic position at the end of line 4, form both pararhyme and *deibhde* rhyme (that is, the rhyme sound is on the stress but out of tonic position in the first item of the pair making the rhyme). This is more straightforward, because simpler, in the pararhyme 'lógic'/'stick' in the second verse (technically speaking, a trochee half-rhyming with an iamb). The aim – to fruitfully disrupt readers used to the standard rhyme of English tradition – is achieved wittily, musically and with only the mildest complication of syntax. Overall, Clarke's aim of forging in English a new mode which incorporates Irish Gaelic poetic modes is triumphantly fulfilled.

'The Scholar' is also representative in making play with Clarke's name ('clerk' and 'scholar' being covered by the same Irish word). Knowing this, we can see how, by its close, the poem also seems to be dramatising an opposition between the freedom-loving scholar/Clarke and the demands of the 'land lord'. Reaction against sentimentalised forms of the 'Irish mode', and an awareness of some of the ideological contradictions involved in writing essentialist Irishness in English begin to surface in the poetry at this time. The opposition between the 'scholar' and the 'ignorant' in the new Ireland was becoming increasingly evident. A growing dissatisfaction with the darkening cultural climate can be seen in Clarke's use – although 'creation' would be more accurate – of two historical eras. These alternative Irelands differed from the Revival Ireland of myth and legend in being, technically at least, properly historical, but were sufficiently distant and indefinite to allow the imagination free rein – namely, the Celto-Romanesque eighth, ninth and tenth centuries (when, as Clarke put it, 'we almost had a religion of our own'), and the era of the Anglo-Norman earldoms of the fifteenth. The first of these in particular lent itself to juxtaposition with the repressive present in a manner both satiric and celebratory. In such settings Clarke used subversive female figures – Maeve and Gormlai, a *speir-bheánn* or beautiful woman, 'The young woman of Beare' – and attributed to them a pride and sexual confidence unknown in Revival writing. These works parallel Yeats's contemporary mythologising of the eighteenth century ascendancy and celebration of sexual power in works such as the Crazy Jane sequence; but it is Clarke's historical originality which is most striking, and it serves as a reminder of the error of Yeats-centric criticism in discussing his work purely in terms of an agonistic struggle with the older writer.

The poems before *Night and Morning* (1938) are heavily accented (although in ways distinct from the English tradition) and rhythmically forceful. Lexically they are distinguished by unusual choices of verb, qualification of Yeatsian verbal modifiers, and a syntactic complexity which is not merely additive, paratactic rather than hypotactic. Indeed, syntax is frequently twisted to make a poem less immediately intelligible when this accords with subject, as in the labyrinthine 'Secrecy' – a far cry from the discursive simplicity of neo-Revival lyrics. These qualities can be seen in the first verse of 'Pilgrimage':

> When the far south glittered
> Behind grey beaded plains,
> And cloudier ships were bitted

Along the pale waves,
The showery breeze – that plies
A mile from Ara – stood
And took our boat on sand:
There by dim wells women tied
A wish on thorn, while rainfall
Was quiet as the turning of books
In the holy schools at dawn.

The third and fourth lines notably set the unusual and physically force-ful Clarkeian verb ('bitted') against Revival vagueness ('cloudier', 'pale'), earthing the latter in the observed landscapes of the poet's travels. Likewise, the deliberately abrupt interjection of the fifth and sixth lines disrupts the rhythm before it can settle. At the very least, Clarke's use of the 'Irish mode' in stylistic terms involves establishing an interplay of styles in which Revival and neo-Revival effects are constantly undermined.

Clarke's modification of neo-Revivalism was the result of his understand-ing of its limitations, but also of the vicissitudes of his own life. Soon after his striking poetic debut, he had fallen foul of his own religious scruple, and then of those of the authorities of the new state. In 1919, during the Anglo-Irish War, he had suffered a nervous breakdown, during the course of which he was hospitalised for almost a year in St Patrick's Hospital in Dublin. This harrowing cure is the subject of *Mnemosyne Lay in Dust*, a work which did not appear until 1966, and which gives few clues as to the origin of Clarke's collapse. Other writings hint at explanations, however, and in his second volume of autobiography, *Penny in the Clouds* (1968), Clarke would note that 'there is no cure for the folly of youth or the dire consequences of overindulgence in continence'. The almost Wildean *bon mot* cannot conceal the deeply personal, even anguished, tone, and indicates a clash between radical social vision, sensual instinct and religious piety of a kind familiar from Joyce's *A Portrait of the Artist as a Young Man*. Unlike Joyce, it would be many years before Clarke recovered; indeed, *Mnemosyne* is arguably the form his recovery took. As a result, when Clarke married the feminist and writer Geraldine Cummins in a secular ceremony in 1921, the marriage remained unconsummated, and was broken off after only two weeks. The disaster was compounded soon after when UCD refused to renew his contract, apparently because he had married in a registry office rather than a church.

Such facts serve as reminders of the complex fusion of national, religious and sexual trauma which shaped Clarke's poetic identity, the sense in which the stable identity of the young neo-Revival writer was shattered and had to be rebuilt. They also remind us that behind the apparently archaic trappings of some of the poetry lies a very modern sense of betrayal and impotence to which it often obliquely attests. In Clarke's work, public and private spiritual, political and sexual narratives twist together in an overdetermined manner, and the difficulties of their representation hints at (without ever wholly explaining) the delay with which he tackled certain subjects as well as the compression and difficulty of his style. Rather than mere costume drama, Clarke's version of the 'Irish mode' is best seen as a continuation of the utopian impulse of the Revival in the face of its decline into whimsy, repetition and ethnic exclusivity. In this process, the loss of a career in academia may have been no bad thing. Forced to spend the next fifteen years as a literary journalist in London, he could view what was happening at home with some detachment. In an article entitled 'Love in Irish Poetry and Drama', published in October 1932, considering the effects of censorship, Clarke remarked on how the 'gloomy, self-righteous Gaels of today' had adversely affected recent Irish writing, attacking a tradition of 'temptation and love-fear'.[11] Similarly, the origin of the 1950s Satires can be detected in his poetic response at this time; in 'Penal Law' (with its pun on 'penile'), for example, political and sexual freedom are indissoluble, just as they will be in the later poems:

> Burn Ovid with the rest. Lovers will find
> A hedge-school for themselves and learn by heart
> All that the clergy banish from the mind,
> When hands are joined and head bows in the dark.
> (*Collected Poems*, 189)

The ironies in this short piece are multiple and profound. Ovid was banished from Rome (now centre of the *Roman* Catholic Church) for writing an 'improper' love poem ('Ars amatoria'), and we also know that 'Penal Law' was written just after 'Love in Irish Poetry and Drama', at the time of the Nazi book-burnings of January 1933. While book-burning did not occur, on any scale at least, in Ireland, censorship had something of the same effect. Aided by the Catholic Truth Society, bookshops and libraries were regularly vetted. Much contemporary literature, and a great deal of past literature was prohibited (*The Decameron* went the way of Aldous Huxley, and both kept company with American pulp titles such as *Hot Dames on Cold Slabs*).[12] Films, radio music, dance styles and fashions were also subject to pulpit denunciations, or to more direct elimination. Worst of all, censorship was to prove deeply demoralising to the nation, even intellectually infantilising (library holdings could be reduced to what Terence Brown has called 'an Irish stew of imported westerns, sloppy romances, blood-and-murders bearing the *nihil obstat* of fifty-two vigilantes').[13]

Clarke's poem gains its force by juxtaposing the present with the past; 'hedge-schools', once organised by the Church in the teeth of Penal attacks on Gaelic culture are outrageously updated as schools of love held in defiance of the Church, which has swapped its former liberatory role for a repressive one. What is 'learnt by heart' by lovers is not the predetermined responses of the Mass, but the free expression of desire; and so the last line gives us the images of hands joined in passion rather than prayer and heads bowed, not in prayer or in 'the dark' of the confessional, but to kiss. *Amor vincit omnia* (love conquers all), maybe, yet it does so framed by a set of rending historical ironies. Clarke himself, however, was by no means immune to censorship or its effects, either by Yeats or the State. Two novels written not long afterwards, *The Bright Temptation* (1932) and *The Singing Men at Cashel* (1936), had already been banned when he returned to Ireland in 1937 with his family (he had remarried, happily this time, in 1930). Perhaps predictably there was another nervous breakdown, informed by the spiritual crisis charted in the anguished personal lyrics of *Night and Morning*. Again, recovery followed; but it would be seventeen years before Clarke published poetry again.

III

Thomas Kinsella has noted that 'in those flat years at the beginning of the nineteen fifties, depressed so thoroughly that one scarcely noted it, the uneasy silence of Austin Clarke added a certain emphasis'.[14] Such a silence was, of course, the norm rather than the exception for many Irish poets of the time.[15] Wartime neutrality had intensified the isolation of the 1930s and peace did not end it; unlike any other western nation, the Republic was stagnating in the mid-1950s, losing population at a rate which seemed to threaten its very existence. Clarke's reinvention of himself as a poet-critic with the publication of *Ancient Lights* in 1955 was precipitated by this crisis. As we have seen, this remaking had been anticipated. 'Martha Blake' in *Night and Morning*, for example, had had a contemporary setting and was left open for future development. This analysis of the faith of a devout spinster (albeit one whose name emblematically combines self-abasing Biblical character and assertive visionary poet), showed a woman so obsessed with ritual that she remains 'ignorant' of 'The hidden grace that people/Hurrying to business/Look after in the street' (*Collected Poems*, p. 185), and it was precisely to such 'business' that Clarke addressed his post-1955 poetry; as if emphasising the continuity and difference between the phases of his writing, 'Martha Blake at fifty-one' reappears in more realistic detail in *Flight to Africa*.

'Ancient lights' is the legal right to keep unobstructed windows of long provenance. It symbolises for Clarke the right to political, moral and spiritual light, a right he continues to seek, with some softening of satiric energy, in *Too Great a Vine* (1957) and *The Horse-Eaters* (1960). All three collections were pamphlet-length and published by Clarke's own Bridge Press. Each contained short 'satires', plus a longer poem. These long pieces contain autobiographical material and general meditation – as opposed to public particular interventions – in which relationships between a personal past and present are explored. 'Ancient Lights' itself is a celebration of escape from childhood fears, release occurring in remembrance of an epiphanic moment when Clarke had scared away a hawk clutching a sparrow. This memory is matched by a baptismal downpour in the present which washes the city clean as the sun breaks out. 'The Loss of Strength' in *Too Great a Vine* is more ambitious, moving as it does from Clarke's rueful acceptance of age to the taming of the Shannon by the hydroelectric plant at Ardnachrusha. For Clarke the plant represents a 'monk-like' curtailment of the 'natural flow' of legendary stories linked to the river and of sexual expression, reducing the current of imagination and life to 'a piddle and blank wall' (*Collected Poems*, 214). The dam also symbolises the Irish Church, and the poem glosses the collection's title: 'Too great a vine, they say, can sour/The best of clay' (216).

The theme of the present consuming the past informs *The Horse-Eaters'* 'The Hippophagi' yet more menacingly. Like the others, this poem recapitulates Clarke's own past, exploring the formation of subjectivity through a fusion of religious discourse and the instinctual, sensual drives of the child, juxtaposing both with a degraded present. The poem's central symbol for modern loss is the replacement of horses by the internal combustion engine, manifested in the new trade of exporting the animals to be 'Cut up, roast, by French and Belgian' (*Collected Poems*, 234). It is a complaint which, in isolation, might seem a fogeyish incomprehension of modernity. Yet the poem is precisely a critique of the conjunction of sentimental religion and amoral technology which is the Irish present, and in which Church and State collude. More broadly, past repression has produced the vulnerable subject which accepts an unholy and inhumane compact between science and mystificatory religion, which in turn threatens nuclear annihilation ('Man above/His own Jehovah . . . Death-dealing tons can fly alone;/Decimals known') (233). The eating of horses thus becomes synonymous with the devouring of our creaturely selves, a denial of the body; autophagy, or self-cannibalism, prepares the way for destruction. And far from being peripheral in the modern world, poetry – the 'horse-play' of children and of the imagination – is crucial to preventing annihilation.[16] In a bleak final stanza Clarke entertains the notion that the Mind, or self-awareness, supposed to distinguish human beings from animals, may after all be a 'void' (235). The technological overriding of our mortal condition might, paradoxically, ensure our extinction as a species. It is these broader perspectives which contextualise Clarke the 'local complainer' of the short satires and their specific abuses. Like the longer poems, these demand respect for the complexities of Irish history and observance of the duties which that past should be able to expect of the present. Through them, they insist on the inseparability of Irish experience from that of the rest of world.

Critics have been arguing about exactly how satirical the satires are since they first appeared. As Terence Brown claims, the importance of sexuality to Clarke's work lay in the fact that it provided him, in the potential for grotesquerie inherent in the act, with a natural route – via deflation and mockery – to a humane form of satire[17]. Generically, Clarke hovers between the milder Horatian and snarling Juvenalian varieties, and pointedly rejects the association of satire with misogyny which runs from Juvenal's *Sixth Satire* through Swift and Pope to Eliot and the present. Although some have complained about the lack of a 'killer instinct', the point lies in their redefinition of the genre, for simply to invert the terms in which State and Church represent themselves would be to remain within the grip of their reactionary mind-set. The flexibility of approach which results makes for considerable variety of tone and theme, even if the longer poems are left out of consideration. So, the inability to protest at officialdom's refusal to erect a monument to the patriot Wolfe Tone because he was a Protestant is ironically self-reproachful: 'What may we do but rattle his chains . . . We cannot blow his statue up?' (*Collected Poems*, 208). Similarly, the belated discovery by the Church of liberation theology is mocked in 'Inscription for a Headstone', which notes its past attacks on James Larkin, union leader and socialist, at a time when fear of the poor 'harden[ed]', rather than 'soften[ed]', the clerical 'heart' (*Collected Poems*, 202). To fight for the dispossessed is, for Clarke, to write 'our holiest page', but the Church has arrived on this particular scene of battle far too late to be taken seriously, unless it is prepared to show far more humility than hitherto.

Clarke would continue to write satires for the rest of his life, and in 'The Subjection of Women' from *The Echo at Coole* (1968), he listed the outstanding women whom a male establishment had written out of Irish history. The poem underlines the fact that his sharpest attacks were aimed at those who abused marginal social groups – Protestants, women and the working class – and those vulnerable in even more fundamental ways; the poor and unemployed, the aged and children. 'Three Poems about Children' was occasioned by the words of a local bishop on the death of thirty-five children in a fire in a Church-run (and fatally mismanaged) orphanage: 'Dear little angels, now before God in heaven, they were taken away before the gold of their innocence had been tarnished by the soil of this world'.[18] The poem notes that the children are not orphans – they were separated by the Church at birth from their unmarried mothers – before moving to its scathing indictment: 'Cast-iron step and railing/Could but prolong the wailing... flame-wrapped babes are spared/Our lifetime of temptation/Leap, mind, in consolation . . . Those children, charred in Cavan/Passed straight through Hell to Heaven' (*Collected Poems*, 197) The final lines, as Hugh Maxton claims, 'must surely count as Clarke's most effective use of his distinctive rhyme patterns' (*Selected Poems*, 228n).

In its controlled outrage 'Three Poems about Children' serves as a reminder that Clarke's best satires have a Brechtian bite and slyness which the longer poems forego. But as in 'The Hippophagi' (in which it is the *betrayal* of the horses and their slaughter *by proxy* which crystallises national hypocrisy), it is the lack of self-awareness, the ability to admit wrongdoing, which is deemed particularly reprehensible. In this sense the poems focus on the peculiarly modern conflict of *representations*, of justice (or injustice) being *seen* to be done, as well as of the actual deeds involved. 'Mother and Child' is another case in point, published as it was in 1954 after the Church's declaration that the year was to be devoted to the Virgin Mary, and the subsequent issue of a commemorative stamp by Post Éireann:

> Obedient keys rattled in locks,
> Bottles in old dispensaries
> Were shaken and the ballot boxes
> Hid politicians on their knees
> When pity showed us what we are.
> 'Why should we care', votes cried, 'for child
> Or mother? Common help is harmful
> And state-control must starve the soul.'
> One doctor spoke out. Bishops mitred.
> But now our caution has been mended,
> The side-door open, bill amended,
> We profit from God's love and pity,
> Sampling the world with good example.
> Before you damp it with your spit,
> Respect our newest postage stamp.
> (*Collected Poems*, 202)

Despite the date of its appearance, the poem initially refers to the attempt made in 1951 by the radical health minister of a coalition government, Dr Noel Browne, to introduce a Mother and Child Bill. Browne's bill was intended to give help to poor nursing mothers, but had been denounced as 'socialistic' by both the Church and the medical profession for grossly self-interested reasons – fear, respectively, of loss of social control and of medical fees. Browne's cabinet colleagues had abandoned him at this point and he was forced to resign. But the poem is not simply lamenting Browne's fate. It refers also to the fact that when the Fianna Fáil party – who had called for Browne's head – came to power in 1953, they passed legislation almost identical to his.

Clarke's target, then, is not just the hypocritical opposition to, or abandonment of, Noel Browne; it is, rather, the general refusal to admit their earlier error by those involved. The pun on 'mitred' – the bishops 'might' have done differently – suggests, as a device, the fusion of Church and State power, as God's 'love' and 'pity' are subordinated to financial and spiritual 'profit'. Though seemingly simply, a topical linkage of past and present, 'Mother and Child' actually concerns the representation of power which underlies this specific abuse. Clarke is angered because democracy's 'ballot boxes' are being made to serve as a cover for the politics of the side-door – privileged access and patriarchal string-pulling. He takes the stamp as a symbol of the State's subservience to the bishops and doctors; it embodies the duplicity which tries to blur the gap between independence ideal ('to cherish each member of the nation equally') and current actuality. In doing so, the poem mimics the blend of brazenness and secrecy it attacks by being itself both belated and immediate, circumspect and offensive, abstract and vulgar (these qualities summed up in the final 'pity'/'spit' rhyme). Taken together, then, these satires are more than the sum of their parts, transcending the 'occasional' category as individual instances of deprivation, neglect and brutality accumulate into a wider attack on power. In their blend of personal and political, the three satires collections, like *Flight to Africa* (which shares their structure), point towards the final imaginative release of *Mnemosyne* and the long poems of Clarke's last years.

IV

It is usual to relate *Mnemosyne Lay in Dust* to the confessional poetry of the time, initiated by W.R. Snodgrass's *The Heart's Needle* (1959), and popularised by Robert Lowell, Sylvia Plath and John Berryman. Certainly, the poem has its therapeutic dimension, taking as it does the form of a ventriloquised, confessional cure. But it is also the product of Irish circumstances, the rapid modernisation of the years after 1959 in which Sean Lemass was Taoiseach, and the reforms to the Catholic Church brought about by the Vatican II Council of 1963–65. Equally crucially, 1966 was the fiftieth

anniversary of the Easter Rising and was marked with much pomp and ceremony. The appearance, at the ceremonies in the Gaelic Athletic Association's
stadium Croke Park, of the blind and aged President De Valera beside the
technocrat Lemass provided a stark contrast of old and new. In publishing
Mnemosyne in the same year Clarke set his own old and younger selves together with something of the same effect of historical irony, inscribing his
personal collapse in 1919 within the national struggle for freedom. Torment
and insurrection collide, and an occluded history is retrieved from the dust
of oblivion in a work whose overdetermined narrative is written on the body
of its protagonist, Maurice Devane, in the most graphic manner. In keeping
with the classicizing of Clarke's later poetry, this movement from loss to recovery of self is conducted under the aegis of Mnemosyne, the Greek goddess
of memory and the mother of the Muses.

The poem, which is in eighteen parts, opens with Maurice entering the
asylum in mortal 'terror', believing that 'Void' – the key concluding word in
'The Hippophagi' – 'would draw his spirit,/Unself him' (*Collected Poems*,
p. 327). Here he is subjected to a brutal, disorienting regime, violently un-
dressed and 'plunged/Into a steaming bath', 'half-suffocated' by 'assailants
gesticulating' as if in 'A Keystone reel gone crazier' (not just more agitated
and absurd than a Keystone Cops movie, but a more-than-Keystone world
'reeling', even becoming the 'real') (p. 328). Visions, nightmares, terror of
other inmates, bedwetting, force-feeding and petty beatings follow. Maurice's
experiences are rendered with the full resources of Clarke's late style, from
a jostling, compressed, assonantal verse in part II to revulsion and repetition in part IV, from the spine-tingling horrors of part VIII (this is
the poem 'Summer Lightning' from *Night and Morning*, a sign of how
long Clarke had wrestled with his subject) to the meditative lyricism of
part III:

> . . . Drugged in the dark, delirious,
> In vision Maurice saw, heard, struggle
> Of men and women, shouting groans.
> In an accident at Westland Row,
> Two locomotives with mangle of wheel-spokes,
> Colliding: [. . .]

> . . . Weakening, he lay flat. Appetite
> Had gone. The beef or mutton, potatoes
> And cabbage – he turned from the thick slices
> Of meat, the greasy rings of gravy.
> Knife had been blunted, fork was thick
> And every plate was getting bigger.
> His stomach closed: always beef or mutton,

Potatoes, cabbage, turnips. Mind spewed,
Only in dreams was gluttonous.

. . . Napoleon took his glittering vault
To be a looking-glass.
Lord Mitchell, pale and suffering,
Fell to the ground in halves.
The cells were filling. Christopher
O'Brien, strapped in pain,

For all the rage of syphilis
Had millions in his brain. [. . .]

Looking down from bars
    With mournful eye
Maurice could see them beckoning,
    Some pointed, signed.

Waving their arms and hands,
    They wandered. Why
Should they pretend they did not see him
    Lost to mind?

        (pp. 328; 333; 190, 338; 331)

The effect of the range of styles is simultaneously to enclose us in Maurice's tactile experience of confinement and to attenuate a sense of identity through the errant, 'wandering'/wondering, 'beyond the Pale' quality of his thought. We are spared little of his anguish, delusions, self-abasement, blank misery and (literal) self-dissolution.

Neil Corcoran has pointed out that, 'A great many substances flow from [Maurice] in the early parts of the poem', suggesting the crumbling of the bounds of selfhood, as Clarke hints at both the ostensible causes for Maurice's fast – a hunger strike against himself paralleling that of the Sinn Féin prisoners held by the British in 1919 – and the psychic blockages that lie behind it.[19] These are traced in dream imagery and wordplay, such as that on 'prick' and 'erections' in part V:

. . . [he] knew they were the holy ictyphalli
Curled hair for bushwood, bark or skin
Heavily veined. He worshipped, a tiny satyr,
    Mere prick beneath those vast erections.

        (p. 333)

Maurice, in fact, constructs a mythic dream-world of considerable beauty as compensation for the real world he has abandoned, out of guilt at his non-involvement in the independence struggle and his thwarted sexual desires. Having heard the warders talk of a gate, garden and fountain, he elaborates on them. Thus, in part V, he is harassed in a dream by a 'silent form' he calls 'The Watcher', who '[casts] the shadow of a policeman'. The mythic 'release' from his all too well-policed libido abruptly takes oriental, fantastic shape:

> Joyously through a gateway, came a running
> Of little Jewish boys, their faces pale
> As ivory or jasmine, from Lebanon
> To Eden. Garlanded, caressing,
> Little girls ran with skip and leap . . .
>   Love
> Fathered him with their happiness.
>
>   (p. 334)

In reality, as the vision reveals when it recurs in part IX, the gate and 'the primal Garden' are, punningly, as 'guarded' as Eden, the 'leaping' of the children echoing the name of 'tall, handsome, tweeded Dr. Leeper'. 'Pale', too, is a loaded word, hinting at possible historical and psychological meanings of confinement and colonial encroachment. Like Maurice's fantasies of fighting for Ireland as a 'Daring Republican', these lead to nothing but the doctor's reiterated appeal to him to ' "Think . . . Think" '. Nevertheless, in the 'top-room' of a very Yeatsian tower inside the hospital Maurice still finds himself 'stumbling/Where Mnemosyne lay in dust' (p. 334). Release, from delusion, self-loss and destructive fasting, finally occurs in two forms, sexual and gustatory. Mnemosyne herself had not been able to help Maurice, although the encounter with her is the precondition for Clarke's writing of the poem. However, withdrawal to the sexual self-sufficiency of masturbation in part X offers itself as one release and as a form of paradoxical affiliation with his fellow inmates:

> Often in priestly robe on a
> Night of full moon, out of the waste,
> A solitary figure, self-wasted,
> Stole from the encampments – Onan,
> Consoler of the young, the timid,
> The captive. Administering, he passed down
> The ward. Balsam was in his hand.
> The self-sufficer, the anonym.   (p. 343)

Maurice Harmon regards Clarke's Onan as merely 'eerie and destructive', as belonging to a 'perverse priesthood', one whose relief is 'furtive, shameful and associated with madness' (Harmon, *Introduction*, 217). As readers of 'Ancient Lights' and *Twice Round the Black Church* (1962) will recall, masturbation is the subject of the more truly shameful extorted 'confession' of 'tak[ing] pleasure when alone' which was wrung out of the seven-year-old Clarke by an over-zealous priest (p. 199). Onan symbolises Maurice's abjection: both are 'self-sufficers', or 'anonyms' to use Clarke's telling coinage. As Corcoran observes, Clarke also fills the absence at the poem's centre 'with the presence of the conditioning circumstances which have provoked and produced that absence: the impossibility of a true sexual relation; the anxiety induced by a false, neurotic religion; the terror of living through a period of violent political upheaval'.[20] In spite of his mythopoeic and therefore illusory aspect ('Balsam' recalls the 'balsam' tree of Maurice's earlier mythic improvisation), Onan nevertheless grants a physical benediction, a release which makes flow just about the one bodily fluid – semen – which has not yet done so in this poem. Unlike the 'unwanted' semen in Maurice's reliving of his sexually continent relationship with 'Margaret'/Geraldine, an impossibly asexual 'romantic dream', this is much desired, and liberatory. It is no coincidence, therefore, that after accepting the 'Balsam', in parts XI and XII of the poem, he breaks his fast with food brought by his mother.

The moment is a Wordsworthian one – 'Nature', as it is glossed, 'Remembering a young believer . . . Gave him from the lovely hand/Of his despairing mother/A dish of strawberries' (344). But it is also, and equally importantly, a Keatsian one. This is not just because the urge to gratify the senses which sees Maurice reach out to take the fruit beside him ('so ripe, ruddy, delicious') is described in terms of sexual anticipation and deferral which recall the feast 'heap'd' at Madeleine's bedside in 'The Eve of Saint Agnes'. It is also because Mnemosyne herself inevitably reminds us of the Mnemosyne of Keats' *Hyperion* who becomes the main figure (under the name of Moneta, her Roman designation) of *The Fall of Hyperion*. She, like Onan, is a figure who appears 'self-wasted', a monitory but healing and empowering presence. As in *The Fall of Hyperion*, Moneta-Mnemosyne in Keats' poem leads the mortal who encounters her to endure a trial which would kill him, should he fail. 'Nature' helps save Maurice, then, but so too do his bodily appetites and memories (or, as Keats phrased it, in one of his final despairing poems to Fanny Brawne, 'Touch has a memory').[21] Clarke/Devane, like Keats, overcomes an oppressive, archaic and patriarchal mythography through the agency of an all-knowing female figure, but he also overcomes self-hatred through an act of will and the material agency of his birth mother. In doing so, it might be added, Yeats and the power of myth are acknowledged and bypassed in a recovery presided over by female figures. Maurice's recovery, Mnemosyne's restoration from 'dust', and poetry itself, are signified in the difference between the verbs in the poem's first and final lines; between 'the house where he was *got*' (p. 327) and 'the house where his mother was *born*' (p. 352) (my emphasis). It is a difference which charts precisely a progress from inert, animal conception to human origin, and a healing return of the repressed.[22]

V

At the end of his life Clarke chose to explore sexual experience in a positive if less realist light than in his previous poetry. The result was a series of extraordinary narrative poems. 'The Dilemma of Iphis' (1970), 'The Healing of Mis' (1970), *Tiresias* (1971) and 'The Wooing of Becfola' (1974), return to mythology and legend, at least partly in an attempt to outdo Yeats's persona of the wild old wicked man. Typically, Clarke's version of the close of an Irish poet's career is anti-phallocentric, a set of tales about women being more capable of sexual pleasure than men ('The Dilemma of Iphis' and *Tiresias*), a wife's ambiguous loyalty to her husband ('The Wooing of Becfola'), and a past of abuse (and an abusive past) overcome by what Marvin Gaye would have called sexual healing ('The Healing of Mis').

In this latter poem, Clarke adapts a Gaelic original in which Duv Ruis, a harper-poet, takes on the challenge of reclaiming Mis, a woman who has lost her mind and has been living in the forest, wild and unkempt, 'for three centuries' (*Collected Poems*, 509). Failure will mean death for Ruis; but he wins her from savagery with music, kindness, coins, 'a griddle cake', a good bath and much mutually enjoyable sex – what Mis calls 'the feat of the wand' (511) If this sounds too close to an old man's lurid fantasy, or even received sexist wisdom that all an 'unfeminine' woman needs is sex with a 'real' man, Clarke characteristically queries most of the stereotypes the story sets up. Most obviously, the musical, cooking Ruis, who washes Mis 'like a mother' and '[keeps] house' for her is himself the 'feminine' partner in this relationship, and is reliant on Mis when they first make love: 'He waited, obedient as she helped/Him through the hymen' (the later Clarke is almost clinical in his descriptions of the sexual act) (513). More disturbingly, Ruis observes that Mis suffers from the 'stir and dire cry' of bad dreams (514). The anticipation of the 'curative methods of Freud' by the original text, mentioned by Clarke in his note to the poem, is activated (557). Mis tells Ruis her buried memories of volcanic eruptions, of zigzagging through labyrinthine passages, and finally of being 'Unvirgined by the Minotaur – /I knew my father' (515). The passages recall those describing Clarke's own childhood terrors of rooms and passages at the beginning of *Twice Round the Black Church*; and Mis's madness is shown to have its source in the breaking of two primal taboos – cannibalism (the drinking of human blood) and incest. The only cure is the talking cure and its power to help Mis 'rememorise' herself, to use the term applied to Maurice Devane. In the original tale, Ruis is murdered after his success whereupon Mis, now recovered, composes his elegy. But, as Maxton acutely notes, Clarke's version eliminates the retributive, sacrificial element and brings us to a conclusion in which, fittingly, 'poet and woman are united' although, as in psychotherapy, nothing is ever absolutely concluded (*Selected Poems*, 20).

It turns out that 'The Healing of Mis' is less a tale with a happy ending than one of a number of provisional conclusions to a body of work which explores and demystifies the stereotypes which trap individuals and nations. In this work, silencing begins as individual but is made collective and representative through its deployment in a satirically creative demolition of the status quo. At all points, it is worth stressing, this is inseparable from a linguistic reversal of silencing, in the form of stylistic resistance to incorporation within the discourses of others and reduction to instrumental linguistic usage. The complex music of the brilliantly transposed Gaelic metrics found in the earlier poetry is complemented, or supplanted, in the later work by something only apparently ungainly; and style and form are inseparable from content and purpose in a way which is rare in much Irish poetry. The wordplay and foregrounding of the literary device in the later poems is calculatedly excessive and outrageous, including as it does *rime riche,* homonyms, anagrams, acrostics, trisyllabic rhyme, puns and neologisms.[23]

Syntactically, parataxis is the norm in this work, and together with rhymes such as 'Voltaire'/'volt tear' (or 'petrol'/'pet, roll', or the reverse-rhyme 'toenail'/'natoed'), is precisely calculated to disrupt expectations of a smoothly discursive narrative style. Clarke's later use of the device represents a displacement of the more mildly disruptive, pulsional rhythms of the early poetry into an angular style, as if he feels compelled to offset the concessions he is forced to grant to realism and reportage in order to make a public statement. His own comparison of these procedures with those of a certain London street-entertainer is well known: 'I load myself with chains and try to get out of them' (*Collected Poems*, 545), and they embody the struggle for release which informs his poetry at every level. Opposed as he is to utilitarian reductionism and bogus transcendentalism, Clarke's style can be linked to a religious doubt which proves its genuineness by stressing the materiality of its medium, language. As Maxton claims, the desire to 'confront an inability to believe' nevertheless indicates an 'inability to disbelieve', and Clarke's doubt is an 'activity which is religious in itself and not merely in its concerns' (*Selected Poems*, 12). His entire poetic therefore proclaims the materiality and constructedness of the poem, even as it permits a negative theology to emerge from the ruins of an orthodox faith.

Bravura technique, satiric but compassionate social analysis and spiritual self-exploration run together in Clarke's best poems. Though he began his career as a poet of myth in the neo-Revival mould, he developed ways of turning its essentialist tendencies against themselves for demystifying, recuperative ends. It is significant, for example, that *Mnemosyne* sets up, but then dismantles, its big symbolic-mythic apparatus of Fountain, Gate and Garden. Donald Davie, in his early championing of Clarke's post-1955 work, argued that Clarke 'is further from mythopoeia than any poet one might think of', and this at a time when there were 'good hard-headed reasons for the modern Irish poet to take the mythopoeic path against which Clarke set his face'.[24] In the light of *Mnemosyne* and the late narratives, this might seem somewhat rash, but the identification of the demystifying urge is correct. Clarke's achievement in this area is tonic, and ultimately aligns him with Joyce rather than his *bête noir* Yeats.

It might just be that few Irish poets of the past hundred years have quite as much contemporary relevance as Clarke. A feminist, socialist humanist and scathing satirist of the hypocrisy of Church and State, Clarke would surely feel at home in the contentious 'Celtic Tiger' Republic of the early twenty-first century. Far from looking quaint, the poet who, in his seventies, could consider calling a collection *The Pill*, and write verses about napalm, or about what was to become the EU, would be in his element. If Clarke has looked out of place in a society which, by and large, reacted to recession and the Troubles with a reassertion of older pieties, the most recent developments allow us to glimpse a future in which poetry like Clarke's will gain new currency, and our relative ignorance of him seem a merely temporary aberration.

NOTES

1 All page references for poems are given for Liam Miller (ed.), *Austin Clarke: Collected Poems* (Dublin: Dolmen Press, 1974). See also *Austin Clarke: Selected Poems* (Dublin: Lilliput Press, 1991), which contains an invaluable introduction by Hugh Maxton.

2 See Terence Brown, 'Austin Clarke: Satirist' in *Ireland's Literature* (Dublin: Gigginstown: Lilliput, 1988) and Neil Corcoran, 'The Blessings of Onan: Austin Clarke's *Mnemosyne Lay in Dust*', *Irish University Review*, 13: 1 (Spring 1983), pp. 43–53.

3 Seamus Deane in *Celtic Revivals* (London: Faber and Faber, 1985) refers briefly and in passing to the 'randy clerics of Clarke's beehive-hut civilisation' and his 'glamourising' of the medieval clergy; Declan Kiberd, in *Inventing Ireland* (London: Jonathan Cape, 1995), depoliticises him by implying that his critique was directed solely against the 'intolerance' of the Irish Church, which is the purely colonial creation of 'the imperial and evangelical spirit of the British race'. Edna Longley in *The Living Stream* (Newcastle: Bloodaxe Books, 1994) mentions none of Clarke's work after 1938.

4 John Goodby, *Irish poetry since 1950: from stillness into history* (Manchester University Press, 1999), pp. 21–8.

5 Clarke mentions 'my own recent work which is inspired by belief in the immediate needs for an Irish Welfare State' in his short study *Poetry in Modern Ireland* (Cork: Mercier Press, 1951).

6 Samuel Beckett, 'Recent Irish Poetry', in Ruby Cohn (ed.), *Disjecta: Miscellaneous Writings and a Dramatic Fragment* (London: John Calder, 1983), p. 71.

7 See W.J. McCormack, 'Austin Clarke: The Poet as Scapegoat of Modernism', in Patricia Coughlan and Alex Davis (eds.), *Modernism and Ireland: The Poetry of the 1930s* (Cork University Press, 1995), pp. 75–102.

8 See Goodby, *Irish poetry since 1950*, pp. 5–6 and 21–2.

9 Daniel Corkery, *Synge and Anglo-Irish Literature* (Cork University Press, 1931), p. 19.

10 David Cairns and Shaun Richards, *Writing Ireland: Colonialism, Nationalism and Culture* (Manchester University Press, 1988), p. 133. See also Gerry Smythe, *Decolonisation and Criticism: The Construction of Irish Literature* (London: Pluto Press, 1998).

11 Austin Clarke, 'Love in Irish Poetry and Drama', *Motley*, 1: 5 (October 1932), pp. 3–4.

12 See Julia Carlson (ed.), *Banned in Ireland: Censorship & the Irish Writer* (London: Routledge, 1990).

13 Terence Browne, *Ireland: A Social and Cultural History 1922–85* (London: Fontana, 1985), p. 77.

14 Thomas Kinsella, 'The Poetic Career of Austin Clarke', *Irish University Review*, 4: 1 (1974), p. 128.

15 Patrick Kavanagh, Padraic Fallon, Thomas MacGreevy and Brian Coffey all suffered such breaks; many young poets, such as Patrick Galvin, Pearse Hutchinson and Desmond O'Reilly left Ireland. Some, like Valentin Iremonger, gave up writing altogether.

16 The same horse theme is developed in *Forget-me-not*, Collected Poems, pp. 237–43.

17 Brown, *Ireland's Literature*, pp. 134–5.

18 Quoted in Maurice Harmon, *Austin Clarke: A Critical Introduction* (Dublin: Wolfhound, 1989) p. 145.

19 Corcoran, 'The Blessings of Onan', pp. 44–6.

20 Ibid., pp. 47–8.

21 Miriam Allott (ed.), *Keats: The Complete Poems* (London: Longman, 1972), pp. 673–4 and 686.

22 See W.J. McCormack, in Coughlan and Davis, p. 98.

23 Clarke's own note on rime riche in the *Collected Poems* provides a hint as to his usage of the device: '. . . in English the second homonym seems at times to be ironic in effect, and in composite self-rhyme may lead back, perhaps, to the mood of *Pacchiarotto and How He Worked in Distemper* [by Robert Browning], in which the rhyme becomes a running commentary' (*Collected Poems*, p. 555n).

24 Donald Davie, 'Austin Clarke and Padraic Fallon', in Douglas Dunn, *Two Decades of Irish Writing: A Critical Survey* (Manchester: Carcanet, 1975), pp. 38 and 41.

3

JONATHAN ALLISON

Patrick Kavanagh and antipastoral

I'm the only man who has written in our time about rural Ireland from the inside.

(Patrick Kavanagh, 1949)[1]

I

'Pastoral' has been defined in a variety of ways, and has been said to include the 'antipastoral', though some readers will wish to make a rigid distinction between the two, while recognising that both are intimately related. Traditionally, pastoral is a matter of rural life and shepherds, idyllic landscapes in which people corrupted by court and city life are changed and renewed. It suggests a healing antithesis to the corrupting influence of urban experience, but has been characterised simply as poetry of the countryside (however defined), and does not always envision an idealised and falsified, conflict-free zone, transcending the tensions of history, though it can do that, too. 'Antipastoral', on the other hand, suggests a poetics of undermining, in which pastoral conventions are deployed or alluded to, in order to suggest or declare the limitations of those conventions, or their downright falsity. If pastoral suggests that rural life offers freedom, antipastoral may proclaim it is a prison-house, and the farmers slaves. Historically, antipastoral has been associated with Goldsmith's *The Deserted Village* (1770) and George Crabbe's *The Village* (1783), with certain poems of John Clare, and with Stephen Duck who, in *The Thresher's Labour* (1736) wrote, 'No fountains murmur here, no Lambkins play, / No Linnets warble, and no Fields look gay'.[2] A defining feature of such poetry has been its realistic treatment of labour, protest against idealising poetic traditions, and in some cases outcry against political conditions related to land enclosure. For Seamus Heaney, pastoral is a matter of 'idealised landscape with contented figures,' but with antipastoral, 'sweat and pain and deprivation are acknowledged'.[3] Patrick

Kavanagh, in his long poem of 1942, *The Great Hunger*, acknowledged all that, and more.

Early in his career, during an impoverished literary apprenticeship in the 1930s, Kavanagh wrote short, religious pastoral lyrics, before his animus found vent with his celebrated depiction of Patrick Maguire and small farmers in a fictional townland, closely modeled on Kavanagh's home ground of Donaghmoyne in County Monaghan. Later, after a ferocious battle in the law courts and a lung operation in the mid-1950s, Kavanagh entered a period of relative calm, as man and poet, when he composed the Canal Bank Sonnets. Throughout his life, he wrote versions of pastoral, although he is remembered by most for *The Great Hunger*, which did indeed acknowledge sweat, pain and deprivation, and posed an aesthetic challenge to the pastoral myths of the Anglo-Irish Literary Revival, including the myth of the noble peasant and the mythology of 'cosy homesteads' and 'dancing at the crossroads' propagated by Eamon de Valera's new government of the Republic of Ireland.[4] Kavanagh's tirades against the poetry and ideology of the Revival were spoken from the viewpoint of a farmer-poet dismayed by writers of national pastoral who, in many cases, had little genuine experience of rural, let alone agricultural life.

His beginnings were in the mystical pastoral lyrics (what his biographer Antoinette Quinn calls 'decorous pastoral verses'[5]), encouraged by his mentor 'AE' (George Russell, 1867–1935), and collected in *Ploughman and Other Poems* (1936). In these, a beautiful landscape is contemplated by the poet-labourer, a place of divine manifestation, where the privileged viewer may have a mystical vision. It was this aspect of the poetry that urged one derisive reviewer to complain that 'echoes of the factitious Celtic mysticism of nature come trailing like rags of gaudy gauze'.[6] In 'Ploughman', for instance, the meadow is a painterly brown, the field 'lea-green,' and labour (disguised as painting) is performed gleefully ('Gaily now').[7] In 'To a Blackbird,' the poet claims kinship with the eponymous bird, and against a picturesque background of lakes, he hears sweet songs in a gentle wind blowing over the hills (p. 3). Here is rural subject matter, an idyllic landscape, a place of reverie, free of anguish or indeed conflict. 'Ploughman' is a prayer-like, religious pastoral, with Christian diction, where the landscape offers visions of a 'star-lovely art', with the divine immanent in the land: '. . . ecstasy / Like a prayer'. In 'To a Blackbird', men plead for religious conversion 'With the Most High'; in 'Mary' we are told 'Her name's in every prayer' (4); in 'I May Reap' the speaker wishes that he 'By God's grace may come to harvest' (4). The speaker in 'A Star' stretches out his hands to the 'Seraphim' (8). On the other hand, we do find the imagination of disappointment at the stunted growth of a tree, which 'will never hide sparrows / From hungry hawks' ('April', 7). Yet April is welcomed as a harbinger of new life, and hope springs near the meadows where spring is pregnant 'By the Holy Ghost' (18). It is not certain that the seeds of *The Great Hunger* are contained in such delicate but ardent visions.

A much admired early poem, 'Inniskeen Road: July Evening', a Shakespearean sonnet (with Miltonic division between octave and sestet), offers a more complex viewpoint (19). Set in the heart of summer, with nature blooming all around, the speaker's palpable sense of isolation from men cycling to the dance suggests clear ambivalence about his position. After the men have passed him by, the speaker witnesses the silence as peaceful but somehow vacuous. He is more aware of the absence of people than of the presence of a compelling natural landscape: 'no shadow thrown / That might turn out a man or woman'. Loneliness prohibits his enjoyment of nature as a place of contemplation; sympathy with the Crusoe-like Alexander Selkirk suggests alienation from the land, a feeling of being imprisoned, or stranded on a desert island. The rustic scene, therefore, is celebrated for its freedom but recognised as a place of banishment: he is king 'Of banks and stones and every blooming thing'. Such ambivalence helps to sound a troubled and ambiguous pastoral note.

Another celebrated lyric, 'Shancoduff' (printed in *Dublin Magazine*, 1937, later published in *Come Dance with Kitty Stobling*), recognises the bleakness and impoverishment of home, but finds the energy to celebrate it (30). The poet's essay 'The Parish and the Universe' throws light on the assumptions behind this poem: 'The parochial mentality . . . is never in any doubt about the social and artistic validity of his parish'.[8] One must recognise the home turf as fit subject matter for poetry, to affirm it courageously in face of external pressures to denigrate what objectively may seem uninteresting. His hills are 'my' black hills, which strikes the all-important note of ownership (he later says 'They are my Alps'). Bleak, shaded, north-facing and cut off from sunshine, they see no sunrise, 'eternally'. 'Incurious', the hills don't look back, are independent and unchanging. This makes them sound rather dull, until relief comes with the surprising word 'happy': happy when dawn comes to whiten the nearby chapel, echoing the sacramental note of the aforementioned poems. Nevertheless, resistance to idealisation in the poem, its bleak candour and courageous obsession with plainness, does much to distinguish it from 'Ploughman' and similar poems.

'Stony Grey Soil' (written October 1940, published 1947), presents an unillusioned view of the rural landscape, and realises an increase in the poet's critical faculties in relation to that world. As Quinn observes, it is in many respects the poem that anticipates the fury of *The Great Hunger*, and the soil in question 'will become the dispirited "clay" that dominates all rural life in *The Great Hunger*'.[9] The unbeautiful landscape of childhood is admired briefly, but blamed for ruining his life; it stole his laughter, youth, love and passion, and deprived him of his 'vision / Of Beauty'. The plough has destroyed him ('O green-life-conquering plough!'), and marked forever his brow with signs of stress (82). He claims he was treated like an animal, and that his farming life was one of moral cowardice. The poem ends by naming townlands dear to him in youth ('Mullahinsha, Drummeril, Black Shanco'), but the pastoral connotations of such naming are totally undercut by the fact they conjure up in his mind the 'Dead loves that were born for me'. Love-denying, they are places of prohibition, constriction and death. The poem is a direct address to the soil, characterised not as fructive and supportive, but as manipulative and malign (in this one respect the soil resembles the portrait in *The Great Hunger*). However, in terms of the poet's search for subject matter, the stony soil of his past provides a fertile ground for this and further poems on the topic, and the mixed tones of disgust and love anticipate ambivalences to be explored later.

II

The Great Hunger established Kavanagh as the fiercest, and one of the most innovative Irish poets after Yeats.[10] The fourteen-section poem is antipas-toral in several respects: implicitly scorning sentimental depictions of peasant life as popularised by writers of the Revival, it invokes the farming landscape only to depict it as infertile and barely productive; it portrays the life of the peasant as utterly boring, if not utterly degraded, and as unheroic and life-denying, whereas conventionally it had been depicted as noble and heroic. The peasant is not the eloquent, vigorous farmer of national tradition, but mute, petty and jealous; the local community is no harmonious, organic so-ciety, but a collection of individual families which are in many ways jealous rivals. Maguire and his men are depicted at first as merely mechanical labour-ers, and throughout the poem are seen as passive, without agency. Their lives exemplify what Kavanagh in the poem calls 'the weak, washy way of true tragedy' – tragedy not in any classical sense, but in the sense of a restricted life without choice, luck or grace (53). Humans are reduced to commodities – to 'what is written on the label'. Maguire is good-hearted, but dominated by his manipulative, elderly mother. He lives in fear of a vengeful God, or at least of vigilant clergy. The religion practiced in the community smacks of uniformity and convention, though affording occasional consolation and uplift. 'Married' to the fields, fearing sin, and fearing but craving sexual in-timacy, Maguire lives a life of sexual abstinence (despite masturbating into the grate), and is depicted variously as emasculated, impotent, feminised, womanish and as a eunuch. His debility is more than hinted at in the line, 'The pricks that pricked were the pointed pins of harrows' (35). Young women like Agnes, in section seven, crave courtship and marriage, but the men are blind to her needs, or afraid of them, and courting rituals are apparently non-existent. The pub is a gathering place for local men, but their conversation is satirised as pointless, ill-informed and competitive. Meetings at the crossroads are occasions of inertia and bovine lethargy. This is a far cry from the pastoral crossroads dances with 'comely maidens' invoked by Irish Taoiseach Eamon de Valera in a famous speech of the 1930s about the rural basis of Irish society. The agricultural conditions of the farm are inferior: the land is damp and largely clay, and grazing conditions are appalling: the poem ends with the dramatic image of an 'apocalypse of clay' (55).

Section one of the poem begins with the mock-Biblical evocation of the gospel according to John – 'Clay is the word and clay is the flesh' – establishing satirical distance from comfortable views of rural life and religious consolation. Hopeless labourers are reduced to the status of 'crows', or automatons. They are passive in the face of an overwhelming routine of hard work and comfortless bachelordom. If the poem recalls Stephen Dedalus's analysis of Irish national life as conditioned by the nets of religion and nationality, Dedalus, unlike Maguire, had the wherewithal to 'fly by those nets'. Maguire can laugh with his friends 'Of how he came free from every net spread / In the gaps of experience', but in reality he does not escape so lightly (34). His life is conditioned by 'marriage' to the land and the inescapable 'grip of the fields', hence his anger at his mother, who always praised farmers who make the farm their bride. If traditional pastoral suggests social integrity, built upon harmonious family and community relations, the divided family unit in the townland of Donaghmoyne speaks to fragmentation at personal and communal levels. Maguire distrusts his mother, who manipulates him continuously: 'And he knows that his own heart is calling his mother a liar' (36). The grammar of that line, contrasting the knowing faculty with the heart, also suggests division within the self. Divided within, his spirit is 'a wet sack' in the wind; the house of Maguire is 'an iron house', suggesting both the confining structure of a prison cell and the unbending structure of destiny.

In the second section, the 65-year-old bachelor farmer is faithful only to his mother (who lived until she was 91), and to the land. Repetition of the phrase 'O he loved' is ironic in light of his bachelorhood and the absence of fulfillment in his life (37). His chief pleasures are physical but solitary; his only dream is to smoke his pipe or to 'clean his arse / with perennial grass, / On the bank of some summer streams' (37). The vulgar colloquialism contrasts strikingly with the pastoral image of the summer bank. (Indeed, most of this section was bowdlerised because considered too vulgar (too antipastoral?) when published in *A Soul for Sale*.) Depicted as emasculated, diminished by daily farming chores, he is a thwarted figure, a 'eunuch' of the fields.

In section three, Maguire's mother is portrayed misogynistically as tough, ugly and demanding: 'a venomous drawl / And a wizened face like moth-eaten leatherette' (37). The first stanza of this section has thirteen lines, but the second and third stanzas are sonnets. The March scene is desolate, with a cold wind blowing, and the ploughing of the 'virgin' fields is depicted as a kind of rape (38).[11] The relationship between earth and its tiller is violent and invasive. Farmers are jealous of each other, who watch one another 'with all the sharpened interest of rivalry' (38). The sonnet turns after the eighth line to the mysticism more usually found in the pastoral lyrics of the 1930s: 'Yet sometimes when the sun comes through a gap / These men know God the Father in a tree' (38). Many of them perceive fleetingly the natural beauty of their surroundings, understood as a manifestation of the Christian God at Easter. The sacrifice of realism here makes Donaghmoyne seem more of a united, religious community than elsewhere in the poem. This is an example of how pastoral breaks in occasionally to the darker antipastoral narrative, but not disrupting the overall antipastoral tone of the poem.

A church scene, in which Maguire, casually at prayer, is distracted by thoughts of turnips, dominates the fourth section (set one month later, in April): never for long can his thoughts stray from his fields. The dull uniformity of the congregation is delivered bathetically in the image of the entire church coughing 'in unison' (39). Nevertheless, the rhetoric at one point rises to the level of religious vision: 'And the pregnant Tabernacle lifted a moment to Prophecy / Out of the clayey hours' (39). The passage employs the biblical imagery of the sermon to suggest the nature of the peoples' religious aspirations, which provide momentary Christian revelation. The limitations of such revelations are suggested by a phlegmy 'Amen': half-prayer, half-cough.

Maguire recalls a romantic encounter one previous summer's day, spoiled by fear and his puritanical association of desire with sin: 'And he saw Sin / Written in letters larger than John Bunyan dreamt of' (39). Capitalisation of the key word, and the use of half-line, conveys the religious character of Maguire's apprehensions. Comparison with Bunyan's *Pilgrim's Progress* suggests a seventeenth-century religious sensibility, and yet the poet laments the repression of instinct entailed by this kind of response. Alone, Maguire resorts to stroking the flanks of the cattle, 'in lieu of wife to handle' (40). Personification, and heightened diction influenced by biblical language lend the section's closing lines a tone of conclusive authority, implying that the farmer is made cowardly by overwhelming religious fears. With a symbolic 'wet weed' bathetically twined around his boot, cowed by fear of the Lord, he seems inglorious (40).

The fifth section opens with an informal gathering at a traditional country crossroads, but within a few lines, traditional pastoral expectations are dashed by the depiction of this world as meaningless, bovine and lethargic: 'Heavy heads nodding out words as wise / As the rumination of cows after milking' (40). When a boy casually throws a piece of gravel onto the nearby railway line, 'It means nothing' (40). Conversation among those heads is anything but wise, who are described as dreamers, sunk in inertia. Compounding the tone of drift, Maguire returns to a meagre supper, and obscenely masturbates in the grate.

In section six, Maguire sits on a 'railway slope' in May, dreaming of wealth and love, but his hopes are dashed and frustrated by lack of opportunity. Though an idealist of sorts (he dreams of 'all or nothing'), he achieves nothing. The language tends to the mystical when we are told God 'is not all / In one place, complete', and the idea is given a distinctly Catholic resonance with the image of Holy Communion: 'In a crumb of bread the whole mystery is' (41). If the poem has any note of redemption, it can be found here, in the image of the host, but the redemptive note is not sustained. Maguire turns from the world of the senses to an obscure mysticism, which seems unlikely to render lasting satisfaction. It is a door 'whose combination lock has puzzled / Philosopher and priest and common dunce' (41). His wishes are 'frozen', and he is incapable of finding an enabling religious faith. We return to the scene by the 'railway slope', and to the atmosphere of psychological and artistic inertia suggested by 'a speechless muse'.

The seventh section begins with the mother's words, urging him to chapel to pray and confess his sins. It is hoped religious devotion will bring luck and material betterment, but the poem's ironies disallow such good fortune, and the narrator dismisses her words as 'a lie' (42). A young woman, Agnes, lifts her skirts 'sensationally up' to perform for the voyeur Maguire, giving further testimony to the deprivations of this starving world, dominated by religious dualism and fear of the body, '. . . in that metaphysical land / Where flesh was a thought more spiritual than music' (42). Unable to love, lusting in thought, sexually puritanical, no local man would marry her. The risqué pastoralism of the image of a woman baring herself to wet grass, a scene of Lawrentian intensity, is offset by the antipastoralism of this all-pervasive emotional repression and despairing need.

In section eight, Maguire's ennui is conveyed by dull, slack repetitions, expressed in short, childlike lines, many of them end-rhymed. Sitting on the gate, uncaring, he 'inconsequently sang' – without consequence, but also 'inconsequentially' (43). He lived for the moment, was satisfied by the health of his animals, by his cigarette and his pint. Still, however, 'young women ran wild / And dreamed of a child' (43). Although hungry for companionship and marriage, and dressed as provocatively as they could, they were unable to secure the affections of ignorant or 'blind' men. Everyone lived in a purgatory of unfulfilled desire, accepted by Maguire resignedly, as 'necessary pain'.

In section nine, he 'gave himself another year', warding off despair in the face of failure, putting faith in some change – marriage, perhaps – that would come to him soon, when he 'would be a new man walking through unbroken meadows' (44). Yet the peasants are terminally ignorant, overshadowed by the church, physically weak and deprived of vitality. The peasant poet's writing is 'tortured' and likened to 'pulled weeds on the ridge', withering in the sun (45). Emasculated by solitary writing, he is given female characteristics: his writing is 'a mad woman's signature,' his thought process 'an enclosed nun'. The image of his life as 'dried in the veins', oppressed by the chapel's low ceiling, is reminiscent of Yeats's Paudeen, in 'September 1913', or of the imagery of death in Eliot's *The Waste Land*, both of which were familiar to Kavanagh.

Maguire's soul has no essence, is only a hole left by a farm animal: 'the mark of a hoof in guttery gaps'. Yet, despite this, light enters the picture fitfully. Trout playing in the pools, young girls sitting on the river bank paint a picture of pastoral distraction, but Maguire lacks a lover's courage. Buttercups, bluebells and goldfinches contribute to the picturesque background to this peasant drama, stimulants to the imagination of an exotic elsewhere: 'A man might imagine then / Himself in Brazil and these birds the birds of paradise'. However, this edifice of otherworlds is flimsily imagined, like stories told at night by the fireside, which are gloomily contrasted, at the end of the ninth section, with the funereal wind blowing from the tomb.

The relatively short tenth section (29 lines) sketches, in almost anthropological fashion ('Their intellectual life consisted in . . .'), the reading habits of the Monaghan farming community – local newspapers, almanacs, school books – but their main preoccupation seems to be talk in the public bar. The satiric narrative voice skewers the intellectual pretensions of participants in these nightly debates; Maguire aspired to rise 'To a professorship like Larry McKenna or Duffy / Or the pig-gelder Nallon whose knowledge was amazing'.

In the much longer section eleven, Maguire is emasculated, 'more woman than man', controlled by sister and mother – the former a middle-aged virgin, his mother a sharp-voiced nag, whose voice is 'like a rust-worn knife' (47). The feminisation of Maguire is part of the poem's antipastoralism. All clichés about the nobility of masculine labour and the strength of the farmer are challenged here. Maguire is occasionally portrayed with a certain dignity and authority: '. . . his voice was the voice of a great cattle-dealer'. Generally though, the picture is bleak. Bachelordom takes on qualities of the female ageing process: menopause or 'the misery pause' (47). Since fear of the law prevented him from approaching schoolgirls, he resorts to masturbation. Even at such a sordid moment, the poet-narrator urges readers to empathise, as he himself does: 'Illiterate, unknown and unknowing. / Let us kneel where he kneels / And feel what he feels' (48). (We presume this is empathy, not a joke). At this point comes a moment of illumination, similar to such brief epiphanies in earlier lyrics. Inspired by the sight of a daisy to recall his childhood, he wonders 'was there a fairy hiding behind it?' Childish naivety is accompanied by kindness towards others, notably lacking in other family members, such as the sister who 'spat poison at the children' (49). The closing lines indicate the farmers are semi-conscious, 'happy as the dead or sleeping' (50).

Impoverished farming conditions are portrayed in twelve: fields bleached white, the place is 'grassless', and a Siberian wind crosses the fields, scattering the cattle fodder (50). A scene of horrid grazing conditions is set against a forbidding background of 'black branches'. Though dying, Maguire's mother controls her now middle-aged children; likened to puppets, they have little or no agency. When she died, they felt no sorrow. The section's final words might speak for Maguire, his sister, or both; the frustration it expresses prevents anything more elegiac being said, while conveying the despair of the captive farmer: 'I am locked in a stable with pigs and cows for ever' (52).

Section thirteen contains some of the harshest satire in the poem. Kavanagh ridicules the clichés that abound about peasant life: that the farmer's life is healthy and fulfilling; that he is in harmony with the elements, as well as the divine. Clearly, the poet associates this naïve, patronising attitude with the writing of the Revival, which he called elsewhere 'a thorough-going, English-bred lie'. The description of the peasantry in terms of culture, religion and poetry suggests that it is primarily the cultural theorists of the primitivist Revival he aims at here: '*There* is the source from which all cultures rise, / And all religions' (52). While great creating nature all around him is free and fecund, while cows and horses breed, humiliated Maguire is tethered to his mother by an umbilical 'navel-cord'.

The final section, set in October, uses theatrical metaphors to announce a finale. The poet asks for applause, including from the farm animals, but in context, cheering seems like mockery, as the elements of traditional pastoral – homing carts, cows at gates, 'screeching water-hens' – seem to sneer at Maguire's world, with 'the hysterical laughter of the defeated everywhere'

(54). The elements of pastoral scream in protest against the conditions they live among. The funereal, deathly imagery of the opening lines of this section anticipates the note of waning sexual energy depicted in Maguire ('no manhood now') and his sister ('wick of an oil-less lamp'). It also lays the groundwork for the surreal passage imagining Maguire lying in his grave, fearing to see a woman's legs, for fear of sin. Will Maguire's soul survive his death? Will he be reincarnated as a bird, or become an angel? Will there be nothing? – 'Or is the earth right that laughs haw-haw / And does not believe / In an unearthly law?' (55). The tone suggests the latter, despite the poem's pervasive religious imagery. Jeering of the earth (conventionally con-trolled by, or in harmony with and nourishing of its inhabitants) at human aspirations to immortality is the ultimate antipastoral gesture. The dismal conclusion conveys a picture of hopeless impotency on a national scale ('In every corner of this land'). The phrase 'apocalypse of clay' echoes the opening lines, in which biblical authority was undermined by the ubiquity of infertile clay, substituting for the word of God. The notion of a national apocalypse, signaled by the 'hungry fiend' (a Monaghan version of Yeats's rough beast from his poem 'The Second Coming', perhaps), supports the view that the poem is not only antipastoral but national anti-epic.

III

Writing in 1964, Kavanagh criticised The Great Hunger for failing to achieve a comic vision, by which he meant a vision of suffering in the context of a Christian perspective.[12] He complained that the poem had been tied to a civic or utilitarian ethic – arguing 'the woes of the poor' – and was aesthetically impure, and undeveloped. The poem was 'tragedy and Tragedy is underde-veloped Comedy, not fully born. Had I stuck to the tragic thing in The Great Hunger I would have found many powerful friends' (Collected Poems, xiv). The notion of underdevelopment suggests he was moving from a tragic to a comic aesthetic, which is how, in retrospect, he imagined the trajectory of his career. In those terms, antipastoral could only be a phase that one had to go through and grow out of, like adolescence. Kavanagh was famous for dis-owning his own work, for he had voiced misgivings about his autobiography, The Green Fool (1938), which he came to think of as 'stage-Irish', pastoralist, and false. It is something of an oddity that he disowned The Great Hunger for precisely the opposite reason, but he thought antipastoral polemic, too, had its failings. Artistically, the long poem was a hard act to follow, and its tone was a difficult one to sustain, had he wanted to. We find in much of the poetry written after it (collected in the postwar volume, A Soul for Sale), a less bitter approach to the rural experiences that had shaped him.

Admittedly, the harsher tones of 'Stony Grey Soil' anticipate the antipastoral voice of the long poem, but a number of poems in *A Soul for Sale* (e.g. 'A Christmas Childhood' and 'Primrose') explore the theme of lost childhood, an innocent golden age, usually located in Monaghan fields. In 'The Long Garden', he outlines the 'childhood skies', in which realism is balanced with a mythologising gesture, and in 'Art McCooey', memory is integrally related to the shaping of poetry, 'alive in the unmeasured womb'. The tender and idyllic 'Bluebells for Love' is addressed to one to whom the speaker, not without humour, promises a gift of wild flowers. Notable for its attractive repetitions of vivid imagery and phrase, the poem uses pastoral language relentlessly to convey a vision of lovers' intimacy in a remote and lovely setting. Conventional pastoral images accumulate, such as ivy, carts that pass, bluebells, primroses, ferns, briars and violets. In addition, the scene of luxuriant growth is blessed with divine sanction and seal; there is clear continuity of tone and feeling between this and earlier romantic-pastoral poems. The contrast between such poems in *A Soul for Sale* and *The Great Hunger* supports the view that there are several strains in Kavanagh's work, even in the 1940s, when his antipastoralism was most intense. As Padraic Colum argued, in his review of *A Soul for Sale*, Kavanagh's work was transitional at this time, poised between celebration and satire.[13]

Kavanagh's reputation was consolidated in 1960 by publication of the highly-acclaimed *Come Dance with Kitty Stobling and Other Poems*, further enhanced by publication, four years later, of *Collected Poems*. The 1960 volume includes some self-regarding, satirical poems (at times tending toward self-pitiful), such as 'The Hero', 'House Party to Celebrate the Destruction of the Roman Catholic Church in Ireland', and 'The Paddiad', which are amusing but did not particularly impress reviewers. A richer strain can be heard in those poems which have come to be regarded as classic Kavanagh: the Canal Bank Sonnets, 'Epic', 'Kerr's Ass' and 'Shancoduff'. These deal with pastoral motifs and subject matter, married to a deliberate parochial aesthetic, allowing the antipastoral to submerge, and a strong redemptive voice to surface, in which the pastoral is embraced as vehicle for revision, radical self-renewal and affirmation.

In 'Peace' (31), for example, written in 1943, but published in 1960, we find something akin to the earlier voice, though it is roughly contemporaneous with *The Great Hunger*. Demonstrating nostalgia for rural Inniskeen, the poem typifies the occasional backward look of Kavanagh's Dublin years, an aspect of his complicated response to the life left behind. This nostalgic note has been identified by Antoinette Quinn as a regular reflex in poetry after the publication of *Tarry Flynn* in 1948, and can be detected throughout his writing of the 1950s: 'the countryside now became an imaginative hinterland to be revisited momentarily, though often memorably'.[14] Apparently envying the peasant his simple life, the poet evokes a series of typical pastoral images: the hare on the headland, an old plough, a weedy ridge, a saddle-harrow, and refers to a lost 'childhood country', associated with innocence and relative leisure. Such qualities may have seemed particularly attractive from the viewpoint of Dublin during the 'Emergency' (the Second World War). A reference to 'tyrants' is a sign of the times, and line seven – curiously, a line that cannot be integrated into the rhyme scheme – refers to wartime farming conditions, the 'turf banks stripped for victory'.

'Epic' (136) explores the idea that the parish is 'important', central to one's life, and equally significant, as poetic theme, as nationally-acclaimed events and famous places. A farmer's argument in the humble townlands of Mucker or Inniskeen – 'That half a rood of rock' – are just as resonant as the Munich agreement of 1938, from Kavanagh's parishioner perspective. Even Homeric epic was based on 'a local row', such as the feud Kavanagh alludes to here, between Duffys and McCabes. He runs the risk of inflating this feud about land ownership and boundaries into a battle of epic proportions, but faces a related risk of deflating Homeric epic to a squabble in a cabbage patch. The point he wishes to make is the artist's need to base his work on something known, within the contours of his own experience. Make poems out of events in the local parish, which illustrate courage, martial spirit and social conflict just as readily as world wars. Behind this, we hear his argument about the importance of the parish as a node where the universal can be discerned, as outlined in 'The Parish and the Universe'. The poem relies on antipastoral, de-idealising energies, which transform the home ground into a place of conflict, eschewing the religious or mystical aspirations to be found in other poems. Nor is the Monaghan townland envisaged as a garden of childhood, vision or epiphany. Coming to the realisation that the Duffy feud was poetic material was, for Kavanagh, similar to realising that the parish has absolute value. Depicting the place of rural labour as a location of land disputes is antipastoral in intention and effect, and provides a further example of writing about rural Ireland 'from the inside' (Morrow).

In 'Kerr's Ass' (135), chatty iambic quatrains are in tension with a casual ballad stanza. As Quinn has noted, this metrical 'leisurely pace' may reflect the poet's imaginative shuttling in the poem between residence in London and native Inniskeen.[15] Trimeter lines, alternating with pentameters, risk but avoid bathos. References to Dundalk and Mucker establish two geographic poles of the poet's imagination, recalled while in a third, London. In stanzas two and three, he provides a detailed catalogue of farming implements that, truth to tell, not every reader will be actively interested in ('harness', 'straw-stuffed straddle', 'breeching', 'bull-wire', 'winkers', 'choke-band'). He affects to address an audience familiar with such artifacts, or is at least asking the reader to come into his world. Suddenly, following an ellipse in line ten, tone and vantage point change, distinguishing between the homeland of memory and the lonely-sounding 'Ealing Broadway, London Town', from where he recalls those lost implements. Memory and naming feed imagination, and 'the god of imagination' is envisaged in a dawn epiphany, associated with the fog of Mucker. The final vision, including that aestheticising fog, has been earned by strict attention to the act of memory, and the fantastic pastoralism of the finale grows out of the realistic diction and catalogue of the second and third stanzas. This poem is very different in effect from the bitter narrative of *The Great Hunger*, though rooted in a similar world, while achieving the numinous uplift of his early pastoral lyrics.

In March 1955, following upon a difficult and highly-publicised court case for libel the previous year, Kavanagh had an operation for lung cancer at the Rialto Hospital, Dublin; these experiences exhausted him. He spent July of that year recuperating in the sun at St Stephen's Green, or on the banks of the Grand Canal, between Baggot and Leeson Street Bridge. He has described this period as his 'hegira'. The poems written at this time signalled a bold return of pastoral in his verse, after a period of involvement in bitter journalism and satire, when Kavanagh vented in various venues his anger against the Dublin literary and cultural establishment. Many critics agree that one of the high points of Kavanagh's career are the Canal Bank Sonnets, written during this period. As Quinn notes, the two sonnets are given pride of place at the start of the volume, *Come Dance with Kitty Stobling and Other Poems* (1960), printed on the first page – a practice maintained in *Collected Poems* where they both appear on one page (150).[16]

'Canal Bank Walk' is a Shakespearean sonnet with half-rhymes, characterised by informal diction and playful phrasing (e.g. 'Leafy with lovebanks'). A dominant note is one of religious aspiration, indicated by phrases such as 'the will of God', 'the Word' and 'enrapture'. As Quinn writes, 'The baptismal water of spiritual redemption is now as unstinted and accessible as canal water' (421). (Water in Kavanagh is usually redemptive at this phase – in 'Is', water signifies religious purification, washing out 'Original Sin', 154). The poem expresses religious aspirations (it is prayer-like), with a fluent but occasionally informal voice, and is attentive to the quotidian details around him (he would 'wallow in the habitual' – the word 'wallow' suggests a careless, self-indulgent enjoyment of the world). He hears voices, and sees grass, but the voices are 'eternal' and the grass 'fabulous'. This vision of the eternal in nature, the intuition of redemption, and recognition of God's will – helps shape a pastoral meditation on the beneficent influences of divinely-ordained nature. A bird building its nest is a servant to 'the Word'. There is no note of disharmony because the world is appropriated into religious meditation. The sestet begins with a prayer to the 'unworn world' (contrasting with the weary, worn-out speaker), to inspire him: 'Enrapture me in a web / of fabulous grass and eternal cows by a beech'. Resembling an invocation to the muse, this is a request for energy and language, that he might pray 'with overflowing speech'.

The second canal bank sonnet, the self-elegiac 'Lines Written On a Seat On the Grand Canal, Dublin', is a request to posterity to commemorate him 'where there is water, / Canal water preferably'. That final phrase suggests this is a love poem for the canal, a celebration of its healing powers, almost as if its redemptive water is a holy well. The title draws attention to the short lines of the poem, which contrast with the long, sprawling lines of the previous sonnet; Quinn writes: '[W]here the first Canal sonnet pulsates with reburgeoning life, the second is an 'In Memoriam' (423). Again, there is a playfulness with words ('stilly greeny') and neologism ('niagarously'); this suits the poem's sentiment, that 'Noone will speak in prose'. The poem celebrates the beauty of a summer day, where canal waters pouring over a lock roar for those 'who sit in the tremendous silence' ('tremendous' bestows upon the moment heightened intensity). Taking the pastoral out of the rural world, into the green spaces of the city allows Kavanagh to envisage an urban pastoral separated from agricultural labour. Rural labour would always be tainted by the memory of the 'stony grey soil'. However, he can attain to a pastoral voice near the canal, where the world of fruitless labour is held at a distance, but the beneficence of the moments of vision in Monaghan may be experienced anew. The emotions of this poem are linked directly by the poet to the feelings of the farmer at Inniskeen, in his earliest verse. In an essay, 'From Monaghan to the Grand Canal', he wrote that the emotion in the Canal Bank Sonnets 'was the same emotion as I had known when I stood on a sharp slope in Monaghan, where I imaginatively stand now, looking across to Slieve Gullion and South Armagh' (Collected Pruse, 223).

The words 'Parnassian islands' help portray this haven as rooted in the classical notion of poetic inspiration. In the first Canal Bank Sonnet, the quotidian was numinous – the grass was 'fabulous'; here, the light is 'fantastic'. 'Mythologies' – a tribute to the Celtic Revival – sail past on a canal barge. Yet, the heroic world of Celtic mythology is banished, and, in a post-heroic gesture, he desires no 'hero-courageous / Tomb'. Contrasting the sentiments of this poem with Yeats's advice to posterity in his late poem 'Under Ben Bulben', Antoinette Quinn argues that Kavanagh is coming close to articulating a final poetic philosophy. In contrast with Yeats's poetic, Kavanagh's 'Canal school of poetry will focus on the fantastic beauty of an ordinary, unpopulated and unglamorous urban scene' (425). An affirmative, loving, urban pastoral vision.

Again, many poems in *Come Dance with Kitty Stobling and Other Poems* introduce pastoral themes (sometimes with antipastoral elements), and lean towards religious or mystical pastoral. The urban sonnets which begin the volume introduce a theme of transformation which we hear in other poems, and, in line with Kavanagh's parochial philosophy, they celebrate place as hallowed ground, as do poems like 'Peace', 'Shancoduff', 'Kerr's Ass' and 'Epic'. 'Shancoduff' with its bleak picture of sunless 'black hills' and desolate 'sleety winds', uses antipastoral imagery to express unbending loyalty to the home ground, which ultimately conveys a sense that this rural backwater contains all meaning for the speaker. 'Epic' has antipastoral energies which lend force to the argument that home is 'important'. 'Kerr's Ass' transforms the memory of rurality into the 'god of imaginative vision'. In its insistence that 'God is down in the swamps and marshes', the religious pastoral lyric, 'The One' argues for a parochial aesthetic, valorising the most infertile places (159). The long, third line of the poem is breathless and enthusiastic, in response to the word 'Sensational', with which the line begins. There are playful rhymes ('red/incred-'; 'marshes/catharsis'), evidence of a casual wit not found in other poems, but in accordance with the ludic quality of the Canal Bank Sonnets. The reference to 'sensational April' invokes a time of regeneration, but the tone is very distant from the cruel springtime of Eliot's *The Waste Land*, sometimes thought to be an influence. Kavanagh's waste land is charged with religious presence, though it were 'A humble scene in a backward place / Where noone important ever looked'. This place of wild flowers and weeds is remote, but blessed. The poet is messenger of the gods, revealing the ultimate truth that 'beautiful, beautiful, beautiful God' breathed his love on the bogs. Overdone in its repetitions, the only antipastoral coloring here might be the recognition that this backwater is remote and humble, but it is never disgraced.

IV

Kavanagh is paradoxically the most uneven and one of the most influential Irish poets since Yeats. His early verse established him as a religious pastoral lyricist, but he made his fame in the early 1940s, with his sceptical, antipastoral anti-epic. The fact that this poem contained moments of lyric intensity and fleeting mystical epiphanies, resembling the numinous visions of his earlier pastoral lyrics, highlighted rather than detracted from the general antipastoral impulses of the poem. The Canal Bank Sonnets do offer so-phisticated echoes of earlier poems, but are rooted in a beloved but adopted place, with new emphasis on a radically-renewed selfhood. Terry Gifford has written that certain poets – Stephen Duck, John Clare and Kavanagh–got accepted by the literary establishment of their day, and their antipastoralism was pastoralised.[17] This is not quite true of Kavanagh, since he pastoralised himself; he explicitly rejected his major antipastoral poem as false, and much of his later work is pastoral, despite a bracing and vigorous rebuff to Revival modes, in a certain sense of the word. That is, he revives pastoral as an urban genre associated not with artificial conventions but with redemptive, self-renewing and religious energies. He also yoked it to his liberating parochial aesthetic so that pastoral at its best could be a vehicle of self-affirmation for the marginal and minor.

Because of his challenge to Revivalist pieties and iconoclastic treatment of rural life, and because of his impact, as journalist, critic and poet, on the Dublin literary world of his time, he has been influential for subsequent poets, including John Montague, who wrote that Kavanagh 'liberated us into ignorance', and Seamus Heaney, author of some of the finest critical writing on Kavanagh to date. Other poets touched by his example include Eavan Boland, Paul Durcan, Desmond Egan, Eamon Grennan, Michael Hartnett, Brendan Kennelly and James Liddy. Modern Irish antipastoral and pastoral are incomprehensible without an understanding of his achievement.

NOTES

1 Larry Morrow (The Bellman), 'Meet Mr. Patrick Kavanagh'. *The Bell*, 16, 1 (April 1949), pp. 5–11. See Jonathan Allison, *Patrick Kavanagh: A Reference Guide* (New York: G.K.Hall, 1996), p. 13.

2 Cited in Terry Gifford *Pastoral* (London and New York: Routledge, 1999), p. 121.

3 Seamus Heaney, *Preoccupations: Selected Prose 1968–1978* (London: Faber and Faber, 1980), p. 176.

4 On de Valera's Ireland in the 1930s and Kavanagh's *Great Hunger*, see R.F. Foster, *Modern Ireland 1600–1972*, (Harmondsworth: Penguin, 1988), pp. 537–9.

5 Antoinette Quinn, 'Introduction'. *Selected Poems of Patrick Kavanagh* (London: Penguin, 1996), xiv.

6 F. MacM, 'Two Poets'. *Irish Press*, 6 October 1937, p. 6. (See Allison, p. 2.).

7 Patrick Kavanagh, *Collected Poems* (London: MacGibbon & Kee, 1964), p. 3. All subsequent references are given within the text.

8 Patrick Kavanagh, *Collected Pruse* (London: MacGibbon & Kee, 1967), p. 282. All subsequent references are given within the text.

9 Antoinette Quinn, *Patrick Kavanagh: Born-Again Romantic* (Dublin: Gill & Macmillan, 1991), p. 108.

10 *The Great Hunger* was completed in October 1941, and an excerpt published as 'The Old Peasant' in *Horizon* 5, 25 (January) 1942. The first complete edition was published by Cuala Press in April 1942, and it was later printed as the concluding poem in *A Soul for Sale*. However, the poet omitted lines 9–32, section two, on grounds of obscenity.

11 Each section is set in a particular month: section three in March, four in April, six in May, section eight in July, but the eleventh ('A year passed') is in April again, and the twelfth in February. The fourteenth and last scene witnesses 'the October reality'.

12 'Author's Note', *Collected Poems*.

13 'Tang of Sloes', *Saturday Review of Literature*, 20 September 1947, p. 24. (See Allison, p. 10.)

14 Quinn, *Patrick Kavanagh*, p. 254.

15 Ibid., p. 367.

16 Ibid., p. 421.

17 Gifford, *Pastoral*, p. 132.

4

PETER McDONALD

Louis MacNeice: irony and responsibility

In an uncollected poem of 1995, 'MacNeice's London', Derek Mahon imagines Louis MacNeice in wartime, in 'A bunker of civilised sound, / A BBC studio':

> Thirty years dead
> I see your ghost, as the Blitz carooms overhead,
> Dissolve into a smoke-ring, meditative,
> Classic, outside time and space,
> Alone with itself, in the presence of the nations,
> Well-bred, dry, the voice
> Of London, speaking of lost illusions.[1]

These lines capture, in a brilliant miniature, much of the complexity of Louis MacNeice's cultural and historical situations. While the adjectives here – 'meditative', 'classic', 'alone', 'well-bred', 'dry' – seem to map out the distinctive qualities of the poet's voice, that voice is also working as 'the voice/ Of London' while it speaks from the wartime BBC to the world. Mahon's final line-break allows the reader to sense the distance between the intimacy and solitude of the poet and the prepared voice of the public writer: as 'the voice' turns into 'the voice/ Of London', we feel a mild and complicating shock of something 'outside time and space' that suddenly locates itself in a specific moment and situation.

The resonance of a number of ironies is being relished in Mahon's lines, not least that of 'the voice/ Of London' being spoken by an Irish poet. Of course, Louis MacNeice was an Irish poet, and thought of himself as being an Irish poet, from the beginning to the end of his writing career. Any doubts, quibbles, or equivocations on that point are not MacNeice's, and they can find little ground in the facts of his life and his writing. MacNeice was also a poet who worked and wrote for much of his career in England, and whose writing often dwells on the England of his time, sometimes in extraordinary and illuminating detail. The man who, as a broadcaster in wartime and afterwards, was indeed in some senses 'the voice/ Of London' had already brought the London of the year before the war to life, in his long poem *Autumn Journal* (1939), with a brilliance and intensity unmatched even in his own gifted generation of British writers. Later, MacNeice continued to work largely from London as a broadcaster – a radio producer who was also the prolific author of radio plays and other features – until his death in 1963.

So, it is true that the poetic 'voice' of MacNeice is bound, in some respects, to be one whose most personal turns are complemented by the awareness of more public situations. If we look at his work as a whole (and it is a large body of work for someone who died just short of 56 years of age: thirteen volumes of poetry, three critical books, a volume of autobiography, over 120 scripts for radio, and enough critical and journalistic writing to fill two volumes in selection alone) we are presented with a number of seeming contradictions. Here is, for example, a writer whose own early life provides him with a series of recurring and compelling images that may suggest a lifelong preoccupation with the self, while his subject matter is also – and often in the same poems – the history of his own time or generation, or the history of times remote from his own. Here, too, is a poet who appears to embrace an aesthetic of inclusive observation of the world, often in seemingly journalistic turns of phrase and takes of detail, while remaining committed to an idea of poetry as parable-like, and mythic, in its essential bearing. MacNeice is a poet given to classical allusion and generic resource; he is, also, a poet whose language and diction are both contemporary and unaffected, and whose range of reference embraces popular as much as high culture. MacNeice is Irish, but capable of angry denunciation of the Ireland of his time; he works as a broadcaster in wartime and post-war Britain, but is scornful of 'propaganda' in mass-communication, and celebrates idiosyncrasy and independence. Like any Irish poet of the twentieth century, he feels himself in W.B. Yeats's shadow; but where Yeats's imagination is proudly aristocratic in its affiliations, MacNeice's is determinedly democratic. All these things contribute to what we might mean by MacNeice's 'voice' as a poet, and are subsumed in a more general distinction between 'irony' in that voice – the knowing, sometimes sceptical, haunted and understating qualities in MacNeice's way of writing – and the voice's 'responsibility', its relation to the seriousness of what it means. The 'lost illusions' mentioned in Derek Mahon's poem are both personal and public: that is to say, they are both MacNeice's and our own.

MacNeice's life

Born in Belfast, Louis MacNeice in fact grew up in a seaside town to the north of that city, in Carrickfergus, where his father was rector of the Anglican church. The youngest of three children (one of whom suffered from Downs Syndrome), MacNeice lost his mother at the age of five, and was educated at schools in England, returning for holidays at Carrickfergus, and with his family on trips to the West of Ireland. MacNeice left Marlborough School in 1926 to become a student at Oxford, where he studied Greek, Latin and Philosophy. While there, MacNeice met a number of lifelong friends, most notably the young Auden, who was already hard at work as a rising poet, and it was in these years as an undergraduate (1926–30) that MacNeice came to realise that his own ambitions were primarily literary ones: he precociously published a volume of poems (most of which he later dropped from his *oeuvre*) entitled *Blind Fireworks* in 1929, and was already seen as a member of a circle of young writers likely to come to prominence in the 1930s.

Towards the end of his time at Oxford, MacNeice met and fell in love with Marie Ezra, and the two were married (after overcoming parental objections from both sides) just as MacNeice completed his final exams. As a married man, MacNeice needed a career; and he was unusual amongst his contemporaries in going straight from university into a lecturing post, in the Department of Classics at Birmingham University. It was at Birmingham that MacNeice came under the influence of E.R. Dodds, an Ulster-born Professor of Classics there, who had taken the considerable risk of offering a post to a young man still waiting to graduate. Over the coming years, when he worked with and lived close to Dodds, MacNeice began to write the poems that would bring him to attention in the 1930s, as well as learning much about a social context quite distinct from either the rectory-centred world of his youth or the rarefied and over-aesthetic atmosphere of late 1920s Oxford. It was at Birmingham in the early 1930s that MacNeice grew up – and grew up into a political climate of crisis and foreboding that was to intensify over the course of that decade. In domestic terms, however, life was idyllic to almost a stifling degree: so, at any rate, MacNeice remembers these years in *The Strings Are False*, the autobiographical work written (but not published) in 1940/1. Not long after the birth of a son, Dan, in 1934, the idyll came to a sudden end with Marie's decision to leave her husband and child, and go to the USA with an American student and football-player. In the complicated and sometimes chaotic emotional fallout from this, MacNeice left Birmingham to live in London, where he took up another post in Classics at Bedford College.

By 1936, when MacNeice and his young son arrived in London, the literary world was dominated by members of the so-called 'Auden group', including poets like Cecil Day-Lewis and Stephen Spender. MacNeice, whose first mature volume, *Poems*, had been published by the prestigious house of Faber and Faber in 1935 to warm reviews, moved immediately to the centre of the metropolitan literary scene. By now, it was clear to MacNeice himself that his heart did not lie in the necessarily dry expanses of classical scholarship; partly for this reason, the late 1930s were years of furious literary productivity as MacNeice began writing a great deal of journalism and other commercial material, along with his increasingly assured and original poetry: two plays were produced in London by Rupert Doone's fashionable Group Theatre; there were books on the Hebrides, and on zoos, as well as a book on modern poetry, and trips to Spain before and during the Civil War, in addition to the trip to Iceland in company with Auden, which resulted in *Letters From Iceland* (1937). With the publication of his Faber volumes of poetry *The Earth Compels* (1937) and *Autumn Journal* (1939), MacNeice was widely regarded as among the foremost young British poets.

On the outbreak of the Second World War, however, MacNeice was on his way to the USA, having given up his lecturing job in London for a temporary post in the English Department of Cornell University. The reasons for this decision were as much personal as professional, for MacNeice had fallen in love with the American writer Eleanor Clarke, and hoped to use his time in New York State to put their relationship on to a firmer footing. With Europe at war, MacNeice was, like other British exiles (including Auden and Christopher Isherwood), seen by some as having deserted his country; he defended his position, and that of the other expatriates, but by 1940, with the so-called 'Phoney' war at an end, he was beginning to feel anxious that he was indeed missing out on an experience which he might have some responsibility as a writer to encounter. Decisively, perhaps, the relationship with Eleanor Clarke did not prosper. At the end of 1940, MacNeice made the dangerous crossing of the Atlantic to return to England, where (having been turned down on health grounds for service in the Royal Navy) he began to work as a scriptwriter (and subsequently a producer) for the BBC, covering London's experience of the Blitz, and learning the trade of radio-playwright – a form of drama he found much more satisfying than his pre-war ventures into writing for the stage. It was in London during the war that MacNeice married Hedli Anderson, a singer who had worked with Benjamin Britten and the Group Theatre.

In many ways, MacNeice later regarded London in the hectic (and often dangerous) years of the war as the scene of the most creatively and humanly intense period in his life. Certainly, he was not immune to a general feeling of anti-climax, and some degree of political disillusion, in the immediate post-war years. Experiencing the war from London had, for a time at least, sharpened MacNeice's feelings of scepticism about Ireland and its relation to the modern world. On unpaid leave in the West of Ireland in 1945, he wrote his best work for radio, the grim and powerful play *The Dark Tower*, which makes a compelling parable out of the struggle between history's weight and the individual's need for independence, along with a series of poems about the West of Ireland that complement and answer his immediately pre-war sequence, also set there, 'The Closing Album'. Although the wartime poem 'Neutrality', which condemns Eire's isolation from the European conflict, is an emphatic and pained statement by MacNeice, it tells much less than the whole story about the poet's complicated feelings; especially after his father's death in 1942, MacNeice found himself thinking more frequently about Ireland, and continued to visit the country and his friends and literary colleagues there.

Through the 1940s and 1950s MacNeice lived the life of a busy writer and broadcaster, working steadily on radio plays and features, literary journalism and, of course, more volumes of poetry. In these years, MacNeice's critical stock began to decline somewhat, despite the regular publication of new collections; in this respect, he shared in the fate of his other '1930s poet' contemporaries, like Auden and Spender, whose work was by then more often politely respected than eagerly anticipated. After publishing his *Collected Poems* in 1949, MacNeice moved on to experiments in longer poems, often deriving from his experience of broadcasting, which produced *Ten Burnt Offerings* in 1952 and *Autumn Sequel*, a huge poem written in *terza rima*, in 1954. Neither volume was a success, and by the mid-1950s it seemed that the poet had written himself into a corner, producing long, over-elaborated and sometimes dull pieces that paled beside his earlier work. In 1957, with the publication of *Visitations*, MacNeice returned to shorter poems, and with a new sense of energy, which provided the lyric momentum for the two subsequent collections that were in fact to contain much of his finest poetry, *Solstices* (1961) and *The Burning Perch* (1963).

MacNeice's last years were as productive as any other phase of his career, and they saw the development of a new style and tone in his writing, in which his poetic voice gained a new, and sometimes startling, resonance and originality. Although the last two volumes seem inevitably like 'late' poetry, it is easy to forget that these last poems were in fact written by a man in his fifties: MacNeice's death in 1963, which resulted from the pneumonia following a drenching trip to Yorkshire in search of accurate sound-effects for a play about potholing, was cruelly early, in terms of literature as well as life. It is clear now (though it might not have seemed quite so clear to the poet himself) that, in the early 1960s, MacNeice had begun a new phase of his writing career, and had left behind the sometimes lacklustre work of the previous decade. Had MacNeice lived to be seventy, we would now almost certainly think of him as a senior contemporary of Heaney, Mahon, Longley and Muldoon; and how the poems he did not live to write would have absorbed the events of post-1968 Northern Ireland is one of those futile, but irresistible, speculations to which the early deaths of poets inevitably draw their readers.

Responsibilities

MacNeice came to maturity in a decade (the 1930s) when literature was often thought to stand in a direct relation to events, both as a clear record and as a part of the intellectual conduct of society. Famously, his contemporary W.H. Auden moved, in the space of that decade, from the assertion that art's job was to 'Make action urgent and its nature clear' to the concession that 'poetry makes nothing happen'.[2] MacNeice's views took no such dramatic swerves; but he was more consistent than Auden in his belief that literature stood in some kind of accountable relation to the common life of its time. Issues like these look, at first sight, political; but they are in fact matters of aesthetic decision and commitment, and it is in this respect that MacNeice's work has its distinctive originality and durability.

As a twentieth-century poet, and the more so as an Irish poet, MacNeice was indebted in profound ways to the example of Yeats; additionally, and just as inevitably, he engaged with Modernism as a poetic tendency. In a way, MacNeice negotiates the influences of Yeats and T.S. Eliot, but he does this less in terms of ideas or positions than of matters of writing: the register, genres and techniques of poetry; the long poem and the lyric; the personal and the impersonal voice, and the resonance of complexes of images and sounds. In MacNeice's work, we encounter an enormously wide variety of verse-forms, inherited and invented, and this technical resource is in the cause of something other than just a display of virtuosity. In particular, the poetry of MacNeice's last years seems to work its way into new and subtle mutations of lyric forms and rhythms, escaping what MacNeice called 'the "iambic" groove' of English metrical instinct.[3] All this mastery of form, however, works for a purpose in MacNeice, and is intended at least as a means of speaking clearly, rather than in any code, private or public, of aesthetic exclusiveness.

In 1938, around the time of composing *Autumn Journal*, MacNeice wrote of how 'The poet is once again to make his response as a whole', 'reacting with both intelligence and emotion . . . to experiences'.[4] There is a characteristic flatness about this, but it is also a manifesto which the poetry makes good, and continues to make good in the succeeding decades. It is true that MacNeice's public voice is at its most effective when least self-conscious; some of the longer pieces in the later 1940s and the 1950s are both laboured and lacking in colour, while the poet's commitment to some virtues, especially those of plain-speaking and defence of liberal democracy, led to instances of bathos and dullness in work like *Autumn Sequel*. However, this voice was also capable of penetrating clarity, concision and originality, most of all perhaps in the compressed, haunting and haunted poems of MacNeice's last years.

In 'Budgie' (from the posthumously-published *The Burning Perch*), a caged bird becomes the symbol for both the poet regarding, along with his readers, a threatened and disintegrating world (one in more grave danger by the early 1960s even than it had been in the 1930s), and for the self-regard of the habitually preening *artiste* (which all true artists, however talented, are in danger of becoming). The result is an extraordinary transformation of Yeats's singing bird from the 'Byzantium' poems:

> *Budgie, can you see me?* The radio telescope
> Picks up a quite different signal, the human
> Race recedes and dwindles, the giant
> Reptiles cackle in their graves, the mountain
> Gorillas exchange their final messages,
> But the budgerigar was not born for nothing,
> He stands at his post on the burning perch –
> I twitter Am – and peeps like a television
> Actor admiring himself in the monitor.[5]

MacNeice's imaginative daring is matched, in lines like these, with an extraordinary technical control of phrase and timing. This control itself depends on our sense of the writing as being in an original relation to straightforward speaking – to what MacNeice in the 1930s would have called 'communication' – without existing in a hermeneutic, essentially closed and private, world of its own verbal procedures. In this sense, these lines do indeed negotiate the influences of Yeats and Eliot, producing something that is both its own memorable creation, and in compelling relation to the world in which it is written and read.

MacNeice's sense of poetry's responsibilities included, of course, his feeling for influence. A short poem from the mid-1950s is addressed 'To Posterity':

> When the books have all seized up like the books in graveyards
> And reading and even speaking have been replaced
> By other, less difficult, media, we wonder if you
> Will find in flowers and fruit the same colour and taste

> They held for us for whom they were framed in words,
> And will your grass be green, your sky be blue,
> Or will your birds be always wingless birds?

The vistas that open here are relevant to MacNeice's large sense of what a poetic voice must be in its 'public' aspect. We might notice that the ambitions of the 1930s for direct communication have been tempered, and that the future has become a worryingly unreadable kind of open book. But the poem takes us, nevertheless, to the heart of the matter for MacNeice: words themselves need to live, and life for the poet is always a life of words, and in words. He is responsible for the future, in this sense at least, and the integrity of language is not separable from other kinds of integrity. If this is the lesson of much of MacNeice's best writing that speaks in a 'public' voice, it is also the rule by which his more apparently 'personal' material has to work. In the process, the poetry provides an example of 'a living language' that can exercise the posterity represented by subsequent poets: in Northern Irish poetry alone, the work of Mahon, Longley and Paul Muldoon has responded at deep levels to MacNeice's artistic example and impetus. 'To Posterity' is an artistic manifesto so tight-lipped that its ambition might be missed at first glance; but it is no less serious, and no less consequential for that.

Voice and irony

From almost the beginning, MacNeice's poetic voice struck readers as a distinctive one. In defining this special quality, we need to engage with the quality of stylistic suppleness and acuteness which makes itself felt in that voice, and which it is tempting to characterise as 'ironic'. Of course, irony is a term with a long critical history, but we should remember that it is also a word that tends to carry other than strictly literary-critical connotations in many contexts. To regard the world ironically is, after all, often taken to mean something slightly distinct from taking the world seriously. This shows through when we check dictionary definitions: 'A figure of speech in which the intended meaning is the opposite of that expressed by the words used' (*OED* 1.a.); 'A condition of affairs or events of a character opposite to what was, or might naturally be, expected; a contradictory outcome of events as if in mockery of the promise and fitness of things' (*OED* 2.). Clearly, this does not fit the voice we hear in MacNeice's poetry, as here in the opening lines of 'Now that the shapes of mist', from 1936:

> Now that the shapes of mist like hooded beggar-children
> Slink quietly along the middle of the road

And the lamps draw trails of milk in ponds of lustrous lead
I am decidedly pleased not to be dead.

The fourth line seems on first reading to be striking an attitude, affectedly perhaps: 'decidedly' is the kind of intensifier not usually to be met with in a serious context for being pleased with something – you might be decidedly pleased to have received a birthday present, for instance, but hardly (say) to have survived a major operation. Given this, the formulation 'decidedly pleased not to be dead' starts to look very odd indeed, since its apparent insouciance would sit more comfortably with the pleasure normally expressed as *being alive*. But MacNeice does not say he is glad to be alive; he tells us he is pleased not to be dead. Considering this degree of strangeness in expression, is 'decidedly pleased' an 'ironic' turn of phrase?

In fact, the poetry here makes sure that we do not decide such questions in terms of isolated phrases, since MacNeice's line works as one part of a larger rhythmic, rhyming structure. We hear 'I am decidedly pleased not to be dead' immediately after the long line with which it rhymes, 'And the lamps draw trails of milk in ponds of lustrous lead', and so its brevity is felt as a kind of snapping-tight of the stanza, as the long vowels and crowded stresses of one line ('lamps draw trails', 'ponds of lustrous lead') speed up into rhythms of clipped conversation ('pleased not to be dead'). The 'irony', then, is something working to make us aware of form, an acknowledgement of the way a poem shapes and controls the order and sound of what it has to say. The whole of this first stanza is concerned with perceiving visual shapes, and the 'beggar-children' of the first line, who so much dominate the stanza, are in fact twice-removed from direct presence there: once, in their being 'hooded', and twice in their being in fact a simile for the 'shapes of mist'.

The remainder of MacNeice's poem continues to make the most of instabilities, as it becomes clearer that the road is being seen from a car, and that the mist is part of a threatening night's weather. The poet braves this, and braves too the possibilities of bathos or infelicity in the final line of his second stanza:

Or when wet roads at night reflect the clutching
Importunate fingers of trees and windy shadows
Lunge and flounce on the windscreen as I drive
I am glad of the accident of being alive.

Avoiding an accident on the road, the poet celebrates the 'accident of being alive', bouncing his language in a way that reinforces the subtlety of 'decidedly pleased not to be dead'. Those 'beggar children' are still present in 'clutching/ Importunate fingers', and the distance between them and the figure of the driving poet is one between death and life: the poet lives at their expense. As the poem ends, we learn more about this ironic distance, and learn in the process about the self-awareness this involves:

> There are so many nights with stars or closely
> Interleaved with battleship-grey or plum,
> So many visitors whose Buddha-like palms are pressed
> Against the windowpanes where people take their rest.
>
> Whose favour now is yours to screen your sleep –
> You need not hear the strings that are tuning for the dawn –
> Mingling, my dear, your breath with the quiet breath
> Of sleep whom the old writers called the brother of Death.

The elements and the night are still being figured as outsiders, beggars or visitors, who crowd in upon the private space, but they allow the person being addressed some respite, in the form of sleep, before they make their final and unrefusable request. At the end of the poem, MacNeice finally sounds the 'breath'/ 'Death' rhyme, but he allows death into the poem with its literary history on view, so that the uneasy proximity between sleep and death is something with a precedent in the works of 'the old writers'. We might notice at the same time as we register this moment of literary distancing, that MacNeice's final line-break – 'your breath with the quiet breath/ Of sleep' – does not allow a speaking voice the time to pause for breath.

Irony, then, is really a technique of self-awareness for MacNeice in these lines, rather than an effect of verbal 'mockery'. The particular case has a more general bearing, for MacNeice's supposedly ironic writing has often been held to be a sign of some more widespread, and perhaps fundamental, position of disengagement on his part. This is the case, certainly, for a number of MacNeice's critics, who have tended to see irony as a lack of serious commitment. But it is because it is so seriously poetry that MacNeice's work can appear deficient to those whose demands on verse have no room for the complications of language, pitch, rhythm, figure, or rhyme. In poetry, and especially in MacNeice's poetry, irony can never be separated from matters of technique: to ask *why* something is said is also to ask *how* the poet says it. Auden recognised this in MacNeice when he wrote, in 1939, of how the 'marriage of a wayward anarchist nature to a precise technique has been happy; his nature prevents him from becoming academic and pedantic, his technique from romantic excess'.[6]

A poet's voice is an amalgam of 'nature' and 'technique', and MacNeice's particular pitch is one in which the technical precision and variety of his metrical practice are informed by a presence and sensibility that seem always on the alert. 'Now that the shapes of mist' can be compared with a poem from near the end of MacNeice's career, 'The Taxis' (1961), in which again there is a running conceit of life as a car-journey, or a series of bought rides. Now, however, MacNeice's formal self-awareness has become more extreme, something that appears at first almost a casual matter of a throw-away refrain:

> In the first taxi he was alone tra-la,
> No extras on the clock. He tipped ninepence
> But the cabby, while he thanked him, looked askance
> As though to suggest someone had bummed a ride.
>
> In the second taxi he was alone tra-la
> But the clock showed sixpence extra; he tipped according
> And the cabby from out his muffler said: 'Make sure
> You have left nothing behind tra-la between you.'
>
> In the third taxi he was alone tra-la
> But the tip-up seats were down and there was an extra
> Charge of one-and-sixpence and an odd
> Scent that reminded him of a trip to Cannes.
>
> As for the fourth taxi, he was alone
> Tra-la when he hailed it but the cabby looked
> Through him and said: 'I can't tra-la well take
> So many people, not to speak of the dog.'

Two elements develop in the course of the poem, and finally give it its shape, both of them ironic in some of the more harsh senses of the word. First, there is the recurring 'tra-la', a filler phrase along ballad lines perhaps, which strays out of what seems its proper place at the ends of lines into the middle ('nothing behind tra-la between you', 'I can't tra-la well take/ So many people'), so that we hear it as a strange blank, or a filling of time. Second, there is the odd logic of the narrative through these four stanzas, as the subject is accompanied by more and more people he cannot see. If we read the poem as a miniature parable, it is an account of the way in which the individual accrues increasingly numerous company – present in memory – in being conveyed through life, until the numbers grow impossible, and the journey can no longer be made. In the poem's alarming world, what is present to memory becomes prosaically present to the eye of a cabby, as a matter of extra fares. What might in another context seem intimate and utterly individual (that 'odd/ Scent', for example) is here only another commonplace, and the subject for some gruff bad temper. Similarly, in another late poem MacNeice has Charon, the ferryman over the Styx, tell would-be passengers that 'If you want to die you will have to pay for it' (*Collected Poems*, 530.) Against this irony, MacNeice plays the recurring 'tra-la', in which the very movement of the verse seems to break up, and we hear a blank as something potentially threatening and incursive.

Like much of MacNeice's late poetry, 'The Taxis' has made irony into a technique, rather than just a tone of voice or a pose of detachment. A great many of the late poems show how the properties of poetry – its rhythms and shapes – can be made to absorb and refigure the less reflective aspects of language – its clichés and dead-ends – and so become charged with a strange and unsettling energy. MacNeice himself saw this as a 'nightmare' aspect of his work, and it is true that much of the writing in his last two collections seems grimly braced against life's attritions, fears and catastrophes. In so far as MacNeice's own life became more overcast in these late years, the condition of irony for which his verse found the technical means was something he found himself living in, and (as it turned out) not living through. Here, perhaps, we encounter what Mahon means by 'lost illusions' as an undertone in MacNeice's voice; here, too, the world of private disappointment, guilt and dismay finds its expression – and transformation – in poetry.

Lost illusions

In the early 1940s, MacNeice's poem 'The Satirist' includes something close to a self-portrait:

> Who is that man with eyes like a lonely dog?
> Lonely is right. He knows that he has missed
> What others miss unconsciously.

The insistence on 'lonely' is in a context that disables any merely sentimental reading, while the whole notion of missing things stretches from the missing associated with personal loss to the kind of missing that is a missing out on something. MacNeice's work as a whole spans a similar gap between intimate losses and more public, shared experiences of history's passing. In his long poem, *Autumn Journal*, MacNeice makes this gap vividly palpable. The poem ranges from the day-to-day life and work of its author in the period from August, 1938 until the New Year, as he goes to work in a London visibly preparing itself for war, to sustained considerations of education, philosophy, Ancient Greece, and the Munich crisis, and of personal memory (schooldays, a broken marriage, love-affairs) as well as of Ireland. In this largely autobiographical poem, MacNeice never lets his own life slip away too far from the life of a particular time and situation; this is what he means by calling *Autumn Journal* 'both a panorama and a confession of faith'.[7]

The genre of a journal – a series of reports on life, with no overarching 'plot' to facilitate narrative or formal techniques of shaping the material – sets MacNeice free from several of the difficulties inherent in writing 'political' poetry. As the poet puts this in his prefatory note: 'It is in the nature of this poem to be neither final nor balanced' (*Collected Poems*, 101). The verse form itself, in which long and short lines alternate, but do not stick to any predictably set lengths, and in which rhyme is the norm, but a rhyme-*scheme* as such is seldom present, answers to the open-ended nature of MacNeice's undertaking. Having said all this, we might still see something of a centre to the wide and various panorama which *Autumn Journal* presents: this is the notion of loss, and of the missing that follows loss. It is this which brings together the 'public' and the 'private' in the poem: the historical events that press most on the poem, which include the Munich Crisis and the perilous condition of the threatened Spanish Republic, as well as an important by-election in Oxford (fought on the issue of appeasement) are all situations that spell out various kinds of defeat; personal losses are given almost as much weight, whether they involve the loss of a wife or a lover, or even that of a dog gone missing for a day, or whether they are both more general and more perplexing, as in the loss of childhood, or of youthful enthusiasms, or that of a homeland. *Autumn Journal* is an act of stocktaking on all these kinds of loss, in which MacNeice's voice finds registers for both what he calls the 'didactic' (describing the particulars of how things are) and the 'lyric' (making personal shapes and sense out of how things were, and how they might be).

One entire section of *Autumn Journal* is given over to Ireland, and it sits at the centre of the long poem as a meditation on the fate of political illusions and dogmas, which MacNeice intends to cast a sombre shadow over the English and European politics that dominate the rest of his poem. Again, this is done first in *personal* terms, since the poet makes it clear that it is his own childhood memories which fuel the meditation. As often in Mac-Neice's poetry, these memories are rendered as sounds: 'the noise of shooting/ Starting in the evening at eight/ In Belfast in the York Street district', or 'the voodoo of the Orange bands/ Drawing an iron net through darkest Ulster'. As the poetry gathers momentum, MacNeice's voice moves emphatically into a mode of denunciation, putting a curse on both Irish houses:

> Up the Rebels, to Hell with the Pope,
>> And God save – as you prefer – the King or Ireland.
> The land of scholars and saints:
>> Scholars and saints my eye, the land of ambush,
> Purblind manifestoes, never-ending complaints,
>> The born martyr and the gallant ninny;

The grocer drunk with the drum,
    The land-owner shot in his bed, the angry voices
Piercing the broken fanlight in the slum,
    The shawled woman weeping at the garish altar.
                        (*Collected Poems*, 132.)

Both 'traditions' in Irish politics have failed, and the force of MacNeice's writing through this section of the poem is one that constructs a kind of parallelism in denunciation: the poet is not so much even-handed as two-fisted in his response. The pitch of this voice is one that gains energy from the brutal stripping away of illusion and pretension; its condemnation of 'Kathaleen ni Houlihan' allows us to be touched – just for a moment – by the apparent pathos of 'The shawled woman weeping at the garish altar', but then lets us know how easy (and fatal) it is to wallow in such feelings. Similarly, the male, Protestant icon takes a hammering, while permitting us – again, just for an instant – to enjoy the misconceived historical glamour of his 'tradition':

Drums on the haycock, drums on the harvest, black
    Drums in the night shaking the windows:
King William is riding his white horse back
    To the Boyne on a banner.
Thousands of banners, thousands of white
    Horses, thousands of Williams
Waving thousands of swords and ready to fight
    Till the blue sea turns to orange.

As section XVI progresses, we share both the possible intoxications of Irish atavisms, and the sharp pangs of the contemporary hangovers they leave behind; MacNeice's procedure builds to a climax of across-the-board de-nunciation ('I hate your grandiose airs,/ Your sob-stuff, your laugh and your swagger,/ Your assumption that everyone cares/ Who is the king of your castle'). The truth is, as the poet adds immediately, that 'Castles are out of date', and this truth is something the reader of *Autumn Journal* has experienced at MacNeice's first hand, in the panorama of loss, indifference, and international wickedness which the poem so meticulously records. For Mac-Neice in 1938, Ireland's collective imagination is living out a complete, and disastrous, illusion: 'Let the round tower stand aloof', he writes savagely, 'In a world of bursting mortar'.

What Ireland misses historically cannot be dissociated from MacNeice's sense of what he misses in Ireland. This is a complex state of affairs, and not one which a single poem can disentangle. In terms of the poet's own life, the scene of a profound early loss (that of his mother) is also a place to be revisited with perpetually mixed feelings; Carrickfergus is remembered as both a family home and a place of exile ('We were in our minds', MacNeice's sister recalled, 'a West of Ireland family exiled from our homeland')[8]; Northern Ireland is figured as somewhere very distinct from the West, in terms of personal mythology as well as of politics and geography; and the pitched antitheses of *Autumn Journal* are complicated increasingly by the competing pulls of loss and affection. In 'The Strand' (1945), a poem written in memory of his father, MacNeice finds his most subtle and haunting image for the mixture of alienation and belonging which he feels, in the recollection of his father by the sea on Achill Island, 'Carrying his boots and paddling like a child':

> Sixty-odd years behind him and twelve before,
> Eyeing the flange of steel in the turning belt of brine
> It was sixteen years ago he walked this shore
>
> And the mirror caught his shape which catches mine
> But then as now the floor-mop of the foam
> Blotted the bright reflections – and no sign
>
> Remains of face or feet when visitors have gone home.

The poem balances those 'bright reflections' against the erasing inevitability of 'the floor-mop of the foam', the vividness of recollection (and, by implication, loving recollection) against the flat facts of leaving and absence. Many of MacNeice's poems about Ireland are about light, and light's ability to transform or withdraw: 'An Irish landscape', he wrote, 'is capable of pantomimic transformation scenes; one moment it will be desolate, dead, unrelieved monotone, the next it will be an indescribably shifting pattern of prismatic light'.[9] Although in 'The Strand' 'no sign/remains', it is the poem which inscribes the 'visitors' on this western landscape: MacNeice's writing here manages to concede the ephemerality of belonging at the same time as it celebrates its reality.

'Visitors' is, of course, a word heavy with implication, for however at home they may feel, these holidaymakers are also away from home. But from almost the beginning, MacNeice's poetry returns to images of homes, of houses and other dwelling-places, as the scenes of alienation and sometimes even dread. In his later poetry especially, MacNeice visits these strange, often haunted properties, which seem to contain much of his own childhood and adult life. 'Selva Oscura' (whose title alludes to the dark wood in which Dante finds himself, in mid-life, at the beginning of the *Divine Comedy*) begins by saying that 'A life can be haunted by those who were never there/

If there was where they were missed', and then goes on, in its second stanza, to re-shape and complicate this claim:

> A life can be haunted by what it never was
> If that were merely glimpsed. Lost in the maze
> That means yourself and never out of the wood
> These days, though lost, will be all your days;
> Life, if you leave it, must be left for good.

MacNeice's sense of his own life as something 'haunted/ By what it never was' certainly includes his feelings for and about Ireland. It is easy, and it has been too tempting over the years, to see this as symptomatic of a personality split in terms of its nationality, and fated by class and religion to be a perpetual tourist in a land to which it can never properly belong. But this is an oversimplification which MacNeice's poetry resists. The complexities of 'home' are certainly intended by MacNeice to be more than merely personal in their application, however intimate may be the sources of their images and recurring motifs. As far as Ireland is concerned, the poet's acute feeling for the ambiguities of belonging, the difficulties and awkwardnesses of leaving and returning, and the allures and liabilities of a tangled history, are not without their relevance for the too clear-cut schemes of 'Irishness' that crop up in a great deal of cultural and political discussion. Here as elsewhere, the poet's instinct for lost illusions seems richer and more fruitful than the continued promotion of those illusions.

In contemporary criticism, MacNeice remains a name to divide Irish critics. For some, he is still not quite 'Irish' enough, or under suspicion on account of the supposed allegiances of his modern advocates. It would be difficult, on the other hand, to find many poets (Irish or British) for whom such suspicions are meaningful, and MacNeice's work looks much more securely established now, in canonical terms, than it did at the time of his death. The poet's significance in contemporary poetry is more to do with the resources, complexity and memorability of his voice than it is with the endlessly-debatable definitions or appropriations of his nationality. In this respect, he is a central and indispensable presence, and remains one of the most exhilarating, haunting and substantial Irish poets since Yeats.

NOTES

1 Derek Mahon, 'MacNeice's London', *Poetry* (Chicago), vol. 167, no. 1–2 (October 1995), p. 36.
2 W.H. Auden, 'August for the people and their favourite islands' (1935), and 'In Memory of W.B. Yeats's (1939), *The English Auden: Poems, Essays and Dramatic Writings* ed. Edward Mendelson (London: Faber and Faber, 1977), pp. 157, 242.

3 'I notice that many of the poems here have been trying to get out of the "iambic" groove which we were all born into.' 'Louis MacNeice writes . . . [on *The Burning Perch*]', *Poetry Book Society Bulletin* 38 (Sept. 1963), repr. in Alan Heuser (ed.), *Selected Literary Criticism of Louis MacNeice* (Oxford: Clarendon Press, 1987), p. 247.

4 Louis MacNeice, *Modern Poetry: A Personal Essay* (Oxford: Clarendon Press, 1938), pp. 29–30.

5 Louis MacNeice, *Collected Poems* ed. E.R. Dodds (London: Faber and Faber, 1966), p. 539. Henceforth cited in the text as *Collected Poems*.

6 W.H. Auden, 'Louis MacNeice', in *We Moderns: Gotham Book Mart 1920–1940* (New York: Gotham Book Mart, n.d. [1939]), p. 48; repr. in Edward Mendelson (ed.), *W.H. Auden: Prose Volume II 1939–1948* (London: Faber and Faber, 2002), p. 35.

7 Louis MacNeice, letter to T.S. Eliot, 22 Nov. 1938, quoted in Robyn Marsack, *The Cave of Making: The Poetry of Louis MacNeice* (Oxford: Clarendon Press, 1982), p. 43.

8 Elizabeth Nicholson, 'Trees were green', in Terence Brown and Alec Reid (eds.), *Time Was Away: The World of Louis MacNeice* (Dublin: Dolmen Press, 1974), p. 217.

9 Louis MacNeice, *The Poetry of W.B. Yeats* (1941), (2nd edn. London: Faber and Faber, 1967), p. 50.

5

ALEX DAVIS

The Irish modernists and their legacy

Modernism and Ireland

'Dublin Modernism? The term has a cheeky disregard of its absurdly obvious self-cancelling simplicity.'　　(Hugh Maxton, *The Puzzle Tree Ascendant*)[1]

Notwithstanding Joyce's representation of the Irish capital in *Ulysses* and *Finnegans Wake*, Dublin is not generally perceived as having been a vibrantly productive location of avant-garde experimentation, as were Paris, Berlin, London and New York. While the Irish Literary Revival is arguably a strand in the knotted skein of early modernism, in the eyes of writers as dissimilar as Thomas MacDonagh and Samuel Beckett its Celticism appeared remote from the dissonant tones and epistemological preoccupations of the historical avant-garde.[2] In *Literature in Ireland* (1916), MacDonagh had proposed that it was not the Revival's 'Celtic Note', but poetry written in the 'Irish Mode' – a style that preserved in English some of the sound-patterns of Gaelic verse – that was to some extent comparable in its disjunctive effects to Italian Futurism. In the light of this thesis, MacDonagh's translations might be profitably read alongside those of Ezra Pound – an admirer of *Literature in Ireland* – whose revolutionary 'translations' from Chinese poetry, *Cathay*, had appeared the year before MacDonagh's critical book. But MacDonagh's poetic and critical career was brutally truncated in 1916, when he was executed for his part in the Easter Rising; and it was to be in the poetry of his successor as lecturer in English at University College Dublin, Austin Clarke, that the Irish Mode was most rewardingly developed during the 1920s.

Clarke's striking defamiliarisation of the English-language lyric in *Pilgrimage and Other Poems* (1929) bears some resemblance to Hugh MacDiarmid's contemporaneous experiments in Synthetic Scots in *Sangschaw* (1925) and *Penny Wheep* (1926). However, in contrast to the Scottish poet, Clarke maintained throughout this decade and the next a frosty antipathy towards literary modernism, especially the poetry of Pound. The antinomy in Clarke's thinking at this date between cultural nationalism and modernist poetics simply had not existed for older militant Republican poets such as Mac-Donagh and Joseph Campbell. Praised in the *Egoist* by T.S. Eliot,[3] the free verse of Campbell's *Earth of Cualann* (1917) fruitfully employs Imagist techniques that the Ulsterman had encountered in avant-garde circles in London in the first decade of the century, to which are conjoined assonantal patterns imitated from Gaelic models. Campbell's work is admittedly mild fare besides that of F.T. Marinetti or Wyndham Lewis's *Blast*; nevertheless it exemplifies the fusion of nationalist politics and experimental poetics that had marked the pre-war European avant-garde.[4]

Clarke acknowledged this dimension to Campbell's poetry in the early 1960s (by which date he had made a rapprochement with Pound), but he continued to conceive of modernism as an international, transcultural phenomenon, and thus bereft of a fructifying relationship with region or nation. In this respect, his thinking was by and large faithful to the self-representation of modernist literature and art in Ireland between the wars. In the visual arts, the enthusiastic response made by Evie Hone and Mainie Jellet, among others, to Cubism in the 1920s constituted an allegiance to 'the Modern Movement', which, though centred in Paris, transcended national boundaries. (In later life, however, Jellett would increasingly press home the affinity between Celtic art and modern abstraction.) In a more complex manner, Flann O'Brien's novels, *At Swim-Two-Birds* (1939) and *The Third Policeman* (written by 1940), as J.C.C. Mays has argued, parodically emulate modernist devices in an overdetermined riposte to the example of Joyce's later fiction and the 'pretensions of international modernism'.[5] In this respect, the early poetry and fiction of Samuel Beckett – also influenced by Joyce – might be read as the reverse of O'Brien's hilariously purgative engagement with high modernism (the latter's project culminating in the doubt surrounding Joyce's authorship of *Ulysses* and the *Wake* in *The Dalkey Archive* [1964]).

Conditioned by Anglo-American and European modernism, Beckett's formative avant-gardism is squarely set against the nationalism of those Irish poets he derisively described as 'delivering with the altitudinous complacency of the Victorian Gael the Ossianic goods'.[6] This interest in poetic modes distinct from both those of the Celtic Twilight and the more robust, folkloric forms exploited by J.M. Synge and others, was one shared by Beckett's acquaintances, Brian Coffey and Denis Devlin. In the inter-war period, only Beckett's friend and confidant, Thomas MacGreevy (whose *Poems* was published in 1934), attempted to conjoin nationalist politics and a poetic conditioned in part by the examples of Eliot, Joyce and the surrealists. But Ireland in the 1920s and 1930s was an unpropitious locale for poets like MacGreevy and Beckett. The introspective literary scene of the Free State was understandably largely absorbed in adjusting to the often disheartening realities of independence, as shown in the commitment by many to what were essentially mimetic modes of writing – the short stories of Seán O'Faolain and Frank O'Connor and, in the war years, Patrick Kavanagh's *The Great Hunger* (1942). As Terence Brown gloomily observes, 'It was as if the challenge to realism effected by both the Revival writers and the modernist movement had not taken place'.[7]

Irish poetic modernism since the 1930s

During the 1930s, Denis Devlin viewed the Irish Mode of Clarke and F.R. Higgins with contempt. His first publication, *Poems* (1930) – with Brian Coffey – appeared in the same year as Samuel Beckett's *Whoroscope* and, like Beckett's poem, is characterised by disjunctive poetic procedures. Beckett's 1934 appraisal of 'Recent Irish Poetry' for the *Bookman* emphasised the importance of the French Surrealists and Eliot to Devlin's early poetry. The essay situates Devlin and Coffey as members of a 'nucleus' of Irish modernist poetry opposed to the ruralism and cultural nationalism of those Irish poets dubbed – and damned – by Beckett as 'the antiquarians'. Beckett astutely singled out for especial praise Devlin's 'Est Prodest', a poem which frantically probes for religious certainty in the midst of the political and economic disarray of the 1930s. The titular allusion to Horace's dictum that poetry exists in order to be beneficial is a pointer to Devlin's anxious preoccupation with justice in many of the poems collected in *Intercessions* (1937); and in this respect his early poetry, while more surrealist than engaged, is coloured by the debate over the nature of 'committed' literature central to this decade.

The dream-logic of the longest poem collected in *Intercessions*, 'Communication from the Eiffel Tower', for instance, owes much to the poetic procedures of André Breton; yet its deployment of a central Futurist icon of technological modernity is in the service of a critique of totalitarianism not unrelated to that of the pylon-poetry of Devlin's British contemporaries, W.H. Auden, Cecil Day Lewis and Stephen Spender. In the course of Devlin's poem, the identity of the persona leaches into that of François-Nöel Babeuf, the French Revolutionary, whose radical egalitarianism is brought to bear upon the racist ideas of the French ethnologist Joseph-Arthur de Gobineau. The topicality of the latter's racial theories are brought home to the reader through the Dali-like transformation of de Gobineau into the Germanic 'Gobethau'; the Frenchman's *Essai sur l'inégalité des races humaines* melting and mutating into contemporary fascist notions of Aryan supremacy.[8]

Devlin's poetry of the 1940s – collected with earlier pieces in *Lough Derg and Other Poems* (1946) – continues to demonstrate his intense concern for the human detritus of a world in which, with the Second World War, 'mullioned Europe [is] shattered' ('Lough Derg'; *Poems*, 132), and to whom a Pascalian God remains indifferent. Formally, the poems of this period, and for the remainder of his career, have largely dispensed with the heady avant-garde mannerisms of Devlin's previous work. In their place, one finds in the main symbolic, densely-patterned poems in various stanzaic forms which, recalling the example of T.S. Eliot in *Poems* (1920) and Hart Crane, accord with the poetic principles laid down by the American New Criticism. Many of Devlin's poems of this period were published in New Critical journals, including the *Southern Review* and the *Sewanee Review*; and following his diplomatic posting to New York in 1939 and Washington in 1940, as a member of Ireland's Department of External Affairs, Devlin formed friendships with the influential poet-critics Allen Tate and Robert Penn Warren (who were to edit a *Selected Poems* in 1963, after Devlin's death).

The New Critical stand-alone quality of these poems is at one with the metaphysical alienation experienced by Devlin's personae in such notable works as 'Lough Derg' and 'Jansenist Journey'. A similar predicament confronts the speakers of his love poetry, the concerns of which – after the example of San Juan de la Cruz – overlap with those of his religious poetry. The erotic poems frequently address an absent beloved, whose status is more the product of the desiring male poet's imagination than that of a referential woman, and whose potential to allay the lover's solitariness is, therefore, highly problematic: they are consoling images, linguistic constructs pitted against existential privation. In 'Farewell and Good', to take a representative instance, the speaker is forced to acknowledge the fact that 'She I loved so much will not appear again', except in imaginary form, as the poet 'in phantasms of sleep assembl[es] her form' (*Poems*, 213). But such an idealised love-object is necessarily a wish-fulfilling poetic construct, and thus meagre compensation for the literal, and now lost, object of desire.

In Devlin's late masterpiece, *The Heavenly Foreigner* (first published in 1950, and subsequently revised), the sequestered self of the love poems is equally the Jansenist subject of his religious lyrics. Based in part on Devlin's reading of Maurice Scève's *canzonerie* of love poems *Délie* (1544), and drawing upon Occitan poetry of *fin'amor*, *The Heavenly Foreigner* is constructed around memories of a lover in whose finite beauty the speaker hopes to discern the atemporal deity of the title. The woman is a variation on the *dompna soiseubuda* ('composite lady') of the provençal poet, Bertran de Born: an idealised, recomposed figure, around whom the male weaves imaginative conjectures, making her 'his emblem, / Making her the absolute woman of a moment' (*Poems*, 266). Yet, in the process of idealising the female, her sentient being vanishes, and with her recedes any hope of grasping the essence of the Heavenly Foreigner. For the poem's lushly metaphorical argument entails that the images denoting the woman constitute a fetishistic symbolism – 'How she stood, hypothetical-eyed and metaphor-breasted', exclaims the persona, 'Weaving my vision out of my sight', to leave but 'a light smoke in my hands' (*Poems*, 273).

Beckett's *Echo's Bones and Other Precipitates* (1935) also draws upon the poetry of the troubadours – the titles of over half of the volume's contents are provençal poetic forms – and the collection as a whole is coloured, as Lawrence E. Harvey suggests, by *amour lointain*, that is, desire unrequited and its ensuing anguish and pain.[9] Beckett's variation on the Occitan dawn song, 'Alba', moulds the subgenre's concentration on the torment of lovers' parting to metaphysical ends. The Alba is a character in Beckett's youthful *Dream of Fair to Middling Women* (written 1932) and *More Pricks than Kicks* (1934); in the poem – as in the prose – her 'beauty' is a 'statement of itself drawn across the tempest of emblems';[10] in other words, she eschews the emblematic and 'metaphor-breasted' nature of women in Devlin's poetry. This is at one with the poem's refusal to entertain her as a spiritually redemptive Beatrice figure. The literal dawn ushers in a metaphorical darkness in which the persona, who corresponds to the prose's Belacqua, submits to existence shorn of the illumination of revelation: 'there is no sun and no unveiling' (*Poems*, 15).

The relentlessly paratactic structures and, in Patricia Coughlan's words, 'too fully furnished'[11] quality of Beckett's early poems gives way, with the turn to French, to an enabling austerity, to haunting cadences free from the bulgingly allusive (both literary and autobiographical) content and staccato rhythms of *Echo's Bones* and related poems. While the speakers of a number of the earlier poems misanthropically perambulate through cityscapes (Dublin, London) transmogrified by Dante, the persona of *'je suis ce cours de sable qui glisse'* threads his course, in Beckett's translation, 'between the shingle and the dune'. The shoreline provides a powerfully evocative objective correlative for the speaker's liminal condition, 'treading these long shifting thresholds' (*Poems*, 59). His desire to 'live the space of a door / that opens and shuts' is, it would appear, a death-wish, the condition of non-being preferable to that monadic existence which *'que ferais-je sans ce monde'* describes as 'peering out of my deadlight [*mon hublot*]' at 'the living / in a convulsive space' (*Poems*, 61).

The *'espace pantin'* into which Beckett gazes is, in the words of his 'Recent Irish Poetry', 'the space that intervenes between [the poet] and the world of objects' (*Disjecta*, 70). Beckett maintains that a 'rupture of the lines of communication' has occurred, a crisis in representation or 'breakdown of the object' to which the 'antiquarians' such as Clarke and Higgins appear oblivious, but one recognised by MacGreevy, Devlin and Coffey. Like Beckett's *Whoro-scope*, Coffey's *Three Poems* (1933) is indebted to *The Waste Land* rather than to recent Irish poetry; but, whereas Beckett's poem is, on one of its levels, a successful pastiche of Eliot's annotated pocket epic, Coffey's chapbook is merely derivative. By way of contrast, his 1938 lyric sequence, *Third Person*, explores the complexity of human and divine love in a style utterly Coffey's own, and introduces the richly ambiguous texture, and hypnotic rhythms, central to his mature poetry. *Third Person* also demonstrates the importance to Coffey of Thomism, and the late 1930s would see him at the Institut Catholique de Paris, working under the Neo-Thomist philosopher, Jacques Maritain, research which would bear fruit in his doctoral thesis on the idea of order in the thought of Aquinas (presented in 1947). Whether Maritain's speculations on the difficulty for the artist in conjoining Catholicism and modernism had any impact on Coffey is difficult to ascertain, but Coffey ceased publishing poetry (though not philosophical papers and reviews in *The Modern Schoolman*) at the end of the 1930s. He returned to print at the beginning of the 1960s with a number of poems published in the *University Review* (Dublin), including *Missouri Sequence* (1962), which he had begun composing nearly a decade before. The composition of *Missouri Sequence* overlaps with Coffey's work on his translation of Stéphane Mallarmé's *Un Coup de dés*, which, as *Dice Thrown Never Will Annul Chance*, was published in 1965. Dónal Moriarty has persuasively argued that Coffey's translation of Mallarmé's poem should be read as a *reply* to the French poet's original text, rather than simply its rendering into English.[12] In this respect, *Dice Thrown* dovetails with *Missouri Sequence*, some of the preoccupations of which can be read as a Thomistic rejoinder to aspects of Mallarmé's atheist poetic.

Subsequent to *Missouri Sequence*, Coffey published *Advent* (1975), a long poem that recalls *Third Person* in its reflections on God and love, but which extends its speculations into the fields of beauty, ethics and environmental issues, to name but a few. *Advent*'s is a large canvas; but linking its many concerns is an emphasis on humanity's existential plight, this universal given grounded throughout the sequence in the particularities of the poet's life (including the death of his mother and one of his sons). *Death of Hektor* (1979) reflects upon Homer's treatment of the Trojan hero, and upon the heroism of war in general, in the sobering light of the potential for nuclear conflict at the time of its writing. Like *Advent*, the later sequence develops its case not through logical argument, but through an associational accretion of images and motifs. Both sequences deploy remarkably various rhythmic units, in contrast to the conversational tone of *Missouri Sequence*; and, in a fashion reminiscent of *Un Coup de dés*, make use of typographical layout to underscore their semantic content. The 'visuality' of these two poems is a feature they share with other poems by Coffey, some of which have a concrete poetic form, while others, such as *Leo* (1968), are the fruit of collaboration with visual artists.

The critique of patriarchal aggression mounted in *Death of Hektor* chimes with Sheila Wingfield's preoccupation in *Beat Drum, Beat Heart* (1946) with the violence of warfare, though Wingfield's poem, unlike Coffey's, counterpoints male brutality with an exploration of the ferocity that subtends female sexual desire. In its focus on the universal human impulses underpinning the particular circumstances of love and war, Wingfield's long poem has points of resemblance to H.D.'s *Trilogy* and the principal work of the neglected Welsh modernist Lynette Roberts, *Gods with Stainless Ears* (1952). Wingfield's sequence, in contrast to H.D.'s and Roberts's, was composed largely before, rather than during, the Second World War; and the poem strikes a recognisably 'Thirties' note in its apocalyptic forebodings, ambivalently censuring the vicissitudes of war and love while embracing the redemptive potential of martial and sexual immolation. Despite Wingfield's admiration for *Orlando* and *The Common Reader*, the sexual politics of the final two sections of the poem are closer to those of D.H. Lawrence than Virginia Woolf (the penultimate part is perhaps revealingly entitled 'Women in Love'), as the final female persona seeks subjugation by a male lover, beseeching him to 'Reflood the desolate ebb: / Renew me, make me whole'.[13] Such Lawrentian life-affirming rhetoric conjoins an urgent topicality reminiscent of Louis MacNeice's *Autumn Journal* (Wingfield refers to the Spanish Civil War and the Long March, among other contemporaneous events); but the poem's representation of history looks back more to the example of *The Waste Land* in its temporal concatenations, as well as in its deployment of a welter of male and female speakers.

That said, *Beat Drum, Beat Heart* (and Wingfield's oeuvre as a whole) eschews the disjunctions of Eliot's 1922 poetic collage; rather, its various stanzaic and free verse forms are juxtaposed in a manner resembling that of the less discordant transitions of *Four Quartets*. Wingfield, after all, believed that *Ulysses* and *Finnegans Wake* constituted a literary impasse rather than an enabling revolution of the word, a view at one with the misgivings of her admired Woolf over the merit of Joyce's later work.[14] In its tangential relationship with high modernism, Wingfield's work contrasts with that of Eugene R. Watters, whose major poem in English, *The Week-End of Dermot and Grace* (1964), takes its formal bearings from both the elliptical structure of *The Waste Land* and the compacted linguistic brio of *Ulysses*, while its delight in homonyms is clearly indebted to the *Wake*. Watters's poem, like its modernist precursors, shows what Eliot famously discerned in *Ulysses*: a 'mythical method'[15] by means of which the poem's overt narrative of a couple's amorous escapade, in flight from a Dublin employer for the pleasures of the seaside resort of Castlefinnerty, is shaped by the legendary pursuit of Diarmuid and Gráinne by Fíonn. The poem's absorption of Eliot and Joyce brings to mind MacGreevy's most ambitious poem, *Crón Tráth na nDéithe* ('Twilight of the Gods', 1929), the ruptured narrative of which is comprised out of the shards of its persona's perceptions of, and reflections on, the Irish Free State in the aftermath of both the Civil War and the Great War. Watters's poem is also conditioned by warfare, though of a more remote kind: set in August 1945, Hiroshima casts its horrendous pall over the lovers' jaunt. John Goodby has adroitly noted that Hiroshima 'represents a crisis not just for Dermot but of human self-understanding', the nuclear conflagration constituting 'a crisis of representation, of language' in the poem.[16] In *Crón Tráth na nDéithe*, conflict in Ireland and Europe exerts a similar pressure on MacGreevy (an Irish nationalist who had served as a combatant on the Western Front). The carnage of the trenches compounded with the Civil War's internecine strife shatter MacGreevy's persona's attempts to totalise or order his experiences into any comprehensive or meaningful pattern – 'Remember Belgium! / You cannot pick up the / Pieces'.[17] So too, in *The Week-End*, Watters's contrapuntal poetic – in which myth counterpoints contemporary existence – threatens to deconstruct, as the discordant reality of nuclear annihilation jars the endlessly cyclical vegetation myths on which the poem is premised: 'Hero. / He Rose? / Hiroshima'.[18] The fertility myths in the poem (derived from *The Golden Bough* by way of Eliot) represent the continuity of humanity, its death and rebirth, figured forth in the slaying of the 'Hero', Dermot, in a train crash towards the beginning of the poem. The remainder of the poem comprises the protagonist's disintegrating consciousness, a narrative strategy which, in the context of Irish poetry, might be seen to foreshadow that of Paul Muldoon's 'Madoc', in which the bulk of the poem is a retinal scan of the dying character, South. In *The Week-End*, the technique accounts for the poem's disorientating shift from a basically 'realist' opening to an increasingly phantasmagoric purview, the tenor of which is the possibility of Dermot's rebirth – and, by extension, the future of humanity – a resurrection which has been thrown into question ('He Rose?') in the atomic age.

Nevertheless, Watters's poem ends with the cycle of life reasserting itself, as, like the *Wake*'s crucified Shaun, Dermot is reborn 'into birth's wounds' (*Week-End*, 44). In Joyce's text, this 'Surrection' of Earwicker is punningly – and ironically – identified with the 1916 insurrection of 'Eireweeker' (the risen son/sun of this Easter week is 'Sonne feine' or Sinn Fein).[19] It is tempting – and early appraisals of the poem were quick to succumb – to see in *The Week-End*'s occasional references to the Easter Rising and its framing allusions to the Crucifixion a similar conflation of nationalist and metaphysical events. But Dermot's 'sacrifice' is only tangentially linked to national struggle. Both the Emergency and the A-Bomb lie between Joyce's last work and Watters's Cold War pocket-epic. In Dermot's prolonged battle with Thanatos, the latter work shows its cognisance of an irrevocably changed historical conjuncture.

The Week-End was published two years before the Republic of Ireland celebrated the fiftieth anniversary of the Easter Rising, one year after which Thomas Kinsella's jaundiced anatomy of 'THE NEW IRELAND', *Nightwalker*, appeared.[20] If Watters sees the date of Hiroshima's bombing as of more import to the future of post-war Ireland than that of 1916, the Holocaust provides Kinsella with a benchmark of depravity against which the ideals of the Irish Republic have to be measured. In this respect, *Nightwalker*, like his 1962 poem, 'Downstream', looks aghast at 'the European pit' of the recent past from the vantage-point of one who grew up in the war's shadow (*Poems*, 49). But, whereas the earlier poem had been primarily concerned with the possibility of art after Auschwitz, *Nightwalker* 'gropes for structure' in the political as well as the aesthetic realm (*Poems*, 76). The later poem also marks the point in Kinsella's career at which he jettisons traditional verse-forms, such as the *terza rima* of 'Downstream' and the blank verse of 'A Country Walk', another early probing into Irish history.

The mordant *Nightwalker* instead refracts recent Irish history through the prism of a poetic form the antecedent of which is *The Waste Land*, and, in this respect, its fragmentary form resembles that of MacGreevy's *Crón Tráth na nDéithe*. Kinsella's poem, like *The Week-End*, also has an intertextual relationship with the *Wake*, and the conclusion to Kinsella's poem can be read as a bleak and arid revision of the overflowing ebullience ('a long the . . . riverrun', *Wake*, 628, 3) with which Joyce's text wheels back to its fluid beginnings. 'A true desert . . . / I think / This is the Sea of Disappointment', muses Kinsella's persona, the parched lunar landscape providing a cruel summary image of the inadequacies of post-revolutionary Ireland charted in the course of the poem (*Poems*, 84). Written in the wake of the expansionist economic reforms inaugurated by the First Secretary at the Irish Department of Finance, T.K. Whitaker – for whom Kinsella had served as private secretary – *Nightwalker* is, on one level, a baroque critique of the compromises and opportunism attendant upon the drive for 'Productive Investment' from abroad (*Poems*, 78). Its satirical devices include outright Juvenalian scorn, oblique political allegory, and a nightmarishly surreal vision, quoting the *Wake*, in which the apparently emblematic figure of the controversial minister Charles Haughey, later scandal-ridden Taoiseach, 'On his big white harse', leads a 'pack of lickspittles' to hunt (*Poems*, 80–81). This topical dimension to the poem has affinities with the satires Clarke was concurrently directing against both Church and State. But Kinsella's poem is both less parochial and less impotently splenetic than many of Clarke's in that its misanthropy has an existential as much as a local application: the Dublin cityscape is a 'Necropolis' in which the Nightwalker is 'Patrolling the hive of his brain', his restless peregrinations propelled by the desire to elicit order from the 'shambles' of contingent experience (*Poems*, 77, 76).

The dual focus of *Nightwalker*, as it looks for meaningful structures in what it calls 'the madness without, / The madness within', looks forward to the Janus-faced nature of Kinsella's subsequent poetry (*Poems*, 76). In his disillusioned response to the killings in Derry on Bloody Sunday, 1972, *Butcher's Dozen* (1972), and his elegy for John F. Kennedy, *The Good Fight* (1973), Kinsella flays the skin of idealism and justice from the body politic. The extended metaphor of *A Technical Supplement* (1976) identifies rationality with a shambles or slaughterhouse, one in which the poet's own rage for order is itself a rendering of the carcass of his subject matter. In sequences such as *Notes from the Land of the Dead* (1972) and *One* (1974), Kinsella looks to the madness within, developing a complex Jungian psychodrama, at the heart of which is an archetypal journey in search of an enlarged, individuated selfhood. Though this dimension to his poetry is thematically comparable to Ted Hughes's internalised quest-romances of the 1970s, *Crow*, *Gaudete* and *Cave Birds*, the structure of Kinsella's interwoven sequences is closer to that of another poetic enterprise inspired by Jung and informed by the procedures of Pound and William Carlos Williams, *The Maximus Poems* of Charles Olson. Like Olson, Kinsella brings together autobiographical, historical and mythological materials with a minimum of connective tissue. Thus, in *Notes from the Land of the Dead*, ancestors alarmingly mutate into archetypes, as fearful grandmothers become avatars of the male psyche's anima, while, in *One*, reminiscences of family history are interlarded with accounts of the legendary origins of Ireland. Lacking authorial *dicta* or determinate narrative, the reader confronts a kaleidoscopic array of poetic segments, the meaning of which emerges from their synchronic patterning, as images and themes recur in different contexts throughout the work.

Kinsella's sequences, in this regard, possess the kind of 'spatial form' Joseph Frank discerned in the high modernist literary work, pre-eminently *Ulysses* and *The Waste Land*.[21] Yet Kinsella's poetic project is not geared towards the construction of the fully 'closed', autotelic artwork – the kind of entirely self-referential *Livre* of which Mallarmé dreamed. While indebted to Eliot, Kinsella's work cannot be wholly characterised as a late example in the line of poetic modernism stemming from the French symbolists. Kinsella's is an 'open verse', in Olson's parlance: a variety of 'allegory', as Kinsella uses the term, in which the shifting patterns that evolve in the course of the poem register the kinetic energies of reality.[22] The craving for poetic order is an appetite for poetry that recognises it is imbricated in a universal hunger. Poetic creation, in Kinsella, is an imaginative devouring, while the probing for order is equally a murderous dissection of the sensuous particular. Order and disorder, chaos and design, comprise the unresolved dialectic of Kinsella's poetry.

In Walter Benjamin's analysis of the allegorical *Trauerspiel*, the symbol represents unity with the universal, whereas allegory recognises our disjunction from the absolute, to which it can only gesture.[23] Kinsella exists in the fallen world of the allegorist. In *Out of Ireland* (1987), while the polyphony that the ninth-century Irish philosopher, Johannes Scotus Eriugena, heard in the created world clearly stands as a figure for Kinsella's dialogic poetry, Eriugena's sanguine belief in a return to 'God's light' is one Kinsella cannot share. He too 'ach[es] for a containing Shape', but the poet's designs are transitory allegorical arrangements (*Poems*, 257). In *The Good Fight*, the possibility of ordered political justice embodied in Kennedy succumbs to the antithetical appetites of the nightwalker, Lee Harvey Oswald, whose isolation and scrambled jottings, the poem darkly implies, are a distorted version of the poetic vocation.

The appetitive violence embodied in Oswald is, elsewhere in the poem, simply called 'the Jaw' (*Poems*, 149). In a poem dedicated to Kinsella, 'Low Water, Howth, 1999', Hugh Maxton (the poetic *nom de plume* of the literary historian W.J. McCormack) depicts Irish politics in equally bestial terms: 'Life lives on life say the wise / Minders of the Minotaur'.[24] Though the harshly satirical tone of the collection in which this poem appears, *Gubu Roi* (2000), is clearly modelled on that of Clarke (whose work, both Maxton and Kinsella have edited), the volume extends in a bitingly uncompromising direction his reflection in a note appended to *Jubilee for Renegades* (1982): 'politically, I consider the poems metaphysical notations of answerable poignancy'.[25] In the poems and sequences succeeding this pronouncement, Maxton has increasingly found such answerability in a poetic inflected by the aesthetic theories of the Frankfurt School. In 'Bomb Culture', Maxton refers to Theodor Adorno's famous reading of Beckett's *Endgame*, and tentatively argues for the on-going validity of modernism's 'dying art-form'; its non-realism 'Shedding as it realises / A world of power inverted knowledge / Redeemed from its mimetic image' (*Gubu Roi*, 38–9).[26] *Gubu Roi*'s lambasting of what it takes to be postmodernism's dissolving of historical atrocities into 'Fictive history' or a 'terrorism of the text' (*Gubu Roi*, 34, 36) does not signal a call for poetic mimesis or a crudely 'committed' literature. Rather, Maxton's predilection for satire – as in 6 *Snapdragons* (1985) and the poetic 'postcards' aptly entitled *Swift Mail* (1992) – interlocks with his interest in the political efficacy of the avant-garde artwork.

Maxton's *The Puzzle Tree Ascendant* (1988) is a mixed-genre work of verse and prose, accompanied by a series of drawings by Mary FitzGerald. The juxtaposition of Maxton's text and FitzGerald's non-representational *Geometric Progression* is a formal justification of that seemingly problematic term, 'Dublin Modernism', which I quoted at the beginning of this chapter. In a mock-essay, '[A Mortuary of Disused Mottoes Overheard]', included in *Puzzle Tree*, Maxton considers another Irish abstract painter, Cecil King, in whose paintings he identifies 'a finer critical knowledge (Thomas Mann's phrase) of society than arm-pit expressionism or metrical polemic. They are acts of discreet self-denial . . . [a] negation of present modes and re-lations while working from and against them' (*Puzzle Tree*, 36–7, 38). The 'critical knowledge' of King's paintings is not dissimilar to the truth-content Adorno located in what he took to be the denial, and consequent refutation, of empirical reality in Beckett's oeuvre and other 'dark works of modernism'.[27] Maxton, however, considers that such 'negation' in the fullest sense is unattainable by literature, which cannot dispense entirely with ref-erence or 'jettison its bump of clay' (*Puzzle Tree*, 38).

A solution to this poetic dilemma is proffered, in *Puzzle Tree*, by recourse to citation: the composition of a new work through the quotation of pre-existing texts, a technique that bears a structural resemblance to the use of found materials in the visual arts. At one point, Maxton refers to Benjamin's unfinished *Passagenwerk*: a vast collection of files (*Konvoluten*) of quota-tions, spliced with a smaller amount of aphoristic commentary. Benjamin believed his enormous montage of citations would release into the twentieth century the utopian potential that inhered in the commodifed culture – the 'phantasmagoria' – of the nineteenth. Maxton's literary-collage follows the *Passagenwerk*'s historical methodology, as pre-existing texts are torn from their original contexts and repositioned in a constellation of illustrations and poetic fragments. The wilfully opaque text which Maxton creates through this procedure is, so *Puzzle Tree* argues, its own guarantee of authenticity: 'such modernism as may remain still struggles towards the moment of its ar-rival, mercifully protected from embrace and acclaim by the comprehending' (*Puzzle Tree*, 38). Unlike Benjamin's, Maxton's is not a redemptive aesthetic: in line with his satirical bent, it has a purgative drive. In resisting easy con-sumption, Maxton's literary collage is the expression of a poetics of disso-nance (art music as much as abstract painting is central to *Puzzle Tree*), the discords of which are made in response to a society envisaged as a 'shopping complex break[ing] out in a *horor-vacuous* chorus of life-advertisement, lies, and harmony' (*Puzzle Tree*, 24).

In a fugitive publication formally related to *Puzzle Tree*, and bearing the Benjaminian title, *Passage* (1985), Maxton's *Konvoluten* include extracts from an article on the anti-nuclear demonstrators at Greenham Common and portions of an account of the Eleusian Mysteries associated with Demeter and Persephone. One effect of the juxtaposition of these source-texts is to align Olympian male violence – Zeus's brutal fathering of Persephone and her abduction by Hades – with the patriarchal forces, political and military, ranged against the women protesters at Greenham. The latter's fires on the common thus find a parallel in the sanctuary light of the Mysteries, while the hierophant's rebirth at the heart of the pre-Hellenic ritual is set against the possible casualties of a nuclear offensive. Structurally, *Passage* is divided into thirty-one sections, each of which has a year-date in lieu of a title, spanning, with omissions, the period from 1947, the year of Maxton's birth, to 1982. The occluded years, plus 1983, provide the titles of a brief section of lyrics, *The Widewater Poems*, which close the collection as a whole. The effect of this arrangement is to map the poet's life against the history of the Cold War: absent from the mythico-political collage, the lyric subject of the shorter poems is appended to the text as a sort of latter-day hierophant at 'petrol Eleusis', his *Koré* an endangered earth.[28]

Maxton's evacuated autobiography bears some comparison with Trevor Joyce's *Trem Neul* (2001), 'an extended auto-biographical essay in prose and verse from which everything personal has been excluded'.[29] Joyce's text, like *Passage*, is constructed out of found materials, its erasure of the authorial subject in favour of a plurality of voices a further example of Joyce's mistrust of a monologic 'poetry of expression'.[30] For Joyce, the expressive lyric is essentially monadic, its closed bounds warding off any genuine dialogue with the world. By way of contrast, Joyce proposes an intersubjective poetic, as witnessed by his 'writing through' of others' poems (those of Randolph Healy, Tom Raworth and Michael Smith), and his experiments in a procedural poem such as *Syzygy* (1998), in which the content of the first section is dictated by a structure encoded in the second. In these works, the illusory immediacy of the lyric utterance is absent: the poet's voice is mediated either through other texts or certain controlling procedures. This is poetry hopefully adequate to an age of information technology, its dialogic forms a recognition of, and a response to, the growing deformation of communicative action by the various media.

Joyce's *Without Asylum* (1999) is a meditation on deformation of various kinds. It opens by reversing normal chronology, with a destructive act run backward in time (an event repeated, in different guises, three times in the course of the poem):

> true we may surmise
> how a knife hatched
> out of meat
> should fledge
>
> span with blade
> then unexpectedly
> take flight onto some sill
> moult there with clutch
> (*with the first dream*,
> 184).

The effect of these lines is of a film in rewind, the knife's blade emerging out of meat, the 'span' of a hand reappearing on the haft, thus giving rise to the defamiliarising image of a fledgling taking flight. The final word of the verse-unit, 'clutch', holds together the initial image of the hand-held knife, and the bird's eggs, and makes a subject-rhyme with 'hatched' in the first verse-unit. This replaying of a destructive act, and its transmutation into a scene redolent of new life (the 'clutch' of eggs), imaginatively reverses the act of violence; but the poem is at pains to stress that this is merely poetic wish-fulfilment ('true we may surmise . . .'). Rather, the text continues by stressing 'murderous / intent and disturbed / dreams', its reversal of chronology a reversal of causality, an attempt to 'surmise' those agents whose intentions, more often than not, cannot be discerned in their destructive consequences.

As the poem progresses, spoliation extends from the individual act of sticking a knife into the 'meat' of a human body to the 'murderous' exploitation of the environment, encapsulated in the destruction of timber in Ireland, both during the Cromwellian era and during the 1970s and 1980s. Such devastation is the result of impersonal 'companies', 'tellers and their firm / controllers', whose culpability is obscured through the sheer scale of the structures involved ('sound / is severed from the dogs throat'; *with the first dream*, 186). The poem closes with a nightmarish image of 'an armoured beast', a postmodern variant of Yeats's 'rough beast', the grotesque hybridity of which testifies to the carapace – the state's armature, perhaps – protecting the savagery of corporate self-interest. Confronted by this, the poet cannot trace 'in this / realm of agents deeds / and instruments', and is left with 'only a sustained bewilderment' (*with the first dream*, 186).

Such 'bewilderment' may well be analogous to the reader's experience of *Without Asylum*. The 'meaning' of the poem, like that of much of Joyce's recent work, is hard to construe; his works instead yield partial readings, like the thread from *Without Asylum* unravelled above. Of interest here is the extent to which this suggests that the 'difficulty' of Joyce's poetry implicates it in precisely the kind of abrogation of responsibility atomised in *Without Asylum*. Is Joyce's poetry *symptomatic* of the malaise it interrogates? *Without Asylum* investigates human agency and intentionality by means of a poetry that, for some, may exemplify the kind of de-personalised 'textuality' celebrated by a narrow form of post-structuralism. However, Joyce's poetics are more accurately described as liminal between a conception of poetry as governed by authorial intentions, and one that maintains that the writing subject, including the lyric 'I' is merely an 'effect' of the impersonal matrix of language. The latter model of language leans heavily on the linguistic theories of Ferdinand de Saussure, and is one that underpins much of the writing of the American L=A=N=G=U=A=G=E poets, such as Charles Bernstein and Ron Silliman. In Joyce's poetry we do not witness the kind of radical dissolution of subjectivity to be found within language writing. Of relevance here is Robert Sheppard's disagreement with Peter Ackroyd's claim, in *Notes for a New Age*, that the poetry of the English late modernist poet, J.H. Prynne, witnesses a dispersal of the humanist self into a 'completely written surface'. Sheppard argues that 'Ackroyd's cultural history pays too little attention to the productive *tension* between the lyrical voice and Language'.[31] Joyce's poetry is conditioned by precisely such 'tension'. Hence his interest in the cyborg, the human-machine hybrid: if *Syzygy* originated with a text produced by a human individual (the 'author'), its subsequent mediation through prescripted procedures entails that it is the product of both human agency and computer programming.

Joyce's early poetic career was closely associated with Michael Smith's New Writers' Press. This was founded by Joyce and Smith in 1967 simply as a means of getting into print new Irish poetry. By the early 1970s it had become a vehicle for Smith's 'corrected history' of Irish poetry – a literary history in which Coffey and Devlin were perceived as major players and as progenitors, of a kind, to poets including Joyce and Geoffrey Squires.[32] While the Irish modernist poets of the 1930s do *not* in fact number among the influences on Joyce's early work, it is not erroneous to trace, *à la* Smith, a counter-tradition of Irish avant-gardist poetry from Beckett, Devlin and Coffey to the New Writers' Press poets such as Joyce and Squires. Smith's account is a publisher-poet's polemic and, as such, tends to smooth-over the complex contours of the literary revival, suppresses the far from homogenous nature of the poetry produced by the poets of the 1930s, and ignores the projects of a number of women poets of that decade, such as Wingfield, Rhoda Coghill and Blanaid Salkeld. It also neglects the extent to which poets not normally read in the context of literary modernism, Clarke and Padraic Fallon, self-consciously wrote at the mid-century in response to Pound as much as to Yeats, thus further testifying to the blotchy permeation of Irish poetry by modernism.

By way of conclusion, the work of a small number of other contemporary Irish experimental poets, including Randolph Healy, David Lloyd, Billy Mills, Maurice Scully and Catherine Walsh, should be mentioned. The poets named do not comprise a coherent 'group' of any kind, rather, their work shares an abjuration of lyric and narrative poetic modes, favouring instead writing practices that proliferate reference, generate indeterminacy. These are texts that violate generic expectations, the authors of which self-consciously, even aggressively in some cases, position themselves against a poetic 'mainstream' and its critical and publishing apparatus. To this extent, they can be said to constitute a neo-avant-garde in Irish poetry, along the lines suggested by the art historian, Hal Foster (his emphasis): *'historical and neo-avant-gardes are constituted in a similar way, as a continual process of protension and retension, a complex relay of anticipated futures and reconstructed pasts—in short, in a deferred action that throws over any simple scheme of before and after, cause and effect, origin and repetition'*.[33]

NOTES

1 Hugh Maxton, *The Puzzle Tree Ascendant* (Dublin: Dedalus, 1988), p. 35.

2 See Thomas MacDonagh, *Literature in Ireland: Studies Irish and Anglo-Irish* (1916; Dublin: Relay, 1996), pp. 5–6; and Samuel Beckett, 'Recent Irish Poetry' (1934), in *Disjecta: Miscellaneous Writings and a Dramatic Fragment*, ed. Ruby Cohn (London: John Calder, 1983), pp. 70–6.

3 See rev. of *Earth of Cualann*, by Joseph Campbell, *Egoist*, 411 (Dec. 1917), pp. 172–3. The attribution of this unsigned review to Eliot is made in Donald Gallup, *T.S. Eliot: A Bibliography*, 2nd edn. (New York: Harcourt, Brace, 1969), p. 200.

4 See Paul Peppis, *Literature, Politics, and the English Avant-Garde: Nation and Empire, 1901–1918* (Cambridge University Press, 2000), pp. 1–19.

5 J.C.C. Mays, 'How is MacGreevy a Modernist?', in Patricia Coughlan and Alex Davis (eds.), *Modernism and Ireland: The Poetry of the 1930s* (Cork University Press, 1995), p. 110.

6 Beckett, *Disjecta*, p. 70.

7 Terence Brown, 'Ireland, Modernism and the 1930s', in Patricia Coughlan and Alex Davis (eds.), *Modernism and Ireland: The Poetry of the 1930s* (Cork University Press, 1995), p. 38.

8 Denis Devlin, *Collected Poems of Denis Devlin*, ed. J.C.C. Mays (Dublin: Dedalus, 1989), p. 71.

9 Lawrence E. Harvey, *Samuel Beckett: Poet and Critic* (Princeton University Press, 1970), p. 78.

10 Samuel Beckett, *Collected Poems 1930–1978* (London: John Calder, 1984), p. 15.

11 Patricia Coughlan, ' "The Poetry is Another Pair of Sleeves": Beckett, Ireland and Modernist Lyric Poetry', in Patricia Coughlan and Alex Davis (eds.), *Modernism and Ireland: The Poetry of the 1930s* (Cork University Press, 1995), p. 196.

12 Dónal Moriarty, *The Art of Brian Coffey* (University College Dublin Press, 2000), p. 16.

13 Sheila Wingfield, *Collected Poems 1938–1983* (London: Enitharmon, 1983), p. 72.

14 See Sheila Powerscourt, *Sun Too Fast* (London: Geoffrey Bles, 1974), p. 121.

15 T.S. Eliot, '*Ulysses*, Order, and Myth' (1923), in *Selected Prose of T.S. Eliot*, ed. Frank Kermode (London: Faber, 1975), p. 178.

16 John Goodby, *Irish poetry since 1950: from stillness into history* (Manchester University Press, 2000), p. 99.

17 Thomas MacGreevy, *Collected Poems of Thomas MacGreevy*, ed. Susan Schreibman (Dublin: Anna Livia, 1991), p. 15.

18 Eugene R. Watters, *The Week-End of Dermot and Grace* (Dublin: Allen Figgis, 1964), p. 5.

19 James Joyce, *Finnegans Wake* (London: Faber, 1939), p. 593.

20 Thomas Kinsella, *Collected Poems 1956–2001* (Manchester: Carcanet, 2001), p. 81.

21 See Joseph Frank, *The Widening Gyre: Crisis and Mastery in Modern Literature* (Urbana: Indiana University Press, 1963).

22 See Kinsella's 'Ballydavid Pier': 'Allegory forms of itself: / The line of life creeps upwards / Replacing one world with another' (*Poems*, p. 57).

23 See Walter Benjamin, *The Origin of German Tragic Drama*, trans. John Osbourne (London: New Left Books, 1977).

24 Hugh Maxton, *Gubu Roi: Poems & Satires, 1991–1999* (Belfast: Lagan, 2000), p. 55.

25 Hugh Maxton, *Jubilee for Renegades: Poems 1976–1980* (Dublin: Dolmen, 1982), p. 80.

26 Maxton / McCormack discusses Adorno's essay in *From Burke to Beckett: Ascendancy, Tradition and Betrayal in Literary History* (Cork University Press, 1994), pp. 410–27. On the relationship between McCormack and his *alter ego*, see Hugh Maxton, *Waking: An Irish Protestant Upbringing* (Belfast: Lagan, 1997), p. 212.

27 Theodor W. Adorno, *Aesthetic Theory*, trans. Robert Hullot-Kentor (Minneapolois: University of Minnesota Press, 1997), p. 318.

28 Hugh Maxton, *Passage (with surviving poems)* (Bradford on Avon, 1985), n. pag.

29 This is from the description of the poem on the dustjacket to Trevor Joyce, *with the first dream of fire they hunt the cold: A Body of Work 1966/2000* (Dublin: New Writers' Press/Cullompton: Shearsman, 2001).

30 Trevor Joyce, 'The Point of Innovation in Poetry', in Harry Gilonis (ed.), *For the Birds: Proceedings of the First Cork Conference on New and Experimental Irish Poetry* (Sutton: Mainstream Poetry/Dublin: hardPressed Poetry, 1998), p. 19.

31 Robert Sheppard, *Far Language: Poetics and Linguistically Innovative Poetry 1978–1997* (Exeter: Stride, 1999), p. 12.
32 See Smith's editorials to New Writers' Press journal, *The Lace Curtain* (1969–78), and his polemical article, 'Irish Poetry since Yeats: Notes Towards a Corrected History', *Denver Quarterly*, 5 (1971), pp. 1–26.
33 Hal Foster, *The Return of the Real: The Avant-Garde at the End of the Century* (Cambridge, MA: MIT, 1996), p. 29.

6

FRAN BREARTON

Poetry of the 1960s: the 'Northern Ireland Renaissance'

I

In August 1970, Eavan Boland published a series of three articles in the *Irish Times* entitled 'The Northern writers' crisis of conscience'. In the concluding article, Boland asks: 'how . . . will writers in Northern Ireland articulate the crisis in progress outside and within them, the retrospect on communities it must force, the needs it imposes to reorder increasingly chaotic impressions?'. How will writers cope, she continues, with 'such intractable, yet urgent material'?[1] Criticism may since have become more circumspect in approaching these questions, but their underlying assumptions still prove contentious in reading contemporary Irish poetry. In effect, Boland implicitly assumes here that Northern writers are a distinct group; that they have responsibilities towards the Troubles which are not necessarily shared by their Southern counterparts; that individual anxieties and conflicts manifest the anxieties of the state; that writers are identifiable with, or speak from, a particular religious community; and that poetry will, in MacNeice's phrase, 'make sense of the world . . . put shape on it' in 1930s generation style.[2]

This is one of many early indications that contemporary poetry in Northern Ireland, rapidly becoming of interest to the media, was not likely to be read outside the context of the Troubles, thus positing a symbiotic relationship between poetry and violence; the reputations and public profiles of these and other writers developed beyond their own shores in tandem with Northern Ireland's own growing international profile. The political problems of the province spiralled out of control to reach a wider audience as Northern Irish poetry simultaneously began to make its mark on an international stage. Consequently, any reading of 1960s poetry in Ireland may succumb to more than one temptation, not least of which is to read the story from a post-1969 perspective, and bring expectations about poetry engendered in part by the Troubles to bear on writing from the early and mid-1960s (among which, notably, are the first collections by Seamus Heaney, Michael Longley and

Derek Mahon). Critics scour the early collections by these poets for poems about the violence. Many discussions of contemporary Northern poetry take 1969 as their starting point. The Troubles link also encourages parallels between the Revivals – literary and cultural – of the early part of the century, and what has been termed the 'Ulster Revival' of the 1960s and 1970s. The Irish Revival, with its nationalist agenda, its emergence from a context of political stalemate and literary silence, and its link with violence through the poet-revolutionaries of Easter 1916, appears to set a precedent for a further literary revival in the North, also inextricably intertwined with Irish/British politics, and running parallel to, if unconnected with, campaigns of violence: the 'ghost of analogy', as Richard Kirkland points out, 'shadows events'.[3] 'Yeats to Heaney' is more than merely a convenient marketing ploy. It has proved equally tempting, if misleading, to compare the Ulster poetry 'phenomenon' of the late 1960s and 1970s to the deliberately regionalist school of Ulster poetry in the 1940s and 1950s – the attempt by John Hewitt and others to collapse unionist and nationalist division into loyalty to the 'region', from which, it was hoped, would emerge 'a culture and an attitude individual and distinctive, a fine contribution to the European inheritance'.[4] Both analogies implicitly attribute some kind of shared agenda to contemporary Ulster poets, although the agendas themselves – regionalist and nationalist – conflict. To read poetry according to the imperatives of time and place (the Troubles, Northern Ireland) is also too often to miss the broader poetic context in which that work should properly find its 'place'. Poets from Northern Ireland have been the focus of extensive academic and media attention over the last thirty years, sometimes to the detriment of proper consideration of their work in the island's poetic traditions as a whole, and in the context of British, Irish and American cultural exchange and influence.

'Decades', as John Montague writes, 'are untidy things'.[5] In contrast, 'Northern poetry post-1969' is a critical package that is temptingly coherent, a narrative with a logical starting point, and one that ultimately strives towards (political) closure. But it places the 1960s themselves in historical limbo, in turn detaching post-1969 poetry from some of its origins and its aesthetic moorings. The 1960s mark the emergence of the concerns, achievements and influences that were to ensure a reputation for much contemporary Irish poetry in spite of, rather than because of, Irish politics. While one possible narrative is of endings in poetry, marked by the (premature) deaths of MacNeice (1963) and of Kavanagh (1967), the more dominant narrative – for these poets too – is one of beginnings. A renascent interest in the poetry and influence of Kavanagh and MacNeice brings them into play in contemporary debate in the 1960s. Mahon suggests that MacNeice's reputation finally 'come[s] to rest' in Ireland;[6] in retrospect he might more accurately say comes to life. And while Kavanagh may have bewailed the lack of an audience in Ireland, that audience was already in place in as much as his challenge to the insular, rural and sentimental Celtic lyricism popularised by Yeats's followers was bearing fruit in a new generation free from the shadow of late Revivalist poetics. John Montague, Thomas Kinsella, Richard Murphy and John Hewitt provided, in the late 1950s and early 1960s, both precedent and example for younger poets. In the cases of Kinsella and Montague in particular, their own emergence as poets through the 1950s, and in apparently unpropitious circumstances, offered a more immediate encouragement for the emergence of the 1960s generation than the revivals in the earlier part of the century.

Since the media interest in poetry from Northern Ireland began, John Montague has been inclined alternately to promote and condemn the concept of 'Northern poetry', a fluctuation which probably fairly accurately represents the varying degrees of attention given to his own work in the context of a 'Northern renaissance'. Nevertheless, there is some truth in Montague's own claim that he can be seen as the 'missing link' in Ulster poetry between the regionalist activities of the 1940s and 1950s, and the younger generation of the 1960s.[7] The regionalist agenda was optimistic – Montague's own background, for instance, engendered an antipathy towards its implicitly unionist sympathies – and the failure of regionalism partly accounts for the fact that, as the 1950s ended, neither John Hewitt nor Roy McFadden had published a full-length collection since the 1940s, W.R. Rodgers since 1951. Hewitt left Northern Ireland in 1957, to what might be seen as involuntary exile, and was not to return until 1972. If the North's repressive unionist Stormont parliament perpetuated a presbyterian ethos that offered its own form of censorship, as it also perpetuated a social and political structure of inequality, the Republic, for Montague, was equally dominated in the 1940s and 1950s by the conditions of exile, censorship and literary isolationism. He describes it as 'a limbo land', its literary culture as 'a procession of sad and broken poets and complaining novelists', and his own condition as one of 'stunned isolation'. 'There was', Montague writes, 'no tradition for someone of my [Ulster Catholic] background to work in'.[8] Effectively suggesting that his isolation in the South in the 1940s and 1950s is a consequence of his Northernness, and in the North a consequence of his Catholicism, Montague mythologises his departure from Ireland in 1952 as a (Joycean) 'flight' from both, a form of exile, from which he was not to return until the late 1950s. As Robert Garratt argues, in Montague's first two collections, *Forms of Exile* (1958) and *Poisoned Lands* (1961), the 'posture' of the early poems is 'struck partly out of fascination with Ireland but also out of regret and rejection'.[9]

Montague responds to the complexity of his environment by explaining his poetic identity in terms of internationalism, claiming a 'natural complicity in three cultures, American, Irish and French', and the possession of a 'world consciousness' as well as 'local allegiances'.[10] One consequence of this convoluted, and perhaps over-argued formula is an uneasy relationship with the Northern poets who come to prominence on an international stage later without the need to claim internationalism. But Montague's poetry in the 1960s both resists the insularity and anti-modernity that had been symptomatic of Irish culture and simultaneously validates the importance of the local and traditional – a difficult but important balance to find. *The Rough Field* (1972) is a poem often, and easily, read in the context of the Troubles, appearing as it did in its final form when the violence was at its height. But its influence begins much earlier. Written in fits and starts between 1961–71, the poem is, in a way, a barometer of the conflicts and shifts in perspective – between repression and freedom, tradition and modernity, optimism and pessimism, beginnings and endings – characteristic of its decade of composition. The 'Rough Field' is Montague's home town of Garvaghey (*garbh achaidh*, a rough field); but the local context is also broadened since the rough field is simultaneously the sweep of (often violent) history that runs alongside the poem's lyrics and destroys the pastoral idyll – 'Our finally lost dream of man at home / in a rural setting!' (*The Rough Field*, p. 83)[11] That history deliberately disrupts the conventional lyric flow of the poem, which is interspersed with sixteenth century woodcuts, and presented alongside extracts from speeches, historical documents, journalism and traditional Irish verse, in a manner which makes the poem as a whole unconventional in its stylistic experimentation, but within which Montague's own poetry adheres to traditional form. Throughout, Montague both regrets a culture that has disappeared; he also validates its existence in the act of recording that which was previously forgotten. The landscape, for Montague, is 'a manuscript / We had lost the skill to read' (p. 35) but the poem implicitly, in its form and structure, also finds a new way to read it. 'Like Dolmens Round my Childhood', his best known poem from the early 1960s, which appeared in *Poisoned Lands* (1961) and was subsequently collected in *The Rough Field*, both mocks 'ancient Ireland', in all its stereotypical guises, but is simultaneously seduced by, and seduces its reader with, its 'dark permanence of ancient forms' (16–17). While Montague flirts with ideas of internationalism and experimentalism, in terms of example, his significance – certainly for Seamus Heaney – lies more in the poetic validation of his home ground in a wider European context, a context that Hewitt, a less accomplished poet, failed to reach. Thus, Heaney's debt to Montague is evident in the early Montague poems – 'The Trout', 'The Water Carrier', 'Like Dolmens

Round my Childhood' – which speak to Heaney's own rural background and tradition.

II

For Mahon, encountering Montague's 'Like Dolmens Round My Childhood' in 1960 proved that the North was not, after all, 'barren of poetry'.[12] As Montague himself notes, when he was awarded a prize for the poem, it was announced in the Irish press as 'Dublin poet wins Belfast Prize', 'so little were they used to someone of [his] background' ('Preface' to *The Rough Field*, p. 7). That attitude suggests that the post-war generation of Longley, Mahon and Heaney started out in equally unpropitious circumstances. Longley describes Northern Ireland in the late 1950s as 'godforsaken'. For Mahon it was a 'cultural desert'. Heaney borrows Mahon's own phrase to describe the stagnant mood of the time: 'If a coathanger knocked in a wardrobe / That was a great event'.[13] But by the late 1960s, that state of affairs had become unrecognisable. The decade, with its modernisation programmes, scientific developments, civil rights movements, social and religious destabilisation, and new educational opportunities (facilitated by the Butler Education Act of 1947), may be seen as a period of change sufficiently extraordinary to render the illusion of (sepia-tinted) pre-Troubles Irish tranquillity as inaccurate as the characterisation of an innocent and stable pre-First World War Edwardian England. The new energies in social and political life also reverberated culturally, and *vice versa*. In Ireland, the Dolmen Press had provided new publishing opportunities for poets; new journals appeared or were revived, among them *Poetry Ireland*. This upsurge in the indigenous life of Irish poetry was also paralleled by an increased engagement with writers and audiences 'across the water': Faber beckoned as much as Dolmen. In Britain, Alvarez's influential anthology, *The New Poetry*, with its call for a 'new seriousness' in poetry and its rejection of the 'gentility principle' indicated a new energy that also reverberated in Ireland, as Alvarez's general editorship of the Penguin Modern European Poets series brought work by Mandelstam, Akhmatova, and others into creative dialogue with British and Irish poetry during the 1960s.[14] The changes through the decade also prompted significant re-evaluations for Montague and Hewitt: they found little common ground in the 1950s, but by 1970 they were working together on the 'Planter and Gael' tour, and as Hewitt noted, poems which had triggered no response at their time of publication took on a new relevance at the end of the 1960s.[15] MacNeice's last collection, *The Burning Perch* (1963), far from marking an ending, took the lyric into a new dimension. The black humour, irony and parabolic approach of his later lyrics haunt the work of later poets such as Paul Muldoon and Ciaran Carson, in a mode of writing all the more telling in its obliquity. Kavanagh's *Come Dance with Kitty Stobling* (1960) contains the resurgence of confidence in his roots, the desire to 'wallow in the habitual',[16] that was to prove inspirational for Heaney in the mid-1960s, and the publication of his *Collected Poems* (1964) redressed the bleak situation in which much of his work had been out of print.

Michael Longley's comment that for him the 1960s 'began quietly in Dublin and ended tumultuously in Belfast' thus encompasses more than simply the move from a context of political stability to one of sectarian strife.[17] One consequence of the poetic developments of the 1960s was that the old stereotype of literary Dublin *versus* philistine Belfast – elegance as opposed to industrialisation – lost much of its force as poetic maps were, of necessity, redrawn to include the North. The publication in the second half of the decade of new collections by young poets North and South – including Derek Mahon, Seamus Heaney, Michael Longley, Eavan Boland, Brendan Kennelly, Michael Hartnett and James Simmons – some of whom would eventually establish international reputations and cast many of their predecessors into the shade, marked a new (and on-going) phase of poetic activity. Of these poets, the fact that an unprecedented number are Northern writers inevitably fuels talk of an 'Ulster Revival' or a 'Northern Renaissance' of poetry. For Thomas Kinsella, the idea of a 'Northern Ireland Renaissance' is 'largely a journalistic entity', a shorthand way of accounting for a coincidence of talent.[18] The idea has also led to over-simplifications: if poetic maps were redrawn to include the North, one might now say that they were redrawn in popular perception to the extent that they seemed to encompass *only* the North after 1969. But Northern writers themselves have always been at once more ambiguous and less dismissive about the idea of a Northern Renaissance than their Southern counterparts: as Mahon points out, Kinsella is 'right up to a point', but 'there *is* more to it than that'.[19] One reason for that ambiguity is Northern writers' sense of a shared social, economic and political as well as cultural environment in the mid to late 1960s distinct from that of the Republic: the conditions of production, in other words, differ significantly.

That assumption might seem uncontroversial, but it has far-reaching implications. Not least, the concept of a 'Northern Renaissance', or even a 'Northern poetry', carries within it the suggestion that Irish writing is itself partitioned, that writers are working in two different traditions. As Richard Kirkland points out, for some critics at least, 'To acknowledge that Northern Ireland operated under a different political and social regime than the rest of the island was one aspect of the argument, but to suggest that such difference in turn created a distinct literature of its own was ... unacceptable'.[20] The ambiguity surrounding such arguments may be measured in a consideration of the reception of Heaney's own poetry, which in its early stages may be seen to benefit from the partitionist critical viewpoint that stresses his 'Northernness', and yet which later makes its way on to an international stage under the banner of 'Irishness'. 'We cannot be unaware', Heaney writes, 'of the link between the political glamour of the place (Ulster), the sex-appeal of violence, and the prominence accorded to the poets'.[21] Mahon's own sense that 'the poet from the North had a new thing to say, a new kind of sound to make, a new texture to create', implies the emergence, or renaissance, of a distinct literature. But he is also inclined to qualify those implications (Irish writing is 'all one'; 'you can't renasce something that was never nasce'). Mahon, who argues that the 'poetry and the "troubles" had a common source; the same energy gave rise to both', is also careful to point out that 'the poetry preceded the politics'[22] – the Troubles do not inspire Northern poetry. But since they inspire much of the journalistic interest in that poetry through the 1970s, they also engender an increasing caution on the part of poets unwilling to find themselves trapped by a literary terminology that might misrepresent their political viewpoints.

III

If a certain amount of political distancing – which does not necessarily deny a distinctive context of production – takes place, the Northern poets are also concerned to distance themselves from a second, related suggestion that hovers behind the terms 'renaissance' and 'revival': that the poets constitute a distinctive poetic 'movement' or 'alliance'. Since this concerns the issue of shared (or otherwise) aesthetic principles, it affects questions of individual identity as well as poetic reputation. It is in this latter context that the formation and influence of a creative writing group at Queen's University Belfast, known as the Belfast Group, becomes pertinent. The story of the Belfast Group has become the stuff of myth. It has also become a contentious story, since interpretations of the Group's significance bear on perceptions of the shifting relationships between writers, their differing aesthetic practices, and the variable fortunes of Northern poetry and criticism more generally in the years that have followed.

In its first, and most famous phase, the Group began in Belfast in 1963, under the auspices of Philip Hobsbaum, who had joined Queen's English department in October of that year. (Hobsbaum left Belfast in 1966, and the Group lapsed for a short period, but was reconstituted in 1968 by Michael Allen, Arthur Terry and Seamus Heaney.) Hobsbaum, who had been taught by F.R. Leavis and worked with William Empson, came to Queen's with a reputation as a talent spotter, as a formalist 'new critic' who had an avowed aim 'to take Leavis's approach into the modern sector',[23] and as the founder, in 1955, of a creative writing group in London which had published *A Group Anthology* in 1963. The London group's discussions were based on the practice of Leavisite criticism – 'closer and more analytical discussion' and an encouragement to 'pay attention to the text itself'.[24] Other critical promptings came from Empson and T.S. Eliot; London participants included Edward Lucie-Smith, Peter Porter, George MacBeth and Peter Redgrove.

The Belfast Group, with this precedent and Hobsbaum's contacts behind it, thus indisputably gave what Longley has termed 'an air of seriousness and electricity to the notion of writing',[25] something which had been lacking in Belfast, despite the best efforts of the earlier generation of McFadden, Hewitt and Rodgers to promote a Northern cultural energy in the 1940s. It provided, in Arthur Terry's words, 'a meeting place for people of very different backgrounds and interests',[26] something which, in the repressive and socially divisive atmosphere of the North at that time, could not be taken for granted, as it was also a meeting place of aesthetic ideas current in Dublin, London and Belfast. (Perennial talking points were Yeats and Auden.) It brought literary critics into dialogue with creative writers. And as Norman Dugdale, a group member in the mid-1960s, points out, it provided 'an audience, however localised, which was prepared to listen',[27] the lack of which Kavanagh had bewailed in the Republic. Creativity was in the air; the Group provided a talking point on the ground. Heaney attended from its inception; Michael Longley on his return to Belfast in 1964. Other Group members included, at various times, Stewart Parker, James Simmons and Bernard MacLaverty, as well as the critics Edna Longley and Michael Allen. Hobsbaum himself was an experienced writer and publicist who in 'mov[ing] disparate elements into a single action' enabled a public perception of the Group as a phenomenon worthy of attention, and of its individuals as worthy of publication.[28]

That attention began before the Troubles, and, indeed, before the first full collections of any of the new poets had appeared. The Belfast Festival publication, in 1965–66, of pamphlets by various members of the Group generated local media interest: those pamphlets by Heaney, Mahon and Longley contain core poems which were to find their way into their first collections, *Death of a Naturalist* (1966), *Night-Crossing* (1968) and *No Continuing City* (1969) respectively. The cultural flowering of this period may be seen as inspired by a new optimism and an energy that, it was hoped, would see the end of repression and oppression in its various forms. The first issue, in May 1968, of the *Honest Ulsterman*, edited by James Simmons, a journal which was to provide an important local publishing venue for poets and critics in Northern Ireland, captured the mood of the decade in billing itself as 'a magazine of revolution', and advertised its contents as a heady mix of debate on 'Love, Exile, Humanism, Hashish, Courage, History, Louis Mac-Neice . . . '. Simmons's own poetry injected a different dimension into the Northern scene on his return in the late 1960s: his blurring of the edges of the genre through connections to song-writing and the ballad tradition link him with a more general popularisation of poetry in Britain and Ireland at the time; his sense of the interdependence of life and art, and of the urgency of direct and colloquial writing, run slightly counter to the Group's own New Critical preoccupations.

Over the last thirty years, Heaney and Longley, the Group's best-known poet-participants, and Mahon, its most famous non-participant, have, along with others, offered differing versions of its significance in what Dugdale has termed 'obituarial oscillations',[29] oscillations which may be understood partly in terms of divergent aesthetic principles. In that sense, unsurprisingly perhaps, accounts of the Group, even if they implicitly suggest shared contexts and concerns, work first and foremost to validate the individual aesthetic. The well-worn myth of the Group as it appears in most critical narratives is also closely linked to Heaney's own first narrative of the Group, and to his reflections on the nature of criticism and poetry more generally. For Heaney, the group 'ratified the activity of writing' and transformed the state of affairs in which he had no 'sense of contemporary poetry' – as he points out, he graduated in 1962 without having heard Larkin's name mentioned.[30] In his account of the Group in *Preoccupations* it becomes a mythic origin, an apprenticeship which consolidates the craft not only of his own poetry, but also of the mode of criticism, Anglo-American New Criticism, or 'practical criticism', by which that poetry is well-served.[31] Heaney was, as other Group members recognised, Hobsbaum's star. His densely textured, empirically grounded, traditional and accessible mode of writing apparently both validated the English 1950s Movement aesthetic endorsed by Hobsbaum (whose own volumes of poetry carry an obvious debt to Larkin) and gave that aesthetic a rawer edge, Ted Hughes style. Read in these terms, Heaney casts out the gentility principle to give formalism a new lease of life as a possible counter to threats from 1960s experimentalist poetry and emerging structuralist agendas.

In a sense, therefore, the Group, and Hobsbaum, gave Heaney self-confidence, as Heaney's career reciprocally became a means by which Hobsbaum validated his own critical principles. That initial lack of confidence was not a feeling shared by his contemporaries, Longley and Mahon. Consequently, although Larkin and Hughes may stand as the obvious influences on Heaney's early poems (along with other English poets – Robert Graves, Wilfred Owen, and, further back, Wordsworth), a significant part of

Heaney's origin myth is the celebration of Patrick Kavanagh's role in validating a background and experience that had little voice in Irish poetry. The genuine parochial, Kavanagh famously argued, 'is never in any doubt about the social and artistic validity of his parish'. Kavanagh's own 'Epic', with its assertion that 'Gods make their own importance', is thus a paradigmatic poem for Heaney's lyrics.[32] Heaney's home ground of Mossbawn makes its own importance in the 1960s, as his 'Bogland' (c.1966–67), which begins with what it lacks – 'We have no prairies to slice a sun at evening', the seemingly wider horizons of America – ends by validating its own narrow ground as infinitely inspirational space: 'the wet centre is bottomless'.[33] Significantly, therefore, when Heaney evaluates the Group dynamic from the vantage point of the 1970s, he does so, knowingly and slightly mischievously, in terms of his own aesthetic practice as adopted and adapted from Kavanagh's (idiosyncratic) version of provincialism and parochialism: 'now, of course', Heaney writes, 'we're genuine parochials. Then we were craven provincials. Hobsbaum contributed much to that crucial transformation'.[34]

If Heaney's interpretation of the Group is implicated in his appropriation of Kavanagh, his sense of an 'apprenticeship' served in the Group is also bound up with an aesthetic that is invested in the concept of apprenticeship in other ways. Heaney 'learns' the craft of poetry as one would learn the crafts paralleled with poetry in *Death of a Naturalist*: digging, butter-churning, water-divining and so on. The trope continues into *Door into the Dark* to become central to Heaney's aesthetic: 'Bogland', as Heaney describes its composition, 'opened the way wood falls open if you hit a wedge into it along the grain'.[35] In 'The Forge', the blacksmith 'expends himself in shape and music'; he 'grunts and goes in, with a slam and a flick / To beat real iron out, to work the bellows' (*Door into the Dark*, 7). Poetry, in Heaney's terms, is both labour and inspiration (as it is also sexually charged, an implicitly masculine activity), beating real iron out of the language, making the lyric 'eat stuff it has never eaten before'.[36] The Group is thus implicitly and seamlessly incorporated into the rural myth of origins and identity, of continuity between cultural and physical labour, with all the disingenuousness such 'continuity' implies.[37] The real sophistication of Heaney's early writing lies in part in his ability to make an audience believe the process of writing is natural and simple. In its Kavanagh-esque function, the Group, for Heaney, is implicated in the process of recovery and rediscovery of a marginalised community, a cultural project – habitually presented in his poetry in natural terms – which carries important political overtones in the Northern Ireland of the late 1960s. Kavanagh, Heaney argues, 'brought the subculture to cultural power'. The publication of *Death of a Naturalist* – the precocity of which owes much to the Group's existence – was also, he continues, a 'ratification . . . a sense that you had represented something that had happened to your generation, you had broken the silence'. Poems are, he writes, 'elements of continuity'; poetry is 'the restoration of a culture to itself'.[38] In that sense, Heaney picks up not only on Kavanagh's parochial aesthetic, he also follows John Montague's attempted recovery of the 'shards of a lost tradition' in finding the 'skill to read' the landscape, the loss of which had left his predecessor clutching at a vanished world. Heaney's 'tradition' is in one sense a fiction (poetry is not the same as digging); but it is also upheld with an astonishing confidence, partly because its 'continuity' myth has been built from scratch.

That the Group has been implicitly integrated into Heaney's aesthetic in this way – both by Heaney and his critics – partly explains Longley's own restrained judgement that the Group 'meant more' to Heaney than to himself or Mahon.[39] Derek Mahon, in any case, was not a member of the Group (although he attended one or two sessions on his visits to Belfast) and was not resident in Northern Ireland during this period. Both Mahon and Longley have more studiedly downplayed the Group's significance, where Heaney has at times, perhaps unconsciously, gathered the Group under his own aesthetic umbrella (the 'we' of 'we're genuine parochials'?). Heaney's role as critic as well as poet has also opened up an audience for his early prose writings that his closest contemporaries have tended to lack – *Preoccupations* remains the standard resource even though Heaney himself has subsequently retreated from some of its judgements.[40] Consequently, Longley and Mahon have been concerned, in recent years, both to dispel certain Group myths, and to raise awareness of what one might call a counter-myth, one that challenges commonplace assumptions about the emergence of 'Northern poetry' in a troubled Belfast – namely the significance of the 'apprenticeship' served by both Mahon and Longley (along with Brendan Kennelly and, later, Eavan Boland) as students at Trinity College Dublin in the early 1960s.

Importantly, the poetry scene at Trinity from 1960–63 is not claimed by Longley and Mahon as a 'movement', or alliance, but as a confluence of different ideas, perspectives and influences, with a shared publishing outlet, the student magazine *Icarus*. The *Icarus* editorial of March 1961 over-enthusiastically claims that 'there is a strong fluent, centralized, fundamentally pure poetic movement right here in Trinity' which is concerned with 'love, society, nature and philosophy'. Michael Longley refuted this in the June 1961 issue, arguing that a 'happy coincidence' of lyric poets in one place is not a movement, still less, and more presumptuously, a 'Movement'. Nevertheless, that the debate can take place indicates something of the cultural energy of Trinity in this period, comparable to that which emerges in Belfast two years later. Mahon describes Trinity as: 'More than a remarkable experience, a whole way of life . . . We published in the college magazines and even in the books pages of the *Irish Times*. We did readings in the rooms of the Philosophical Society . . . [Longley and I] read as far up as Lowell and Larkin, as far up as Kinsella and Montague . . . University life merged imperceptibly into literary life'.[41] The Northern student who went to Trinity, he argues, 'picked up an all-Ireland view instead of the provincial view'.[42] Longley suggests that Alec Reid, an English lecturer at Trinity who founded *Icarus* in 1950 (and left in 1963), was a 'father figure' who fulfilled the Hobsbaum role.[43] The influences at work on both poets at this time included Yeats, MacNeice and Graves, as well as American poets such as cummings, Crane, Stevens, Lowell and Wilbur. In contrast to Heaney's undergraduate years, both had an acute sense of developments in contemporary poetry, reading Montague's and Kinsella's early collections, as well as work by Geoffrey Hill, Ted Hughes and Philip Larkin.

Some of these influences are seen at work in the poems Mahon and Longley published in *Icarus* in the early 1960s. Mahon's early love poems have an obvious, and rewarding debt to Robert Graves as well as to the French symbolists. The preoccupation with language and the metaphysical uncertainty that carry into his first collection are also present in poems, discarded as juvenilia, that would rival the mature work of others. Mahon's arrival on the pages of *Icarus* in 1960 with 'Subsidy Bungalows' foreshadows his important revision of '[w]hatever we mean by "the Irish situation"' to include the shipyards of Belfast and the suburban, Protestant lower middle-class existence.[44] Similarly, Longley's own poetry, given new energy by Mahon's arrival at Trinity, promises the formal accomplishment that would make his first collection an exceptionally virtuoso performance in contemporary poetry, and manifests the precision in language – also characteristic of Richard Wilbur – that remains a hallmark of Longley's aesthetic, as it was also to become a vital stay against the pressures of Northern Ireland in the 1970s. Some of this work was, of course, subsequently jettisoned. But the Belfast Group's influence here may be measured in part by the fact that a number of poems Longley brought to the Group had been published in *Icarus* two years earlier, and underwent little or no revision in Belfast. Mahon's 'Prayer for an Unborn Child', and Longley's 'Epithalamion', published in *Icarus* in 1963, went into *Night Crossing* (1968) and *No Continuing City* (1969) respectively towards the end of the decade. With the maturity of these poems, it is difficult not to sense the end of an 'apprenticeship' in 1963 comparable to the end of the Belfast Group's first phase in 1966.

Edna Longley argues that the 'aesthetic conflicts that pervaded [the Group's] sessions', and which militate against the notion of a 'cosy fostering', have much to do with the very different contexts in which its poets began to write, and that Hobsbaum himself, in Group sessions:

> did not, as a rule, endorse Romantic, symbolist, mythic, metaphysical and rhetorical tendencies, including those derived from [Yeats, Graves, Crane, Stevens and Lowell] . . . Dylan Thomas was – and remains – anathema. Much of this echoed central emphases of the English Movement and diverged from the aesthetic principles established between Mahon and Longley in Dublin – where, for instance, Lowell represented a walk on the wild side and Larkin's dialogue with Yeats struck more chords than his relation to Kingsley Amis.[45]

Hobsbaum's preference for what Heaney terms 'the bleeding hunk of experience'[46] does not sit comfortably with Longley's formal precision and fascination with myth, any more than with Mahon's urbanity, metaphysical unease and Yeatsian rhetoric. The Gravesian notion of the Muse expounded in *The White Goddess* (a text which had its own 'revival' in the 1960s) in-fluences both poets, and also associates their work with the romanticism of 1940s English poetry, as well as with Yeats, both associations that English Movement poets in the 1950s were anxious to refute. Thus, as Heaney recog-nises, Longley's poems were habitually challenged in Group sessions where his own were praised.[47] Mahon, typically, kept an ironic and literal distance from the whole thing ('Too Leavisite and too contentious'[48]), whilst contin-uing to comment on the Group and its activities with cheerful irreverence.

The ambiguous relation of both Longley and Mahon to the Group mir-rors their ambiguous sense of identity and place. Where Heaney's *Death of a Naturalist* implies the birth of a poet, one seamlessly giving way to the other, Mahon's *Night-Crossing*, even in its title, suggests a permanently transitional identity split between here and elsewhere. The poems play out a debate be-tween belonging and not belonging, opening up an ironic distance between poet and community. Mahon's urbanity becomes a defence against commit-ment to place, as he simultaneously brings a new conception of urban space into Irish poetry. Thus, in 'In Belfast' (retitled 'The Spring Vacation'), the poet, ironically 'Walking among my own', typically finds himself 'between shower and shower', exhorts his mind to 'know its place', but never claims actually to do so. 'Glengormley' might have its nostalgia for an era of saints and heroes, but even if the poem cannot quite bring itself to praise the sub-urban 'worldly time under this worldly sky', it cannot ignore its existence.[49] For Longley, *No Continuing City*, with its multiple voices, marks perhaps an even more complex collapse of boundaries in space and time: that there is no continuing city in material terms suggests both an absence of tradi-tional and communal stability and, implicitly, a belief in imaginative com-pensation – poetry displacing conventional religious consolations. Poetry is 'incorrigible[s]', in 'The Freemartin', but it is also a 'Difficult birth[s]', an oddment that, like the freemartin, resists categorisation.[50] The ambiguity inherent in this also accords with Longley's own feeling that Mahon and Heaney began their careers with what he himself lacked – 'recourse to solid hinterlands – Heaney the much publicized farm in Co. Derry, Mahon his working class background and the shipyards'.[51]

The Group, seen as a Belfast-Dublin-London aesthetic collision ground, also foreshadows in miniature the broader argument that Northern Ireland itself may be understood as a 'cultural corridor', in which Irish and English and other influences meet – Ulster is, in Michael Longley's phrase, 'a limbo between two (three?) cultures'.[52] Such a stance denies aesthetic coherence to the Group – 'northern poets' don't hunt in a pack – but it does also suggest that Northern Ireland, with its industrialisation, its peculiar tensions and cross-currents of influence, demands, in Mahon's phrase, a 'different court of appeal' for its poets 'from that which sits in the South'.[53] Both arguments differ significantly from Boland's earlier implicit assumption that Northern poets have special (Troubles) responsibilities. They suggest rather a desire to widen the parameters of what is understood by 'Irish poetry' as this has been increasingly narrowly defined – an argument made in a different context by Kavanagh in the 1930s – and to allow for an influx of new ideas and influences. In that sense, the Trinity experience, with its cross-currents of influence, also becomes, in retrospect, a mythic paradigm for the aesthetic principles expounded by Longley and Mahon in the late 1960s and early 1970s.

IV

It is perhaps ironic that Longley's early poems, with their precocious formal accomplishment, have been less well-served by formalist New Criticism than Heaney's. One reason may be that they do not lead the reader on a well sign-posted route to a comprehensible sense of 'identity', 'home', or 'religion'. Heaney builds a myth of confidence on the back of cultural marginality, digging deeper and deeper into his home ground for (poetic) nourishment, continuity and confidence – as Mahon suggests, for Heaney 'each new poem is an accretion, an addition, a further step along a known road'.[54] Longley's own aesthetic works instead with a deliberate lack of confidence that stands in marked contrast to his technical accomplishment. The poems unravel potential securities. In 'Emily Dickinson' her poems are 'Gradual as flowers, gradual as rust' (*No Continuing City*, 14): each accumulation is also a starting afresh, growth is decline and *vice versa*, earthly decay (no continuing city) is imaginative regeneration, the moment of achievement also deconstructs itself. Thus, Longley's 'Epithalamion', which opens his first collection, indicates what was and remains the case: that Longley and Heaney, both concerned with form and language, and both implicitly concerned to subvert the rigidity of the political and religious environments in which they grew up, nevertheless, and of necessity, work towards those ends in different ways. Heaney's love poem, 'Scaffolding', builds the scaffolding of the poem and the relationship, making sure 'that planks won't slip', tightening 'bolted joints' with formal precision. The wall that is built is 'of sure and solid stone', able to survive any 'Old bridges breaking' (*Death of a Naturalist*, 37). The poem wears its self-reflexivity too much on its sleeve perhaps, but its construction of an invisible yet ultimately solid support shows some of the 'inside' workings of Heaney's aesthetic, pre-empting the later imaginative ground that is 'Utterly empty, utterly a source'.[55] In Longley's 'Epithalamion' (a poem which carries debts to Robert Graves, and to John Donne), the poem may be the perfected edifice, but its sense works against that formal stability to leave it with only the hope of 'lingering on': the darkness is finite even as the love seeks infinity. As the poem gathers momentum through the complex sentence that comprises its first half, the syntax leads steadily and inevitably towards its centre:

> And everything seems bent
> On robing in this evening you
> And me, all dark the element
> Our light is earnest to,

But the centre once reached, when 'dark will be / For ever like this', is also the point where the poem's centrifugal collapse begins – the 'small hours widening into day' and into the need to begin all over again:

> The two of us . . .
> Must hope that in new properties
> We'll find a uniform
> To know each other truly by, . . .

In contrast to both, Mahon's 'Preface to a Love Poem', in *Night-Crossing*, marks the emergence of the theme that dominates his aesthetic through the 1970s and 1980s: exploring the nature (and inadequacy) of language itself. 'Only words', he writes in 'Glengormley', 'hurt us now'. That ironic revision of the cliché recognises language as a constraint, as a form of imprisonment within particular versions of history and identity (a concern in Mahon that takes on particular resonance in Northern Ireland's own war of words).

'Preface to a Love Poem' is a 'night cry, neither here nor there', a preface 'at one remove' from the love poem that cannot exist, a testament to what lies beyond language – silence. In that sense, it is also possible to see Mahon's aesthetic, at this time, as working in the opposite direction to Heaney's.

The idea of a 'Northern Renaissance', if it is understood as a 'movement', suggests the programmatic approach of, for example, British Movement poetics in the 1950s, (where in fact the major poetic figure of Philip Larkin stood to some extent outside any professed agenda). The diversity of the collections published in the 1960s, the combative poetic environments in which they were forged, and the development of strong and distinctive poetic voices, disallow any easy delineation of a 'group' aesthetic. The different practices evident in the mid-1960s can be related to a broad range of influences, but also to the different traditions in the North from which these poets emerge. Heaney recovers, or in his own language 'restores' a Northern Catholic culture against the odds; Longley and Mahon are concerned to destabilise tradition and language, concerns linked partly to their sense of Protestantism as a 'religion of the Word', and partly to a desire to undermine the Protestant tradition's repressive political ethos prior to 1969. Nevertheless, some of the shared assumptions do bring a collective argument to bear, if implicitly, on the contemporary poetry scene, as they also give Northern poetry a distinctive focus.

Mahon, Longley and Heaney share the sense of art as an alternative spirituality; in varying degrees, this seemingly 'traditional' or romantic assumption makes it a mode of subversion all the more telling in a context where sectarianism is rife. They have been called the 'tight-assed trio', formalist poets in an age of experimentation: as Mahon says, 'No art without the resistance of the medium'.[56] In the 1960s, the assumption that break-up in society should be mirrored by a break-up in form was perhaps an inevitable outcome of a popularisation of the 1950s America 'Beat generation' aesthetic, with its link between experimental form and anti-hierarchical politics. But Northern poets in the 1960s render the argument that formalism implies political conservatism redundant. As Mahon puts it in 'Death of a Film Star' in *Night-Crossing*: 'when an immovable body meets an ir-/Resistible force, something has got to give'. While their poetry can be read as a response to the violent consequences of the break-up of rigid and divisive political structures in the North after 1969, it is also, before 1969, one manifestation of the 'new energy' that helps to engender that break up. As with Yeats earlier, form can become a form of resistance, an antithetical art. In that sense, Northern poetry's radical formalism raises questions as to whether experimentalism may become its own form of conservatism.

NOTES

1 *Irish Times*, 14 August 1970, p. 12.

2 Louis MacNeice, *The Poetry of W.B.Yeats*, 2nd edn. (London: Faber and Faber, 1967), p. 191.

3 Richard Kirkland, *Literature and Culture in Northern Ireland Since 1965: Moments of Danger* (London: Longman, 1996), p. 59.

4 John Hewitt, 'Regionalism: The Last Chance', 1947, *Ancestral Voices: the Selected Prose of John Hewitt*, ed. Tom Clyde (Belfast: Blackstaff Press, 1987), p. 125.

5 John Montague, 'Scylla and Charybdis', *Watching the River Flow: A Century in Irish Poetry*, ed. Noel Duffy and Theo Dorgan (Dublin: Poetry Ireland, 1999), p. 105.

6 Derek Mahon, 'Introduction', *The Sphere Book of Modern Irish Poetry* (London: Sphere Books, 1972), p. 14.

7 John Montague, *The Figure in the Cave and Other Essays* (New York: Syracuse University Press, 1989), pp. 8–9.

8 *The Figure in the Cave*, pp. 8, 36–7.

9 Robert F. Garratt, *Modern Irish Poetry: Tradition and Continuity from Yeats to Heaney* (Berkeley & London: University of California Press, 1986), p. 201.

10 *The Figure in the Cave*, pp. 18–19.

11 John Montague, *The Rough Field*, 3rd edn. (Dublin: Dolmen Press, 1979), p. 83.

12 Derek Mahon, 'Each Poem for me is a New Beginning', interview by Willie Kelly, *The Cork Review* 2.3 (June 1981), p. 10.

13 Michael Longley, 'The Longley Tapes', interview by Robert Johnstone, *Honest Ulsterman*, 78 (Summer 1985), p. 23; Derek Mahon, 'Poetry in Northern Ireland', *Twentieth Century Studies*, 4 (Nov. 1970), p. 90; Seamus Heaney, *Preoccupations: Selected Prose 1968–1978* (London: Faber and Faber, 1980), p. 28. It is worth noting that Heaney modifies this view in the 1990s, arguing that there was a literary life in Queen's University before the Group, though it had scattered. See *Reading the Future: Irish Writers in Conversation with Mike Murphy* (Dublin: Lilliput Press, 2000), p. 84.

14 See A. Alvarez, 'Introduction', *The New Poetry* (London: Penguin, 1962) p. 28.

15 ' "The Colony" appeared . . . in 1953, but no one seems to have paid much heed. When, however, in the winter of 1970 the Arts Council of Northern Ireland organised a tour of poetry readings by John Montague and myself . . . this time it secured some attention . . .'. John Hewitt, 'No Rootless Colonist', 1972, *Ancestral Voices*, p. 155. Hewitt's own *Collected Poems* appeared in 1968.

16 'Canal Bank Walk', *The Complete Poems* (London: MacGibbon & Kee, 1964), p. 294.

17 Michael Longley, 'A Boat on the River', *Watching the River Flow*, p. 137.

18 Thomas Kinsella, 'Introduction', *The New Oxford Book of Irish Verse* (Oxford University Press, 1986), p. xxx.

19 Derek Mahon, Interview by William Scammell, *Poetry Review* 81.2 (Summer 1991), p. 5.

20 *Literature and Culture in Northern Ireland*, p. 75.

21 Seamus Heaney, 'Calling the Tune', an interview by Tom Adair, *Linen Hall Review* 6.2 (Autumn 1989), p. 5.

22 Derek Mahon, 'An interview by Terence Brown', *Poetry Ireland Review* 14 (Autumn 1985), pp. 12–13; 'Q & A with Derek Mahon', *Irish Literary Supplement* (Fall 1991), p. 28; interview by William Scammell, *Poetry Review*, p. 5.

23 Philip Hobsbaum, *A Theory of Communication* (London: Macmillan, 1970), p. 165.

24 Edward Lucie-Smith, 'Foreword', *A Group Anthology*, ed. Edward Lucie-Smith and Philip Hobsbaum (London: Oxford University Press, 1963), p. vii.

25 'The Longley Tapes', p. 22.

26 'The Belfast Group: A Symposium', *Honest Ulsterman* 54 (Nov/Dec 1976), p. 61.

27 Ibid., p. 54.

28 See Heaney's contribution to 'The Belfast Group: A Symposium', pp. 62–3, repr. in *Preoccupations*, pp. 28–30.

29 Norman Dugdale, 'The Belfast Group', *Honest Ulsterman* 97 (Spring 1994), p. 4.

30 *Preoccupations*, pp. 28–9.

31 See Michael Allen, 'Introduction', *Seamus Heaney: Contemporary Critical Essays* (London: Macmillan, 1997), pp. 1–17.

32 Patrick Kavanagh, 'The Parish and the Universe', *Collected Pruse*. London: MacGibbon & Kee, 1967, p. 282; also *Complete Poems*, p. 238.

33 *Door into the Dark* (London: Faber and Faber, 1969), pp. 41–2.

34 *Preoccupations*, p. 29.

35 *Reading the Future*, p. 86.

36 Heaney quoted in Neil Corcoran, *Seamus Heaney* (London: Faber and Faber, 1986), p. 95.

37 For further discussion of this point see David Lloyd, ' "Pap for the dispossessed": Seamus Heaney and the Poetics of Identity', in *Seamus Heaney*, ed. Michael Allen, p. 165.

38 Heaney in *Reading the Future*, pp. 84–5; *Preoccupations*, p. 41.

39 *Reading the Future*, p. 123.

40 See, for example, Heaney's own more restrained comments on the Group in an interview with Frank Kinahan, *Critical Inquiry*, 8.3 (Spring 1982), p. 408.

41 Interview with William Scammell, *Poetry Review*, p. 4.

42 Q & A with Derek Mahon, *Irish Literary Supplement* (Fall 1991), p. 27.

43 *Reading the Future*, p. 123.

44 Derek Mahon. 'Introduction', *The Sphere Book of Modern Irish Poetry*, p. 14.

45 Edna Longley, *The Living Stream: Literature and Revisionism in Ireland* (Newcastle: Bloodaxe, 1994), p. 19.

46 Quoted in Richard Kirkland, *Literature and Culture*, p. 81.

47 Ibid.

48 Interview with William Scammell, *Poetry Review*, p. 4.

49 *Night-Crossing* (Oxford University Press, 1968), pp. 5–6.

50 *No Continuing City* (London: Macmillan, 1969), p. 45.

51 Michael Longley, 'Strife and the Ulster Poet', *Hibernia* (7 Nov. 1969), p. 11.

52 Michael Longley, 'The Neolithic Night: A Note on the Irishness of Louis Mac-Neice', *Two Decades of Irish Writing*, ed. Douglas Dunn (Manchester: Carcanet Press, 1975), p. 99.
53 Mahon, 'Poetry in Northern Ireland', p. 90.
54 'Each Poem for me is a New Beginning', interview by Willie Kelly, *Cork Review* 2.3 (June 1981), p. 12.
55 Heaney, *The Haw Lantern* (London: Faber and Faber, 1987), p. 32.
56 Interview with William Scammell, *Poetry Review*, p. 5.

7

DILLON JOHNSTON

Violence in Seamus Heaney's poetry

> hung in the scales
> with beauty and atrocity
> ('The Grauballe Man')

If, as Seamus Heaney says, quoting Borges, 'poetry lies in the meeting of poem and reader, not in the lines of symbols printed on pages',[1] then we might recognise that the issues involved in the depiction of violence may differ from reader to reader or, more generally, from one national readership – in this case Irish, British, or American and other Anglophone readers – to another. We know readers have registered their approval of Heaney's poetry in the sales figures of Waterstone's, Barnes & Noble's, and other booksellers, and this popularity has been confirmed by most of the prizes. Yet reviewers who might represent these readerships have differed widely in their responses to what the Swedish Academy praised as Heaney's 'analysis of the violence in Northern Ireland'.[2]

This controversy moved to the centre of Heaney criticism with the publication of the poet's fourth book *North* (1975). Among the majority of British critics who praised the book, Neil Corcoran differed from most in his understanding of colonial politics in Ireland and his sympathy with opposing positions. He characterised *North* as 'necessary poems' because they 'articulate those elements of resentment and hostility at the bottom of the republican-nationalist psyche . . .' but do so 'oppressively, self-laceratingly, constrictedly . . . .'.[3] The American critic Helen Vendler offers nearly unqualified approval of *North* as 'one of the crucial poetic interventions of the twentieth century', but she refuses to read the volume as a political statement, such readings of lyric poetry being, in her view, 'a fundamental philosophical mistake'.[4] Less sure of Heaney's achievement, Blake Morrison wrote that in certain poems in *North*, Heaney's 'poetry grants sectarian killing in Northern Ireland a historical respectability which it is not usually granted in day-to-day journalism'.[5] Among the volume's detractors, Belfast critic Edna

Longley and the Belfast poet Ciaran Carson reject Part I's ritualising and mythologising of murder which risk making Heaney, in Carson's phrase, 'the laureate of violence'.[6]

Although from autumn of 1968 on – after the publication of his first two volumes – historical events in Northern Ireland provided Heaney with images of public violence, from the beginning his poetry dwelt on rural violence and the country attitude towards death. He wrote out of his own background as the first of nine children born to a laconic cattle-dealer and small farmer and his more verbally animated wife. Born on the forty-acre farm called Mossbawn on the north side of Lough Neagh in the east of Co Derry, he might have lived his life among small farmers, fishermen and village merchants, had not the 1947 Northern Ireland Education Act allowed him to attend on scholarship St Columb's College in Derry and then Queen's University, Belfast, and, in Michael Parker's words, began 'to prise open a gap between him and his parents'.[7] Poems of the first volume *Death of A Naturalist* (1966) reveal the sensitive rural youth building in language and verse-structures a stay against farmyard barbarity and the violence of nature, in order 'to see myself', he says in 'Personal Helicon', 'to set the darkness echoing'.[8] Among these poems are a group, 'morbid in their infatuation with grotesque detail', according to one American critic,[9] that can also suggest Heaney's political uncertainty.

'The Early Purges' (*Death of Naturalist*, 23), for example, seems at first reading built on opposing urban and rural attitudes toward cruelty, partly in-fluenced by Ted Hughes's poems exploring 'the arrogance of blood and bone'. But Heaney's tone is uncertain. The poem's speaker mixes general popular assertions with the farmer's saws ('"Prevention of cruelty" talk cuts ice in town') and the boy's reactions ('I just shrug'), so that irony is directed both at the animal-rights sentimentalist and the strong farmer. While at the time of this poem's composition, the summer of 1964, Heaney may have been, as Parker says, 'young, relatively unpolitical', he would have observed decades of sectarian politics, a secondary topic of this poem. Although the Taggarts of Derry are not Calvinists (their minds 'a white-washed kitchen/hung with texts . . .',[10] as Heaney says of another neighbour in *Wintering Out*, 1972), Dan Taggart participates in the terseness that characterises both sides of the Northern farming community, and he seems given to facile summaries, such as his 'Sure isn't it better for them now', a sentiment not shared by the drowning kittens, their 'soft paws scraping like mad'. The tercets – seven, mostly end-stopped stanzas that rhyme *aba* but eschew the ongoing narra-tive thrust of terza rima – effectively convey Taggart's disconnected adages that substitute for ratiocination or more engaged, ongoing thinking.

In this and other poems in the first two volumes, the 'grotesque detail' concerns fears in the boy more than the sinister in nature, as the second tercet reveals:

> Soft paws scraping like mad. But their tiny din
> Was soon soused. They were slung on the snout
> Of the pump and the water pumped in.

The eye-rhyme and assonance of 'tiny din', which also evokes *tin*, are enjambed into the next line's variation of *o, oo, ou*, and u sounds that accompany the drowning. The repetition of the plosive *pump* and *pumped in* completes the drowning and allows the sound associated with the kittens, *in*, finally to bob to the surface, as it were. The simile that conveys the image of the kittens – 'Like wet gloves that bobbed and shone . . .' – hides metonymically the agents of death, Taggart's hands within the gloves. Without reading into this image too much of the later, subtler Heaney, we can observe two implications. First, the hidden hand suggests the governmental procedure by which all citizens, subalterns as well as colonisers, help govern the body politic. Second, the mystery of death transpires beneath the water's troubled surface, concealed from the rational, enquiring eye. As suggested in 'Sunlight', a prologue poem to *North*, Heaney evokes, when he cannot depict, what is 'sunk past its gleam' within the unconscious.

From his earliest poetry, certainly from 'Personal Helicon' onward, the poetic speaker's direction was downward, through digging, the 'dark drop', soundings, or 'striking inward and downwards'. Such probings are part of the poet's effort to define the self, in great part by characterising what is notself and part of the unconscious, both of himself and of his society. The boy's first-person probings of the sources of his own fear, central to the first volume, are replaced in the second volume by the adult's presentation, as in 'Vision', 'The Forge', and 'The Outlaw'. In *North*, Heaney's psychological intentions are obscured by the accidental conjunction of history – his personal discovery of P.V. Glob's *The Bog People* and the resumption of the Troubles. During the composition and publication of Heaney's first two books, Northern Ireland had remained restless but peaceful. Early in 1967, inspired in part by the Civil Rights movement in the US, the Northern Ireland Civil Rights Association was founded in Belfast and joined by many of Heaney's students at Queens. Civil rights marches began in August 1968. Eliciting unrestrained police batoning as well as provocative behaviour from diehard loyalists, they soon drew in both the British army and the IRA. Although Heaney participated in at least one march, for many months of the first years of the Troubles he was away from the North, travelling in Spain on a fellowship, teaching in Berkeley, and finally moving to Wicklow in 1972, which would lead to a permanent residence in Dublin.

Heaney's departure from the North hardly eased the pressure on the poet to address issues of the Troubles, to speak out for justice, or otherwise to affirm, in Seamus Deane's words, 'the fidelity of the poet to his community'.[11] Looking back from the present, Heaney's choices may seem determined. Helen Vendler judges that the Troubles 'forced Heaney (who had been raised a Catholic) into becoming a poet of public as well as private life' (*Seamus Heaney*, 1). In reviewing *Electric Light* (2001), Landon Hammer asserts that 'when Heaney began to publish poems, the mere presence of his first name in print had a political force, since it marked him as Catholic and therefore a minority speaker in Northern Ireland, and he learned to weigh the public resonance of every poem'.[12] In 1975 Conor Cruise O'Brien read *North* with much the same sense of Heaney's limited choices: 'Yeats was free to try . . . on different relations to the tragedy. Heaney's relation to a deeper tragedy is fixed and pre-ordained'.[13] Yet, Heaney was not the first Catholic poet from Ulster to write about the Troubles, and from the model of John Montague's *Poisoned Lands*, which Heaney read in 1963, but especially *The Rough Field* in 1972, he could find both encouragement and the basis for his own independent approach to the Troubles. Because Montague composed most of *The Rough Field* before the re-eruption of the Troubles, he sees the sectarian tensions of Ulster through the lenses of Elizabethan and Victorian history and the multi-layered, dream-like perspective of autobiography, 'the bleak moors of dream'. While history and autobiography – the return to a homeland from which he is permanently separated – give Montague's multivoiced narrative greater coolness and distance, Heaney employs myth – images of the bog burials that are detailed and obsessive – and his own composed voice to give warmth and immediacy to his more current account of the Troubles.

Heaney's third volume *Wintering Out* (1972) reveals the poet's concern for continuity between his chosen craft and those of his community. More plausibly than in 'Digging', where pen and spade are finally discontinuous, the analogues between the poet and local craftsmen are extended from such artisans in *Door Into the Dark* as the blacksmith and the thatcher to more marginal figures, such as the 'Servant Boy' and isolated women in *Wintering Out*. He often slips from 'I' to 'we', and in a half-dozen poems he grounds the poet's language in the wet and rocky aspects of his landscape, as he proclaims himself 'lobe and larynx/of the mossy places' (*Wintering Out*, 28). With a few exceptions, the poems of *Wintering Out* back off from violence or signal it obliquely in 'semaphores of hurt . . .' (74).

The most direct representation of violence in this volume occurs in 'The Tollund Man', a prototype of the bog poems in *North* and Heaney's first creative response to the rich imagistic mine of P.V. Glob's *The Bog People*, an archaelogical study of Iron Age corpses recovered from Jutland bogs.[14] In 1974 Heaney said that his profound response to the photographs of these sacrificial victims to the earth goddess Nerthus arose from their parallel to 'the tradition of Irish political martyrdom . . . whose icon is Kathleen Ni Houlihan'. He continued, 'This is more than an archaic barbarous rite: it is an archetypal pattern'.[15] Consequently, one of these recoveries, the Tollund Man, who is described as a 'bridegroom' to the fertility goddess in the poem's first section, is asked to 'make germinate' the bodies of four brothers killed in sectarian violence in the 1920s. Most of the final section records the poet's imagined response as he makes his pilgrimage to this corpse's site in Jutland. Neil Corcoran finds the emotional centre of this poem elsewhere than does Heaney in his 1974 comments. The critic argues that while the analogy between sacrificial killings in Jutland and political murder in Ireland 'clearly supplies the poem with its structure and its rationale, the connection that actually supplies its emotional sustenance is that between the Tollund man and Heaney himself'.

Corcoran concludes,

> In placing its emotional weight where it does, on the relationship between poet and evoked human figure, 'The Tollund Man' . . . dissolves its more ambitious mythical elements into something sharply immediate: the pain of personal incomprehension, isolation and pity.[16]

So 'sharply immediate' is this relationship between poetic persona and this mysterious corpse that the structure of the sentence reflects this emotional disturbance:

> In the flat country nearby
> Where they dug him out,
> His last gruel of winter seeds
> Caked in his stomach,
>
> Naked except for
> The cap, noose and girdle,
> I will stand a long time.

By the time we recover the structure of the simple sentence – 'In the flat country . . . I will stand. . . .' – we will have had to blink at the way the participle *naked* modifies the poet and risks burlesque. If Parker can say that this goddess has a 'soft spot' for her bridegroom, then we might venture that the dangling modifier confuses the identity of poet and victim so that both, through the poet's sympathy and voyeurism, are indecently exposed. We might go beyond Corcoran's supposition about the poet's emotions to suggest that one level of this response must arise from a perfection of the photographic images down to fingerprints that have survived centuries of destruction. That this is one of the poet's deepest wishes, to make poems equally impervious to time, Heaney recognises particularly in *North* where in his 'blazon of sweet beauty's best' – such as the wrist, heel, instep, and chin of 'the Grauballe Man' – he competes with the bog to immortalise distinguishing details of the individual.

Published in 1975, *North* quickly became, and has remained, Heaney's most celebrated and controversial volume. It opens with two prefatory poems, then Part I – a long section on the Antaeus myth, bog-burials, Viking myth and art, turbary linguistics, porno-cartography, and tupping-topography – and a briefer Part II, in which the poet comments more personally on the Troubles. The publicist's blurb for *North* declares 'Heaney has found a myth which . . . gives the book direction, cohesion and cumulative power' and renders this volume 'more profound and authoritative' than his previous books. Most critics focus on Part I, many treating it as just such a myth of Northern violence as a response and tribute to an earth goddess for whom the bog-burials, no less than the current sectarian homicides, provide sacrificial victims.

One may derive a mythic notion from *North*, but the poems are too exploratory, tentative, and dialectical to compose a coherent myth. For example, in 'Kinship' the poet makes no serious claims for the originary myths that might relate current Irish homicides to the Jutland victims: 'I step through origins/like a dog turning/in memories of wilderness/on the kitchen mat'.[17] Although the Irish and Danes share bogland, Heaney does not extend to the Danish his sense of gendered vowels and consonants: 'This is the v*owe*l of earth/dreaming its root/in flowers and sn*ow*' as the maternal seed-bed is sown in the contrasting seasons of spring and winter. This section IV of 'Kinship' opens with a contradiction of Yeats's 'Second Coming' as Corcoran points out: 'This centre holds/ . . . /sump and seedbed'. Where Yeats envisions the dissolution of an historical epoch within a broader historiographical pattern, Heaney affirms a non-historical, generative basis for life. The section ends: 'I grew out of all this/like a weeping willow/inclined to/the appetites of gravity' (*North*, 43) which intends to say not much more than 'dust to dust'. 'Funeral Rites' and 'North' evade history by linking prehistoric Ireland with Norse legend. Recent victims interred within the passage graves of the Boyne valley link by simile to the poet-hero of Njal's Saga, as surrogate for Heaney, making poetry amid violence. Revisiting the setting of 'Shoreline' from *Door Into the Dark*, 'North' conjures from 'the secular/powers of the Atlantic thundering' voices 'warning me, lifted again/in violence and epiphany' (*North*, 19). Although some irony and linguistic complexity (e.g. 'The longship's swimming tongue//was buoyant with hindsight') may qualify our sense that Heaney is forcing mythic connections, the author of these three poems might fairly be labelled, as Carson does, 'a mythmaker, an anthropologist of ritual killing, and . . . in the last resort, a mystifier'.[18]

Other poems in Part I, however, explore the implications of Glob's photographs and dramatise the poet's response rather than imposing meaning. 'Punishment' begins with the poet's reaction ('I can feel . . .', 'I can see . . .', 'I almost love . . .') to photographs of the Windeby girl who at the hands of the tribe suffered death for adultery. The poet compares this 'tribal, intimate revenge' to pitchcapping of Catholic girls in the North for consorting with British soldiers. He confesses that he

> . . . would have cast, I know
> the stones of silence.
> I am the artful voyeur.

Corcoran identifies the Biblical reference to the girl taken in adultery in 'John: 8'. Heaney confesses that he would have violated Christ's injunction not to judge, on the basis of our common human frailty, and he thereby emphasises his own human weakness. His role as 'artful voyeur' is a corruption of his function as poetic observer, and his silence threatens to turn poetic detachment, which he once defended before British journalists as 'a fine, well-earned and constantly renewed condition', into the indifference which he decried in that same speech.[19]

The poem concludes by representing the ambivalence of the poet,

> who would connive
> in civilized outrage
> yet understand the exact
> and tribal, intimate revenge.

Quoting these lines, Edna Longley writes,

> This is all right if Heaney is merely being 'outrageously honest about his own reactions, if the paradox 'connive . . . civilized' is designed to corner people who think they have risen above the primitive, if the poem exposes a representative Irish conflict between 'humane reason' and subconscious allegiances.
>
> (Longley, 154)

Although Longley is sceptical, Heaney, in an interview with Seamus Deane soon after the publication of *North*, insists on maintaining 'a dialogue' between the 'obstinate voice of rationalist humanism' and that of tribal atavisms (Deane, 63). In 'Punishment' and a few other poems in *North*, such as 'The Grauballe Man' and 'Hercules and Antaeus', we can recognise what Heaney calls 'dithering', what Yeats would call 'vacillation', and what we might call a dialectic.

Longley would withhold this designation from 'Bog Queen' which she argues 'renews that well-worn genre the aisling by presenting Ireland as her landscape, weather, geography and history, and by pushing her "old hag" incarnation to an extreme' (Longley, 79). Without specifying this eighteenth-century Irish genre, Corcoran agrees: 'Bog Queen' is 'a kind of Kathleen ni Houlihan, a kind of Mother Ireland . . . a symbol for disaffected native resentment, biding its time underground . . .'. (Corcoran, *Seamus Heaney*, 114). To read this poem as an aisling, we might expect the attributes of this corpse, found in Co Down in the eighteenth century, to be more specifically Irish rather than 'Baltic' or 'phoenician' or Nordic, feeling 'the nuzzle of fjords', and we could expect some final rebirth or disclosure to reveal or promise a radiant Ireland. The emotional centre of the poem, however, is Heaney's lifelong fascination with the body and with its relation to spirit. This cadaver offers herself for interpretation and meaning: 'My body was braille'; 'the illiterate roots/pondered . . .'; her gemstones are '*like* the bearings of history', but she can no more undergo the 'triumphant re-birth' some critics attribute to her (Parker, 136) than she can emerge into the light of reason and understanding. She is interwoven into the bog by apocopated rhyme:

> wrinkling, dyed weaves
> and phoenician stitchwork
> retted on my breasts'
>
> soft moraines.
> I knew winter cold
> like the nuzzle of fjords
> at my thighs –
>
> the soaked fledge, the heavy
> swaddle of hides.

She disintegrates into a paratactic series of parts as she emerges from the dark of the unconscious into the light of reason:

> and I rose from the dark,
> hacked bone, skull-ware,
> frayed stitches, tufts,
> small gleams on the bank.

To paraphrase Yeats, Heaney cannot know rationally what the body as matter means; he can only 'embody' this in a poem, which he does here successfully. Heaney has every right to explore and dramatise his own irrational, atavistic responses to death and violence. As he said in regard to 'The Tollund Man': 'And just how persistent the barbaric attitudes are, not only in the slaughter but in the psyche, I discovered, again when the *frisson* of the poem itself had passed . . .' (*Preoccupations*, 59). Complaints become legitimate, however, concerning those few poems where he suggests that the violence in Northern Ireland and ancient Denmark are cognate and determined by psychological forces present in ancient Northern rituals of sacrifice, a suggestion supported by neither argument nor real evidence. These poems are too few, however, to justify Carson's assertion that all of Part I belongs to 'the laureate of violence'. If critics are fair in finding Carson's review 'fiercely hostile',[20] the basis for such hostility might lodge in the word *laureate* as much as in *violence*.

In spite of the differences between the two parts of *North* and among the four primary texts Heaney had published, readers recognise the poet's voice and his positioning of himself as the poet, representative of his tribe and, progressively, of poetry. Even in his most dramatic poems, such as the monologues of *Station Island*, the voice in the poem remains familiar and the persona congenial and, usually, trustworthy. In a 1974 lecture, Heaney offers his popular poem 'Digging' as 'an example of what we call "finding a voice" ':

> Finding a voice means that you can get your own feeling into your own words; . . . a poetic voice is probably very intimately connected with the poet's natural voice. . . . A voice is like a fingerprint, possessing a constant and unique signature. . . .
> (*Preoccupations*, 43)

What Heaney characterises as a writer's aspiration, Ian Gregson believes Heaney had already fully established:

> As always when reading Heaney, there is a strong sense of the implied author: one of his most remarkable achievements has been to construct a version of himself as a poet which his readers recognise. This is partly a matter of his public persona, the 50-ish year old public smiling man . . . old-fashioned as a poet should be, and above all actually a very nice man.[21]

Whereas Gregson speaks of *constructing* a persona, Heaney would *find* or *disclose* it, sometimes delving to recover some more original or authentic self. In that frequently quoted interview with Deane in 1977, Heaney stated, 'Poetry is born out of the watermarks and colourings of the self. But that self in some ways takes its spiritual pulse from the inwards spiritual structure of the community to which it belongs' (Deane, 62).

A dozen years later in a lecture at Oxford, Heaney said,

> In emergent cultures the struggle of an individual consciousness towards affir-
> mations and distinctness may be analogous, if not coterminous, with a collec-
> tive straining toward self-definition; there is a mutual susceptibility between
> the formation of a new tradition and the self-fashioning of individual talent.
>
> (*Redress of Poetry*, 6)

The echoes of Eliot and Arnold are appropriate for a poet establishing continuities and differences between himself and guardians of English culture. The
author of 'Tradition and the Individual Talent' meant by *tradition* the canon
of European Christendom rather than the Catholic nationalist community
of Northern Ireland and by *individual talent* a depersonalised, 'transforming
catalyst'[22] rather than Heaney's integrated poetic persona.

Poets such as Kinsella, Carson, Muldoon and Ní Chuilleanáin, who offer
fragmented selves and deflect personality, may question the value of such
a consistently recognisable voice. David Lloyd, perhaps Heaney's harshest
critic, identifies this 'strong sense of the implied author' with conservatism
and caution:

> The cautious limits which Heaney's poetry sets round any potential for disrup-
> tive, immanent questioning may be the reason for the extraordinary inflation
> of his current reputation. If Heaney is held to be 'the most trusted poet of
> our [*sic*] islands', by the same token he is the most institutionalized of recent
> poets.[23]

Lloyd's *sic* refers to the proprietariness of the English critic Christopher
Ricks, whom he is quoting. Ricks's trust in Heaney, no doubt, was grounded
on Heaney's frank rebukes to English audiences and critics who were hon-
ouring him. For example, in 1983 he reminded editors who had made him
the keystone in an anthology of 'British' poetry that 'No glass of ours was
ever raised/To toast *The Queen*',[24] and in 1988 upon receiving the *Sunday
Times* Award, the skald turned scold as he candidly told an admiring
English audience that 'policies which Downing Street presumably regards
as a hard line against terrorism can feel like a high-handed disregard for the
self-respect of the Irish people in general'.[25]

Nevertheless, the esteemed English poet and critic Donald Davie, shortly
before his death in 1995, offered Heaney remarkable praise:

> In the world of English language poetry Seamus Heaney has . . . a position
> of unchallenged authority. And that is a boon for all of us who inhabit that
> world; one shudders to think how it would have been for the rest of us if that
> authority, earned by solid accomplishment, had been vested in a person less
> generous and less prudent. . . . It is a main part of Heaney's claim upon us that

he has offered that romantic role, refused the privileges that it offered him. He has consistently refused, in the face of tempting offers, to be either outlandish or partisan.[26]

Such praise, not unique to Davie, may account for some of Heaney's own uneasiness as he balances tribal solidarity with his individual role as the representative poet. As he and many Northern poets – Catholic and Protestant – must have recognised, for critics and readers along the English mainstream, Irish poets were, literally, outlandish and partisan.

To varying degrees in his next two volumes, Heaney's uneasiness will accompany the treatment of violence that appears in elegies in *Field Work* (1979) and poems that bear witness in *Station Island* (1984). The poems of witness in Cantos VII & VIII of 'Station Island' depart from Heaney's intention in the elegies of *Field Work* – 'The Strand at Lough Beg', 'A Postcard from North Antrim', and 'Casualty' – 'to assuage', in Parker's words, 'his sense of loss, and to strike sharp, clear notes in celebration' (Parker, 159). The first of these elegies 'The Strand at Lough Beg' offers gripping details of Colum McCartney's fatal outing and of his grisly corpse. However, from the Dantean epigraph through the recognition that the legendary, Heaney-resurrected Sweeney fled along this same road, we know we are travelling a parallel but separate course, between which and the actuality of death is what Heaney will later call 'the frontier of writing'. These three elegies close with evocations of Dante, perhaps of *The Odyssey*, and of literary ghosts, such as Hamlet's father or the Yeats-Swift apparition from T.S. Eliot's 'Little Gidding' (in *Four Quartets*), as the three victims, all 'dawn-sniffing revenants', observe new curfews and haunt new margins between mortality and literary memorial. The comfort Heaney brings to the reader and to the memory of McCartney, Armstrong and O'Neill derives from the elegiac and legendary side of this divide.

While the poems about victims of violence in the sequence 'Station Island' are as meticulously formed and phrased as the three poems in *Field Work*, they differ from these elegies by conveying what Heaney ascribes to poets of witness, 'the impulse to elevate truth above beauty'.[27] He writes, '"The poet as witness" . . . represents poetry's solidarity with the doomed, the deprived, the victimized, the under-privileged' (*Government of the Tongue*, xvi), so that the poet, who offered ablutions at the end of 'The Strand at Lough Beg', now yields to the victim's viewpoint and voice which upbraids the poet because he 'drew/the lovely blinds of the *Purgatorio/* and saccharined my death with morning dew'.[28] The aestheticising of brutal history, for which Heaney's character upbraids him, was denounced especially by the post-war East European poets whom Heaney was reading in the late 1970s:

In the words of Zbigniew Herbert, the task of the poet now was 'to salvage out of the catastrophe of history at least two words, without which all poetry is an empty play of meanings and appearances, namely: justice and truth'.

(Government of the Tongue, xviii)

Perhaps the narrow but important distinction between elegy and witness emerges most clearly in Canto VII, in which a pharmacist and former football teammate William Strathearn recounts his own late-night murder by two off-duty policemen who roused him from his sleep and shot him through the head. Eschewing the Dantean locomotor of *terza rima*, Heaney gains some of his master's momentum by employing independent tercets rhyming *aba cdc* but whose lines are rarely end-stopped (e.g. lines from the first seven tercets end in only one full stop). Rhyme is usually slant and dissembling, first and third words sometimes claiming kinship through concept rather than sound: '... behind the curtain/... with the doors open'; '... end-all/... jail'; and, most indicative of 'the impulse to elevate truth above beauty', '... sportscoat/... racket', where for meter and rhyme, 'jacket' would seem the obvious choice but where 'sportscoat' makes a slightly more precise class distinction.

Whereas in *Field Work* the poet performs ablutions, invites the victim to 'Get up from your blood on the floor', and challenges him to 'Question me again', in 'Station Island' he apologises for the elegist's self-reflective presumption and returns Strathearn to his mutilated body – 'a stun of pain seemed to go through him' – an archaeologist friend dead at 32 to his disappointment, and his cousin McCartney to his rage. So caustic is the self-criticism of these cantos and so graphic the representation of atrocities that one might have expected Heaney to continue such witness, at least for the duration of the Troubles.

A reader might be surprised, consequently, that violence vanishes from Heaney's next two volumes, appearing only occasionally and at a remove in *The Haw Lantern* (1987) and *Seeing Things* (1991). In *The Haw Lantern* the one poem that explicitly represents an aspect of the Troubles 'From the Frontier of Writing'[29] may also offer clues to the cessation of hostilities elsewhere in this volume and the next. The first four tercets of the poem recount the anxiety and affront many Irish experienced in crossing through British-manned border-checkpoints.

> The tightness and the nilness round that space
> when the car stops in the road, the troops inspect
> its make and number and, as one bends his face
>
> towards your window, you catch sight of more
> on a hill beyond, eyeing with intent
> down cradled guns that hold you under cover

Beginning with *so*, a word that will serve many purposes for Heaney but which here means 'in a similar fashion', the next four tercets repeat much of the content of the poem's first half. Helen Vendler asks, 'Did the (real) road-block turn up as a metaphor for a creative block, or did the subjugation of the writer at a real road-block make him aware of an inner equivalent when writing?' (Vendler, 117) If we look at the closing two tercets, we might find a variation of the second reading more plausible:

> And suddenly you're through, arraigned yet freed,
> as if you'd passed from behind a waterfall
> on the black current of a tarmac road
> past armour-plated vehicles, out between
> the posted soldiers flowing and receding
> like tree shadows into the polished windscreen.

In the first dozen lines, the windscreen provides the poet a clear view of menacing sharpshooters. The second version tames the threat into 'posted soldiers' who metamorphose 'like tree shadows' in the glass. This windscreen transforms its subject less like Joyce's 'cracked looking glass of a servant' than like Wordsworth's transforming memory which in Book IV of *The Prelude* blends the reflection and motion of 'one downbending from the side/Of a slow-moving boat' (247–8) with the submerged contents and current of the stream.

'From the Frontier of Writing' reminds us that from his beginning Heaney's poems about violence have all carried as subtexts – explored or unexplored – questions about the relation of art to life, about those spaces where poetry impinges on political reality and vice versa and which Conor Cruise O'Brien had sign-posted as 'an unhealthy intersection'.[30] Heaney's Ellmann lectures at Emory, one year after the publication of *The Haw Lantern*, locate this junction in the work of post-colonial writers:

> Irish poets, Polish poets, South African poets, West Indian poets (those in London as well as those in the Caribbean) and many others . . . have been caught at a crossroads where the essentially aesthetic demand of their voca-tion encountered the different demand that their work participate in a general debate which . . . concerns the political rights and cultural loyalties of different social or racial groups resulting from separate heritages . . .[31]

In *The Haw Lantern* this crossroads becomes more like parallel motor-ways, roads leading through the Republic of Conscience or the Canton of Expectation or the land visited by mud visions that offer a perspective on the accustomed world without intersecting its path. In a 1988 interview with Rand Brandes, Heaney admitted that 'some of the poems are abstracted versions of what has been fleshed out already in other things, poems of an allegorical sort . . .'[32] Helen Vendler speaks of 'the allegorical and parabolic poetry' of *The Haw Lantern*, but more helpfully she characterises this volume as 'Heaney's first book of the virtual' (113). We benefit from this characterisation of imaginary space – the realm of the aesthetic, peatbog preservations, memorialised life, spaces held out of, while reflecting on, time – because *virtual* avoids the conventional Otherworld of Irish narratives and substitutes a universal concept familiar to children and other cyberspace-cadets while remaining mysterious to adult readers.

Heaney's reflections on the imaginative world and the world we think we share find full expression in *The Redress of Poetry* published in 1995 from lectures delivered at Oxford University between 1989 and 1994 when Heaney was Professor of Poetry. He concludes this volume with a simplified version of these two worlds:

> Within our individual selves we can reconcile two orders of knowledge which we might call the practical and the poetic; . . . each form of knowledge redresses the other and . . . the frontier between them is there for the crossing.   (203)

He then cites a poem from *Seeing Things* (1991) based on a meeting of these two worlds as recorded in *The Annals of the Four Masters*. A ship from the Otherworld gets its tackle accidentally entangled in the altar rail of an oratory. The poem concludes:

> A crewman shinned and grappled down the rope
> And struggled to release it. But in vain.
> 'This man can't bear our life here and will drown,'
>
> The abbot said, 'unless we help him.' So
> They did, the freed ship sailed, and the man climbed back
> Out of the marvellous as he had known it.[33]

He opens *The Redress of Poetry* by speaking about 'crossing from the domain of the matter-of-fact into the domain of the imagined' (xiii), but as we see from the *Annals* poem, in *Seeing Things* traffic sails both ways.

However, as he develops and extends his idea of *redress*, the metaphor of traffic and crossroads yields to an unstated metaphor of a thin partition between these two worlds: 'The nobility of poetry says Wallace Stevens "is a violence from within that protects us from a violence without". It is the imagination pressing back against the pressure of reality' (*Redress of Poetry*, 1). The 'frontier of writing' becomes then a scrim or narrow boundary – what Paul Muldoon has written about, the *féth fiada* or mist-curtain which separates this world from the Irish Otherworld.[34] From either side public reality and personal imagination contend. From within the imagined and poetic, the writer seeks 'reparation of, satisfaction or compensation for, a wrong sustained or the loss resulting from this' (*Redress of Poetry*, 15). More generally, poetry redresses by restoring balance or direction. Poetry does not transgress this boundary but rather exerts its pressure from its own transformative realm:

> Even when the redress of poetry is operative in the first sense in which I employed it – poetry, that is, being instrumental in adjusting and correcting imbalances in the world . . . – even then, poetry is involved with supreme fictions . . . a world to which 'we turn incessantly and without knowing it'. (192)

One gathers from the discussion of John Hewitt in the concluding lecture in this volume that poetic redress within the realm of one audience, in this case Northern Ireland, may redress differently or not redress at all an imbalance in a larger realm, such as the United Kingdom or the West.

This distinction becomes important in understanding the shift back from celebrating the miraculousness of this world in *Seeing Things* to depicting extreme violence in *The Spirit Level* (1996). 'Keeping Going' eulogises the poet's brother for maintaining his equanimity in the face of Northern Ireland's atrocities, a balance he achieves through a transformative imagination. The souvenir for this transformation, a whitewash brush that served as a sporran in the brother's clowning, can continue to redress because like the mug with a cornflower pattern from 'Station Island, X', once it has crossed the frontier into the imaginative realm, it remains 'glamoured from this translation' (*Station Island*, 87). The poem ends with the gesture of one just back or about to enter that otherworld: 'Then rubbing your eyes and seeing our old brush/Up on the byre door, and keeping going'.[35] This icon of redress, however, must weigh against the art-enhanced horror of a murder in the town centre of a part-time reservist, a memory that re-emerges for the brother in the steam of his morning gruel:

> Grey matter like gruel flecked with blood
> In spatters on the whitewash. A clean spot
> Where his head had been, other stains subsumed
> In the parched wall he leant his back against

The poet's representation of memory – the transitional gruel, the animistic 'parched', 'whitewash' connecting the murder scene to the brush – sharpens the terror, to such an extent that the reader may doubt the efficacy of poetic redress.

'Mycenae Lookout' is one of several sinewy poems in *The Spirit Level* that can stand with Heaney's best poetry. In his helpful reading, Daniel Tobin recognises the sentry as a surrogate for the poet, always 'at the ready', but I cannot agree that 'the violent world of Ulster finds its objective correlative in the often savage world of Greek myth'.[36] The tone of the Lookout, 'posted and forgotten', is too cynical, the rhyme too smart-ass, the details too heavy-metal, the abrupt lines too spiky:

> Her soiled vest,
> her little breasts,
> her clipped, devast-
>
> ated, scabbed
> punk head,
> the char-eyed
>
> famine gawk –
> she looked
> camp-fucked
>
> and simple.
> ('Cassandra')

As Vendler says, 'Heaney has never before permitted himself such brutal strokes in delineating a victim', and, she continues, 'Agamemnon . . . is equally violently sketched' (170). Indeed, Heaney's Agamemnon is so menacing he might have sprung from the head of Ted Hughes's Crow. After the ceasefire of 1994 and the ungoing negotiations for peace, the reader might have expected pacific poems such as 'Tolland', the penultimate poem in this volume, in which the site of prehistoric violence has become 'the bright "Townland of Peace"' (Spirit Level, 80). The eruption of 'Mycenae Lookout' into this ceasefire has the effect of reminding us that homicide was not endemic to Ulster and 'That killing-fest, the life-warp and world-wrong/ . . . still augured and endured' (34). For that reason, the attempt to redress seems directed toward a realm larger than Northern Ireland.

The relation of poetry to practical life occupies Heaney in *Electric Light* (2001).[37] Some reviewers found that the book had an insufficiency of joules, although the title poem was universally admired. Because it indirectly but significantly addresses the question of the location of poetry, 'Electric Light' should be the best place to end this essay. In a *Poetry Book Society Bulletin*, reprinted in *The Guardian* on Bloomsday of 2001, Heaney identified the old woman as his grandmother: 'There are clues to show that she is ancient, archetypal and central to the family'. Heaney says further, 'The brightness of my grandmother's house is associated in my mind with a beautiful line from the Mass of the Dead – "Et lux perpetua luceat eis", "And let perpetual light shine upon them . . . ."' He continues, ' "The stilly night" is mentioned and to anyone who knows the Thomas Moore song, the phrase inevitably calls up "the light/Of other days around me" '.[38] Electric Light, then, represented the new and wonderful and lit the boy's aspirations toward the outside world:

> If I stood on the bow-backed chair, I could reach
> The light switch. They let me and they watched me.
> A touch of the little pip would work the magic.
>
> A turn of their wireless knob and light came on
> In the dial. They let me and they watched me
> As I roamed at will the stations of the world.

It also represents the glow of memory and imagination as it lights the past and the dead, appropriate to setting the elegies that fill most of this volume.

Several reviewers were attracted to the description of the old woman's thumbnail which opens the poem:

> Candle-grease congealed, dark-streaked with wick-soot . . .
> The smashed thumb-nail
> Of that ancient mangled thumb was puckered pearl,
>
> Rucked quartz, a littered Cumae.
> In the first house where I saw electric light

The thumbnail also closes it:

> Electric light shone over us, I feared
>
> The dirt-tracked flint and fissure of her nail,
> So plectrum-hard, glit-glittery, it must still keep
> Among beads and vertebrae in the Derry ground.

Beyond connecting this woman to Cumae and, thereby, to the oldest of the prophetesses who served Apollo, god of light and poetry, the nails of this diviner of the future signify her pre-electrical past with candles and lanterns. Moreover, they relate her to the corpses in *North*, those of relatives whose 'nails/were darkened . . .' (15) and those of the bog-burials who had 'bruised berries under . . . [their] nails' (*North*, 33). Of the Grabaulle Man, he writes,

> but now he lies
> perfected in my memory
> down to the red horn
> of his nails
>
> hung in the scales
> with beauty and atrocity

If, as argued earlier in this essay, the bog-corpses in their perfection and their mysterious Otherness, human in origin but inhuman, as much excrescence as the nails themselves, become analogues to works of art, then the old woman represents the translated object of art, poetry itself in its elegiac light.

Heaney's sibyl holds a curious kinship with another demigod called The Nymph who appears in the 'Calypso' and 'Circe' episodes of Joyce's *Ulysses*. Born as a *Photo Bits* gatefold, *The Bath of the Nymph*, framed by Bloom as a 'splendid masterpiece in art colours', serves to illustrate Bloom's explanation to Molly of metempsychosis. More basically, she manifests Bloom's confusion, not of beauty and atrocity, Heaney's distinction, but of art and pornography, a distinction that elsewhere occupies Stephen Dedalus. Accused by her of drafting her into his sexual fantasies, Bloom responds by evoking Keatsian aesthetics: 'Your classic curves, beautiful immortal, I was glad to look on you, to praise you, a thing of beauty, almost to pray'.[39] The wildly comic encounter with its psychological subtext contains a startling confession by the Nymph who associates herself with reproductions of Greek sculpture in the National Museum: 'We immortals . . . are stonecold and pure. We eat electric light' (*Ulysses*, 449). The ingested light provides the art's radiance, what Stephen calls its *claritas*. The coldness arises from the necessary detachment of the work of art, in Stephen's Thomist vocabulary its *integritas*: 'The esthetic image is first luminously apprehended as selfbounded and selfcontained upon the immeasurable background of space or time which is not it'.[40] This frigidity, which Keats calls 'Cold Pastoral', Yeats assigns to all great works of art.

We might deduce three explanations for the reappearance of the term for art's diet in Heaney's title poem: Heaney deliberately recycled the term from Joyce but left it to us to uncover the implications of this exchange; the phrase 'Electric Light' resonates for Heaney beyond its autobiographical associations, but he does not recall its source in his quite familiar *Ulysses*; the recurrence of the phrase Joyce used in Heaney's poetry is purely accidental although the phrase reaves in quite similar aesthetic concerns. Whatever the fuller sources for this phrase, it points to the gravity of Heaney's concerns about the place of art, the possibility of and manner in which art impinges on political realities, the uses of art in facing troubles, and poetry and violence. It may be the frequent expression of such concerns, rather than any superiority of his poetry, that will distinguish Heaney from his brilliant Irish contemporaries, a generation likely to be remembered with the Elizabethan, Jacobean and Romantic British poets and the post-Depression American poets as marvellous gatherings of talent. But that conclusion must wait for another time.

NOTES

1 *The Redress of Poetry* (London: Faber and Faber, 1995), p. 8.
2 Swedish Academy, 5 October 1995. www.nobel.se/literature/laureats/1995/Press. html.
3 Neil Corcoran, *Poets of Modern Ireland* (Cardiff: University of Wales Press, 1999), p. 116.
4 Helen Vendler, *Seamus Heaney* (Cambridge: Harvard University Press, 1998), p. 9.
5 Blake Morrison, *Seamus Heaney* (London: Methuen, 1982), p. 68.
6 Ciaran Carson, "Escaped from the Massacre?" *The Honest Ulsterman*, No. 50 (Winter 1975), 183–6. Coming from a fellow poet who has retained his residency and raised his family in Belfast, Carson's criticism had a particular authority and mordancy. Edna Longley, *Poetry in the Wars* (Newcastle: Bloodaxe, 1986).
7 Michael Parker, *Seamus Heaney: The Making of the Poet* (University of Iowa Press, 1993), p. 11.
8 Seamus Heaney, *Death of A Naturalist* (London: Faber and Faber, 1966), p. 57.
9 Henry Hart, *Seamus Heaney: Poet of Contrary Progressions* (Syracuse University Press, 1992), p. 31.
10 Seamus Heaney, *Wintering Out* (London: Faber and Faber, 1972), p. 35.
11 Seamus Deane, "Unhappy and at Home: Interview with Seamus Heaney", *The Crane Bag*, vol. 1, No. 1 (Spring, 1977), pp. 61–7, 61.
12 'Talking Irish', *The New York Times on the Web*, April 8, 2001. Archiveds. nytimes.com.
13 Conor Cruise O'Brien, review of *North*, *Listener*, 25 Sept 1975.
14 P.V. Glob, *The Bog People* (London: Faber and Faber, 1969).
15 Seamus Heaney, *Preoccupations: Selected Prose, 1968–78* (London: Faber and Faber, 1980), p. 57.
16 Neil Corcoran, *Seamus Heaney* (London: Faber and Faber, 1986), pp. 79–80.
17 Seamus Heaney, *North* (London: Faber and Faber, 1975), p. 40.
18 Carson, ' "Escaped from the Massacre" ', p. 183.
19 Seamus Heaney, "Anglo-Irish Occasions", *London Review of Books*, 5 May 1988, p. 9.
20 Bernard O'Donoghue, *Seamus Heaney and the Language of Poetry* (Brighton: Harvester, 1994), p. 69.
21 Ian Gregson, *The Male Image: Representations of Masculinity in Postwar Poetry* (Basingstoke: Macmillan, 1999), p. 130.
22 T.S. Eliot, *Selected Prose of T.S. Eliot* ed. with intro by Frank Kermode (New York: Farrar, Straus, Giroux, 1975), p. 41.
23 David Lloyd, *Anomalous States* (Durham: Duke University Press, 1993), p. 35.
24 Seamus Heaney, 'An Open Letter', A Field Day Pamphlet, 2 (Derry: Field Day, 1983), p. 9.
25 'Anglo-Irish Occasions', *London Review of Books*, 5 May 1988, p. 9.
26 Donald Davie, 'Donald Davie on Critics and Essayists', *Poetry Review* 85:3 (Autumn 1995), p. 38.
27 Seamus Heaney, *The Government of the Tongue* (London: Faber and Faber, 1988), p. xviii.
28 Seamus Heaney, *Station Island* (London: Faber and Faber, 1984), p. 83.

29 Seamus Heaney, *The Haw Lantern* (London: Faber and Faber, 1987), p. 6.

30 Conor Cruise O'Brien, 'An Unhealthy Intersection'. *The New Review*, 2:16 (1975), 3–8.

31 Seamus Heaney, *The Place of Writing*, intro. by Ronald Schuchard (Atlanta: Scholars Press, 1989), p. 36–7.

32 Rand Brandes, 'Seamus Heaney: An Interview', *Salmagundi*, No. 80 (Fall 1988), p. 18.

33 Seamus Heaney, *Seeing Things* (London: Faber and Faber, 1991), p. 62.

34 Paul Muldoon, *To Ireland, I* (Oxford University Press, 2001), p. 7.

35 Seamus Heaney, *The Spirit Level* (London: Faber and Faber, 1996), p. 16.

36 Daniel Tobin, *Passage to the Center: Imagination and the Sacred in the Poetry of Seamus Heaney* (Lexington: University of Kentucky Press, 1999), p. 287.

37 Seamus Heaney, *Electric Light* (London: Faber and Faber, 2001).

38 'Seamus Heaney on the Making of His Recent Collection, *Electric Light*' *Poetry Book Society Bulletin*, reprinted in *The Guardian*, Saturday, 16 June 2001.

39 James Joyce, *Ulysses* (New York: Random House, 1986), p. 445.

40 James Joyce, *A Portrait of the Artist As A Young Man*, ed. Seamus Deane (London: Penguin, 1992), p. 230.

8

TERENCE BROWN

Mahon and Longley: place and placelessness

Derek Mahon and Michael Longley have been publishing verse since the mid-1960s. Both born in Belfast (Longley in 1939, Mahon in 1941), educated at the Royal Belfast Academical Institution (or 'Inst', as it is known) and at Trinity College, Dublin (where Longley read classics and Mahon French, English and philosophy), they emerged as poets in a period marked both by a remarkable growth in artistic and literary activity in a province long regarded as inimical to the arts, and by the stirring of political energies in Northern Ireland that inaugurated decades of violence and radical change. Their careers as poets display similarities and differences as they have responded to lives lived in a period when the status of Northern Ireland within the United Kingdom has been in constant question. Michael Longley has lived in Belfast since the 1960s, spending summers in Co Mayo. In the same period Mahon has lived in London, Dublin and New York with sojourns in France and Italy, having spent only a brief period in Belfast after graduation. The historical and personal experience with which their work engages, however, is certainly related (whatever their differing career trajectories) to the political crisis of a period in which the relationship between Britain and Ireland has been profoundly affected by the Northern Irish problem. How they both relate imaginatively to the North, to Ireland and the rest of the world in such a period, when violence was endemic, takes the critic to central aspects of their work.

Derek Mahon's first collection of verse was titled *Night-Crossing* (1968). The title (referring to the mail-boat crossing of the Irish sea, then, before the era of cheap flights, often a challenging ordeal) surely signalled that his was a migratory imagination for which journeys away from and occasionally back to a native place would constitute a defining way of being in the world. Where Seamus Heaney two years earlier, in such poems as 'Digging' and 'Follower' in *Death of Naturalist*, announced himself as a poet linked to an ancestral tradition in an immemorial rural world, Mahon presented himself as a self-consciously urban, *deraciné* intelligence, whose birthright was the bitter inheritance of an industrial Belfast, where the dubious blessings of modernity challenged poetic ambition. In 1970, in an article called 'Poetry in Northern Ireland', Mahon acknowledged how social formation as Protestant Northerners set such as Michael Longley, James Simmons and himself apart from an Irish sense of presumed continuities of place and identity. He recognised that John Montague and Seamus Heaney, had distinctive voices in Irish poetry since, as Northerners 'surrounded by the Greek gifts of modern industry and what Ferlinghetti called the hollering monsters of the imagination of disaster', they share 'an ecology with . . . technological society' and so 'insist upon a different court of appeal from that which sits in the south'. Yet 'born within close range' of the Irish literary inheritance 'they can assimilate to the traditional aesthetics which are their birthright some of (to risk pretentiousness) the cultural fragmentation of our time'. By contrast Simmons and Longley (and by implication Mahon himself) as 'ironic heirs of a threadbare colonialism, have as their inheritance that very fragmentation'. Possessed of 'dissociated sensibilities' they take as literary inspiration a 'fragmentary assembly of Irish, British and American models, not necessarily in that order'.[1] Natural access to a presumably coherent Irish tradition was not an option.

I

It is clear that if the young Mahon could not take an Irish patrimony for granted, he was markedly unimpressed by the provincial British life offered as a possible alternative by his native Belfast. He rather half-heartedly confessed of its suburban banality, in the early poem he has chosen to stand at the head of his *Collected Poems* (1999), 'Spring in Belfast', (originally titled 'In Belfast', 1968), 'One part of my mind must learn to know its place'.[2] It is as if Belfast is entered in his world as the obverse of poetry, as a manifestation of a version of modernity which induces deracination, as the place that set him wandering to the many locations that over four decades have engaged his restless, peregrine imagination.

Tellingly one of the most powerful poems in his first collection was a journey poem 'Day Trip to Donegal'. This marked one of Mahon's earliest renderings of the Irish landscape as a zone of being that in its elemental contrast to the Belfast in which he grew up in the 1950s, serves as a reminder of the risky depths of consciousness poetry must tap. The journey by car takes the poet from Belfast to Donegal and back so that his dreams that night in the city after a mere day in such a place are full of wind, rain and sea, intimations of existential vertigo: 'At dawn I was alone far out at sea / Without skill or reassurance'.

The plangent note struck in this poem is one that recurs throughout Mahon's work, frequently sounding in those poems where he contemplates Irish vistas of sea and seashore as tokens of metaphysical perspectives. In such writing the Irish land and seascape, even if possessed of historical associations and political import (as in 'Rathlin' (1982) with its memories of the sixteenth-century massacre of the MacDonnells and its 'metaphysical wind') or of social significance (as in the long poem of 1972, 'Beyond Howth Head') evoke an order of being akin to that imagined in those memorably chiliastic poems in his *oeuvre* which invoke ultimate states of post-history, post-existence ('The Last of the Fire Kings', 'Leaves', both 1975, 'An Image from Beckett', 1972). It offers none of the consolations a poetry of place customarily involves in Irish cultural tradition, with its suggestions of belonging, of familial and tribal continuities, nor does it allow indulgence of romantic concepts of nature as a restorative spiritual agent in consciousness. Rather, the alienated mind of these poems finds a set of expressive symbols in images of storm, rain, wind, cold, waves and elemental emptiness. It especially relishes with a kind of stoical hauteur the idea of the liminal, what is addressed in 'The Sea in Winter' (1979)[3] as 'the heroism and cowardice / of living on the edge of space'. For this poet the peripheral is a vantage point which opens on empty desolation that cuts human pride down to size. 'North Wind: Portrush' (1982), in an entirely characteristic manner, invokes the wind of a 'benighted' Irish coast:

> It whistles off the stars
> And the existential, stark
> Face of the cosmic dark.
> We crouch to roaring fires.

It is not that Mahon does not know that landscape can serve as more than the symbolic expression of a vision of negation, of the rootless consciousness in an empty universe. In 'Going Home'(1975) he acknowledges that pastoral possibilities and classical mythology can invest place with imaginary charm. This poem contrasts a domesticated southern scene (presumably the poem opens in the south of England) with a northern shoreline (presumably Ireland; the poem may unconsciously echo Louis MacNeice's poem of a similar juxtaposition, 'Woods', 1946). In the one are 'mild woods' where, despite the resident nymphs being poisoned by car exhaust, the poet can envisage an Ovidian transformation whereby, as a tree, he might seem as if he 'belonged here too'. But on the northern coast to which he is about to depart there will be only a tree 'Battered by constant rain/And twisted by the sea-wind', which truly belongs in the 'funereal/Cloud-continent of night'.

In his essay 'MacNeice in England and Ireland' (1974) Mahon remarks that only an 'English' poet could have written one of the stanzas of 'Woods' where MacNeice observes

> The patch
> Of sky at the end of the path grows and discloses
> An ordered open air long ruled by dyke and fence,
> With geese whose form and gait proclaim their consequence,
> Pargetted outposts, windows bowed with thatch,
> And cow pats – and inconsequent wild roses.[4]

A brace of poems by Mahon from 1979[5] suggests that he himself, even less of an 'English' poet than MacNeice, was not immune to the attractions of the English rural scene in pastoral guise. 'Ford Manor' allows the flora and fauna of the countryside near Gatwick airport south of London a fragile moment of exquisite existence, when a pregnant mother is 'a smiling Muse come back to life'. 'Penshurst Place' imagines a similar country house scene as an Elizabethan moment, love proposed to a backdrop of lute music, intrigue and rumours of sea-battle. Read as companion poems these elegantly composed verses (each two stanzas of eight lines of rhymed couplets) do however set an imagined England in a broad, disenchanted historical context, for all that they realise a rustic world in traditionally lyrical terms. 'Ford Manor' is aware of globalised modernity with its reference to flights 'from Tokyo, New York or Rome' while 'Penshurst Place' evokes the origins of the modern world in its reference to early modern colonial buccaneering ('Spanish ships around Kinsale'). It is clear that for Mahon the attractions of an English pastoral are no real alternative to the 'chaos and old night' of reality imagined as a metaphysically awesome Irish vista. It is corrupted by a historical legacy of imperialism and poisoned by modernity. In 'The Woods' (1982), a two years' retreat in the grounds of a 'once great estate' readily slips into allusions to the *anciens regimes* of Hapsburgs and Romanovs, Lenin arriving at Petrograd. A post-imperial idyll is indulged for a time, until it sates and the poet acknowledges 'chaos and confusion' as 'our birthright and our proper portion'. If England once possessed a spirit of place able in its intimations of continuity and settled tradition (more numinous than anything encountered in provincial Belfast) to rival the vertiginous infinities of Irish land and seascapes, then it does so no more. 'Brighton Beach' (1982) recalls the journey which had inspired 'Day Trip to Donegal', but now the poet who had been out of his depth in Donegal, strolls where 'the spirit of place' cannot appear, for 'places as such are dead'. Where the poet had once been 'alone far out at sea', the 'loved sea' now 'reflects banality'.

If places are in fact dead in the modern world, the titles of Mahon's poems reflect an obsession with what place might once have been when it was possible to conceive of it as a stabilising point of reference. Many of the titles are simple place names ('Rathlin', 'Old Roscoff', 'Mt Gabriel', 'Achill', 'Kinsale') while the figure *in situ* is recurrent poetic theme ('Brecht in Svendborg', 'Ovid in Tomis'). The prevailing mood of many of these poems is a kind of austere nostalgia, emotion admitted as it is simultaneously ironised in a regretful tone which can modulate from exacting self-mockery to elevated sorrow in a way that is distinctively Mahonesque. 'The Chinese Restaurant in Portrush' (1979), for example, has the poet himself as the figure in a streetscape, contemplating an out-of-season Co Antrim seaside resort.

The first stanza indulges almost sweetly a nostalgia for a possible past: 'Today the place is as it might have been, / Gentle and almost hospitable'. The early spring day composes itself as a lyrical instant after the rigours of winter in a northern clime and before 'the first "invasion"' of tourists. There is even an old wolfhound dozing in the sun to complete the scene as imaginary Irish good place. Stanza two offers the poet as semi-absurd figure with his 'paper and prawn chow mein / Under a framed photograph of Hong Kong'. For a moment the proprietor of the restaurant sees the seascape before him as a Chinese scene ('an ideogram on sea-cloud') and whistling, dreams of home. It is 'as if the world were young'. Yet the reference to Hong Kong in stanza two, comic counter of dislocation, where chow mein can seem an unlikely item on a menu (the Northern Counties Hotel of stanza one would in the past have offered more traditional fare), is disruptive of the poem's composure. As disputed Crown colony (the poem dates from before the British hand-over of Hong Kong to the People's Republic of China) it reminds us of Northern Ireland's ambiguous status in the United Kingdom and makes the phrase 'the first "invasion"' of stanza one, far from innocent. The good place is a momentary trick of light on the mountains of Donegal (across a contentious border), the legacy of history is ineluctable, home the stuff of dreams. Even such a celebratory poem of place as this is rich in ironies.

In his poetry, Mahon recurrently invests the places he chooses as subjects in England and Ireland and in the world at large with this poignant atmosphere of certain loss. It is as if the alienation from a native place has made exile, homelessness, loneliness, the defining conditions of modernity. Empires have come and gone, a continent can bloom and disappear like a flower in a sandstorm ('Another Sunday Morning'), history will repeat itself in the long English aftermath of imperial power ('One of these nights'). The poet's is the voice of a gravely pained belatedness, uncertain of any adequate human future to supersede the failures of the past. Indeed he is drawn to sites where epochal events have taken place, making them the loci of a residual poetry of their meaningful occasions. 'A Postcard from Berlin' (1982), for example, evokes the collapse of the Weimar Republic in 'the fires / Of abstract rage'. The sequence poem 'A Kensington Notebook' (1985) re-creates a London district in terms of its early twentieth-century Modernist associations, but recalls that the work of Ford Madox Ford, Ezra Pound and Wyndham Lewis was conducted at the heart of an empire at war. The fourth poem of the sequence is set in a diminished present 'Beneath the shadow of / A nuclear power plant', in a world of dust. New York in 'The Hudson Letter' is a 'modern Rome', a smorgasbord of cultural reference points (Manhattan as 'off-shore boutique'), which induces millenarian speculations as in 'the thaw water of an oil-drum / the hot genes of the future seeth'. It is a city of ghosts in this long sequence poem of 1995: Dylan Thomas, W.H. Auden, Hart Crane, Frank O'Hara, John Butler Yeats and an emigrant Irish girl. It is a metropolis no longer visited by great sea-going liners, the dinosaurs of a less 'exigent world'.

Occasionally in this poetic inventory of places that have known significance of one kind or another, Mahon includes his native Belfast and Northern Ireland. In such poems the Troubles are treated as a further experience of belatedness by the poet, in a melancholy poetry of place caught up, transformed and abandoned by history. Native places have been made placeless, as is the modern fate. 'Afterlives' (1975) has the poet return to Belfast after five years of war to 'a city so changed' that the 'places' he grew up in are scarcely recognisable. 'Derry Morning' (1982) evokes a 'tranquil place,/ Its desolation almost peace', where a revolution had once seemed to start and the city itself figured on the Richter scale of international import. Now, in a strange music of endings and departures, 'A Russian freighter bound for home/ Mourns to the city in its gloom'.

Mahon's restless, migratory imagination, an intelligence alert to cultural and social decline, a sensibility ironised by a perennial awareness of the peripheral, accordingly finds expression in an *oeuvre* that makes of dissociation a signal poetic resource. Yet the poet remains haunted by the possibility of belonging. However, exile and homelessness, (like that explored in 'The Hudson Letter' in the volume of that name), the traveller's loneliness recorded in many individual lyrics, find only momentary alleviation from a sense of loss, estrangement, separation, as in the masterpiece of temporary sojourn and 'disconsolate' solitude, 'Achill'(1985), which is lit by bright images of the poet's children on holiday in Greece. The poet recurrently finds himself expressing love for a lover, for family members, affection for friends, across empty distances, as if oceanic and cosmic spaces highlight the difficulty of human communication and the fragility of such homes as we can construct.

'The Globe in North Carolina' (1982), for example, has the poet turning a globe in an American twilight, which induces spacious thoughts of continental geographies and New World futures. The poem shifts to a global perspective. The planet itself is imagined for a moment as a 'home from home' in space, before it address one who lies 'an ocean to the east' in a different time-zone. The poet who began his career with a collection titled *Night-Crossing* has become the poet of the trans-Atlantic flight ('Homecoming', 'Imbolc' in 'The Hudson Letter'), the poet of repeated dislocation. 'The Hudson Letter' acknowledges that 'even as we speak, somewhere a plane / gains altitude in the moon's exilic glare'.

Given this peripatetic take on things it is not surprising that occasionally Mahon does admit that he could make a home somewhere. Kinsale, in the poem of that name, on a day of sun, with 'yachts tinkling and dancing in the bay', in a Co Cork seaside town (the poet is attracted to the liminal pleasures of harbour towns, seaside resorts, shorelines, ports) inspires the poet to 'contemplate at last / shining windows, a future forbidden by no-one' (states of blessedness are often intimated in the verse by images of light and sun). 'The Hudson Letter', in its penultimate poem, imagines heading for Dublin as if for 'home', while the final poem of the sequence has as epigraph Marina Warner's hopeful words 'Home lies in the unfolding of the story in the future – not behind, waiting to be regained'. However, *The Yellow Book*, 1997, which comprises the second of the long sequence poems Mahon composed in the 1990s, suggests that Dublin disappointed, like everywhere else. For the city is entered in that work as the site of post-modern decadence, a dystopia for an ageing aesthete: 'The place a Georgian theme-park for the tourist'.

Early in his career Mahon identified a French landscape as an exemplum of a possible good place. For one of the most buoyant of his poems of place was the early 'Four Walks in the Country Near Saint-Brieuc' (1968), which opens with a lyrical morning evocation of *la France profonde*:

> Suddenly, near at hand, the click of a wooden shoe
> An old woman among the primaeval shapes
> Abroad in a field of light . . .

It was, however, in his regard for the poetry of the twentieth-century poet Philippe Jaccottet that Mahon allowed his Francophilia its fullest expression. He published a selection of Jaccottet translations in 1988. In the introduction to this volume he wrote of Jaccottet's imaginative terrain in terms that suggest that he is 'a secular mystic, an explorer of "*le vrai lieu*" ("the real place")' who allows the possibility of presence in elemental, pre-Socratic symbols: 'tree, flower, sun, moon, road mountain, wind, water, bird, house, lamp'.

He notes that Jaccottet's characteristic posture is that of 'a man alone in a garden watching the sun rise . . . or seated at his desk at dusk', in a world (so different from his own), where there 'is (almost) no *sea*: this is an inland poetry of river and mountain, the country road, the lake in the woods'.[6] Even death, in such a primal setting can be imagined without a sense of absolute loss. 'Words in the Air', has a spirit accept that others have taken the place of the clear air that was once its home. So the poem concludes with 'tears of happiness' as the living reflect on the departed inhabitant, 'who liked it here so much': 'He has changed into what shade pleased him best'.

Mahon's version of Jaccottet renders his world as essentially calm, ahistorical, touched mysteriously by the numinous in the natural order of things. In the body of his own historically and culturally alert work the volume serves as a signpost to those moments in his own poetry where a similar secular mysticism finds intimations of presence amid the flux of time. The sequence of Haiku-like miniatures published in 1977 as *Light Music* has something of Jaccottet writ exquisitely small in it (though with Mahon's characteristic geographic range), as in 'A stone at the roadside/watches snow fall/on the silent gatelodge' ('Twilight'). It is, however, in two of Mahon's poems on European paintings from 1982 that his own sense of the numinous finds its fullest expression. In famous pictures by the Dutch Pieter de Hooch and the Norwegian Edvard Munch Mahon finds himself before arrested, almost sacral time. In 'Courtyards in Delft' and 'Girls on the Bridge' (there is a series of Munch canvases on this theme), life seems permanently composed at a significant moment in a particular place. Both poems imagine the people of the pictures – the humble artisans of de Hooch's canvas, Munch's adolescent girls on a bridge – as unconscious of the terrible histories of colonialism and modernity that their worlds will give way to. They seem possessed of the apparent permanence of art, yet the poems they inhabit render such transcendence as illusory. The timeless place art can seem to conjure into existence – a girl waiting 'For her man to come home for his tea' until 'the paint disintegrates', girls on a bridge at twilight, their 'plangent conversational quack/Expressive of calm days/And peace of mind' – is not immune from history in Mahon's imagining. No place, however invested with luminous intensity or emotional depth ('late afternoon/ Lambency informing the deal table'; 'girls content to gaze/At the unplumbed, reflective lake') is bulwark against pain and loss which in Mahon's sense of things, is a given of the European and global inheritance.

It is this, perhaps, that makes 'A Disused Shed In Co Wexford' (1975) his quintessential poem (and one of his finest works). This too is a place poem that imagines, in a world where anywhere might be anywhere else observed by the traveller with a 'light meter and relaxed itinerary', places that retain the authenticity of the suffering they have known. Such surviving 'places where a thought might grow' could be Peruvian mines, 'Indian compounds' and 'a disused shed in Co Wexford' where since civil war days, mushrooms have been expectantly awaiting release from the long dark they have endured. A sombre fantasy, touched with atmospherics of science fiction ('stalked like triffids' of stanza five, derives from John Wyndham's sci-fi novel of botanical threat *The Day of the Triffids*), the poem builds with assured gravity into a modern threnody for universal victimage. It is dedicated to J.G. Farrell, and the allusion in stanza two to 'the grounds of a burnt-out hotel' summons to mind *Troubles*, that author's novel of 1920s violence in Ireland. Yet the work expands its purview from the particular time and place to encompass millennia: 'Lost people of Treblinka and Pompeii!' The sci-fi aspect of the poem gives to it an eerie strangeness, as if the residually human, with its places, lives and histories, is an anachonism which nevertheless makes its claim on the present.

II

Michael Longley's first collection was titled *No Continuing City* (1968) as if to alert his readers to expect a pilgrim soul (the title refers to the Pauline text "We have no continuing city', Letter to the *Hebrews* 13, 14). The title poem, however, was a piece of Metaphysical bravura ('my picture in her eyes'[7] in line two is an obvious borrowing from Donne), more concerned with arrivals than departures. A man says farewell to former loves as he salutes his bride and wife-to-be. It was a poem that anticipated a settled married life in a collection marked, in contrast, by recurrent imagery of sea, water, weather, journeying, and by what the poet in 'A Personal Statement' (dedicated to Seamus Heaney) termed 'excursions for my heart and lungs to face'. In this poem these are journeys of the mind in the sensory world. Elsewhere in the volume actual geographies are imagined (the Hebrides in two poems, Inishmore, Essex) but they are treated as metaphors of possible states of consciousness explored by a poet inventing himself in his art. For Longley's early poems (influenced by the poetics of English Movement verse of the late 1950s and 1960s) were highly-wrought, tautly versified, self-conscious artifices, that set urbanity of manner and civilised panache, against wilder territories of feeling. 'The Hebrides' is a key early poem, with its elegant verse form, verbal punctiliousness, syntactical and rhythmic precision, deployed to ponder a region of the mind for which a wild, rocky Atlantic world is appropriate metaphor. There is in this extended meditation a sense of the poem's formal structure about to topple over in the risky zone of feeling it has entered. The poem concludes with a dizzying image: 'I fight all the way for balance – /In the mountain's shadow/ Losing foothold, covet the privilege/ Of vertigo'.

One of Longley's early poems, 'In Memoriam', does allow the carefully controlled mental space of his imaginative engagement with the world to be invaded by powerful feeling. Indeed the impression of deeply buried emotion finding eventual expression is a poetic effect Longley achieves in the best of his work. Here the record of a father's First World War experience is allowed an expansive, elegiac narration. The conceitful troping of the early poetic manner is scrupulously minimised and put to the service of compassionate recollection (with a muted allusion to Wilfred Owen to root the poem in a specific tradition of war poetry)[8]:

> Now I see in close-up, in my mind's eye,
> The cracked and splintered dead for pity's sake
> Each dismal evening predecease the sun. . . .

The local 'war' which began in Northern Ireland in 1969, early in Longley's career as poet, entered his *oeuvre* in his second collection, *An Exploded View* (1972). Three verse letters to fellow poets, James Simmons, Derek Mahon and Seamus Heaney have as their occasion the outbreak of political violence in their shared native province ('Blood on the curbstones, and my mind/Dividing . . .'), which has forced the poet to reflect on his own political and literary alignments. 'To James Simmons' entertains the possibility that in a violent time an insouciant bravado has its merits ('Play your guitar while Derry burns'). 'To Derek Mahon', by contrast, is a guilty acknowledgement that as 'Two poetic conservatives/In the city of guns and long knives', and implicitly as Northern Protestants, they had engaged insufficiently with 'The stereophonic nightmare/Of the Shankill and the Falls'. Yet as he recalls how they had in the violent August of 1969 together become fully conscious of the sectarian realities of their natal city, he also remembers a joint trip to the Aran island of Inisheer with two companions, where they had understood how foreign they both were to the Gaelic and Catholic traditions of the islanders. The poem registers a Northern Protestant crisis of identity which cannot easily be resolved. 'To Seamus Heaney' is a circumspect address to a poet whose early work had been palpably rural in focus, assuming that they both might turn from the grim life of Belfast at war to 'That small subconscious cottage where/ The Irish poet slams his door/On slow-worm, toad and adder'. Yet Longley cannot, he suggests to Heaney, slip into that easy Irish role, for he knows rural life can be as violent as urban. He must make do as best he can, 'Mind open like a half-door/To the speckled hill, the plovers' shore'.

This telling couplet does in fact allow the critic to read Longley's many Nature poems (and he has been Ireland's foremost Nature poet in the twentieth century), in which the flora and fauna of the Irish countryside are reverently itemised and described with a naturalist's knowledge and precision, as careful acts of attentiveness to the natural order, amounting to a spiritual resource in a time of cruelty and violence. This sets his Nature poems apart from the long-held English observational tradition of natural history and topographical verse with its roots in eighteenth-century science, to which such poetry might initially seem to belong. Longley might have joined Mahon in a poetry of dislocations, placeless places, but for him exact naming of species becomes a complex way of Irish belonging, of remembering, of situating himself in a difficult cultural terrain, while remaining true to his sense of a complex inheritance.

Longley's natural world, principally apprehended in the Irish West, particularly in Co Mayo, is a thing of exquisite particulars – of wings, feathers, petals, birds' eggs, nests, bones, wild flowers, pebbles, footprints and traces. His imagination is drawn to its vulnerable fragility, as if the gross forces of history were an affront to its miniature perfections. The poet in his landscapes, amid its flora and fauna, is an intent figure, simultaneously gentle and resolute in his fidelity to a material reality that merely includes the human and the historical. Indeed Longley's sensibility is Lucretian in its scientific rigour and instinctively ecological in its lack of anthropomorphic feeling. Nature for Longley is a marvellous miracle, recorded lovingly but without piety or easy sentiment. The characteristic tone of his Nature poetry is that of delight and clear-eyed wonderment before the world's manifold detail.

This sense of Nature as an intricate order of being in which humankind takes its place with badgers, otters, birds – especially larks, the almost iconic lapwing – wild flowers, beasts, rivers, lakes, rocks, earth and sky, stars, allows Longley to write of historical disasters as if they were unwarranted assaults upon the nature of things. Indeed his contemplative respect for the processes of the natural world gives to his poems on warfare and on violence a tone of compassionate anger that is central to their emotional force.

For Longley the violence of the twentieth century has its representative occasion in the slaughter of the Great War in which his English father served as a soldier in the British Army. The killing fields of that war, especially as they were rendered in the verses of the English war poets, have constituted for this poet a kind of metaphor for all conflict, in which human life is cruelly, even wantonly wasted (allusions to and treatment of Great War themes recur almost obsessively in his work, as in the repeated deployed phrase 'No Man's Land', also the title of a poem of 1985, or in such poems as 'Master of Ceremonies', 'Second Sight', 'The War Graves'). Accordingly in those poems in which Longley confronted the violence of the Northern Irish conflict most directly (in 'Wounds', 1972 and 'Wreathes', 1979) it was with a consciousness that the conflict there was notable for its victims, not its heroes, that poetry was in the pity not the glory of war. In 'Wounds', piteous events (the murder of three soldiers seduced into danger, a bus-conductor murdered in front of his family in his own home) draw from the poet memories of his father's Great War experiences. Both father and new victims are buried by the poet with 'military honours of a kind', which pay respects not to the martial valour his father had admired in the Ulster Division at the Somme, but to the victims' very ordinariness, caught up as they all were by a force they could not comprehend. In this poem his father has a 'spinning compass', out of control, as well as badges and medals. Three teenage soldiers die 'bellies full of beer, their flies undone', a bus conductor collapses 'beside his carpet slippers', shot by 'a shivering boy who wandered in'.

'Wreathes' offers funerary respects to the victims of three acts of violence: a civil servant murdered in his home, a greengrocer in his shop and ten linen workers massacred by a roadside. Once again terrible events are associated with the victimhood and waste of the Great War (the allusion to burial rites for his father links the poem to 'In Memoriam' and 'Wounds'):

> Before I can bury my father once again
> I must polish the spectacles, balance them
> Upon his nose, fill his pockets with money
> And into his dead mouth slip the set of teeth.

The holocaust of European Jewry has also been registered in Longley's *oeuvre* as a terrible assault on the human and natural worlds. 'Buchenwald Musuem' in *The Ghost Orchid* (1995), with an allusion to a wreath of poppies barely visible beneath a covering of snow, links that horror to the piteous victimage of the Great War. 'Ghetto' in *Gorse Fires* (1991) implicitly associates the ethnic cleansing of the Nazi period with the sectarian atrociousness of Irish history. For this poem of seven heartbreaking vignettes from the Polish Jewish experience includes, as the poet imagines a meagre ghetto diet, a feast of Irish potatoes, named precisely like propitiatory gifts. It is as if the whole weight of Longley's work as Nature poet can allow him to invest a mere list with great ethical import – the cruelty of humankind is rebuked by the tenaciousness of nature 'resistant to eelworm,/Resignation, common scab, terror, frost, potato-blight'. Elsewhere in his recent work, Irish atrocity, the murders of an ice-cream man in his shop ('The Ice-cream Man' in *Gorse Fires*) and of a group of fishermen in 'The Fishing Party' (in *The Ghost Orchid*) are made to seem obscene by similar litanies of names of flowers and fauna.

Longley's early poetry was marked by locational uncertainty. Not exactly rootless in the Mahonesque mode, it was, however, the poetry of undecided mental states associated with diverse territories in the British Isles. As he developed into a poet of the natural world his imaginative centre of gravity became unshakeably Irish. Indeed the townland of Carrigskeewaun in Co Mayo became a settled point of reference, balancing the home territory of his native Belfast as when in 'Remembering Carrigskeewaun' (in *Gorse Fires*) 'the animals come back to me . . . /From a page lit by the milky way'. The distinctly cerebral quality of the early work (in which the word 'mind' recurs) gives way as the poet matures to poetry marked by bodily awareness. The imaginative centre of gravity is Ireland, the site of consciousness the self in physical, even physiological engagement with its world. Arms, calves, shoulders, breasts, nipples, buttocks, hands, fingers, feet, skin, hair, eyes, eyelids, teeth, bones, skulls, intestines, lungs and bodily fluids make Longley's world one in which feeling is embodied in the palpable, in the actual living, physical person with a biology, a physiology, as well as a history. The poem's formal qualities, often deploying well-stocked stanzas, big with elaborate syntax and imagery, with their steadily cumulative, intimately precise rhythmic advance on their material, also make Longley a poet of somatic awareness.

Yet for all the substantiality of Longley's sense of things, the poet is also haunted by dissolutions, altered states, posthumous conditions. For a profound emotional engagement with how things are also induces in this poet a countervailing apprehension of their impermanence. A characteristic impulse accordingly is to imagine a future in which 'the children/Are drawers full of soft toys' ('Company', 1975) and a couple 'hesitate together/On the verge of an almost total silence', or to ponder the poet's own disappearance in a vanishing trick or in death itself. The idea of his own death-bed fascinates, as in 'Three Posthumous Pieces', as does his own funeral in 'Detour' (1991), that makes its circuitous progress through typical Longley territory, but ends with an image of the futile postponement of finality. 'Oliver Plunkett' (1979) is absorbed by the bizarre perceptual effects of decapitation, and ends with a consciousness that both the Christian saint and his killers have been absorbed by the void:

> He has been buried under the fingernails
> Of his executioner, until they too fade
> Like the lightning flash of their instruments.
>
> There accompanies him around the cathedral
> Enough silence to register the noise
> Of the hairs on his arms and legs expiring.

'Obsequies' (1979) reflects most curiously on the poet's own body on a dissecting table, eyes and other parts made available to medical science, awaiting 'A final ocean, tears, water from the tap,/ Superstitious rivers to take me there'. For Longley's is a sensibility that admits no conventional religious consolation to its awareness of mutability and mortality. His mind, it could be said, is classical rather than Christian, life being greeted with a Horation sense of its brevity. Afterwards there is only the world of the shades.

The superstitious waters invoked in the final line of 'Obsequies' are, of course, the rivers Styx and Lethe, introduced with consummate assurance from Longley's pervasive intimacy as poet with Graeco-Roman perspectives. For throughout his career the classical authors have afforded him imaginative sustenance in dark times almost to the degree that the Irish landscape and its natural history have done, giving his work a European as well as Irish amplitude.

In his early poetry, Longley's classicism had it must be said a bookish, rather mannered quality. In *No Continuing City*, 'Circe', 'Nausicaa', and 'Narcissus' read like the self-conscious, conventional experiments of the Classics student Longley had recently been at Trinity College, Dublin. It was in his second collection *An Exploded View* (1973) that Longley's classicism took on a markedly distinctive note related to his developing vision of the palpable Irish world and of the body. A poem in that book which realises in imagistic detail the folklore of Irish rural life is titled 'Lares'. It links immemorial practice and religious belief in Ireland with the protective Roman deities of farmland and household, the guardians of roads and wayfarers and of the state itself. And 'An Image From Propertius' associates the Roman love poet with Longley's intent concern for posthumous disintegration ('Ankle-bone, knuckle/In the ship of death') while 'Altera Cithera' salutes the same Latin poet as an 'old friend' who espoused an erotic, bodily aesthetic of the lyric in a time when events seemed to call for 'all the dreary/epics of the muscle bound'.

Peter McDonald has astutely identified 'Altera Cithera' as an intimation of later poems that would prove to be 'among Longley's most powerful performances'. These are poems in his volume *Gorse Fires* (1991) which 'are best characterised as transformations into lyric of narrative material'. McDonald is referring here to a set of seven poems which 'condense Homeric episodes, employing long lines and a syntax which maintains a degree of complexity without falling into convolutedness'.[9] *The Ghost Orchid* (1995) collects seven further poems of this type. In these works Homeric incidents from an epic narration are rendered as occasions best apprehended in terms of lyric feeling. The effect is not to reduce the import of what is enacted in the poems (Odysseus' return to Ithaca, for example, his meeting with his nurse, with his aged father, the destruction of the suitors), but to invest the events recalled from the Homeric text with an accompanying sense of pity. The poems become in their way further 'war poems' in the Longley *oeuvre*, for the poetry is still in the pity. Great events are granted their epic significance but the human participants are given the privilege of individual emotion in intimately realised settings. And the intimacy of setting in these poems is augmented by a subtle blend of formal and demotic language (a shadowy cave is 'full of bullauns', Laertes is seen 'in his gardening duds' wearing a 'goatskin duncher', the soul of the slaughtered suitors are led 'Along . . . clammy sheughs'). The landscape is Mediterranean, imagined with the exactitude of Longley's botanical eye, modulating at moments into an Irish topography (as it does in 'The Camp-Fires' in *The Ghost Orchid*, when men at their fires waiting for dawn on a battlefield are compared, in an epic simile within a skilfully controlled parentheses, to the stars above a Mayo townland). The effect is to suggest that an ancient text can sustain the poet's ethical commitment to the personal life, even when it involves suffering and atrocity.

The Ghost Orchid, in which passages from both the *Odyssey* and from the *Iliad* are employed as the basis of lyric verse, is also notable for a series of poems which derive from the Latin poet Ovid. As poems that highlight 'the fundamental interconnectedness of things' ('According to Pythagoras'), they endow Longley's pervasive ecological awareness with an air of sacred mystery. They also allow him to indulge a deepening interest in gender exchange in poems of the body which allow human sexuality to appear as a botanical process. 'A Flowering' begins 'Now that my body grows woman-like' and concludes in imagery that makes of sexual intercourse a biological miracle:

> Creating in an hour
> My own son's beauty, the truthfulness of my nipples,
> Petals that will not last long, that hang on and no more,
> Youth and its flower named after the wind, anemone.

'Mr $10\frac{1}{2}$' is good-humouredly delighted that even the most well-endowed male began life in the womb, 'As a wee girl, and I substitute for his two plums/Plum blossom, for his cucumber a yellowy flower'.

Poems in this volume where the body is a site of Ovidian gender exchange and the loves of plants, extend the range of Longley as love poet. For beginning with 'No Continuing City', the title poem of his first volume, the intimate strangeness of erotic experience has been a constant preoccupation of this poet. In a body of work that has admonished history with its manifold victims in a poetry which precisely apprehends the physical and natural worlds and which makes epic occasion the stuff of lyric emotion, Longley has repeatedly allowed sexual love to seem humankind's most profound, even sacral, experience of 'interconnectedness' with a material universe. 'The Linen Industry' in *The Echo Gate* is a key poem, with its elaborate conceit of the process whereby flax is transformed into linen likened to the transformative power of the erotic. *The Weather in Japan* (2000) contains poems that take patchwork quilting, sewing, embroidery, as controlling metaphors. They invest traditionally female activities with the power of gender-exchanging sexuality itself and with the tenderness of erotic mutuality which, in Longley's cosmos of feeling, is the ultimate force for good in the face of death.

> You love your body. So does Sydney. So do I.
> Communion is blankets and eiderdown and sheets.
> All I can think of is a quilt called *Broken Dishes*
> And spreading it out on the floor beneath his knees.
>
> ('Broken Dishes')

NOTES

1 Derek Mahon, 'Poetry in Northern Ireland', *20th Century Studies* (4, November, 1970), 90–2.
2 Derek Mahon, *Collected Poems* (Loughcrew: Gallery, 1999) and *The Hudson Letter* (Loughcrew: Gallery, 1995) and *The Yellow Book* (Loughcrew: Gallery, 1997).
3 In Derek Mahon, *Poems 1962–1978* (Oxford University Press, 1979).
4 Louis MacNeice, *Collected Poems*, ed. E.R. Dodds. (London: Faber and Faber), 1966, 231.
5 Both in *Poems 1962–1978*.
6 Derek Mahon, 'Introduction', *Selected Poems: Philippe Jaccottet* (Harmondsworth: Penguin, 1988), 11–14.
7 All Longley quotations and references from Michael Longley, *Poems 1963–1983* (Edinburgh: The Salamander Press; Dublin: Gallery, 1985); and *Gorse Fires* (London: Jonathan Cape, 1991), *The Ghost Orchid* (London: Jonathan Cape, 1995) and *The Weather in Japan* (London: Jonathan Cape, 2000).
8 The First World War poet Wilfred Owen in his Preface to a projected volume of 'war' poetry had asserted: 'Above all I am not concerned with Poetry. My subject is War, and the pity of War. The Poetry is in the pity'. *The Poems of Wilfred Owen*, edited with a Memoir by Edmund Blunden (London: Chatto and Windus, 1965), p. 40.
9 Peter McDonald, 'Lapsed Classics: Homer, Ovid and Michael Longley's Poetry' in *The Poetry of Michael Longley*, eds. Alan J. Peacock and Kathleen Devine (Gerrards Cross: Colin Smythe, 2000), p. 41.

9

FRANK SEWELL

Between two languages: poetry in Irish, English and Irish English

'Do you hear me whispering to you across the Golden Vale?
Do you hear me bawling to you across the hearthrug?'
(Paul Durcan, 'Ireland 1977')

Introduction: the position of Irish in contemporary Irish poetry

Irish literature has historically possessed what Thomas Kinsella calls a 'dual tradition', and continues to be written in the country's majority and minority languages, English and Irish, respectively. As the two languages keep up what Kinsella terms their 'dynamic interaction',[1] many Irish readers have increasingly turned at least one of their two ears to Irish language literature, in the original, in translation, and via critiques that take into account both languages for a more comprehensive representation and understanding of Ireland's art and eras. Therefore, whereas in some quarters a narrow, monoglot view of Ireland's poetry still exists,[2] recent critical studies of contemporary work recognise the need to account for the polyphony of voices which make up what Seán Ó Ríordáin called the 'fuaim na habhann' / river-sound[3] of the living stream of Irish writing.

Regarding the notice that poets in Irish, English, or both languages, take of each other, it must be said that Irish authors, like all others, freely tap into whatever international sources they wish; reading, translating and responding to the forms, styles and subject matter of literature from both far and near. But the 'near' in this equation does include the 'home' tradition, both past and present, and there is evidence that a growing number of Irish writers in either English or Irish are deeply engaging with work by their comrades in Irish and / or their comrades in English. The evidence is in the large amount of translation from Irish to English by most leading twentieth-century Irish poets, and the smaller amount of translation from English to Irish. There are dedications and conversations across the two languages, shared stages and pages, and regular reviews and criticism (by writers in one language) of poetry (in the other language), revealing mutual awareness, appreciation, and even disagreement.[4]

Twentieth-century poetry in Irish can be divided into three main periods. The first is the 1910s–1930s, the period of Patrick Pearse (1879–1916) and, afterwards, poets such as Liam Gógan (1891–1979) and Piaras Béaslaí (1881–1965). The second period is the mid-century era of Máirtín Ó Direáin (1910–88), Seán Ó Ríordáin (1916–77), and Máire Mhac an tSaoi (b. 1922). The third period is that of the Cork *INNTI*[5] generation and after, characterised by youthful vigour, modernity and internationalism. It includes poets such as Michael Davitt (b. 1950), Liam Ó Muirthile (b. 1950), Gabriel Rosenstock (b. 1949), Nuala Ní Dhomhnaill (b. 1952), Cathal Ó Searcaigh (b. 1956), Biddy Jenkinson (b. 1949), Louis de Paor (b. 1961) and Gearóid Mac Lochlainn (b. 1967).[6] The work of these poets will be discussed here in relation to significant themes in modern Irish poetry (including language, gender and sexuality). Following each generation of poets' handling of these themes is one way to appreciate the shifts in sensibility that mark key stages in the development of twentieth-century Irish poetry. Also, in order to highlight some of the main ways in which the two main languages of Irish literature interact, I will focus on bilingual writing, translation and influences across and between languages, and literary traditions, from within Ireland and beyond.

Language as a theme in modern Irish language poetry

Patrick Pearse was the founding father of twentieth-century poetry in Irish for one main reason: he was the first of his century to produce, in Irish, short lyric poems of personal feeling. He wrote to the contemporary moment, and did not tend to write about Irish itself as a subject in his literary work. Instead, he demonstrated, through his own work, the creative potential of the language. Yet, a decade later, Liam Gógan wrote this dispirited account of his own engagement with Irish:

Dom féin is duit-se b'fhearra choidhch	For me and you it would've been better
Go deo gan tigheacht id' ghoire	If I had never gone near you.
Do bheifeá féin id' bhláth gan teimheal	You'd still be an untarnished bloom
Is ní bheinn mar taoim gan toradh.	And I'd not be, as I am, rewardless.[7]

Gógan sometimes felt 'rewardless' but persevered, producing nine collections of poetry between 1919 and 1966. Moreover, he must have taken some pleasure from the wordplay and formal craftsmanship in the above poem. His sense of being rewardless was due to a discouraging lack of public recognition or appreciation – a condition that many modern poets could identify with, but far exaggerated for the minority-language poet.

In his prose work *Feamainn Bhealtaine* ('May seaweed', 111–13), Máirtín Ó Direáin invented the story of a poet called James Millane who wrote only in the 'Ifish' language (known to him alone), and who would never (as James Joyce did) have a book published with the words 'the Essential' before his name in the title. Irish, however, was essential for Ó Direáin, keeping him in touch with his roots in the Aran islands. Still, his fidelity to 'the dialect of the tribe' was balanced with his lesson from T.S. Eliot that the poet's job was partly to 'purify' that dialect.[8] His generation, therefore, not only retrieved neglected gems (words and phrases) from the vernacular but 'made their own of the language'. Also, if an idea or subject was first encountered, say, in English, it had to be de-Anglicised, deconstructed and rebuilt word by word (like stones in an Aran wall) in Irish. Then it could stand the test of linguistic surveyors such as 'Sean-Mhíchil' ('Old Michael'),[9] a guiding spirit from Ó Direáin's Aran childhood, whose native ear for Irish assures qualities such as authenticity and native-ness for his poetry. However, while traditional and natural use of his language was important for this Irish language poet, the point is that he was a genuine pluralist regarding languages and ideas: 'Ariamh níor dhiúltaigh solas / Ó na ceithre hairde nuair tháinig; / Ach iarraim ar an solas iasachta / Gan mo sholas féin a mhúchadh.' (I never knocked back light / from anywhere when it came / but I ask the foreign light / not to put out my own.)[10]

Seán Ó Ríordáin wrote that 'it wasn't always the subject that moved me to write poetry, but the language itself. Many poems [. . .] came from the stirring, the excitement of the language itself'.[11] Some critics felt that his linguistic excitement and thoughts 'stolen' from English[12] could produce a Hopkins-esque that was neither Irish nor English. Occasionally, his language was perhaps strained to an artificial-sounding level, but even the early Heaney had difficulty in shaking off Hopkins' influence. Silenced briefly by his critics, Ó Ríordáin made language a subject of his second collection, *Brosna* (1964); and had the last satiric word in 'Údar' ('Expert' or 'Author'), a poem about a character who takes so long to pursue 'perfect' Irish that he dies as he acquires it.[13]

Michael Hartnett, in 'Teanga Mise' (1978, 'I am a Language') gave the language its own voice as narrator: 'I am a language, the net that gathers every fish'.[14] Here Hartnett presents the language as a fisherman's net that can surprise by landing any kind of fish, regardless of strictures and expectations about the shape and size, etc., that an 'Irish' fish, or poem, should be. Language, he adds, is 'more noble' than any one country, religion or patriotic ideal, all of which tend or try to harness language to their cause. Such causes, religious and / or political, have taken a utilitarian view of language (in Ireland and other countries) by turning it into a sacred or

avenging (national) 'weapon'. For Hartnett, such a view of language is re-
ductive. However, he finds that, in the past, even Irish writers (including
James Clarence Mangan, W.B. Yeats and Padraic Pearse) have sometimes
been guilty of reducing language to a cypher, a symbol, in the service of a
cultural nationalist struggle. Consequently, language, as a narrator in Hartnett's poem, replies: 'I am not a hag, or ancient crone: / I am not Dark
Rosaleen, or A Poor Old Woman: / I am not a young woman with the walk
of a queen'. Here, the first line echoes Pearse's 'Old Woman of Beare' (a representation of Ireland and, by extension, the Irish language); the second line
recalls James Clarence Mangan's 'Dark Rosaleen'; and the third line clearly
quotes from Yeats's *Cathleen Ní Houlihan*.

The three works to which Hartnett alludes are key texts in the pantheon
of Irish political writing; all of them are highly emotive and effective literary works but also, to an extent, propaganda. The contemporary critical
argument is that these works reduce woman to a one-dimensional image
for Ireland; here Hartnett levels a similar criticism, but this time against a
mis-representation of the Irish language itself as a national symbol. Notably,
Hartnett does not respond by romanticising the language, or making it 'something sacred'; on the contrary, he delights in the language's liberty and capacity to be both 'the soul's music' and 'the bad talk you hear in the pub'.
Irish, for Hartnett, is 'a ribald language / anti-Irish' and, for that very reason,
is both essential for the Irish, and essentially Irish. The poet utters neither
a po-faced paean nor puritan prayer for the Irish language. Instead, he repeats, first and last, a simple image that conveys the breadth, scope and
unpredictability of Irish: 'I am a language, the net that gathers every fish'.
With this one line, Hartnett deftly counterbalances the negativity that Joyce
cast with Stephen Dedalus' famous remark in *A Portrait of the Artist*, that
'when the soul of a man is born in this country there are nets flung at it to
hold it back from flight. You talk to me of nationality, language, religion. I
shall try to fly by those nets'.[15] Hartnett's poem shows that the net of language (Irish as well as English) still hauls in unpredictable, necessary and
mouth-watering catches. Sometimes contemporary poets worry about the
minority status, and future, of the Irish language[16] but they are writing out
their worries, and much more, in Irish language verse. Their original and
translated work is reaching, and teaching, a growing audience at home and
abroad – an audience that includes, and inspires, language-learners.

Gender in modern Irish language poetry

Eavan Boland has written of Irish literature as a male-dominated tradition
where, previously, women were presented as symbols and one-dimensional

objects under the male gaze. The journey from being represented as 'fictive queens and national sibyls', to becoming the authors of their own fates and poems ('dáin') is, therefore, often mirrored in the many 'journey' motifs in women's writing: see Boland's 'The Journey' and Nuala Ní Dhomhnaill's 'Turas na Scríne' ('Journey to the Shrine'). Irish women poets, including Medbh McGuckian, have looked to, and beyond, the Irish literary tradition to find models and examples of first-rate women poets. They have often tapped into the Russian and American traditions: to Anna Akhmatova, Marina Tsvetaeva, Denise Levertov, Tess Gallagher and the feminist Adrienne Rich. Why look to these international poets for aesthetic solidarity? Ní Dhomhnaill, for one, has described Ireland's literature as 'sexist and masculinist to the core'. She has labelled women's contribution to that tradition as 'the hidden Ireland' – redeploying Daniel Corkery's cultural nationalist book title in a feminist light. Looking to the tradition, even with the benefit of her Celtic studies, Ní Dhomhnaill finds little evidence of female foremothers' work, although there is occasional mention of their existence in legend and history.[17]

Historically, it seems that women's poetry, especially laments, were not deemed worthy of inclusion in the handwritten manuscripts. One rare example of a work that was recorded, is the 'Lament for Art O'Leary' by Eibhlín Ní Chonaill. This international classic could not have emerged from a literary vacuum; therefore, there must have been an underclass of women poets and keening women. Yet, even folk tradition could be a cold place for a woman poet: she was viewed as taboo, or a curse, signalling either a tongue-lashing or that poetry (a hereditary gift) would die out in the family whose daughter inherited it. More recently, Seán Ó Ríordáin expressed surprise at the concept of a woman poet, and saw verse-making as a male activity, requiring masculine strength and fatherhood:

An é go n-iompaíonn baineann fireann	Is it that the feminine turns masculine
Nuair a iompaíonn bean ina file?	when a woman turns into a poet?
Ní file ach filíocht an bhean.	A woman is not a poet, but poetry.[18]

Ó Ríordáin's word-play suggests he was half-joking, as the poem ends with the bathetic remark that 'a man is not a poet either; he is nothing'. But he must also have been half-serious in this poem, which is one of several that explore notions of what is feminine and masculine; the division between them; and, perhaps, Ó Ríordáin's own mid-century, male crises and confusions about gender and masculinity.

Meanwhile Boland and others were striving to prove that they could be poets, and no longer 'poetry', by producing work to surpass the males. A new generation of feminist critics also emerged and cast doubt on the accepted, mainly male, version of the canon. Some past women poets did come to the attention of Celtic scholars.[19] Their absence from the manuscripts (the anthologies of their day) mirrors, in Ní Dhomhnaill's view, the relatively small amount of space currently allowed for women writers, whose exclusion and limited representation points to a fear and repression of the 'deep feminine' in Irish minds and society.[20] In response, Ní Dhomhnaill has reversed the male gaze of earlier poetry and cast a bold eye on life and love, challenging male tradition and authority. Her poems can be sexy, funny, tragic, exultant, rebellious – neither the sky nor subconscious is the limit. She has also ransacked history and mythology for female masks and voices, in poems characterised by female agency; where the 'she' is in the driving seat; and when 'she' talks, even the male warrior Cú Chulainn listens.[21]

From female warriors to male worriers

Gender, as a subject, has been diversely treated by male writers. Early twentieth-century poetry by Yeats, Pearse (executed leader of the 1916 Easter Rising) and others was dominated by the warrior image of Cú Chulainn and the mitre of St Patrick and the Church. Certainly, the rifle and ecclesiastical staff, rather than Dubh Ruis's gaming-stick,[22] loomed large as images on the national totem pole.

In the mid-century poetry of Ó Direáin, manly fortitude and constancy were often symbolised by phallic symbols of standing trees and stout oars; but also 'masculine' stone as compared to 'feminine' wax. This sharp delineation increasingly troubled the poet himself: he feared that his youthful abandonment of risky, physical toil on Aran for desk and artistic work in the city, was responsible for a 'softness' that he detected and detested in himself. Softness, inconstancy and malleability were qualities which he distrusted (in himself and other males) and associated with the feminine or female who, in some poems, could be swayed or 'turned' by a false whisper.[23] What Ó Direáin admired was the constancy and steadfastness of those who do not deviate from their vision, faith, love or loyalty; consequently, his eulogies are for dedicated artists (including J.M. Synge and Máirtín Ó Cadhain) and uncompromising rebels such as 'Mná na hAiséirí' ('Women of the 1916 Easter Rising').

Ó Ríordáin's imagination was saturated with the language and symbolism of Catholicism, including the Fall that 'split the beautiful morning / into male and female' (*Eireaball Spideoige*, 71). This division (as in Ó Direáin's work) was not always so clear cut. In 'An Bás' ('Death'), Ó Ríordáin recalled a period of illness when, accepting the immanence of death, he 'understood / the joy of a woman / expecting her partner, / although I am not female'.

Not female, Ó Ríordáin's aesthetic, nevertheless, demanded that he fly from self to self to occupy a horse's hooves, ('Malairt', 'Swapping Places'), a cat's paws, ('Eireablú', 'Tailed' in *Tar Éis Mo Bháis*) or somebody else's stilettos:

> I look at a bottle and I am bottled. I think of a woman and I am womaned. That is, the bottle and the woman lift me out of myself, take away the burden of 'me-ness'. To think of them is to be bottled, womaned. A thought is a kind of magic wand. This flight is necessary. You'd go insane if you were always yourself. Life and self are multifarious. We have to be bottles, horses, prayers or else we'd be mad. A lunatic is someone who has tripped and fallen into himself and can't get out . . . or into a bottle and can't get out. That's the way it is. 'No Loitering'. A person must keep travelling from self to self.[24]

Such 'travelling' points to a key transgressive element in Ó Ríordáin's aesthetic. For example, if it took masculine strength to wrest poems from memory and rock, to struggle like a Gandhi or St Barra with metaphysics (in 'Oileán agus Oileán Eile' / One Island and Another'), he elsewhere presented versemaking as a feminine birthing process (in 'A Sheanfhilí, Múinídh Dom Glao' / 'Old Poets, Teach Me the Call').

Sexuality in modern Irish poetry

The early twentieth century in Ireland was the period of a national movement towards independence. Members of resistance movements developed a holier-than-thou attitude to their imperialist enemies. This attitude was evident in writings by Pearse and other nationalists. The effect on Pearse's poetry was a tendency to 'renounce' physical pleasures and worldly goods, in favour of abstract concepts (the sovereign nation) and holy ideals (sacrifice). Sexuality, in his poetry, is repressed because of his Victorian morality, and / or because of his Irish Jansenist Catholicism, and / or because of possibly the latent homosexuality of which he may, or may not, have been aware.

Male poets of the mid-century mostly avoided writing about sex. Yet, occasionally, they surprised readers with a frankness about sexuality: see Ó Direáin's 'Ó Morna' and Mhac an tSaoi's 'Quatrains of Mary Hogan'.[25] In 'Ó Morna', Ó Direáin sympathises with a dissolute landlord who forces himself on some peasant girls and is welcomed by others, including 'Cat' of the Glen. The poem has been called immoral but Ó Direáin's stance was amoral, honest and influenced by Nietzsche's *Beyond Good and Evil*. Mostly, however, Ó Direáin was influenced by Eliot to 'rubbish' modern life and sex, in the city: compare 'Ár Ré Dhearóil' ('Our Wretched Era') with Part 3 of *The Waste Land*. Both present a bleak and passionless portrait of twentieth-century relationships. For Ó Direáin, in 'Ár Ré Dhearóil', women are either too free with their sexuality, or too repressed. Either way, the 'wretched era' of Ireland's mid-century appears a 'sterile' and 'infertile' time in Ó Direáin's mid-career poems which themselves seem born of frustration. As a traditionalist, however, he apparently approved of healthy sex-lives in long-term, marital, relationships; and he wasn't beyond using sexual metaphors. He once lampooned his critics as 'eunuchs' envying the man with 'rocks'.[26]

Ó Ríordáin (like Ó Direáin) was disappointed in love, as suggested in the poem in *Eireaball Spideoige*, 'Ní raibh sí dílis' ('She was not faithful'). Afterwards, partly because of his TB and post-Catholic conscience, Ó Ríordáin led a common mid-century Irish life of frustration. Repressed sexuality is one source, perhaps, of the 'masculine' and 'feminine' imagery and vocabulary of his poems. Certainly, in his last poems, as in 'Préachán' ('Crow'), he regretted the bad timing that left him too old to enjoy the sexual revolution:

Tá mná na haoise seo	Women these days
Níos féile féna gcuid	are more generous with what they've got
Ná bantracht óige an fhir:	than the women of this man's youth:
Trua cás an fhireannaigh	what a pity for the man
A chaill a chumas fir	who lost his virility
Sara mbog an bhaineannach.	before womanhood shifted/softened/loosened.

Another late poem, 'Do Striapach' ('For a Prostitute'), eulogises a prostitute for openly plying her trade with the courage and honesty of a saint.

Máire Mhac an tSaoi's first poems caused a sensation partly for their frankness about female desire and attraction: her poems feature a male 'big blonde' called 'Jack'; and the dark-haired, red-lipped 'Naoise, son of Ushna'.[27] More openly sexual and defiant in content, is 'Ceathrúintí Mháire Ní hÓgáin' ('Quatrains of Mary Hogan'):

Beagbheann ar amhras daoine,	Indifferent to people's suspicions,
Beagbheann ar chros an sagart,	Indifferent to ban of priest,
Ar gach ní ach bheith sínte	Indifferent to everything except
Idir tú is an falla.	Lying between you and the wall.[28]

Since *INNTI*, the 1970s generation, writing about sexuality is part of a general modern Irish attitude of saying boo to taboos: Michael Davitt celebrates a pair of lovers' 'mysterious union' by focusing on menstruation; while Liam Ó Muirthile sensitively celebrates the first 'tearing of the knot' of sexual experience, which leaves streaks of blood 'setting in a seal of love over my heart and over us'.[29] But most notorious for sexing the cherry of Irish literature, is Nuala Ní Dhomhnaill whose *Selected Poems* and *Pharaoh's Daughter* contain poems about women engaged in illicit relationships; women 'looking at a man' as a mouth-watering sex-object; teasing male authority; declaring war on 'all the men of Ireland'; and cutting 'Masculus Giganticus Hibernicus' down to size. She has magically revised the canon of Irish literature by transforming the male, this time, into an embodiment of an island or landscape in 'Oileán' ('Island'). And, if earlier male poets were worried about female constancy, Ní Dhomhnaill presents them, in *Pharaoh's Daughter*, with the nightmare Mrs of 'An Bhean Mhídhílis' ('The Unfaithful Wife'). If Ó Direáin was concerned that individuals should be as rock-steady as a 'standing tree', Ní Dhomhnaill's trees have lovely bunches of coconuts and yearly how's your father, despite male/female tree-segregation.[30] Sexuality, in Ní Dhomhnaill's work, also has mythic, psychological and social dimensions: it offers (even if fleetingly, as in 'Dún' / 'Stronghold') moments of balance and harmony, as symbolised by the union of the Celtic earth goddess and sky god. Some Ní Dhomhnaill poems are suffused with the afterglow of sexuality, including the 'silk-sheet' sensuousness of 'Leaba Shíoda'; some are sensationally mouth-watering in sound and sense; some are intensely moving in their evocation of the pain of separation.

Cathal Ó Searcaigh's love poetry matches that of Ní Dhomhnaill in its stirring evocation of past passion and tender longing. Whereas Pearse started the twentieth century quelling his passions, Ó Searcaigh ends it, summoning his passions and revelling in the physical joys and pleasures of life. Whereas Pearse asked 'Cad Chuige Díbh Dom' Chiapadh?' ('Why do you torment me / desires of my heart?'), Ó Searcaigh, eighty years later, invites the 'passions of [his] youth' to take him over, in 'A Mhianta M'Óige'.[31] Whereas Pearse's desires are an unleashed houndpack, greedily hunting him down, and he wishes them held back, Ó Searcaigh calls for the houndpack of his senses to be unleashed and unbound. Comparison of these two poems is invited by similarities of diction, rhythm and imagery. However, the contrast between the sensibilities of the two poets could not be more stark, and is indicative of the journey of twentieth-century Irish poetry (and society) from the repression of the 1910s to the gradual freedoms of the 1990s.

Even between the mid-century and its close, there was a remarkable shift in attitudes towards sexuality and its expression in society and poems. Ó Searcaigh, like Davitt, is a great admirer of Ó Direáin ('the liberator of the word'). Yet, when Ó Searcaigh recycles Ó Direáin's image of the steadfast tree, one finds that if the arms aren't openly embracing, the roots are playing footsie under the surface.[32] Ó Searcaigh's 'Crainn' ('Trees'), in *Homecoming*, have more in common with Ní Dhomhnaill's 'Coco-de-Mer'[33] and Paul Muldoon's 'Wind and Tree' than with Ó Direáin's lonelier trees in a colder decade: 'Géag-uaigneach gach crann / Scartha leis an uile' (Branch-lonely is every tree, / Separated from everything.)[34] Ní Dhomhnaill's male and female trees were at least allowed to tryst once per year; Ó Searcaigh would extend this license to same-sex trees and lovers 'any season of the year'.[35] Recently, Ó Searcaigh invoked the guiding spirits of the Greek poet Constantin Cavafy and the Greek Irishman Oscar Wilde, to speak out openly and honestly about 'Greek' or gay love, which turns out (in *Na Buachaillí Bána* and *Out in the Open*) to be the same as any other in longing, longevity, lust and loss. Sadly, some readers have been as loud in their condemnation of the erotic poems, as others have been silent regarding the sexual abuses which the poet highlights in 'Gort na gCnámh' ('The Field of Bones').[36] Ó Searcaigh is brave in tackling topics which include gay love, sex and sexual abuse. There was gay and erotic poetry earlier in the tradition but it has re-emerged with a vengeance and confidence since the civil, women's, gay rights eras.

Bilingual writers

In the twentieth century, Pearse was Ireland's first major bilingual author, producing work in Irish, English, and sometimes both. In diction and rhythm, he was a faithful and effective translator of his own work, if one ignores the outmoded use of 'thy' and 'ye' in his English versions. After Pearse, the list of Irish bilingual poets is an impressive roll-call, including Brendan Behan, Pearse Hutchinson, Michael Hartnett, Eoghan Ó Tuairisc, and recently, Mícheál Ó Siadhail, Eithne Strong and Celia de Fréine.

Introducing the anthology *The Bright Wave*, the writer and critic Alan Titley remarks that 'the bilingual writer in Ireland runs the danger of being treated with suspicion by both traditions without gaining the entire respect of either'. In Eoghan Ó Tuairisc's case, the writer wasn't so much viewed with suspicion as, often, not viewed at all by one language group or the other. Confusion resulted partly because Ó Tuairisc wrote in Irish under his Gaelic name, but in English, as Eugene Watters. Therefore, it was not always clear that the author of 'Aifreann na Marbh' was, simultaneously, the author of *The Weekend of Dermot and Grace* (both published 1964). However, Ó Tuairisc was a typical example of a plurilingual author, writing in two languages just as freely as he read from several other languages and literary traditions, including Chinese. He saw no reason to deprive himself of linguistic and literary roots or routes. Moreover, in his view, Irish was just as necessary for Irish writers in English as it was for their comrades-in-Irish: 'the Anglo-Irish writer without a mastery of Irish will always be a colonial writer, member of a satellite culture, speaking and writing a provincial dialect'.[37] That statement may not sound very generous to his comrades-in-English-only, but Ó Tuairisc as a man and writer was generous, giving of himself, his talent and time by writing in two languages, and helping to make Irish language literature accessible to readers without Irish: for example, he translated short stories by Máirtín Ó Cadhain in *The Road to Bright City*, and edited a unique and revealing, early bilingual anthology, *Rogha an Fhile / The Poet's Choice*. Like other bilingual authors, Ó Tuairisc, writing in Irish and / or in English, was deeply engaged with his craft and whichever, at the time, was his language of composition. It happens that the bulk and best of Ó Tuairisc's work is in Irish.

The author most successful in both languages, however was Michael Hartnett. From Co Limerick, Hartnett was the author of twenty books of poetry and many volumes of translated work. Writing in English, he came to fame at an early age. One of his best poems is 'Death of an Irishwoman' which concludes powerfully and movingly with two triads back to back – an example of the use of traditional Irish (Gaelic or even Celtic) techniques in English language poetry. Hartnett generally identified with the subaltern or downtrodden. In the mid-1970s, when a coalition government was further marginalising the Irish language in Ireland, he decided to bid publicly *A Farewell to English* (1975), and to write exclusively in Irish. Partly, he was reacting against a new spirit of Anglicisation and materialism which was evident in the Irish establishment. Yet, because he was a very accomplished and successful writer in English, Hartnett's move to writing in Irish was dramatic and daring. His motives were complex, mainly aesthetic, linguistic and cultural rather than simply the result of any narrow form of nationalism:

caithfidh mé mo cheird	I have to hone my craft
a ghearradh as coill úr:	in a wood that's new:
mar tá mo gharrán Béarla	for my English grove
crann-nochta seasc.	is naked, barren.[38]

Despite some raised eyebrows at the new 'convert', Hartnett's first work in Irish was welcomed. The poets Liam Ó Muirthile and Seamus Heaney felt that he was fusing Irish and Spanish influences (especially Lorca) in a vital and revitalising fashion. Several critics even claimed that Hartnett's poetry was more native or traditional than work by the Anglo-American influenced *INNTI* group. This critique irked writers such as Ó Muirthile who was impressed by Hartnett's work, especially the shorter lyric poems.[39] Yet, among some readers, including Cathal Ó Searcaigh, the preference for Hartnett's shorter lyrics is accompanied by a slight doubt regarding the much longer poems, including 'An Phurgóid' ('Purgatory') and 'Cúlú Íde' ('The Retreat of Ita Cagney'). For native speakers, Hartnett's acquired Irish does not always read as naturally as his work in English to which he later returned: 'my English dam bursts and out stroll all my bastards. / Irish shakes its head' (from *Inchicore Haiku*).

Hartnett's return to writing in English was as natural as that water image suggests, and the damming of English as artificial as that image suggests. Most importantly, he remained a productive poet, writing in, and between, two languages, and translating from past and present, home and abroad. He left behind him a unique body of work with many aspects and layers. For Hartnett was never one-dimensional: he was creative with a destructive personality (an alcoholic); he was partly a 'stranger' and partly a Gael; he saw poetry both as a gift and a curse. Shortly before he died, he said of poetry that 'we met at the crossroads, and we got married'. To the end, he was still at the crossroads, where languages and cultures, lives and times meet:

> Chonaic mé, mar scáileanna,   I saw, in the form of shadows,
> mo spailpíní fánacha,   my 'economic migrants',
> is in ionad sleán nó rámhainn acu   and instead of shovel or spade,
> bhí rós ar ghualainn cháich.   there was a rose on every shoulder.[40]

English language poets and Irish

Conversations between writers in Irish and in English (in the form of listening-in, dialogue and translation) have become most common in the twentieth century. The conversation has not always been conducted on an equal basis: Ní Dhomhnaill once remarked that 'if Lady Gregory came round to me I'd give her all the seanchas [folklore] she wanted, but in my heart of hearts I'd be thinking [. . .] how come she's up there with her silk skirt, and I in my báinín [peasant dress]; and how's she better than me?'.[41] One recalls also the image of Yeats in the 'peasant' cottages, collecting folklore to fill and decorate his own voluminous pages; or the shadowy Synge noting what he heard through chinks in floorboards or by the fire, to inspire his own dramatisations.[42] Were these spy-like authors cannibalising the 'native' roots and branches of Irish culture? And / or re-potting them in Irish English?

Irish language promoters, including Pearse, first felt suspicious of (then-called) 'Anglo-Irish' authors, and believed that truly Irish literature could only be written in Irish. Increasingly impressed, however, by 'Anglo-' Irish writing, Pearse, and most others, soon took the view that Ireland could benefit culturally and internationally by having high-quality literature in two languages. Meanwhile, Irish writers in English were convinced that a fusion of 'Gaelic' literature (syntax, imagery, style, personae, etc.) with their English language and international aesthetics, would prove uniquely inspiring and liberating both culturally and politically. Some leant heavily on translations from Irish to English by Douglas Hyde and other Celtic scholars. Others such as Gregory and Synge learnt and translated from Irish. They also encouraged

Irish language authors, prompting Hyde to write his play *Casadh an tSúgáin* ('The Twisting of the Rope').

In the mid-twentieth century, there were some deaf and blindspots between Irish writers in English and those in Irish: Eavan Boland was unaware of Máire Mhac an tSaoi's encouraging example; and Seán Ó Ríordáin heard on the radio (from two leading poets in English) that 'poetry in Ireland had been quiescent in the 1950s' – the period when his generation was blossoming.[43] Contrastingly, there were poets in the tradition of Yeats, including Austin Clarke, who sought to apply the techniques of Irish language verse to their English language poems, increasing their aesthetic range and options. This, however, was sometimes viewed as a shallow attempt at authenticity, that is, to sound more Irish (or what today would be seen as cringingly 'Oirish'). 'Irishness' as a criteria for art was rejected by Patrick Kavanagh who perceived cultural nationalism, by the mid-century, as 'anti-art', detrimental to the imagination. Kavanagh doubted whether Irish language writers could produce the real McCoy of art when, it seemed to him, they would get away with anything as long as it was written in Irish. Unable to read Irish, what he really distrusted was the critical and cultural climate of his day; he did, however, evoke the spirit of an earlier local Gaelic poet in 'Art McCooey'.

Before Kavanagh, Louis MacNeice betrayed hostility to the Irish language and the cultural movement to promote it in literature and society. In his autobiography, for example, he wrongly assumed that Gaelic Leaguers were 'one-minded'[44] when they were, at least, bilingual and (like Seán Ó Ríordáin) subject to as many cultural divisions as MacNeice himself and most other Irish people. Also, rather oddly for a reader of classical languages, MacNeice dismissed still extant 'Gaelic' as a 'half-dead' language in Part XVI of his occasionally ill-tempered masterpiece, *Autumn Journal*. Writers in Irish, however, were neither suspicious nor hostile to the work of their comrades-in-English. Actually, they were appreciative: Ó Ríordáin of Yeats for his honesty, and of Joyce for his craft and daring; while Ó Direáin eulogised Synge in 'Homage to J.M. Synge'. The Irish language poets occasionally even learnt strategies from Irish writers in English whom they celebrated in poems and criticism.[45]

In 1999, John Montague returned some of the compliment and the spotlight (mostly given to writers in English due to the prevalence of that language at home and abroad) to his peer in Irish, Seán Ó Ríordáin.[46] Montague has also produced translations from Irish; written of his personal experience of the two-tongued, and sometimes tongue-tied, condition of the Irish people; based poems on the tradition of dinnseanchas / place-lore and placenames, and on personae from Irish language literature, including 'Mad Sweeney'. He has even built poems on Gaelic Irish and Scottish models. For example, the poem 'Like Dolmens round my Childhood, the Old People' consists of self-contained verses, and testifies to the continuance of 'ancient' ways.[47]

Most Southern Irish, and Northern Catholic, poets encounter Irish language and literature at school, meeting poetry in both languages around the same time. One upshot is the large amount of translation from Irish (among other languages) that Irish poets in English produce: key examples are Thomas Kinsella's *The Táin* and *Poems of the Dispossessed*; and Seamus Heaney's *Sweeney Astray*. These texts represent modern poets' engagement with earlier Irish literature (which is mostly in Irish), and their attempt to synthesise their strand of the Irish tradition (in English) with the pre-existing, strand in Irish. Their interest is not simply antiquarian or nationalistic, but stems from genuine aesthetic interest in the content and forms of (among others) the 'home' tradition, which includes poems that give insights into the Irish past and present, and pointers to images, concepts and techniques for new work. However, one difference between the translations of Kinsella and those of Heaney, is that Kinsella mostly limits himself to past classics, while Heaney translates works by past masters but also by contemporaries, including Ó Searcaigh and Ní Dhomhnaill.

It would be wrong to think that only poets from an Irish, nationalist or Catholic background, have engaged with Irish language literature. Twentieth-century Irish Protestant poets have found their own inroads into, and mirror images in, the 'Gaelic' tradition. Yeats as a cultural nationalist embraced the latter. MacNeice was suspicious but identified with, notably, the voyager St Brendan in the poem 'Western Landscape'. And Derek Mahon observed, circa 1971, that, *previously*, some poets, such as Michael Longley and James Simmons, had deprived themselves of the 'benefits of the "Irishness" at their disposal'.[48] Mahon accounted for the refusal of such poets to engage with their native Irish inheritance by explaining that they had first to be true to their own 'dissociated sensibilities' and to their 'diffuse and fortuitous' Anglo-American and Anglo-Irish interests and influences.

Mahon's own example, however, suggests that a dissociated sensibility like his, is free also to engage deeply with the native Irishness at his disposal: see 'I am Raftery' and 'An Bonnán Buí' ('The Yellow Bittern').[49] Significantly, both Longley and Simmons later did engage with their Irish inheritance and Irish-ness. Longley has become a close reader (in translation) of poetry in Irish, translating a poem by Ní Dhomhnaill and reviewing poetry by Ó Searcaigh. But the most dramatic turn-around has come from Simmons who once mockingly entitled a poem 'From the Irish'. Instead of the expected translation, the poem satirically delivers a bomb-shell 'from the Irish'. Later, Simmons crossed over 'to the Irish', sighting his neo-bardic Poets' House in the Donegal Gaeltacht, with the help of Ó Searcaigh, and the enrolment of international students writing in English and / or Irish.

In the post-Heaney generation, Irish has surfaced diversely in English language poetry: Paul Durcan has mocked tokenistic and 'official' use of Irish in the southern state in the sexual revolutionary poem 'Making Love outside Áras an Uachtaráin' (the President's residence); and there are also some deft, macaronic turns of two languages in his farewell address from the bilingual writer and translator 'Mícheál Mac Liammóir'. Paul Muldoon first wrote poems in Irish before switching to English, feeling he had a greater command of the latter. Yet Irish remains an influence: his early poetry included dinnseanchas / placename poems such as 'Clonfeacle', playing on the sound and sense of the name; his vowel rhymes, which surprise non-Irish commentators, are influenced by the Irish language poetry which he studied at school; he is also known as a technically and imaginatively gifted translator who plays, simultaneously, with both languages. For instance, the word 'Astrakhan' is something Muldoon added to his translation of Ní Dhomhnaill's 'clóca uaithne' ('green cloak') in 'Deora Duibhshléibhe' ('Dora Dooley'). The phrase *The Astrakhan Cloak* then became the title of Ní Dhomhnaill and Muldoon's 1993 bilingual collection, partly because 'astrakhan' is a pun on the Irish 'aistriúchán' which means 'translation'. Muldoon also confessed that the only worthwhile image 'worth a fuck' in his 1994 sequence, *The Prince of the Quotidian* was borrowed from Ní Dhomhnaill (pp. 38–40).

Ciaran Carson was brought up in Belfast in an Irish-speaking household, and his narrative poems are influenced by his father and other traditional storytellers and techniques. In *First Language*, Carson included one poem in Irish (untranslated); and he has kept up-to-date with Irish language verse, translating the newest poets (Gearóid Mac Lochlainn), contemporaries (Ní Dhomhnaill), and Ó Ríordáin's 'Malairt' ('Second Nature') which, he writes, 'I have been trying to translate for about half of my life'.[50] Medbh McGuckian has written about language shifts and loss in 'The Dream-Language of Fergus': 'conversation is as necessary / among these familiar campus trees / as the apartness of torches'.[51] She herself has recently 'conversed' along with Eiléan Ní Chuilleanáin (an Irish speaker who writes in English), by co-translating Ní Dhomhnaill's poetry in *The Water Horse*.

Irish language poets and English

In 'Solas', quoted above, Ó Direáin had stated the position of all twentieth-century Irish language poets: 'I never knocked back light / from anywhere when it came / but I ask the foreign light / not to drown out my own'. This 'light' has come in the form of international poetry, criticism and philosophy, and favourite writers from wherever, whenever. Their 'light' or inspiration has been trans-lated (borne across), not to 'drown' or dilute the Irish language tradition but to shake and stir its own inner lights and those of its writers.

Meanwhile, relationships between Irish language poets and English, have been varied: Ó Direáin was a native Irish speaker, less comfortable in English – though he carefully translated one of his poems for Ó Tuairisc's anthology *The Poet's Choice*. Ó Ríordáin, however, first wrote poems in English, but quickly realised that his work in Irish was better, and that he was more involved with the Irish language. An insufficient number of poems by these authors have been translated (by various poets) in bilingual anthologies, and also to accompany some criticism. Their peer, Máire Mhac an tSaoi translated some of her own poems for anthologies, and also edited and translated one bilingual anthology (*Trasládáil/* 'Ferrying across'). Her English versions, however, sound rather folksy, and misrepresent the originals, which can be difficult to translate.

Many poets of the *INNTI* generation have published translations of their work in anthologies and in popular bilingual 'selected poems'. The translations are often by the best of their contemporaries in English – some of whom (including Heaney and Muldoon) know Irish well. Poets and translators often collaborate on the translations, and some of those in the bilingual anthology *The Bright Wave / An Tonn Gheal* have become as famous as the originals. (This anthology, together with *The Flowering Tree / An Crann faoi Bhláth*, provides a useful introduction to modern poetry in Irish.)

Arguably, one reason for the concentration of critical interest in poetry by Ní Dhomhnaill and Ó Searcaigh is the success and wide-availability of their bilingual editions. Their work is remarkable in itself, of course; it is impressive in quality, originality, imagination, language and range. Yet, it sometimes seems unfair that these two poets are often spotlighted without reference to others, especially those (including Biddy Jenkinson and Louis de Paor) who don't allow their work to be published in English language translation *in Ireland*. In future, more room should be allowed for critics to highlight the full range of authors writing in Irish.

Ní Dhomhnaill's early *Selected Poems* features translations by the bilingual author Michael Hartnett but also carefully-worded versions by Ní Dhomhnaill herself. They resemble the 'cribs' which she provides for poet-translators with little Irish. These cribs, as she calls them, are underrated by the poet herself, but often provide the groundwork for English versions that could stand as poems in that target language. Publication of the original poems with facing translations by Heaney, Muldoon, *et al.*, in *Pharaoh's Daughter* have run into many editions, and even more languages. Muldoon stood out as such a fine interpreter of Ní Dhomhnaill's Irish that he was a welcome choice as translator for *The Astrakhan Cloak*. The decision to have one translator, her leading peer in English, engage with Ní Dhomhnaill's work at length, was inspired and productive. Bilingual readers of this bilingual book were doubly entertained, if sometimes puzzled, by Muldoon's own characteristic formalism and some other informed (and approved by Ní Dhomhnaill) deviations from the originals. Ní Dhomhnaill, meanwhile, had already been reading Muldoon's own work, and there are some signs of his influence in this volume (including the journey / 'Immram' sequence). All in all, it makes for a unique and multifaceted collaboration. Most recently, Ní Dhomhnaill chose two female writers in English (Medbh McGuckian and Eiléan Ní Chuilleanáin) to represent her in that language. This creative experiment yielded fantastic (feminist) results in *The Water Horse* (1999).

Cathal Ó Searcaigh's bilingual collection *An Bealach 'na Bhaile / Homecoming* includes translations by a range of poets and translators, from Heaney to lesser known writers. This text, with facing translations, is immensely popular with poetry-lovers and also with students of the language, who compare or rely upon the two versions together. Ó Searcaigh's second bilingual volume uses the present author as translator. The project attempts to heed Alan Titley's warning that 'the rustle of sheets in one language' could become 'the scratching of the bedpost' in another.[52] This warning was important because Ó Searcaigh was unleashing his 'coming out' and most erotic poems to date, which required that the translations should attempt to be as 'fresh' as the originals.

Much thought has recently been given to the subject of translation, in an Irish context, by Gearóid Mac Lochlainn in *Sruth Teangacha / Stream of Tongues*. The 'author's notes' in this collection express the worry (shared by Louis de Paor and Biddy Jenkinson) that English language translations 'often gain an autonomy of their own and eclipse the Irish', the original poem. Jenkinson and de Paor respond by not allowing their work to be translated in Ireland because Irish people should either take the effort to read the original, or leave it. Mac Lochlainn, however, essentially an Irish language poet and musician, has increasingly played on the two languages to produce macaronic sound and sense effects. He has also played around with the questions and contexts surrounding translation:

Amanna, éiríonn tú tuirseach	Sometimes you get tired talking
de chluasa falsa Éireannacha.	to lazy Irish ears. Tired
Féinsásamh an *monoglot* a deir leat –	of self-satisfied monoglots who say
'It sounds lovely. I wish I had the Irish.	– *'It sounds lovely. I wish I had the Irish.*
Don't you do translations?'	*Don't you do translations?'*[53]

Reading this, and other twentieth-century poetry from Ireland, I am convinced that 'monoglots' are missing out by restricting themselves to (what Ní Dhomhnaill has called) linguistic and cultural apartheid. 'Culture', James Stephens wrote, 'is a conversation between equals'.[54] The Irish and English languages may not be equal in terms of power relationships and numbers of speakers, but the conversations (including silences) between these languages, make up a huge portion of what we can uniquely call Irish literary culture.

NOTES

1 Thomas Kinsella, *The Dual Tradition: An Essay on Poetry and Politics in Ireland* (Manchester: Carcanet Press, 1995); and (ed.), Preface, *The New Oxford Book of Irish Verse* (Oxford University Press, 1986), p. xxvii.

2 See, for instance, Dillon Johnston, in *Irish Poetry After Joyce*, 2nd edn. (Syracuse University Press 1997), p. xix: ' "Irish Poetry" means what most of the English-reading world recognises: "poetry written in English, from or pertaining mostly to Ireland" '. But see also his 'Afterword', pp. 286–98.

3 Seán Ó Ríordáin, 'Éist le Fuaim na hAbhann' ('Listen to the River-sound'), *Eireaball Spideoige* (Dublin: Sáirséal and Dill, 1952, 1986), p. 47.

4 Gabriel Rosenstock has translated a selection of Seamus Heaney's poetry into Irish; while two-way translation has occurred between Nuala Ní Dhomhnaill and Michael Longley. See Rosenstock, *Conlán: dánta le Seamus Heaney* (Dublin: Coiscéim, 1989); and Ní Dhomhnaill, *Pharaoh's Daughter* (Loughcrew: Gallery, 1990) and *Cead Aighnis* (An Daingean: An Sagart, 1998). See also mutual reviewing by Ní Dhomhnaill, 'The Irish for English' (a review of Ciaran Carson's *The Irish for No*), in *The Irish Review*, 4 (1988), pp. 116–18 and Michael Longley, 'A Going Back to Sources' (a review of Cathal Ó Searcaigh's *Homecoming*), in *Poetry Ireland Review* 39 (Autumn, 1993), pp. 92–6. Disagreement can be found in Seamus Heaney, 'Forked Tongues, Céilís and Incubators', *Fortnight*, 197 (Sept. 1983), pp. 113–16. See also the journal *Irish Pages*, edited by Chris Agee and Ó Searcaigh, English and Irish poets respectively.

5 *INNTI* was founded as a poetry broadsheet by students at Cork University in March 1970, and relaunched as a journal by Michael Davitt, a founding editor, in 1980.

6 Introductions to these poets can be found in Robert Welch (ed.), *The Oxford Companion to Irish Literature* (Oxford University Press, 1996), and Gregoir Ó Dúill (ed.), *Fearann Pinn: Filíocht 1900 to 1999* (Dublin: Coiscéim, 2000).

7 Liam Gógan, 'An Ghaeidhilge' ('To Irish', trans. by Bernard O'Donoghue). See Duffy, N. and T. Dorgan (eds.), *Watching the River Flow: A Century in Irish Poetry* (Dublin: Poetry Ireland, 1999), p. 58.

8 This and subsequent Máirtín Ó Direáin quotes are from his essay 'Mise agus an Fhilíocht' ('Poetry and I'), in Ó Direáin, *Dánta: 1939–1979* (Dublin: An Clóchomhar, 1980), pp. 216–17.

9 Ó Direáin, *Béasa an Túir* (Dublin: An Clóchomhar, 1984), p. 15.

10 Ó Direáin, 'Solas' ('Light'), in *Craobhóg Dán* (Dublin: An Clóchomhar, 1986), p. 23. My translation. Unless otherwise stated, all translations are by F. Sewell.

11 Ó Ríordáin, quoted in S. Ó Coileáin, *Seán Ó Ríordáin: Beatha agus Saothar* (Dublin: An Clóchomhar, 1982, repr. 1985), p. 209.

12 Ó Ríordáin, *Brosna* (Dublin: Sáirséal and Dill, 1964, 1987), p. 10.

13 Ó Ríordáin, *Tar Éis Mo Bháis* (Dublin: Sáirséal and Dill, 1978, 1986), p. 20.

14 Michael Hartnett, *Adharca Broic* (Dublin: Gallery, 1978), p. 14.

15 James Joyce, *A Portrait of the Artist as a Young Man*, in H. Levin (ed.), *The Essential James Joyce* (London: Jonathan Cape, 1950), p. 327.

16 Cathal Ó Searcaigh, 'Caoineadh' ('Lament'), *An Bealach 'na Bhaile / Homecoming* (Indreabhán: Cló Iar-Chonnachta, 1993), p. 208; Nuala Ní Dhomhnaill, 'Ceist na Teangan' ('The Language Issue'), *Pharaoh's Daughter*, p. 154.

17 Ní Dhomhnaill, 'The Hidden Ireland: Women's Inheritance', in *Irish Poetry since Kavanagh*, ed. by Theo Dorgan (Dublin: Four Courts Press, 1996), pp. 106–15.

18 Ó Ríordáin, 'Banfhile' ('Woman Poet'), *Tar Éis Mo Bháis*, p. 45.

19 See Biddy Jenkinson, 'A View from the Whale's Back', in *Poetry Ireland Review*, 52 (Spring, 1993), pp. 61–9.

20 See Ní Dhomhnaill, 'The Hidden Ireland: Womens' Inheritance'; and 'Mis and Dubh Ruis: A Parable of Psychic Transformation', in R. Welch (ed.), *Irish Writers and Religion* (Gerrards Cross: Colin Smythe, 1992), pp. 194–201.

21 See Ní Dhomhnaill, 'Mise ag Tiomáint' ('In Charge', literally -'I'm doing the driving'), *Pharaoh's Daughter*, p. 102; and 'Agallamh na Mór-Ríona le Cú Chulainn' ('The Great Queen Speaks. Cú Chulainn listens.'), *Selected Poems / Rogha Dánta* (Dublin: Raven Arts Press, 1988; repr. 1991), p. 116.

22 A folkloric reference to the penis as a symbol of sexual union, mutual pleasure and harmony between the sexes. See Ní Dhomhnaill, 'Mis and Dubh Ruis', p. 195.

23 See Ó Direáin, 'Cloch is Céir' ('Stone and Wax'), 'Teagmháil' ('Contact'); 'Boige' ('Softness'), 'Caoin Tú Féin a Bhean' ('Cry for yourself, woman'), in *Dánta*, pp. 116, 141, 143 and 54.

24 Ó Ríordáin, quoted in S. Ó Coileáin, *Seán Ó Ríordáin: Beatha agus Saothar*, pp. 155–6.

25 Ó Direáin, *Dánta*, 36; and Kiberd and Fitzmaurice (eds.), *The Flowering Tree*, p. 80.

26 Ó Direáin, *Dánta*, p. 102.

27 Máire Mhac an tSaoi, *An Cion go dtí Seo* (Dublin: Sáirséal – Ó Marcaigh, 1987, repr. 1988), pp. 22 and 32.

28 See Kiberd and Fitzmaurice (eds.), *The Flowering Tree*, p. 80.

29 D. Bolger (ed.), *The Bright Wave / An Tonn Gheal* (Dublin: Raven Arts Press, 1991), pp. 28 and 166.

30 Ní Dhomhnaill, *The Astrakhan Cloak* (Loughcrew: Gallery, 1993), p. 90.

31 Compare Padraic Pearse, *Selected Poems / Rogha Dánta*, ed. by Dermot Bolger (Dublin: New Island Books, 1993), p. 52, with Cathal Ó Searcaigh, *Out in the Open* (Indreabhán: Cló Iar-Chonnachta, 1997), p. 132.

32 Ó Searcaigh, *An Bealach 'na Bhaile / Homecoming*, pp. 186 and 160.

33 Ní Dhomhnaill, *The Astrakhan Cloak*, p. 90.

34 Ó Direáin, *Dánta*, p. 79.

35 Ó Searcaigh, *An Bealach 'na Bhaile / Homecoming*, p. 82.

36 See Dúghlas Sealy, untitled review of *An Bealach 'na Bhaile / Homecoming*, in *Comhar* (July 1993), pp. 21–2; and Noel Duffy and T. Dorgan (eds.), *Watching the River Flow*, p. 223. Also, Ó Searcaigh, *Out in the Open*, p. 66.

37 Comments from an RTE radio interview; broadcast July 6, 1980.

38 'Dan do Rosemary' ('Poem for Rosemary'), trans. by Gabriel Fitzmaurice, in *The Flowering Tree*, p. 183.

39 See G. Denvir (ed.), *Duanaire an Chéid* (Indreabhán: Cló Iar-Chonnachta, 2000), pp. 76 and 77.

40 M. Hartnett, 'Fís Dheireanach Eoghain Rua Uí Shúilleabháin' ('Last Vision of Owen Roe O'Sullivan'), in G. Denvir (ed.), *Duanaire an Chéid*, p. 77.

41 See 'Question and Answer: Nuala Ní Dhomhnaill', an interview by L. McDiarmid and M. Durkan, in *Irish Literary Supplement* (Fall 1987), p. 42. Lady Augusta Gregory (1852–1932) was a dramatist, folklorist, translator and founder (with Yeats and others) of the Irish National Theatre, later to become The Abbey Theatre.

42 See John Millington Synge (1871–1909), *The Aran Islands*, in which he describes listening in to Irish language and oral tales. These later resurfaced in the content and language (Irish or Hiberno-English) of his creative work.

43 See Nuala Ní Dhomhnaill, 'Why I Choose to Write in Irish', *The New York Times Book Review*, January 8, 1995, p. 27.

44 'There was a huge crowd of Gaelic Leaguers, all wearing their *fáine*, one-minded partisans'. Louis MacNeice, *The Strings are False* (London: Faber and Faber, 1965), p. 212.

45 For Ó Ríordáin's negotiation of Corkery's and Joyce's diverse influences, see Frank Sewell, 'Seán Ó Ríordáin: Joycery-Corkery-Sorcery', in *The Irish Review*, No. 23 (Winter 1998), pp. 42–61.

46 John Montague, 'The Two Seáns', *Smashing the Piano* (Loughcrew: Gallery Press, 1999), p. 58.

47 John Montague, *New Selected Poems* (Loughcrew: Gallery, 1989), p. 12.

48 Mahon, 'Poetry in Northern Ireland', *Twentieth Century Studies*, 4 (November 1970), p. 92.

49 Mahon, *Poems 1962–1978* (Oxford University Press, 1979), p. 50; and *The Yellow Book* (Loughcrew: Gallery Press, 1997), p. 26.

50 See N. Duffy and T. Dorgan (eds.), *Watching the River Flow*, p. 86.

51 M. McGuckian, *Selected Poems* (Loughcrew: Gallery, 1997), pp. 48–9.

52 See the Preface of Cathal Ó Searcaigh's *Out in the Open*.

53 G. Mac Lochlainn, 'Aistriúcháin' ('Translations'), *Sruth Teangacha*, p. 62.

54 J. Stephens, 'The Outlook for Literature with Special Reference to Ireland' (1922), in M. Storey (ed.), *Poetry and Ireland Since 1800: A Source Book* (London: Routledge, 1988), p. 179.

10

GUINN BATTEN

Boland, McGuckian, Ní Chuilleanáin and the body of the nation

> He lies in his English envelope
> like the Greek word for Greekness,
> defender of Throne and Altar,
> while the frontier is guarded
> by the small wombs of two chickens.
>
> (Medbh McGuckian 'Life as a
> Literary Convict', *Soldiers of
> Year Two*, 2002)[1]

> The modern Irish poet is not a man in the foreground, silhouetted against
> a place.... like a Gaelic bard the creature can be male or female, nomadic
> without losing a tribal identity.
>
> (Eiléan Ní Chuilleanáin)[2]

In an Irish context it may not be possible to imagine poetry in relation to the 'body' of the 'nation' without evoking the still-existent border to which Medbh McGuckian starkly alludes, a political and historical fact that divides 'Ireland' into two states and at least two bodies politic. Neither is it possible, despite the growing popularity of these three women poets, to imagine the term 'Irish poet' without picturing the foregrounded and masculine body emerging from the landscape which Eiléan Ní Chuilleanáin challenges. Bringing together both implications, the phrase 'body of the nation' implicitly recalls the nationalist literary text to which Eavan Boland, probably Ireland's most influential feminist, alludes in her essay 'Subject Matters', *The Spirit of the Nation*. Concerning these 'sixpenny booklet' anthologies of nationalist ballads compiled by *The Nation* newspaper from 1843, Boland writes: 'in its pages the public poem and the political poem were confused at the very moment when the national tradition was making a claim on Irish poetry which would colour its themes and purposes for a century'. As she has clearly and forcefully insisted in that essay and elsewhere, Ireland's particular literary history, with its closely related politics and poetics of embodiment, has led to a 'mixing of the national and the feminine'[3] that has disempowered the woman writer. Boland's argument may, at the risk of overstatement, be briefly summarised and slightly enlarged as follows. Irish cultural nationalism, in defining claims for poetic authority as the reclamation of the motherland, has defined the poet as it has the hero: as a specially endowed (male) subject who can repossess the maternal body – the aisling, Sovereignty, Kathleen ni Houlihan – who has been overcome by a foreign father. Such repossession, a restoration of family property, allegedly offers to the (male) poet not only a lost land but also, more importantly, a previously thwarted vision of 'Ireland' in its totality.

In the chapter that follows, I depart from the excellent work of two scholars of both Boland and McGuckian, Clair Wills and Catriona Clutterbuck. Beginning with quite different bases for understanding nationality and gender in relation to Irish women's poetry, Wills and Clutterbuck not surprisingly reach different conclusions concerning, broadly speaking, the consequences and, indeed, the efficacy of representative politics and poetic representation.[4] My own reading of Boland and McGuckian has acquired a different focus largely through the presence of a third poet, Eiléan Ní Chuilleanáin. A comparative reading of these three poets through the inter-related terms 'body' and 'nation' requires us to look beyond the limits as well as the possibilites of, in its various senses, representation.

Political representation and the representative poet

Interestingly, Boland's prescription in 'Subject Matters' for a political woman's poetry that refuses the representative role of the poet as (to adapt Yeats's title) a 'spirit medium' for nationalism coincides with David Lloyd's critique of *The Spirit of the Nation* in his *Nationalism and Minor Literature* (1987). Both have argued that the Romantic tradition has in Ireland (as others have claimed it has in England) reinforced a definition of canonical, or 'major', poetry that continues into the present to favour the lyric poem. Both have further claimed that through that particular genre the (male) poet discovers and strengthens 'spirit' *as* the self by surmounting and transcending the object or body that first kindled desire and sparked the alleged revolutionary 'spirit'. That desire leads to the creation of a national and Irish literature that remains bound by an ideology that frustrates real political change. Genuine revolution is undermined from within by the delusions of an ideology of Romantic genius, a mistaken belief that the individual subject, aggrandised by the very process of writing Romantic, 'revolutionary' poetry or translating powerful poems from Ireland's past, may represent through his 'national spirit' a united Ireland whose unity of body and spirit is always only symbolic, always (like desire itself) deferred,[5] and always united hierarchically: the spirit rules the body. The maternal body and the united motherland underwrite a masculine fantasy that gives the male body/spirit 'unity' through its narcissistic mirroring in the fantasmatic mother of the psychoanalytic mirror stage. What keeps the wished-for unity always at one step removed is precisely the expansion of what is perceived to be a unified, individual subjectivity at the expense of a community that is thereby only further removed from, and further sutured by, the rise of the newly postcolonial subject.

Indeed, the very priority of spirit to body in this paradigm may be portrayed as mollifying in a political situation that shows no signs of fully democratising. The body, as always, is to blame for not fully conforming to 'form', but, according to this view, we may at least take comfort in the survival of spirit in 'art'. Lloyd disparages not only the self-aggrandisement behind the urge for national unity that underwrote various poetic ambitions; more particularly he indicts its aesthetic consequences: a canonical Irish literature that has failed to take advantage of the alternative, empowering strategies of its very alterity as a 'minor literature'. Lloyd concludes that Irish cultural nationalism was misled by the Enlightenment dream of an 'archetypal or representative man' (the gender is deliberate) who could at once represent the nature and the 'total essence of the human' (16–17). Yet if Lloyd is correct – that the drive toward canon formation misshaped a masculinist and nationalist mission in the cracked looking glass of its Enlightenment and English Romantic models – then we can well imagine how that mistaken purpose has affected the writings of women who were doubly estranged, through gender bias as well as through postcolonial disempowerment.

If Irish cultural nationalism has, as Lloyd and Boland have argued from their different perspectives and agendas, assumed the role of a national (and, indeed, racial or ethnic) *spirit* of individual and representative genius at the cost of genuine community, then we might well ask where one might locate – and what has happened to – the *body* in a nationalist poetry that Boland describes as a 'confusion' of 'the public poem and the political poem'. Boland in 'Subject Matters' proposes that one of the two choices available to her as an Irish woman who also writes was to 'write my life into the Irish poem in the way tradition dictated – as mythic distaff of the national tradition'. But she chose what she implies was a more challenging route:

I could confront the fact that in order to write the Irish poem, I would have to alter, for myself, the powerful relations between subject and object which were established there. That in turn involved disrupting the other values encoded in those relations: the authority of the poet. Its place in the historic legend. And the allegory of nationhood which had customarily been shadowed and enmeshed in the image of the woman.

But in reality I had no choice. I was that image come to life. I had walked out of the pages of *The Nation*, the cadences of protest, the regret of emigrant ballads. And yet I spoke with the ordinary and fractured speech of a woman living in a Dublin suburb, whose claims to the visionary experience would be sooner made on behalf of a child or a tree than a century of struggle. I was a long way from what [Thomas] Davis thought of as a national poet. And yet my relation to the national poem – as its object, its past – was integral and forceful and ominous.   (*Object Lessons*, 184–5)

Boland concludes that, 'given the force of the national tradition and the claim it had made on Irish literature', only a 'subversive private experience' could now offer to the political poem 'true perspective and authority'. And that authority, according to Boland, 'could be guaranteed only by an identity – and this included a sexual identity – which the poetic tradition, and the structure of the Irish poem, had almost stifled'.

What is the relation between the sexual identity of the individual poet, her chosen poetic structure (or form), and the form that is the feminine and maternal body that has structured the myths, and the contextual realities, of the Irish poetic tradition? While Boland, co-author of the *The Making of a Poem: A Norton Anthology of Poetic Forms* is of the three poets considered here the one most associated with such matters, in the works of Medbh McGuckian and Eiléan Ní Chuilleanáin we also encounter quite powerful formal responses to a history in which the (male) cultural nationalist 'expresses' (finds the form for) the national spirit that the (female) body at once inspires and grounds. How these women poets define 'spirit' in relation to the bodies in their poems that are – like postcolonial culture itself in relation to the dominant culture of the coloniser – anomalous or exceptional suggests some surprising answers to Lloyd's unavoidable question: 'If the function of literature is to form and unite a people not yet in existence, how will a writer of sufficient stature arise, given that it is from the people he must arise if he is to express the spirit of the nation?' (Lloyd, 73) Indeed, as feminists have argued for some time, the 'people' are likely to unite precisely *not* in their identification with the exceptional individual (the hero or leader, for example) but through the exclusion of an otherness within the body politic that expresses itself as sexual difference, which means that 'the people' are very likely to express a 'humanity' that is by this very process of exclusion therefore male. Hence the 'form' that community takes in response to literature may itself prove to be, in Judith Butler's paradigm for *Bodies that Matter*, one that coheres only by excluding from its total vision certain exceptions, certain bodies that *because* they are visible only as 'matter', 'ground', 'not-spirit' do not matter sufficiently to include them in the form of community.[6] And there is a further dilemma for the woman poet whose 'spirit' occupies a body that is (in Luce Irigaray's terms) not 'one'. With whom is she to identify if there is not only not yet (in Lloyd's terms) a community, much less a nation, emerging on the ground and through the figure of Mother Ireland but also no clear model at the level of the individual psyche for how she might desire and then dominate that female body which will then represent unity? While there is insufficient space here to address all of these issues, we will see that for each of these three women poets questions of the self and its problematic relation to body and spirit are not separable from questions of community, questions that themselves *question* – particularly through their poetic figuration of absence – the very possibility of either a unified self or a unified community.

In none of these Irish women poets can the body be defined fully in opposition to 'spirit', and in none can we easily derive an alternative poetics or politics of the nation that is 'grounded' or 'rooted' in a body that is maternal. But in McGuckian and Ní Chuilleanáin we might find a surprising alternative to Boland's own insistence that the woman poet must cease to be an object in poems and become (in her words) a 'subject' who 'matters'. Contrary to Boland's extension of a secular and Enlightenment ideal of representative subjecthood to women, McGuckian and Ní Chuilleanáin have increasingly offered in their poems bodies that, as objects, become vehicles and even forms for the reincarnation of (in various senses) 'spirit'. That fascination with an embodied spirit links these two poets less to twentieth-century Anglo-American feminist traditions (to which Boland is herself in part indebted for her international success) than to the subject matters of the most influential Irish poet of that century, W.B. Yeats. To Boland's argument that women writers become political when they eschew victimhood while representing those women who remain victims, McGuckian and Ní Chuilleanáin often present speakers or historical figures who acquire agency through bodily surrender. To Boland's anger that women in Ireland have been historically silenced or absent they offer a poetry that figures silence and absence as replete with strategies for rethinking the course of narrative and of history. And to her objections to an Irish and Catholic iconography of woman, its veiling of her 'actual' or 'real' body, they suggest that the body is itself phantasmatic, a broken relic that is in excess of history and yet remains, in Ní Chuilleanáin's 'The Brazen Serpent', 'real':

True stories wind and hang like this
Shuddering loop wreathed on a lapis lazuli
Frame. She says, this is the real thing.
She veils it again and locks up.
On the shelves behind her the treasures are lined.
The episcopal seal repeats every coil,
Stamped on all closures of each reliquary
Where the labels read: *Bones
Of Different Saints. Unknown.*

Her history is a blank sheet,
Her vows a folded paper locked like a well.
The torn end of the serpent
Tilts the lace edge of the veil.
The real thing, the one free foot kicking
Under the white sheet of history.[7]

In this poem Ní Chuilleanáin offers a brief narrative based on the story of the brazen serpent, Moses' icon of brass offered to heal those bitten by the serpents sent as punishment by God. Like that talisman, the saint's relic offers special properties: in becoming a broken piece of a once-living body, the body that has suffered accrues value as each fragment of the body is pieced out and labelled. While the symbols of patriarchal authority are also real in this poem – the episcopal seal, the sister's own veil, a bishop's command that the real world be sealed from view – the secret authority of the sister's relics, as of her own hidden life and body, persists in the very blankness of the sheet, paper and veil, a story just at the edge of which lies the ambiguous serpent and that other, missing narrative of woman and desire.

Lloyd has suggested that the martyr is a metaphor for 'the individual's relation to the nation' (71). In this sense the martyr serves the same function as literature, for both exist as 'the medium of the spiritual nation . . . the very form of the national constitution' that prefigures the actual and political document. Here and elsewhere he defines as ideology the following related acts of representation: 1) the aesthetic, 2) the martyr who represents the 'spirit' which establishes the relation between individual and nation, and 3) the ideals of equal representation for all in the nation coming into being. While Boland likewise investigates how these mutually reinforcing versions of representation maintain the force of an invisible but nevertheless repressive ideology, locating in their operation the violent erasure of the female body, McGuckian and Ní Chuilleanáin are more interested in how the body reshapes or even metamorphoses under conditions of threat, becoming itself at once form and content, structure and substance, history or story and resistant event. In so doing McGuckian and Ní Chuilleanáin are writers who in fact follow more closely than does Boland the 'minority' model offered by Lloyd: far from being merely a literature that fails to achieve major or canonical status, minority literature as Lloyd adapts it from the model used by Gilles Deleuze and Félix Guattari, refuses 'the production of narratives of ethical identity' and, indeed, refuses the very notion of 'the narrative as productive' (Lloyd, 21).[8]

What may be most exciting about these two poets and the different ways in which they evoke the body by refusing to represent it either through language or through the role of 'poet' is that they also avoid conventional tropes about the female body as inevitably maternal and therefore reproductive. In this sense their work may be viewed as aligned to Gayatri Spivak's work on gender and postcolonialism. In her recent discussion of what she defines as the too-easy homology of political and aesthetic representation, Spivak argues in *A Critique of Postcolonial Reason* that in postcolonial theory certain contemporary oppositions to theory itself – as in the statement 'there is no more representation; there's nothing but action' – fails to make the distinction she prefers to make between political and aesthetic representation: that 'running them together, especially in order to say that beyond both is where oppressed subjects speak, act, and know *for themselves*, leads to an essentialist, utopian politics'.[9] Ironically, such a conflation of representations merely reinforces the postcolonial theorist as a 'subject' who speaks *for* the silenced subaltern female who, like the body, is suppose to precede and ground representation: 'representing them, the intellectuals represent themselves as transparent' (Spivak, 257), or, as Lloyd might say, as 'spirit' to their 'body'. The silenced figure, male and female, returns in the poetry of McGuckian and Ní Chuilleanáin as itself a sometimes sinister but nonetheless corrective spirit; a revenant that reveals the gaps and silences that shaped the past and misshape the present, the female poet who speaks through that palpable absence does not claim to make either nation or history 'whole'.

Representation, reincarnation and bodily remainders

Whereas in Boland's poetry after 1995 what she calls the 'public poem' becomes 'political' when the (female) object of the Irish past becomes the (female) subject who is the present and – as she has said – 'entitled' poet, McGuckian reverses that process in her 1998 *Shelmalier*, turning the poet/subject into an object through which the dead – and the past – come back to life. Boland in 'Subject Matters' and throughout her 1998 volume *The Lost Land* makes clear her wish to replace the male hero with the unsung Irish female.[10] McGuckian, on the other hand, celebrates those Irish heroes as 'feminine Christs', making them, like the speaker, not a subject in history but a 'collected object' *of* history, their bodily pulses still beating beyond death, directed simultaneously to the past and to the future:

> Their pulses are differently timed, mule-
> powered, safely poured in two directions
> into time, into the collected object.
>
> All their fingers are together, they are
> tight-lipped, unwakeable mothers
> embraced to the hilt and reconceived.
>   ('The Feminine Christs')[11]

The differences between the two poets' responses to their different communities' commemorations of one moment in what Boland calls in 'Subject Matters' the 'hopeful past' – the 1798 Rising – are striking. Ní Chuilleanáin, on the other hand, while she published no book in 1998, in her 1995 volume *The Brazen Serpent* 'embodies' history, whether as blank sheet, in the snapshot of a crime victim ('Vierge Ouvrant', 36), or in 'signatures on slips of ravelled paper' ('The Secret', 42).

Of the three poets, McGuckian and Ní Chuilleanáin are the two who have been by turns praised and criticised for being obscure. Referents are typically elusive in McGuckian's poetry because of her compounded similes that lack stable grounds and her innovative and exciting manipulations of syntax that require the reader to wander endlessly and aimlessly, like desire itself, from the point of connection between subject and predicate. As critics have observed, she deploys metonymic displacement and metaphoric condensation (the strategies Freud identifies in the syntax of dreams) in ways that violate expectations of a mimetic, one-to-one correspondence of word and object that underwrites the agency of the subject. In the Ní Chuilleanáin poem, the elusive referent is more often narrative, manifested as a secret around which the poem draws and by which it is energised. If Boland's poetry, on the other hand, is more accessible, it is in part because, despite her frequent castigations of the privileged male speaking subject of the lyric poem (a topic to which I will return), she is not so much interested in reconceiving a less traditional form for the voice of her typically unified subject as in ensuring that women have an equal right to that form and its Romantic and lyric tradition.

While Boland's poems increasingly use a syntax that separates subject and predicate, the effect is the news bulletin or the pithy, bitten off, statement of fact. The point of her politics as a poet is to achieve equal privilege so that she may represent, albeit self-consciously and even ironically through what are acknowledged as the limited forms of art, the lost women of the past who may now be embodied in the poetic subject of the present who is, herself, a woman. And for a woman poet, her own private, even ordinary, life offers 'a politic of its own' (*Object Lessons*, 194). It offers it because of the very disjunction of that private world from the 'context of public opinion and assumption' (195). Women, she argues, once the objects of the Irish poem, are now, like Pygmalion's Galatea, assuming life and subjectivity:

> The obstinate and articulate privacy of their lives was now writing the poem, rather than simply being written by it. If this did not make a new political poem, it at least constituted a powerful revision of the old one. As more and more poems by Irishwomen were written, it was obvious that something was happening to the Irish poem. It was what happens to any tradition when previously mute images within it come to awkward and vivid life, when the icons return to haunt the icon makers. That these disruptions had been necessary at all, and that they were awkward and painful when they happened, had something to do with the force of the national tradition.
>
> (*Object Lessons*, 197)

Boland concludes that 'my womanhood', once the 'object and icon' of the political poem in Ireland 'became part of its authorship' (200). But that did not diminish the difficulties inherent in the political poem: 'How to draw the reality into the poem, and therefore into a subversive relation with the rhetoric, is the crucial question' (200). Thus while the 'emergence of women poets in Ireland guarantees nothing' because they, too, are subjects in and to language (rhetoric), nevertheless 'where icons walk out of the poem to become authors of it, their speculative energy is directed not just to the iconography which held them hostage but to the poem itself' (200). This requires a double strategy, she writes, of 'dismantling the poetic persona which supported' the male and bardic tradition of the political poem and 'to seek the authority to do this not from a privileged or historic stance within the Irish poem but from the silences it created and sustained' (201). Where do we find those silences in Boland, and how do they compare with the haunting spirits and haunted absences of the other two poets?

Representing women: Eavan Boland

In *The Lost Land*, Boland opens with reference to the national tradition as it was represented by a bardic order that, by the nineteenth century, had lost its authority with the loss of the land and language once guaranteed by aristocratic privilege. Toward that authority Boland has ambivalence if not hostility, for 'whatever the dispossession and humiliation of an outer world, maleness remained a caste system within the poem', as she writes in 'Subject Matters': 'The shadow of bardic privilege still fell on the Irish poem when I was young. It was hard to question and harder to shift. Yet I knew

I would have to do both if I wanted access to the political poem in Ireland' (*Object Lessons*, 191). Because women 'had for so long been a natural object relation for the Irish poem', when women began to write poems themselves it 'was as though a fixed part of the Irish poem had broken free' (191). As in her much-praised earlier poem 'Mise Eire', Boland in *The Lost Land* turns frequently to that fixed poetic part as it assumes personhood, a process whereby Mother Ireland becomes an ordinary (but therefore exemplary) Irish woman. In 'Mother Ireland' (*Lost Land*, 42–3), the motherland itself acquires language and subjectivity. Indeed, she might be said to be either emigrating or, like a housewife, leaving home in order to find herself.

> At first
> I was land
> I lay on my back to be fields
>
> . . .
> I did not see.
> I was seen.

Once a subject of language ('words fell on me. / Seeds. Raindrops'.), she moves from learning her name, to rising up, to remembering. The narrative of this poem is history itself, a straightforward teleology even if told (literally) from the ground up as the base, one might say, acquires the tools of the superstructure:

> Now I could tell my story.
> It was different
> from the story told about me.

When she looks back with nostalgic, maternal love 'they misundersrtood (sic) me': '*Come back to us*/they said./ *Trust me* I whispered'.

But the speaker of the poems is as much a colonial Prospero as she is a ready wielder of prosopopoeia on behalf of the dispossessed:

> Out of my mouth they come:
> The spurred and booted garrisons.
> The men and women
> they dispossessed.
>
> What is a colony
> if not the brutal truth
> that when we speak
> the graves open.
>
> And the dead walk?   ('Witness')

Interestingly, in this poem that echoes Yeats's 'Fragments', Boland takes back the agency that Yeats gives to the female director of the séance: 'Where got I that truth?/Out of a medium's mouth,/Out of nothing it came'. Like the spiritualist, but as an Irish native rather than as a medium, she makes the graves of history open. Boland has made clear her refusal of the supernatural and, indeed, of any testimony from such paranormal events as the statues some claimed to have seen move in Ireland in 1988. She writes in 'Moving Statues' (a title that might have led her audience to anticipate another Pygmalion/Galatea theme from Boland) that many in Ireland were duped by such visions (she calls the phenomenon first the 'dark forces at the crossroads' [16], then the 'hysteria of collective superstition', then later 'a dark hysteria in religion' [20]). If their impulses, she contends, are strikingly similar to those of the visionary male poet, they are also betrayed by the privileged culture he represents: in Ireland as in England poetic tradition derives its authority from 'distance from such forces' (16) and a usurpation of them (a secularised 'religion of poetry' [18]). That privileged culture denies the authority of a woman poet who insists on claiming that 'however ordinary' the routines of her own domestic world she nevertheless insists on standing 'at the lyric center of my experience and . . . wished to make a claim for that experience' (17). 'A shadow fell between me and my sense that I could get from that historic poetic past the sanction I needed', Boland writes, 'both for my subject matter and the claim I wished to make for it in formal terms' (17).

Nationalism as reincarnation: Medbh McGuckian

Whereas in Boland's poems the dead are unlikely to walk except through tropes that the poet openly and self-consciously controls in a deliberate process of reclaiming a lost history of woman's reality, McGuckian writes in her 1998 collection *Shelmalier* that 'Keeping magic out has itself the character/ of magic':

> . . . – a picture held us captive
> and we could not get outside it
> for it lay in our language in the uniform
> of a force that no longer existed.
> Peace was the target he was aiming at,
> the point at which doubt becomes senseless,
> the last thing that will find a home.
> ('Pulsus Paradoxus')

McGuckian shares Boland's scepticism of language's capacity to liberate, given its complicity with oppression ('force'), but she goes beyond Boland's Platonic understanding of language as political 'rhetoric', implying here that it operates at the unconscious level of ideology. The ambiguity of reference here – Who wears the uniform and what side is he on? If the picture no longer exists, when did it? Why is it still a force? – offers a complex and sophisticated understanding of what Boland so often calls simply the 'shadows' of power, for in the McGuckian poem power may be held by the heroes who lost as well as by those who won the wars of the past. Further, the poem's syntax makes it unclear as to whether the uniform may not itself be, like the language in which it is clothed, a veil that may be duplicitous. If there is no getting outside language in this poem, then how may the woman poet locate an alternative to its sexist or colonialist constructions of history? Can an aesthetic that, like language, captivates also liberate?

A word appears here that we might associate with a Boland claim for the authority of the domestic – 'home' – but in the McGuckian poem it is, like 'peace', and like 'unity', deferred. Only when doubt – a sceptical consciousness that Boland prefers in 'Moving Statues' to credulity – sinks into senselessness, can that unconscious state in the McGuckian poem become the object which, in this poem, is like 'peace' the 'point'. Yet peace is also a state of mind that is already, even before it is reached as a 'target', also, sadly, an object of further contestation. The contest is not simply *for* a home (whose Ireland?) but also for an object whose home, like desire itself or, indeed, like the full unification of the 'subject' or the state, by definition is deferred. In McGuckian's bleak view of the hopefulness of the Northern Ireland peace process, she recognises that hope, in taking for granted the appeal to what she calls (in the lines that follow) an 'incorruptible' colour, refuses to see the totality ('everything') that would turn the perhaps all-green promise of the future into an all 'brown' and soiled history. Behind and beneath hope are the returning and cautionary ghost heroes of past wars who are backlit by the glare of the present.

They may either promise or prevent the fulfillment of hope, as the poem's first stanza suggests:

> At first something like an image was there:
> he had for me a pre-love which leaves
> everything as it is. We do not see everything
> as something, everything that is brown,
> we take for granted the incorruptible
> colouredness of the colour. But a light
> shines on them from behind, they do not
> themselves glow. As a word has only
> an aroma of meaning, as the really faithful
> memory is the part of a wound
> that goes quiet.

The presumably female speaker here is the object of a 'pre-love' that is offered by a male subject ('he') who is given form by the speaker as 'the really faithful/memory': he is 'the part of the wound /that goes quiet'. To Boland's 'scar' of language, McGuckian offers instead a notion of the word as an entity whose meaning is scented but silent, related through simile ('as') to 'part of a wound'. The speaker hears that 'part' of something *not* because she has assumed what once was a male privilege but because she has been called by masculine 'pre-love', and called as its object, to witness an *image* (indeed, more significantly, 'something like an image') that has found its home in her as a calling which seemed to leave 'everything as it is'. While that phrase may be read as 'leaving alone . . . unchanged', it may also be read as a moment of vision in which 'everything' '*is*': a moment when totality is glimpsed. If this is poetic vision, it may require us to understand that seeing, often associated by feminists with a masculine gaze that desires and seeks to possess its object, does not necessarily mean that totality – again, 'everything' – is an object: 'something'. Neither is the colour (like 'uniform') of what is seen necessarily what it seems.

In this poem by a woman, a masculine image from the past has found its embodiment in what is now her memory, and her wound, both of which are now 'his' home as well as hers. Far from rejecting the maternal implications of such an act of imagination *as* incarnation, McGuckian uses in 'Pulsus Paradoxus' images that recall another of her poems that is explicitly about motherhood. Dedicated to her daughter, Emer, 'On Her Second Birthday' is written in the voice of the daughter. She remembers a time that may well evoke a moment before life begins as inception and incarnation: 'In the beginning I was no more/Than a rising and falling mist/You could see through without seeing'. In the second stanza, McGuckian uses simile (as she does frequently) at once to displace and to embed within figural speech the content/meaning of the poem. Figuration thereby, unexpectedly, becomes matter or body. She refers to 'soul' only indirectly, but it seems, like writing in the lines below, to precede bodily birth:

> A flame burnt up the paper
> On which my gold was written,
> The wind like a soul
> Seeking to be born
> Carried off half
> Of what I was able to say.[12]

As the child in this minus time of being dallies in the trees, a 'shadow' hovering at the edge of the horizon 'Which I mistook for my own' gradually guides the daughter-to-be into life by offering to her a model of embodiment not as being but as metamorphosis:

> The more it changed
> The more it changed me into itself,
> Till I regarded it as more real
> Than all else, more ardent
> Than love. Higher than the air
> Of a dream,
> A field in which I ripened
> From an unmoving, continually nascent
> Light into pure light.

At last the daughter-speaker acknowledges that her own life is a 'flowing' 'outwards', not toward a reunion with that shadow as 'spirit' but, more miraculously, as 'body': 'I know its name: / One day it will pass my mind into its body'.

Throughout *Shelmalier* the minds of spirits, or more particularly ghosts, pass through the speaker's mind. Likewise, in these poems as in early McGuckian collections we have a sense that the objects surrounding, enclosing, even imprisoning the speaker are more alive, more connected to the world, than she. The subject in such poems exists only negatively, through what she is 'not' in relation to material circumstances. But in these poems, which are so often sinister, the negation cuts in two directions: in a refusal to recall the injuries of the past and in the erosion of that repression. In 'Dream in a Train' a 'house is a perfect body/Surpassing, unwriting me'. The poem concludes with the image of negative form that hints at (but does not promise) 'awakening': 'a swimmer/whose sigh is a fold/imposed upon the waves,/*suggestive* of an awakening' (my emphasis). These are poems very much concerned with what McGuckian has called her own, personal awakening to the history and ideologies of an Irish nationalism about which she heard little as a Catholic girl growing up in Northern Ireland. While Boland in *The Lost Land* seeks to usurp the privilege of Ireland's male heroes, making herself a subject at their expense, in McGuckian's *Shelmalier* the martyrs of 1998 repossess the speaker's body, speaking through her even as 'door' and 'window' – openings that are framed and that thereby become inanimate objects – embrace 'as if they were living, not speechless':

> the frozen hedge lipped and flared
> so every inch is thick
> with a different flower,
> not a flower escapes.
> . . .

> The dead among the spices of words
> brush their eyes over me, as if
> all my limbs were separate.
> They are pearls that have got
> into my clothes, they stir about
> briskly with a form of tenderness
> like a bird on its nest. I may
> glide into them before they become set.
> ('The Sofa in the Window with the
> Trees Outside', *Shelmalier*)

Even as an object (in this poem the hedge) 'lipped' and therefore reproduced ('flowered'), so does the speaker find herself identifying with the dead (the seeds or eggs that are 'pearls') who themselves in turn will incarnate *her* in the nest of a bird over which they brood as simile. She not only hears their speech but also finds that it has usurped her own, even as the dead look through her own eyes (evoking from Ariel's song in Shakespeare's *The Tempest* the dead pearls that were once living eyes) at a world made different for her by their looking. In a final and remarkable inversion, their gaze returns us to the first image of the hedge's lips, an image that might on first reference have suggested the hedge school for Irish Catholics under the Penal Laws, but the hedges are now trees whose bodies, while sunken, also have the organs of speech: 'they / are bodily sunk to the lips / in the age of the garden'. Notably, these trees (of knowledge? of life?) are sunk not in an Ireland 'racy of the soil' or in the golden age of a sinless past to which the term 'garden' so often refers but, rather, in *time*: the 'age' of the garden.

Bodily remainders: Eiléan Ní Chuilleanáin

Of Eiléan Ní Chuilleanáin's poetry John Kerrigan has written that it 'gives hiddenness a location beyond the specificity of place'.[13] And one location to which she is drawn as a poet, he argues, is what Daniel Corkery called 'the hidden Ireland' of a persistent Gaelic culture. But at Trinity College in Dublin she is a scholar of the sixteenth- and seventeenth-century English literature that rose on what Boland calls the 'bardic shadows' of a dying literature in Ireland. And beyond those two locations and literatures Ní Chuilleanáin often associates herself with a third to which the 'nomadic' that she refers to in this essay's opening citation no doubt alludes: an Irish tradition of 'nomadism' or even exile in Europe, learning other languages and looking back critically at Ireland through their resources. While Boland defines the 'bardic tradition' as inexorably male and Irish, Ní Chuilleanáin reclaims it as neither, upsetting the oppositions that patriarchal colonialism itself sets into place between the terms male and female, English and Irish. Indeed, like the nineteenth-century poet James Clarence Mangan, who published in *The Nation*, she uses translation, in Seamus Deane's words, to question 'the very basis of Irish cultural nationalism, which, after all, assumes the translatability of Irish spirit into English words',[14] a questioning that, in both cases, in fact respects and even empowers that which lies beyond the powers of language. We might witness this nomadism in the title poem of Ní Chuilleanáin's 2002 volume, 'The Girl Who Married the Reindeer', or in another poem in that volume which takes up the linguist's journey of discovery and leads, at last, not to the possession of a possessive ('his', 'hers') but, rather, to a ghostly woman 'panting on the other side', who has been evoked by an Irish word ('glas') that means both 'green' and 'lock':

> Until he reaches the language that has no word for *his*,
> No word for *hers*, and is brought up sudden
> Like a boy in a story faced with a small locked door.
> Who is that he can hear panting on the other side?
> The steam of her breath is turning the locked lock green.
>
> ('Gloss/Clós/Glas')[15]

Kerrigan suggests that part of what remains occluded in Ní Chuilleanáin's carefully locked poems is bodily suffering, particularly as she has experienced it in her visits with the ill and the dying. Those bodies in pain become parts of other and unrelated narratives in her poems, even as they persist in her poetry as troubling, underground currents. For example, he notes that in 'Passing Over in Silence', a poem whose line 'A hooked foot holding her down' seems to evoke sexual violation, in fact 'hooked foot' is a reference to cancer.[16] 'Studying the Language', which begins with 'hermits coming out of their holes/Into the light' had its inception in a sickroom visit. Ní Chuilleanáin's intimacy with and insipiration from the injured body also relates to her attraction to such elements of Catholic iconography as the Sacred Heart and the Virgin. In his study of art and bodiliness in her poetry, Dillon Johnston has suggested that the poet's foregrounding of such figures is part of her scholarly and poetic fascination with the Counter Reformation, a history that Johnston notes has its own ties to Irish nationalist culture and whose art, the Baroque, figures frequently in Ní Chuilleanáin's poetry. He cites her response to one 'proto-Baroque' work, Correggio's *Leda*: 'Here was a body at the centre of a story, female and pleased in all its dimensions. I was suddenly back in a world before the upheaval of the Reformation, before the Protestant war on icons of the body, rituals and material ceremonies' (191).[17] Of Ní Chuilleanáin's 'Daniel Grose' (1995) Johnston offers an illuminating reading, revealing the ways in which Ní Chuilleanáin differs from Boland in her understanding and use of the male gaze. He notes, for example, the presence of the *cailleach* (one embodiment of Kathleen ni Houlihan) in this poem.

We might further note that the female poet, in becoming that *cailleach*, assumes as in the tradition of the Hag of Beare the position of a speaking subject whose haggardness expresses the impoverishment and even ruination of Ireland. Indeed, in this poem she assumes the role of the male figure backlit in the essay's first citation of Ní Chuilleanáin ('a man in the foreground, silhouetted against a place'), offering to the military draughtsman in the poem what he takes only to be an object of perspective:

> Where is the human figure
> He needs to show the scale
> And all the time that's passed
> And how different things are now?
> (*Brazen Serpent*, 34)

In Ní Chuilleanáin's poem, as often in McGuckian's work, the very building – in this case, a ruin – seems to be giving birth: 'The breach widens at every push'. Yet this opening is also indicative of a despoliation that bespeaks a traumatic silence until 'a taste for ruins' brings the male gaze (with its own wounding apertures) to measure both the (female) openings that themselves gaze outward ('The way the pierced loop keeps exactly/The dimensions of the first wounding,/Holding in the same spasm the same long view') and the male 'upright of the tower'.

If 'things are different now', the catalogue of what such aesthetic measuring, such hygienic transformation of the sexualised body of the ruin into a 'draught', leaves out of the story tells the reader that difference depends on perspective, on who occupies the ground, and on the violence of what isn't heard as well as what is in the allegedly enlightened, non-threatening perspective of the nineteenth-century surveyor: 'The old woman by the oak tree / Can be pressed into service / To occupy the foreground./ Her feet are warmed by drifting leaves'. Where Boland would speak for that figure, embody her in the speaker's more authoritative perspective, Ní Chuilleanáin at least twice removes the old woman from a speaker who is watching her through his instruments of measure – the imperial, empirical extensions of the organs of sense – instruments through which he fails either to see or to hear her. Perhaps not surprisingly, this lends to the *cailleach* more power than the female figures in Boland's poems are usually granted. It is she who controls not only the 'measures' of 'verse' but also what Boland calls the 'rhythm of the crime', the 'rictus of delight' that is an incantory opening into, and an evil eye capable of blighting, the landscape hidden from view:

He stands too far away
To hear what she is saying,
How she routinely measures
The verse called the midwife's curse
On all that catches her eye, naming
The scholar's index finger, the piper's hunch,
The squint, the rub, the itch of every trade.

Finally in this poem the body of the woman persists as an irreducible remainder of the Enlightenment perspective that would represent the landscape as map or as art. Precisely in doing so, she prevents the surveyor from obtaining a unified perspective, further shattering both landscape and woman into the part objects of science and of art. A reminder, stuck in the opened gap between subject and object, male and female, colonist and coloniser, of what the masterful perspective does not enclose in its grasp of totality, the body therefore serves precisely as the 'breach' that will produce an alternative to representation itself. It offers its own perspective on what and whom history, and community, hurts.

Indeed, perhaps the image of community that remains most compelling in Ní Chuilleanáin's poetry is that offered in 'Studying the Language' of the 'cliff . . . as full as a hive' of hermits who do sometimes come 'Into the light', for the poet who writes 'I call this my work, these decades and stations – / Because, without these, I would be a stranger here'. In the gap between Boland's view that a woman writer finds her voice by becoming her own subject and representing it faithfully, and Ní Chuilleanáin's that the woman writer finds that voice *through* the objects of her poem who lead her from a hermit's estrangement into human connection, we might locate an important and ongoing theoretical debate concerning the possibility of a fully democratic community. As three of its major contestants – Judith Butler, Ernesto Laclau and Slavoj Zizek – have agreed in their separate contributions to *Contingency, Hegemony, Universality: Contemporary Dialogues on the Left*, the very possibility of a democracy that represents fully and equally all subjects requires that there be competing claims for the occupancy of the unfulfilled, and probably unfulfillable, position of the 'subject' in the representative 'bodies' of the state.[18] Ní Chuilleanáin, finding throughout her career subtle strategies for representing by *not* claiming to represent authentic 'muscle and blood', for serving others by *not* serving as a subject who represents what she calls in the following poem 'the absent girl', redefines what is, and can only be, missing in every effort to achieve justice in the court of history or in the canon that revises – the body and its own irrecuperable time that carries with it its own shadows:

She can feel the glass cold
But with no time for pain
Searches for a memory lost with muscle and blood –
She misses her ligaments and the marrow of her bones.

The clock chatters; with no beating heart
Lung or breast how can she tell the time?
Her skin is shadowed
Where once the early sunlight blazed.[19]

NOTES

1 Medbh McGuckian, *The Soldiers of Year Two* (Winston Salem: Wake Forest University Press, 2002).

2 Quoted in John Kerrigan, 'Hidden Ireland: Eiléan Ní Chuilleanáin and Munster Poetry', *Critical Quarterly* 40.4 (Winter 1998), p. 86.

3 Eavan Boland, *Object Lessons: The Life of the Woman and the Poet in Our Time* (Manchester: Carcanet, 1995), pp. 183 and 182.

4 See Catriona Clutterbuck, 'Irish Critical Responses to Self-Representation in Eavan Boland, 1987–1995', *Colby Quarterly* 35.4 (Dec 1999), pp. 275–87 and 'Irish Women's Poetry and the Republic of Ireland: Formalism as Form', in *Writing in the Irish Republic: Literature, Culture, Politics*, ed. Ray Ryan (London: Macmillan, 2000), pp. 17–43; Clair Wills, *Improprieties: Politics and Sexuality in Northern Irish Poetry* (Oxford: Clarendon Press, 1993).

5 David Lloyd, *Nationalism and Minor Literature: James Clarence Mangan and the Emergence of Irish Cultural Nationalism* (Berkeley and London: University of California Press, 1987), pp. 70–1.

6 See Judith Butler, *Bodies that Matter: On the Discursive Limits of 'Sex'* (New York and London: Routledge, 1993).

7 Eiléan Ní Chuilleanáin, *The Brazen Serpent* (Loughcrew: Gallery & Winston Salem: Wake Forest University Press, 1991), p. 16.

8 See Gilles Deleuze and Félix Guattari, *Kafka: Toward a Minor Literature*, trans. Dana Polan (Minneapolis: University of Minnesota Press, 1986).

9 Gayatri Chakravorty Spivak, *A Critique of Postcolonial Reason: Toward a History of the Vanishing Present* (Cambridge, MA: Harvard University Press, 1999), pp. 256–7.

10 Eavan Boland, *The Lost Land* (Manchester: Carcanet, 1998).

11 Medbh McGuckian, *Shelmalier* (Loughcrew: Gallery & Winston Salem: Wake Forest University Press, 1998).

12 Medbh McGuckian, *Marconi's Cottage* (Loughcrew: Gallery & Winston Salem: Wake Forest University Press, 1991).

13 John Kerrigan, 'Hidden Ireland: Eiléan Ní Chuilleanáin and Munster Poetry', p. 90.

14 Seamus Deane, 'Poetry and Song 1800–1890' in *The Field Day Anthology of Irish Writing*, ed. Seamus Deane. (Derry: Field Day Publications, 1991), vol. 2, p. 6.

15 Eiléan Ní Chuilleanáin, *The Girl Who Married the Reindeer* (Loughcrew: Gallery & Winston Salem: Wake Forest University Press, 2002).

16 Kerrigan, 'Hidden Ireland'.
17 Dillon Johnston, ' "Our Bodies' Eyes and Writing Hands": Secrecy and Sensuality in Ní Chuilleanáin's Baroque Art', in *Gender and Sexuality in Modern Ireland*, ed. Anthony Bradley and Maryann Gialanella Valiulis (Amherst, MA: University of Massachusetts Press, 1997), p. 191.
18 Judith Butler, Ernesto Laclau and Slavoj Zizek. *Contingency, Hegemony, Universality: Contemporary Dialogues on the Left* (New York and London: Verso, 2000).
19 Eiléan Ní Chuilleanáin *The Second Voyage* (Loughcrew: Gallery & Winston Salem: Wake Forest University Press, 1997), p. 13.

II

SHANE MURPHY

Sonnets, centos and long lines: Muldoon, Paulin, McGuckian and Carson

> One way or another, it does seem that Irish writers again and again find themselves challenged by the violent juxtaposition of the concepts of 'Ireland' and 'I'. Irish writers have a tendency to interpose themselves between the two . . . either to bring them closer together, or to force them further apart. It's as if they feel obliged to extend the notion of being a 'medium' to becoming a 'mediator'.
>
> (Paul Muldoon, *To Ireland, I*, 2000)[1]

According to Paul Muldoon, Irish writers experience an often disabling tension between the urge to express private concerns in their work and the compulsion to address identity politics, inherited atavisms and the legacy of sectarian strife. His comments restate the competing definitions of what Seamus Heaney terms 'the government of the tongue'. This is an obligation to 'concede to the corrective pressures of social, moral, political and historical reality'. Yet it is also a liberating manifesto, allowing the poet to submit to 'the jurisdiction of achieved form', with poetry 'as its own vindicating force'.[2] Heaney has consistently attempted to address these apparently conflictual imperatives. In *Wintering Out* and *North*, he engaged with what are euphemistically termed 'the Troubles' by advancing images of bodies drawn from the bogs at Tollund, Grauballe and Windeby as archaeological emblems of victimhood. This poetic reflex, whilst deep-felt and instinctive, was interpreted as providing decontextualised analogies (if not unintentional justifications) for the killings in Northern Ireland. Heaney had become, according to his fellow-poet Ciaran Carson, 'the laureate of violence – a mythmaker, an anthropologist of ritual killing, an apologist for "the situation", in the last resort, a mystifier'.[3]

The application of mythical parallels and quotations from exemplary authors gave rise to a poetry that exhibited a tormented self-reflexivity. For instance, citing Shakespeare, Heaney said,

I am Hamlet the Dane,
skull-handler, parablist,
smeller of rot

in the state, infused
with its poisons,
pinioned by ghosts
and affections
    ('Viking Dublin: Trial
    Pieces', 1975)

Similarly, in 'Away from It All' in *Station Island* (1984), the speaker is about
to have a guilt-laden meal of lobster, when quotations are said 'to rise / like
rehearsed alibis'. The poet cites a passage from Czeslaw Milosz's *The Native
Realm*:

> *I was stretched between contemplation*
> *Of a motionless point*
> *And the command to participate*
> *Actively in history.*[4]

In his preface to *The Crane Bag Book of Irish Studies*, Heaney quotes these
same lines and provides Milosz's own interpretation of this inner conflict.
Fearing the 'delusiveness of words and thoughts', the poet must maintain
'a firm hold on tangible things undergoing constant change; that is, control
over the motor that moves them in society – namely politics'.[5] In the poem,
however, Heaney cannot resolve the conflict between the demands of poetry
and those of politics. The quotation, cited out of context, signifies an opposition between the two seemingly dichotomous positions, with the speaker
unable to comprehend how to participate actively in history: '*Actively?* What
do you mean?'

While for Northern Irish writers such a dialectic is commonplace, signalling a heightened sense of their role in a time of violence, nevertheless
the poetic responses of the generation represented by the four poets under discussion constitute a significant conceptual, if not a formal, departure
from the response of their precursor and contemporary, Seamus Heaney. As
John Goodby says, for those poets whose formative years coincided with the
eruption of the Northern Irish Troubles since 1968, conflict becomes 'more
insistently part of their mental furniture, less to be deplored in a simply moral
sense than incorporated and worked out within the poetry itself'.[6] In what
follows, it will be argued that, in their respective oeuvres, Muldoon, Paulin,
McGuckian and Carson, all address issues stemming from the Northern Irish
conflict without being inhibited by strict demarcations between private and

public discourse. They all employ structures of quotations not as 'rehearsed alibis' but as part of a complicating, oblique approach to issues of historical memory, identity and politics.

I

Paul Muldoon's poetry is reknowned for its precocious word-play and linguistic experimentation. However, reluctant to concur with the poet's contention that 'For "ludic" read "lucid" ', ('Errata', 1998)[7] critics have reacted with disquiet over the increasing obscurity of his poetry. Given free reign, its associational logic tends towards obliquity, indecipherability and a maddening lack of closure, all of which makes the reader's task onerous. Literary humour abounds in his capricious oeuvre. For instance, the final poetic enjambment of 'Why Brownlee Left' depicting the horses 'shifting their weight from foot to / Foot' is a literal translation of '*enjamber*'. The fifth line of the tenth sonnet of 'The More a Man Has the More a Man Wants' quotes the fifth line from Shakespeare's tenth sonnet ('for thou art so possessed with murd'rous hate'). And when joined together, the first letter of each line from 'Capercaillies' reads 'Is this a *New Yorker* poem, or what'. Yet such formal complexity has equally been regarded as the enviable technical ingenuity of a poet at the height of his powers; heralded as a practitioner of the 'New Narrative' by the editors of *The Penguin Book of Contemporary British Poetry*, his work has come to be seen as deploying reflexive, fragmentary fictions suited to postmodernity.

'Something Else', an extended sonnet from *Meeting the British* (1987), is typical of his impish, prismatic style. Its narrative thread flows with both rhyme and reason from the contemplation of a dinner companion's lobster, to thoughts of different kinds of dye. It alludes to the infamous anecdote of how the nineteenth-century author Gérard de Nerval used to take his pet lobster for a walk on a leash and to his tragic suicide in 1855 in the *Rue de la Vieille-Lanterne*. All this makes the speaker 'think of something else, then something else again'. The reader follows the narrative through a process of analogic association, gleaning a scenario of ill-fated or misplaced desire through, first, the recurrence of the colour red and, second, through the poet's subtly constructed web of intertextual allusions. The cited texts upon which the speaker muses, Nerval's dark, melancholic 'El Desdichado' and his evanescent, non-linear romance *Sylvie*, both hint indirectly at his own precarious relationship with the unnamed and silent companion. The form of Muldoon's text is central to its meaning. Its *mise-en-page* and the clever enjambment between the second quatrain and first tercet both mimetically represent time inexorably passing. The disrupted traditional sonnet rhyme scheme and the supplementary final line indicate a latent wish to deny both the passing of time (the deaths of the lobster, Nerval, the relationship) and writing's *différance*: its 'fugitive inks' complement the equally chimerical objects of desire. Muldoon's choice here of Nerval as a literary exemplar is symptomatic of his penchant for narrative indirection and signals his abiding concern for the reader's activity. 'The point of poetry', he argues, is to be acutely *dis*comforting, to prod and provoke, to poke us in the eye, to punch us in the nose, to knock us off our feet, to take our breath away'.[8] In contrast to Heaney's lobster from 'Away from it All', a symbol of the poet out of his element and struggling to survive, 'out of water, / fortified and bewildered', Muldoon's lobster stands for a work which can survive in both the aesthetic and public realms: it is the author who firmly guides the crustacean, not the other way round.

Muldoon's associational logic may suggest arbitrariness as the paratactic arrangement of his narratives and structures of imagery disrupt hierarchies. In his sonnet 'The Marriage of Strongbow and Aoife', (1987) the reader wonders which narrative is more important, that of the marriage between Strongbow and Aoife MacMurrough, a union leading to the Norman conquest of Ireland, or the tense stand-off between the speaker and his dinner-guest, Mary. Yet herein lies Muldoon's oblique approach to political concerns: by personalising the distant, historical account, and by granting the intimate encounter the enormity of historical significance, he intensifies the sense of betrayal inherent within both accounts ('It's as if someone had slipped / a double-edged knife between my ribs'). Similarly, in the marriage poem, 'Long Finish' from *Hay* (1998), Muldoon incorporates an anecdote detailing the senseless death of a man 'who'll shortly divine / the precise whereabouts of a landmine / on the road between Beragh and Sixmilecross'. While with Heaney such a death would feature prominently in a text, giving rise to a moral on stoic fortitude in the midst of the Troubles (as in 'Keeping Going' from *The Spirit Level*, 1996), with Muldoon it becomes an affective detail amongst other narratives which tell of the fine line between 'longing and loss'.

As in Heaney's poetry, quotations, allusions and literary references are not included for their own sake. In 'The More a Man Has the More a Man Wants', Muldoon refers to Pablo Picasso's 'Guernica' as a symbol of artistic response to the Spanish Civil War. In '7, Middagh Street', he stages an intertextual debate between Louis MacNeice and W.H. Auden over W.B. Yeats's artistic politics. Auden quotes from Yeats's 'The Man and the Echo' ('"Did that play of mine / send out certain men" (*certain* men?) / "the English shot . . .?"'), only to reply 'If Yeats had saved his pencil-lead / would certain men have stayed in bed?' While Muldoon has disavowed 'the notion of poetry as a moral force, offering respite or retribution',[9] nevertheless poems such as 'Meeting the British' and 'Madoc – A Mystery' engage with identity politics by re-examining the material forces involved in the colonial encounter, refusing the simplistic equations of coloniser/colonised. The latter text implicates both the Native Americans and the Irish in the colonisation of America and is a prime example of his self-reflexive metafictions which use quotations and historical narratives to question the processes of mediation.

'Madoc – A Mystery' (1990) is broken up into 233 sections, each surtitled with the name of a philosopher. It deals with, amongst other themes, Thomas Jefferson's expansionist policies, the Lewis and Clark expedition and the Aaron Burr conspiracy. The narrative inscribes its own structural flaws into the text. The speaker is unreliable and appears to be making it up as he goes along. At times he is forced to admit the sheer implausibility of his own tale with ironic asides: nearly half-way into the poem he concedes that things have fallen 'a little too patly into the scheme / of things'. The historical events to which the poem alludes are thus rendered suspect:

> [Jefferson]
> Has today received (1) a live gopher (2) a magpie (3) a piece of chequered skin
> or hide and (4) a cipher that reads . . . 'A-R-T-I-C-H-O-K-E-S'.

This extract relates to the articles sent back to Jefferson by the Lewis and Clark expedition. However, the veracity of Muldoon's account is put into question if one refers back both to the actual invoice forwarded by the explorers at Fort Mandan to the President and to subsequent letters by Jefferson. Equally dubious is the encrypted letter sent to Jefferson. Although the mathematician Robert Patterson developed a cipher based on the key-word 'artichokes', the code was never used on the expedition. By including carefully edited extracts from travel memoirs, letters and diaries, Muldoon guides the reader along the path of intertextual detection: while the reader is the ultimate arbiter of meaning, it is the poet who places the clues, helping the reader to see how historical experience becomes mediated through selective editing. According to Linda Hutcheon, such writing 'shows fiction to be historically conditioned and history to be discursively structured': it foregrounds 'the politics of human agency'.[10] 'Madoc – A Mystery' continually alerts the reader to a disjunction between official history and fictional re-creation, not only by including obvious disruptive elements, but also by tonal modulations and withholding information.

For Muldoon, there is a discernible tension between imaginative free play and the ordered manipulation of the reader's textual experience. Rather than opening up his poems to limitless readings, Muldoon subscribes to the notion of limited connotation: 'I'm one of those old fogies who was brought up on New Criticism and practical criticism; I believe that one of the writer's jobs is to reduce the number of possible readings of a text'. He 'argues for the primacy of unknowing yet insists on almost total knowingness on the part of poet as first reader'. In this regard, he cites Robert Frost as his exemplar, admiring, as he says in an interview, 'his mischievous, sly, multi-layered quality under the surface'.[11] However, this is only half the story. Whilst Muldoon resists pre-determination on a thematic level, in his form he often seeks fixity. In the elegy for Mary Farl Powers, 'Incantata' (1994), one can see how Muldoon's structure of quotations directs the reader's reception of the poem. 'Eyes abrim' at his lover's determination to accept her death, Muldoon alludes to Lucky's monologue in Samuel Beckett's *Waiting for Godot*, presenting grief reduced to the despairing inarticulacy of Lucky's '*quaquaqua*'. He refers also to the dumb speaking in James Joyce's *Finnegans Wake* ('quoiquoiquoiquoiquoiquoiquoiq!')

> I crouch with Belaqua
> and Lucky and Pozzo in the Acacacac-
> ademy of Anthropopopometry, trying to make sense of the
> '*quaquaqua*'
> of that potato-mouth; that mouth as prim
> and proper as it's full of self-opprobrium,
> with its '*quaquaqua*,' with its 'Quoiquoiquoiquoiquoiquoiquoiq'.

Thematically, the speaker's anguish in the face of Powers's acceptance of her pre-ordained fate is evident. Yet, paradoxically, in a text which adopts a rigid rhyme scheme, Muldoon deliberately leads the reader to view this passage as the poem's emotional centre, placed as it is at its mid-point.

II

Tom Paulin shares Muldoon's thematic preoccupation with history and politics, yet his pugnacious style as both poet and critic is, in some respects, antithetical to the latter's teasing obliquity. Reviewers have been quick to allude to Paulin's aggressive style and his reputation for verbal truculence. This was firmly established when his third (and most celebrated) collection, *Liberty Tree*, was published in 1983. In 'Desertmartin', the final stanza reductively conflates two forms of what the speaker perceives to be political extremism, namely Northern Irish Loyalism which has fostered 'a culture of twigs and bird-shit / Waving a gaudy flag it loves and curses', and Islamic fundamentalism's 'theology of rifle-butts and executions'. It may, however, be misleading to argue that the cultural clichés expose the author as ill-informed since the poem itself foregrounds the speaker's limited perspective: whereas Hegel's owl of Minerva flies only at dusk, signifying that wisdom only comes after the event, Paulin has the owl driving in a rented car across 'the territory of the Law' in the present, a visitor at a remove from his environment. Nevertheless, the structure of oppositions established within the text neatly contrasts a 'free strenuous spirit' with 'servile defiance'. This accords with the over-arching dialectic set up by the collection as a whole between the radical, dissenting Presbyterian spirit of the United Irishmen and the apparent diminishment of these ideals in contemporary Northern Irish society. This is precisely summarised in the closing lines of 'Father of History', where the United Irishmen appear 'like sweet yams buried deep, these rebel minds / endure posterity without a monument, / their names a covered sheugh, remnants, some brackish signs'.

Like Muldoon, Paulin abhors fixity, and a recurring motif in the collection is that of imprisonment, with the poet consistently registering a sense of enclosure. In 'Trine', he rails against the 'patterned god'. In 'What Kind of Formation are B Specials', he lives in 'a frozen state'. In 'From the Death Cell: Iambes VIII', rewriting a text by André Chénier in the context of the 1981 Republican Hunger Strike, the speaker accepts having to live 'dishonoured, in the shit' because, he says, 'it had to be'. And in 'Of Difference Does It Make', a poem about Unionist misrule in Northern Ireland prior to the imposition of direct rule by Westminster, we are presented with the image of 'a mild and patient prisoner / pecking through granite with a teaspoon'. Such antipathy towards Calvinist pre-determinism, rigidly linear historical narratives and the Kafkaesque implacability of governmental institutions is a direct continuation from his previous collection, *The Strange Museum*, in which the past is regarded as 'an autocracy', 'somewhere costive and unchanging'. In 'A Partial State', the territory is 'Intractable and northern', a place where the prevailing atmosphere is one of disempowerment and disillusionment: 'Stillness, without history; / until leviathan spouts, / bursting through manhole covers'. The biblical 'Leviathan' is emblematic of the forces that lurk beneath Northern Irish society and recurs in 'In the Lost Province', a poem which conveys the apparently cyclical inevitability of conflict. The speaker despairingly asks, 'Is it too early or late for change?' However, in *Liberty Tree*, Paulin re-orients his conception of history; rather than viewing it as deterministic, his poetry signals its contingent nature. Like Muldoon, he collapses the distinctions between the objectivity of historical record and the subjectivity of fictional narrative. In 'L'Envie de Commencement', history as a narrative construct is foregrounded as the speaker pictures the historian before his text as a blank canvas, 'seeing a pure narrative before him'. Similarly, in 'Martello', the speaker asks whether one can '*describe* history' and asks 'Isn't it a fiction that pretends to be fact / like *A Journal of the Plague Year*?'

Paulin's fervent engagement with issues affecting Northern Irish society has established him as the foremost political poet of his generation; as he argued in his preface to *The Faber Book of Political Verse* (1986), he does not believe 'that poems exist in a timeless vacuum or a soundproof museum, and that poets are gifted with an ability to hold themselves above history, rather like skylarks or weather satellites'.[12] In 'Purity', for example, the speaker speculates that 'a maritime pastoral / Is the form best suited' to Belfast, only to have this disallowed by the appearance of 'a crowded troopship'. Commenting on the poem, he reiterates his disavowal of any crude distinction between the private and public realms, stating that 'what I'm agonizing about is how the public life – which is cruel and involves seeing people as statistics or mass aggregates – subsidizes certain people who are able to escape it, to get beneath their duvets and supposedly relate to each other'; as a poet, he rejects what he terms 'the cult of the intimate', arguing that 'the privatization of life' involves a deplorable 'retreat from any commitment to the public world'.[13]

A distinction needs to be made, however, between texts in which Paulin usefully juxtaposes different historical contexts and incorporates enlightening intertexts, and those weaker poems which resemble cyclopic, ill-tempered tirades. In *Fivemiletown*, his fourth and most challenging collection, the poet offers an implicit indictment of the Anglo-Irish Agreement, signed by the British and Irish governments at Hillsborough, Co Down on 15 November 1985. Based on a speech by Harold McCusker, the then deputy leader of the Official Unionist Party, and one included by Paulin, as editor, in his section on 'Northern Irish Oratory' in the third volume of *The Field Day Anthology of Irish Writing*, the poem displays a rare empathy with the solitary, disregarded figure who has suddenly been forced to question not simply his political affiliation, but also his identity:

> All that Friday
> there was no flag –
> no Union Jack,
> no tricolour –
> on the governor's mansion.

Following the Agreement, what constitutes 'my own province' and 'my own people' is left uncertain for the disaffected Unionist. Paulin registers the speaker's deep, religious faith and compares his position with that of the Three Hebrew Children from the Book of Daniel (Shadrach, Meshech and Abednego), refusing to bow down before a foreign power.

In the introduction to his 1996 collection of essays, *Writing to the Moment*, Paulin explains his deep fascination for writing which is 'instant, excited, spontaneous, concentrated', for journalistic texts that are 'provisional, off-hand, spontaneous, risky in this volatile mindset', and for writing which 'seeks but never finds absolutely definitive judgments'.[14] When applied to poetry, such a style can risk appearing impetuous, unfinished and off-the-cuff; yet this is Paulin's way of counteracting, both formally and thematically, the strictures of order and determinism. In his fifth collection, *Walking a Line* (1994), his lines acquire austere brevity, avoiding iambic pentameter and punctuation; his lines of thought become less rigid. '51 Sans Souci Park' hears 'a voice thrashing in the wilderness' and then effectively presents his poetic manifesto (Paulin's italics): *'action's a solid bash / narrative a straight line / try writing to the moment / as it wimples like a burn / baby it's NOW!'*

By 'writing to the moment', his poetry becomes more immediate, fore-grounding orality and the vernacular. In an interview with Tom Raphael, the poet argued against viewing 'English' as a 'pure language'; for him, language 'goes on, recreating itself, playing games, breaking down old structures and forming new ones'; using the vernacular involves 'the total remaking of everything, and that sense of the absolute present moment'.[15] Indeed, countering the perceived inflexibilities of both English received pronunciation and print culture, Paulin writes in his introduction to *The Faber Book of Vernacular Verse* that 'the vernacular imagination distrusts print in the way that most of us dislike legal documents. That imagination expresses itself in speech and feels untrammeled by the monolithic simplicities of print, by those formulaic monotonies which distort the spirit of the living language'.[16] While in his previous collections he had liberally used Northern Irish dialect words, slang and neologisms, it had been deemed counter-productive by the critics, who argued that, far from revivifying and celebrating oral culture, it was merely 'something of a self-conscious poetical gesture'.[17] However, with 'The Wind Dog', the title poem of his collection published in 1999, Paulin had found an appropriate poetic form: the cento. In an interview with Jane Hardy he explains how he finally managed to produce this poem:

> I began to write and got interested in the cento as a literary form through Hazlitt and Eliot. A cento means a patchwork, and I found myself writing a cento with different lines, or thoughts, coming in. It's a poetic form where you take bits of other poems and put them together. The idea is that somehow, like taking bits from elsewhere to make a quilt, you make your own thing of it.[18]

Paulin has recently written about Hazlitt's prose style, describing it as 'a version of Milton's poetic centos'. So the function of the cento, is to provide old ideas with 'a redemptive life'; in Hazlitt's prose, there is 'a new quickening spirit which melts down or decomposes quotations, sources, and subjects in order to recompose'.[19] In his introduction to the recent Penguin edition of Hazlitt's writings, Paulin expands upon this theme: 'If the critic is an epic compiler of centos, a Cellini melting down prefabricated materials, he is also an actor, someone who imaginatively participates in the works he evaluates'.[20] The writer who creates centos is not equated with the lowly jobbing copyist; rather, he is a creative artist, one who all the while performing the task of iteration is also carrying out one of evaluation.

If 'The Wind Dog' is a cento, then Robert Frost lies at the heart of its bewildering myriad of citations. Paulin has long regarded Frost as an exemplar, but for very different reasons to Muldoon: 'His concept of writing', Paulin explains to Eamonn Hughes, 'was that it should come out of vernacular rhythms and trust in the speech around you. Rather than looking to received pronunciation or to a language which exists in printed texts, writing should look to that primitive, original orality, which any child is given from the moment they try to talk'.[21] Paulin imbeds two key quotations from Frost into his text, each taken from the essays 'Sentence Sounds' and 'The Figure a Poem Makes', both collected in James Scully's *Modern Poets on Poetry*:[22] 'A sentence is a sound in itself on which other sounds called words may be strung . . . The ear is the only true writer and the ear only true reader' (Frost in Scully, 50 and 52). For Paulin, Frost's poetry is accessible, democratic and non-elitist; it embraces vernacular rhythms and is to be apprehended by the ear. Embracing this *ars poetica*, Paulin cites quotations from street ballads as well as from texts by Joyce, John Clare and Thomas Hardy, each emphasising the variety of regional dialects. Crucially, however, this acts as a reaffirmation of his beliefs, as he states in the poem, 'so let me trawl and list / a couple or three sounds in my archive'.

Writing centos has, in some respects, become an artistic principle for Paulin. By joining together citations and remembered quotations, he incorporates the writing styles of others in his own text, often offering either a critique or analysis of the author in the process. For example, in 'The Four', a prose text based on the Versailles Treaty negotiations from *The Invasion Handbook* (2002), he creates an assemblage from sections taken from John Maynard Keynes's *The Economic Consequences of Peace*, inserting occasional lines of his own to augment the vitriolic attack on the policies dictated by the presiding heads of state (Clemenceau, Wilson, Lloyd George). By adopting the cento form, Paulin not only succeeds in presenting a condensed version of Keynes's treatise, he also deflects the earlier criticism concerning his verbal truculence: not only are his arguments a matter of ventriloquism, he presents the antithetical arguments in the very next poem, 'Mantoux', based on Étienne Mantoux's rejection of Keynesian economics in *The Carthaginian Peace*.

III

Medbh McGuckian is another poet who, in each of her seven collections to date, composes centos; however, while both Muldoon and Paulin guide the reader, wearing their knowledge on their sleeve, McGuckian hides hers in the seams, usually avoiding the use of italics, quotation marks, footnotes and other indicators that a text is being referred to. For this reason her texts have baffled critics with their paratactic arrangement of metaphors and dislocated syntax.

Typical of her style is the intriguingly titled 'Frost in Beaconsfield' from her collection *On Ballycastle Beach* (1987), in which she enigmatically states, 'A voice beyond a door that cuts off / The words was my coverless book to you, / Myself the price of it'. The key to her method of composition is contained in a recent cryptic statement: 'I have a certain number of gathered words (liked and chosen and interesting to me and maybe never used before) that I try to mould into a coherent, readable argument that might parallel what is going on deep in my subconscious or somewhere unreachable by words'.[23] However, far from being 'never used before', these words are compiled by the poet from biographies, memoirs, essays and other literature and subsequently used to construct poems in the form of centos. 'Frost in Beaconsfield' borrows heavily from the letters collected in *Robert Frost and John Bartlett: The Record of a Friendship*. The 'coverless book' refers to a manuscript of *A Boy's Will*, Frost's first collection which was finalised when the poet was staying in Beaconsfield. Frost prepared this particular copy himself, trimming the galley proofs and stitching the pages together, sending them to Bartlett as a gift. In a letter of 1913, he wrote to Bartlett saying, 'About now you are in receipt of my coverless book. Now you are reading it upside down in your excitement. What's the matter? You look pale. I see it all as true to life as in melodrama. . . .'[24] McGuckian's embedded quotations from Frost's letter provide a crucial context for the poem: an author, having just prepared his collection, is in need of praise, and sends it to his former pupil, and McGuckian's poem too, shares the questioning about her own poetry.[25]

Like Paulin's 'The Wind Dog', McGuckian's text expresses one of Frost's theories of poetry. She cites from another letter of 1913, in which he argues:

The best place to get the abstract sound of sense is from *voices behind a door that cuts off the words*. . . . These sounds are summoned by the audible imagination and they must be positive, strong, and definitely and unmistakeably indicated by the context. The reader must be at no loss to give his voice the posture proper to the sentence.[26]

There is a problem here. McGuckian does not clearly indicate the context in her own poem. To what extent does McGuckian lose authority, her role and status as author, by appropriating another author's words? The phrase is ambivalent: her self is certainly in the book (it is autobiographical), but she is also giving up her self and using Frost as a touchstone and literary exemplar. Her book is, therefore, 'coverless': her name does not appear as author.

There is one vital way in which McGuckian's texts follow Frost: her words are indeed 'voices behind a door that cuts off the words'. They strive towards the irrational, or that which is not-English. In recent interviews she has consistently emphasised her antipathy to English: 'I am more and more aware of English as being a foreign medium'; 'I resist and I'm angry – we're always angry, because every time we open our mouths we're slaves'. For McGuckian, the psychological discord arising from her mother tongue is not a recent phenomenon, as is evident from thoughts recorded in her 1968/69 diary: 'English is very sour upon the tongue . . . I keep finding fault with English these days, like a mother with her child'. What is particularly noteworthy is her desire to redress the situation: 'John says English here is sterile – maybe I will inseminate it'. Her decolonisation of the mind does not take the usual approach of actively appropriating English or foregrounding Hiberno-English; instead her work deterritorialises the English language, subjecting it to a radical displacement. Her deterritorialisation attempts to disrupt its structures: 'I feel perhaps in poetry a meta-language where English and Irish could meet might be possible, and disturbing the grammar or messing about like Hopkins is one method of achieving this'.[27] But her poetry is nothing like that of Hopkins. Her palimpsests do not bespeak an anxiety of influence; they manifest a deliberate estrangement from the English language.

Such a dislocation of the English language would lend credence to those critics who claim that her work is both apolitical and irrational; however, this would neglect the careful way in which she crafts her assemblages and would minimise the very real politics in her work. McGuckian's poetry has consistently sought to address the Troubles obliquely, as can be seen from her quotation from Picasso for an epigraph to her 1994 collection *Captain Lavender*: 'I have not painted the war . . . but I have no doubt that the war is in . . . these paintings I have done'. Similarly, in the title poem of her 2001 collection, *Drawing Ballerinas*, she commemorates Ann Frances Owens, a neighbour and schoolfellow who was killed in the Abercorn Café explosion in 1972 by composing a cento from extracts taken from John Elderfield's *The Drawings of Henri Matisse*:[28]

> but the page stays light, the paper with ease, at ease,
> possesses the entirety of the sheets they occupy.
> (McGuckian)

> They share an absolute sureness – a sense of having been drawn *with ease, at ease* . . . *The entirety of the sheets* is addressed (p. 128) The design 'bleeds over the whole page' and '*the page stays light*', Matisse said.
> (Elderfield, 74, 128 and 104; emphasis added)

The immediate context for these lines is the progression from Matisse's brief experiment with Cubism (*Madame Matisse*) to the less 'disquieting' *Plumed Hat* series. The artist is at ease with his medium and subject matter, and is under no obligation to respond to social strife. Summarising the rationale behind the poem, McGuckian (after Matisse) states that 'the pain and outrage continue, and one still feels obliged to draw one's ballerinas against that background'.[29]

This stance regarding the poet's social responsibility is akin to that of Muldoon's diasavowal of 'the notion of poetry as a moral force, offering respite or retribution'. In an interview with John Brown he states that '[t]he poems I've written about the political situation . . . tend to be oblique, and I think properly so: they tend to look slightly further back at the society from which the situation erupted, at *why* we are how we are now'.[30] In 'Visiting Rainer Maria' from *Marconi's Cottage* (1991), McGuckian borrows from Nadhezde Mandelstam's biography of her husband, the Russian poet Osip Mandelstam, obliquely to parallel his position as a poet in a time of state repression with her own. In 'The Disinterment' from *Drawing Ballerinas*, she draws on a critical study of the Greek playwright Aristophanes by Carlo Ferdinando Russo to establish an analogy between the treaty established between Sparta and Athens (421 BC) and the precarious first IRA ceasefire (1994). And in 'Manteo' from the same collection, she uses Angela Bourke's book *The Burning of Bridget Cleary* (about a woman violently killed because she had supposedly been abducted by the fairies) to counteract nineteenth-century anti-Irish stereotypes.

Equally, McGuckian examines the roots of conflict, imaginatively reconstructing the lives of important Irish figures. In 'The Truciler', for instance, McGuckian engages with Irish civil war politics of the 1920s by fashioning a collage of phrases taken from Tim Pat Coogan's biography of the Irish political leader, Michael Collins.

> The bullet cleared the briars
> off the top of the ditch, drove
> particles of his bone at a four

miles per hour walk, to rejoin a road
like a swine with a tusk
which has grown round into the head.

Within minutes of that noontide
priceless manuscripts floated over
the city, releasing the scent
of partition, and the stray light
in the straitjacket of the Republic
paid out the head money of his soul.

Many of the *'Trucileers'* as they were called were poorly disciplined. [. . .]
And McPeake cleaning *the briars off of the top of the ditch* [. . .] *The bullet*
apparently *drives* not only *particles of bone* but also an air pocket before
it [. . .] [T]he pair went back to Dublin at a *'four miles an hour walk'* [. . .]
[P]riceless manuscripts . . . floated over the city [. . .] Firstly, the election, which
made Craig the Six Counties' first Prime Minister . . . had the more important
long-term result of definitely and unmistakably *releasing the scent of Partition*
into the Irish electoral air. . . . 'That', said he, 'is me, in *the straitjacket of the
Republic*'.[31]

Chronologically, the poem works backwards, beginning with a description
of the assassination in 1922 of Michael Collins, leader of the pro-Treaty
faction during the civil war and head of the Free State Army ('Trucileers').
We follow the bullet's trajectory as it passes inexorably through his head, its
speed linked to a different journey, a friendly, though perilous 'four miles an
hour walk' across Dublin with Liam Deasy, a leading figure in the Cork IRA,
the organisation which ultimately sealed his fate. Here, McGuckian intimates
its tragic nature: as the Volunteers' Director of Intelligence during the guerilla
insurgency of 1919–21, Collins trained those who would later oppose him
after the Treaty was signed with Lloyd George. The weapon used against the
British ('tusk') becomes self-defeating for Collins ('grown round inside his
own head'). McGuckian blurs cause and effect by conflating three distinct
elements which led up to (but were not a result of) Collins's death. In the first
place, she refers to an event on 30 June 1922, when surrendering anti-Treaty
forces destroyed irreplaceable manuscripts at the Public Records Office in
Dublin's Four Courts. Second, Sir James Craig was elected as the first Prime
Minister of the newly partitioned Northern Ireland. And third, McGuckian
alludes to the concept of 'external association' (in which Ireland remained in
the Commonwealth while independent in internal matters). Michael Collins
brought this plan to his negotiations with the British in 1921, but it failed
to keep him out of what the plan's author, and Collins's nemesis, Eamon de
Valera termed, 'the straitjacket of the Republic'. McGuckian's lines dwell on

the political fall-out rather than their specific causes, establishing an apparent tension between freedom and restriction: the limitations of 'straitjacket' and 'partition' are picked up later by the 'dwelling house' that 'is always/ locked' and the 'towels/ framed all round the railings'. Parallel to this is the bullet clearing the briars and the released scent, both as destructive as the enclosed tusk 'which has grown round into the head'.

It is open to speculation as to whether McGuckian considers Collins to be a tragic figure manipulated by De Valera into a no-win situation or as someone who has made a Faustian pact and is to blame for the legacy of partition. However, the speaker does address Collins in Churchill's derogatory terms:

> Corner boy in excelsis, with towels
> framed all round the railings,
> Ireland is yours: take it.
>
> (McGuckian)

Churchill, . . . was coming to view Collins as a 'corner boy in excelsis' [. . .] [W]ith towels framed all around the railings to show they were on pleasure bent [. . .] 'Ireland is yours for the taking. Take it.'

(Coogan, 365, 219 and 320)

IV

Just as Medbh McGuckian's approach to identity politics can be described as veiled ('This oblique trance is my natural / Way of speaking' ['Prie-Dieu']), that of Ciaran Carson is equally indirect ('I tell it slant' ['I']). Although his two best-known collections, *The Irish for No* (1987) and *Belfast Confetti* (1989), are packed with references to defensive architecture, surveillance gadgetry and the armaments of both State and paramilitary warfare, his poetic narratives refuse to make summary judgements. In 'Campaign' (originally entitled 'Wrong Side of the Fence'), we are told bluntly that 'They took him to a waste-ground somewhere near the Horseshoe Bend, and told him / What he was. They shot him nine times'. Similarly, in 'Cocktails', 'There was talk of someone who was shot nine times and lived, and someone else / Had the info. On the Romper Room. We were trying to remember the facts'. Like David Crone's street-scene painting *Shop Window* (1980), or Jack Pakenham's series of paintings entitled *A Broken Sky* (1995),[32] both of which feature Belfast viewed from multiple perspectives and differing sightlines, there are rapid shifts of perspective between (and often within) poems. In a realistic manner, at once documentary and psychological, the poems convey the disorienting complexity of life during the Troubles, a time when location and locution become key signifiers of identity. Carson's poetry recounts quotidian instances of interrogation when names, appearances and personal histories are all assessed to ascertain religious (and political) affiliation. In 'Last Orders' the speaker and his companion are first scrutinised by CCTV before passing through 'the steel mesh gate' that surrounds the entrance to the bar. Appearances are deceiving, however, as we are told that the speaker is a Catholic ('Taig's written on my face') and, once inside, they both order the beer *Harp*, failing to notice in time 'the *Bushmills* mirror' (signifying a Protestant establishment). 'Night Out' replays the initial scene of optical surveillance with the speaker forced to wait outside 'the galvinized wire mesh gate', and when inside 'we get the once-over once again'.

Carson's poetry insists on repetition and circularity within the 'narrow ground' of Ulster geography and history. The historian A.T.Q. Stewart uses the phrase 'narrow ground', for his analysis of the Northern Irish conflict as cyclical and inflexible. 'The Ulsterman carries the map of this religious geography in his mind almost from birth', says Stewart, '[h]e knows which villages, which roads and streets, are Catholic, or Protestant, or 'mixed'. It not only tells him where he can, or cannot, wave an Irish tricolour or wear his orange sash, but imposes on him a complex behaviour pattern and a special way of looking at political problems'.[33] 'The Brain of Edward Carson' from *First Language* (1993) is one poem which promulgates such a thesis, featuring a map of Ulster, 'opened up, hexagonal and intricate, tectonic: / Its shifting plates were clunked and welded into place by laws Masonic'. The text centres on the 'riveted, internal gaze' and cognitive mapping of 'the uncrowned king of Ulster', Edward Carson. The rhymes of the poem place emphasis on such a rigid mindset ('static', 'cataleptic', 'Masonic', 'catatonic').

Like Muldoon and Paulin, Carson does not subscribe to a deterministic outlook and uses cartographic discourse to foreground contingency. In attempting to write 'the fractious epic that is Belfast' and to render the city itself as a text, using 'alphabet bricks', recording how 'the storeyed houses became emboldened by their hyphenated, skyward narrative',[34] Carson uses the crucial image of the map. Cartography in his work has many functions: it marks out territory and records the location of peace-walls, security barriers and republican/loyalist enclaves; it is an *aide-mémoire*, facilitating an ultimately doomed project of reclamation, retrieval and remembrance; it instigates a reflection both on the inexactitude of memory and on the intersection between story and history. Carson realises what cultural geographers have increasingly come to accept, that a map is not a text which presents a simple mimetic representation of a territory. A map constructs the world rather than simply reproducing it, since the knowledge which it embodies is socially constructed. And a map can be redrawn in any number of ways and can symbolise change rather than fixity.

In 'Punctuation' the speaker is walking the streets and the 'frosty night is jittering with lines and angles, invisible trajectories: Crackly, chalky diagrams in geometry, rubbed out the instant they're sketched'; the lines may be familiar, yet the speaker feels lost. Similarly, the maps of 'Turn Again' are all provisional. There is the blueprint for the bridge that was never built and an inaccurate cartographic plan of the city depicting 'the bridge that collapsed' and 'the streets that never existed'. The map's materiality itself is prone to change ('The linen backing is falling apart'). What interests Carson about cartographic representation is not verisimilitude. Rather, it is 'the idea that a map has a secret, or that it is an essential part of a narrative, or that it is in itself a narrative, a sidelong version of reality. It's interesting to me that a map is only useful by how far it deviates from reality'.[35] We see the world not as it is, but as it is perceived. Belfast is consistently represented as fearful and complex, frustrating the quest for meaning at every turn. In 'Smithfield' the speaker glimpses 'a map of Belfast / In the ruins: obliterated streets, the faint impression of a key. / Something many-toothed, elaborate, stirred briefly in the labyrinth'. While the 'key' has the potential to unlock mysteries and make the map intelligible, it is also as forbidding and 'many-toothed' as a Minotaur.

Carson's emphasis on provisionality is compounded by the form of his poetry. After his first collection, *The New Estate*, was published in 1976, he became intensely self-critical, viewing poetry as a furtive pursuit, removed and academic. He gained renewed self-confidence in his art from a number of sources, each of which dictated the form of his later work. Initially, he began to read the work of C.K. Williams who composed narrative poetry using expansive long lines. But he was also influenced by the digressive, convoluted oral narratives of Joseph Campbell from Mullaghbawn. His job then as Arts Council Officer also took him around Ireland to study and record traditional music, an activity which led him to see how '[t]he 8-bar music unit of the reel – which can be further divided into smaller units, 2 or 4 or whatever – corresponds roughly to the length of, and stresses within, the poetry line'.[36] Employing the long line, his poetry adopts an associative logic and becomes both conversational and metamorphic; eschewing closure, it features multiple (often disjunctive) narratives, mixing personal anecdotes with excerpts from ballads, literature and historical documentation. The beginning of 'Dresden' (which opened *The Irish For No* in 1987) is typical of this new style: 'Horse Boyle was called Horse Boyle because of his brother Mule; / Though why Mule was called Mule is anybody's guess. I stayed there once, / Or rather, I nearly stayed there once. But that's another story'. Time frames overlap, stories mutate into one another and all are held together by a complex structure. Commenting on the effect of Cathal McConnell's music,

Carson states that '[o]ur knowledge of the past is changed each time we hear it; our present time, imbued with yesterday, comes out with bent dimensions. Slipping in and out of notes of time, we find our circles sometimes intersect with others'.[37] Likewise, his own use of the musical long line allows him to convey place, history and identity as palimpsests, resistant to unitary readings.

Representation for Carson becomes even more problematic since his first language is Gaelic. '*La Je-Ne-Sais-Quoi*', the opening (love) poem from *First Language* attempts to express the ineffable though synaesthesia, the mixing of the senses:

> I bhfaiteadh na mbéal
> I bhfriotal na súl
> Fáscadh agus teannadh
> Do dtí nach raibh ann
> Ach scáth an scátháin eadrainn,
> Tocht i do chluais istigh.

(In the blink of a mouth, in the word of an eye, embraced and tightened, until there was nothing there but the shadow of a shadow between us, I reach into your ear.) Yet even here one witnesses the difficulty language has in describing the interstitial or liminal. The poet lapses into silence, struggling to describe the emotions evoked 'I gclapsholas domhain do phóige' (by the twilight world of your kiss). His English poems describing Belfast life become fragmented, straining to contain a veritable babble and hubbub. 'Sonnet' is parodic of the neatly constructed form it names, made up of fourteen random, disjointed lines taken from overheard conversations, films and advertisements. His suspicion of, and playful attitude towards, language becomes evident in 'Ark of the Covenant' in which he imitates Wallace Stevens's 'Sea Surface Full of Clouds', having each section as a variation of the other: using synonyms gleaned from a thesaurus, Carson constructs four differing narratives based on a single text.

All four poets under discussion have faced hostile criticism during their respective careers. Muldoon has been charged with an elitist intellectualism. Paulin has been castigated for his blunt directness. McGuckian's hermetic verse has led to incomprehension and bafflement. And Carson levelled criticism at himself for the costive nature of his early work. While one must concede that interpreting their poetry involves difficulty for the reader (finding the sources, comparing the quoting text with that from which it cites, translating the 'foreign' language), nevertheless each poet has found a form best suited to tackling different aspects of identity politics. Muldoon's historiographic metafictions allow him to interrogate the veracity and assumptions behind historical narratives. Paulin's poetic centos enable him to celebrate oral culture. McGuckian's palimpsests facilitate a more oblique approach to the Troubles. Carson's long lines and fragmented narratives, borrowing sources as poetic material and competing voices, make possible a poetry which disrupts the very idea of a single, unitary national story or identity.

NOTES

1 Paul Muldoon, *To Ireland, I* (Oxford University Press, 2000), p. 35.
2 Seamus Heaney, *The Government of the Tongue* (London: Faber and Faber, 1988), pp. 101, 92.
3 Ciaran Carson, 'Escaped from the Massacre', *Honest Ulsterman*, 50 (Winter, 1975), p. 183.
4 Seamus Heaney, *Station Island* (London: Faber and Faber, 1984).
5 Milosz cited by Heaney, Preface, *The Crane Bag Book of Irish Studies*, eds. Richard Kearney and Mark Patrick Hederman (Gerrards Cross: Colin Smythe, 1983), p. i.
6 John Goodby, *Irish poetry since 1950: from stillness into history* (Manchester University Press, 2000), p. 9.
7 Paul Muldoon, *Poems, 1968–1998* (London: Faber and Faber, 2001).
8 Muldoon, 'The Point of Poetry', *Princeton University Library Chronicle*, 49.3 (Spring, 1998), p. 516.
9 Muldoon, 'Getting Round: Notes Towards an *Ars Poetica*', *Essays in Criticism*, 48, 2 (April, 1998), p. 127.
10 Linda Hutcheon, ' "The Pastime of Time Past": Fiction, History, and Historiographic Metafiction', *Genre* 20.3–4 (Fall-Winter, 1987), p. 299; and *Irony's Edge: The Theory and Politics of Irony* (London: Routledge, 1994), pp. 11–12.
11 Lynn Keller, 'An Interview with Paul Muldoon', *Contemporary Poetry*, 35.1 (Spring, 1994), 13l; Muldoon, 'Getting Round', p. 127; Muldoon in John Brown, *In the Chair: Interviews with Poets from the North of Ireland* (Clare: Salmon Press, 2002), p. 188.
12 Paulin, 'Introduction', *The Faber Book of Political Verse*, ed. Paulin (London: Faber and Faber, 1986), p. 17.
13 Paulin, interview by John Haffenden, *Viewpoints: Poets in Conversation with John Haffenden* (London: Faber and Faber, 1981), pp. 164–5.
14 Paulin, 'Introduction', *Writing to the Moment: Selected Critical Essays, 1980–1996* (London: Faber and Faber, 1996), p. xii.
15 Paulin, interview by Tom Raphael, 'The Promised Land', *Oxford Poetry* 7.1 (1983), p. 9.
16 Paulin, 'Vernacular Verse', in *Writing to the Moment*, p. 260.
17 Kate Flint, 'Face to Face', *The English Review* 4.1 (September, 1993), p. 15.
18 Paulin, 'The Dust over a Battlefield', interview by Jane Hardy, *Poetry Review* 87.1 (Spring, 1997), p. 33.
19 Tom Paulin, *The Day-Star of Liberty: William Hazlitt's Radical Style* (London: Faber and Faber, 1998), p. 95.
20 Paulin, 'Introduction', *William Hazlitt: The Fight and Other Writings* (London: Penguin, 2000), p. xii.

21 Eamonn Hughes, 'Q&A with Tom Paulin', *Irish Literary Supplement* 7.2 (1991), p. 31.

22 Quotations from Frost, 'Sentence Sounds', Modern Poets on Poetry, ed. James Scully (London: Collins, 1966), are cited on the left of Paulin's text. See Paulin, 'The Wind Dog', *The Wind Dog* (London: Faber and Faber, 1999), pp. 21–36.

23 McGuckian, interview by Brown, *In the Chair*, p. 176.

24 Margaret Bartlett Anderson, *Robert Frost and John Bartlett: The Record of a Friendship* (New York: Holt, Rinehart and Winston, 1963), p. 35.

25 In a letter to the author (15 September 1999), McGuckian reveals that the poem was written for her cousin, a scientist living in Beaconsfield, who was trying to understand her work.

26 Frost in Anderson, pp. 52–3.

27 Rand Brandes, 'Interview with Medbh McGuckian', *Chattahoochee Review* 16.3 (Spring, 1996), p. 60; John Hobbs, ' "My Words Are Traps": An Interview with Medbh McGuckian', *New Hibernia Review* 2.1 (Spring, 1998), p. 114; McGuckian, 'Rescuers and White Cloaks: Diary 1968–69', *My Self, My Muse: Irish Women Poets Reflect on Life and Art*, ed. Patricia Boyle Haberstroh (Syracuse University Press, 2001), p. 150; Brandes, p. 61.

28 John Elderfield, *The Drawings of Henri Matisse* (London: Thames and Hudson, 1984).

29 McGuckian, 'How Being Irish Has Influenced Me as a Writer', *Wee Girls*, ed. Lizz Murphy (Melbourne: Spinifex, 1996), p. 201.

30 Muldoon, interview by Brown, *In the Poet's Chair*, p. 190.

31 Tim Pat Coogan, *Michael Collins: A Biography* (London: Arrow, 1991), pp. 311, 420, 418, 138, 332, 212 and 231.

32 See David Crone, *Paintings, 1963–1999*, ed. S.B. Kennedy (Dublin: Four Courts Press, 1999), p. 35; Jack Pakenham, *A Broken Sky* (Derry: Orchard Gallery, 1995).

33 A.T.Q. Stewart, *The Narrow Ground*, 1977 (London: Faber and Faber, 1989), p. 181.

34 Ciaran Carson, *The Star Factory* (London: Granta, 1997), p. 126.

35 Carson, interview by Frank Ormsby, *Linen Hall Review* (April, 1991), p. 5.

36 Carson, interview by Rand Brandes, *Irish Review* 8 (Spring, 1990), p. 82.

37 Carson, *Last Night's Fun: A Book about Irish Traditional Music* (London: Jonathan Cape, 1996), p. 90.

12

LUCY COLLINS

Performance and dissent: Irish poets in the public sphere

The poetry of dissent, indeed the dissenting position in literature as a whole, has a long and distinguished tradition in Ireland. For reasons of political and personal sensitivity, writers have found themselves in, and often cultivated, a marginalised, observing status. The presence of aesthetic and political tensions can be linked closely to Ireland's continuing absorption of differing influences and experiences: these can both conflict with and build upon existing ideas of tradition and continuity. The adversarial position adopted by Irish writers earlier in this century focused on oppositional relations such as those between Ireland and England or between individual freedoms and the Catholic norms of the evolving state. Now violence, materialism and social exclusion have become the focus of attention and with these forms comes a complex matrix of affects neither easy to define nor to address. The poets dealt with in this chapter – Brendan Kennelly, Paul Durcan, Rita Ann Higgins and Nuala Ní Dhomhnaill – are aware of the tensions inherent in these issues and of the fact that they are never fully subject to artistic or personal control. Indeed it is this lack of control that heightens the risks taken by these poets to allow their voices to be heard. All four poets are widely read, in a culture where the critical attention to poetry still far exceeds popular readership, and all the poets use vibrant humorous language and frequent public performance to maintain the dissenting voice within contemporary Irish poetry.

The notion of dissent itself foregrounds the issue of authorial position: from what or from whom do these writers dissent? Is it from political norms, or prevailing social values? The evolution undergone by Irish society in the past half-century has some bearing on this question, for the recurring backdrop to discussion of social change is the stereotypical model of de Valera's Ireland: conservative, isolationist, dominated by the Church and its rigid moral codes. Indeed it is the once close connection between the State and Catholicism that is thought to underlie many of the difficulties with which Irish society has sought to come to terms over recent decades. It now moves

away from a period in which social ills are seen as sanctioned by the ma-
chinery of state, and towards one which accords global forces the shaping
power of change. Yet when considering literature within a particular cultural
framework – here an Irish one – it seems impossible to remove the specific
nature of that state and, more especially, its relationship with its citizens,
from consideration. This dynamic is a complex one since the perceptions of
the individual concerning political authority are notoriously changeable and
open to endless reinterpretation. The cultural force-field within which the
writer works makes palpable the tensions between historical and contemporary understanding, as well as between fluctuating public opinion and slow-
moving political and legislative developments. It is clear then, that poets
adopting a dissenting position must often contend with ill-defined, and
scarcely remediable, areas of human experience.

The relationship between the private and the public assumes particular
importance here. These poets must negotiate their own personal position in
relation to society while also speaking for others – they do not represent an
entirely individual perspective but also a changing role within that society. If
the theme of change itself calls attention to ideas of tradition – so strong in
formulations of Irish literature – these poets must be aware of the burden of
that tradition while concertedly seeking fresh views, aiming to make poetry
speak to a wider audience. The conflict between experiencing the injustices
of society and rendering them objectively in art has always been a troubled
one. It accounted for the struggle marking Austin Clarke's satirical works as
he sought to represent the extremity of despair in disciplined forms. Thomas
Kinsella's *Butcher's Dozen*, uncharacteristic among his works for the outspoken nature of its political comment, was also criticised for its intemperate
stance and for its supposed aesthetic failure. As early as 1962 Sean O'Faolain
registered the 'writer's battle for honesty' in these terms: 'The danger of becoming embittered, or twisted, threatens creativity itself, and here we come
to the real battleground of contemporary Irish writing. For the first time Irish
writers have to *think* themselves into personal release ... We need to explore
Irish life with an objectivity never hitherto applied to it ...'[1] The combined
necessity of objective judgement and personal conviction means that the poet
occupies several positions at once: never simply the marginalised observer,
the writer's own identity and process of writing is implicated in the social
dynamic represented.

The scrutiny of critics often turns on the ability of the poet to sustain
the highest attention to form while rendering the immediate world in direct
and uncompromising terms. Yet in the context of performance this may be a
misplaced demand, as Richard Poirier suggests: 'Because performance is [...]
inevitably caught up in the social and political exigencies of the moment – the

formal dimensions of an artist's particular medium might even be said to impede the action of performance'.[2] Thus while the relationship between form and theme is an important one in poetry, it becomes necessary to adjust our expectations of aesthetic achievement in this context. If the poem is to challenge, especially at the level of performance, it must question as well as utilise the demands of its genre. Indeed the kinds of interrogation attempted by these writers may also strike at the heart of fixed attitudes to the role and norms of poetic reception. If these poets are of their time in their attention to the social and political nexus that they occupy, they also take pleasure in unsettling established perceptions.

Performance is a key element in the formation of poetic identity for these four writers. All give well-attended readings and, in the case of Brendan Kennelly and Paul Durcan, their appearance on discussion programmes and chat shows has greatly enhanced their public profile, as well as suggesting that accessibility and contemporary relevance are popularising attributes. This kind of exposure has also reinforced their identity as specifically Irish poets, personally recognisable to their readership in a way that few British or American poets could claim. Such visibility can emphasise the persona of the poet at the expense of the work, however, and encourages a view of Irish culture as more concerned to reinforce a literary ambience than to read poems. The performative aspect of the work also has implications for the immediacy – and perhaps even the brevity – of its impact, though many performance poets state that they do not write with this specific context in mind.[3] In drawing attention to the voice and to the presence of the poet within the work, a reading emphasises the directness and the topicality of the form as well as making oblique connections to the oral tradition of the poem in history. Yet in spite of the importance of performance in forging a direct connection with the listener, the availability of the written text also obliquely suggests the ways in which that moment of connection can be transcended by the fixity of the written word. Even during the performance then, the attuned listener will be evaluating the experience against that of reading the text. Alternatively, an audience less familiar with the work may be discouraged from an analytical response by the proximity between the writer's persona and the poetic content, deferring such a development to a time of private reading.

These complex levels of engagement signal the value of an intellectual approach to the relationship between poem itself and its public reading, yet to theorise the act of performance may be to diminish its power. Performance poets, Paul Beasley argues, 'up-hold the sheer physicality of language [. . .] which a communication model would de-materialize'.[4] In the performance situation involvement in the poetry becomes more important than judgement of it, even though a complex commentary on the society under scrutiny may be in the process of being formed. Are the listeners part of that society or also canny observers of it? The use of humour, irony and shock tactics in the poetry has the potential to disrupt the comfortable position of the audience. Yet the sheer familiarity of the performer may counteract this effect. It is possible for the shocking utterance to become a parody of itself, internalised by a willing audience who can become comfortable with the dissenting voice, so long as it is kept within bounds.

Out of bounds: Brendan Kennelly

The enduring popularity of Brendan Kennelly's poetry is perhaps its most striking feature, not least as his readership has grown considerably since his transition from lyric to epic mode. Frequency of publication also keeps his work firmly in the public arena, though now watched for more keenly by committed readers than by poetry critics. His popular appeal owes as much to the attitude and energy of the work as it does to its scope and style. Cultural context also plays a heightened role in both the reception and creation of these poems: Kennelly's expression of his opinions in interviews and conversation shows an inquiring, flexible mind full of incongruities and surprises. These qualities are found also in his poetic voice and are responsible for the engaging yet often disconcerting quality of his writing, especially in the exuberant long sequences: *Cromwell* (1983), *The Book of Judas* (1991) and *Poetry My Arse* (1995).

From his earliest work Kennelly has been attuned to the weaknesses and cruelties inherent in human behaviour and has placed these decisively, even relentlessly, in an Irish context. The characters and stories of his native Kerry provided structure for the first collections of lyrics, rendering Kennelly's childhood with immediacy yet keeping him rooted in a particularised world that did not force him to extend the limits of his understanding or of his art. Few of these early poems show any attempt at experimentation either in thematic or technical terms, though at their most successful they create a cumulative picture of the contradictory emotions, the fear and stubbornness, of the human struggle. Critical consensus suggests that the prolific output of these years encouraged Kennelly's tendency towards indiscriminate writing and his reluctance to edit his work. These judgements, based largely on failures of technique, have frequently relegated Kennelly to the role of minor poet and they remain difficult to elide. Nevertheless, Ake Persson, in *Betraying the Age: Social and Artistic Process in Brendan Kennelly's Work*, has argued for new criteria to be used in any assessment, suggesting that the social function of the poetry must be at the forefront of interpretation.[5]

Such a reading emphasises the dynamism of the work and its explicit engagement with difficult and contentious topics rather than its limited formal achievements.

Some acute and aggressive works from the early period specifically challenge an unthinking acceptance of received opinion. A poem such as 'Baby' draws startling social commentary and the harsh realities of rural existence together: it refers specifically to the 1984 Kerry Babies case[6] yet surprisingly moves towards a celebration of human endurance:

> I find it interesting to be dead.
> I drift out here, released, looking down
> At men and women passing judgement
> In the streets of that moneymad little town.
>
> . . .
>
> There was a hope of love at the back of it all
> And in spite of clever men making money
> That small hope still survives.[7]

By choosing to give the dead baby a voice, Kennelly not only brings a vital – even shocking – new perspective to a topical issue but makes the reader think further about what it means to lack a voice, or to have others speak on our behalf. In this poem as in a number of others, Kennelly's subversion of established viewpoints implicitly extends far beyond his chosen subject, yet is made the stronger by the particularity of the context. It seems, paradoxically, that the poet's work needs this firm anchor in order to make its range clearly felt.

Kennelly's desire to let the voiceless speak through his work is linked by him to a conviction that poetry is a force for change, yet one that must accommodate multiple – and often distinctly marginal – viewpoints within its scope:

Eliot's line, 'the awful daring of a moment's surrender' has often come into my head when I am trying to work on the notion that poetry is an attacking force born of a state of conscious surrender. For me, this surrender is made possible by listening to voices, letting them speak, especially if these voices are of those who are outcasts in history and myth, reviled, damned, and not worth a second thought.[8]

The idea of reclaiming these voices, not only from the present but from personal and collective memory, is important in Kennelly's continuing evocation of the rural world and provides the momentum for the most significant of his projects to date. *Cromwell*, published in 1983, has been seen as a turning point in the poet's career, marking a decisive move towards an ambitious, historically focused work unique in its approach to Irish history. This is an epic poem constructed from a series of sonnets, allowing this normally distant form to be brought close to the reader and availing fully of the consequent emotional range. The inclusive imagination of Buffún, the central narrating figure, is the key to the meaning of this poem and to its measured success: he 'could not endure the emptiness' and initiated a dialogue with Cromwell who will later remind him – 'you invited me here. I am the guest of your imagination, therefore have the grace to hear me out'.[9] This act of invitation must also be the reader's, though the going will be tough. The strands of Kennelly's early storytelling impulse remain strong here; at times made taut by the presence of raw experience – violence, religious ferocity, humour; at times slackening under the numerous digressions that readers have found distracting.

The opening poem 'A Host of Ghosts' begins: 'Night: the pits are everywhere,/I am slipping into the pit of my own voice,/Snares and traps in plenty there' (*Cromwell*, 1) warning that though the voice can liberate us from fixed emotions, it can also misuse us, manipulate us. In slipping among the voice of Cromwell himself (excerpts from letters and speeches are used directly in places) and other characters and stories, Kennelly rejects fixed notions of history and probes the psychology of the most reviled figure in Irish history. To dissent from this inherited hatred is to call into question the emotional responses of both individual and nation and to question assumptions concerning recent events in the continuing story of British-Irish relations. The digressions of the poem then, can be seen at this stage as part of the poet's desire to render alternative ideas and positions fully. By using versions of the sonnet form Kennelly encloses each idea firmly within its own boundaries, yet in the grouping of poems we see how one expression finds continuity in the next. 'A Language' emphasises the cultural and personal isolation of language loss picked up again in the subsequent poems 'That Word' and 'What Use?':

> I had a language once.
> I was at home there.
> Someone murdered it
> Buried it somewhere.
> I use different words now
> Without skill, truly as I can.
> A man without a language
> Is half a man, if he's lucky.

For all the loquacious qualities of narrator and of poet, this collection concerns the struggle to make the self understood amid the misrepresentations

of history and the narrow-minded judgements of society. In this sense performance itself becomes a dissenting act, a demand for the voice of the individual
to be heard against the assumptions of the majority. Ultimately though, even
the sense of personal identity comes under erasure, as the penultimate poem
suggests: 'When I consider what all this has made me/I marvel at the catalogue:/I am that prince of liars Xavier O'Grady,/I am Tom Gorman, dead in
the bog . . .' (*Cromwell*, p. 145). To break down certainties of identity is also
to risk incoherence, both personal and poetic.

These risks are taken still further in *The Book of Judas* (1991) to the point
where the meaning imparted by the experiment begins to be lost.[10] Again
Kennelly picks an icon of hatred and explores the contemporary implications
of betrayal and greed. This work has the body at its centre – whether it is the
betrayed body of Christ or the self-destructive Judas, this visceral quality im-
bues almost all the poems with their omnipresent sexual concerns. In addressing a culture comparatively recently grown from sexual timidity, Kennelly
again places explicit expression against a background of stultifying Catholic
morality, but here excess almost destroys the power of the voice. The directness of the utterance is a rebuff to conservative attitudes towards religion, sex
and history as well as an attempt to render the realities of passion directly.
'[T]his Christian culture itself is a parody of what may once have been a passion', Kennelly writes in his preface to the poem, locating his reworking of the
Christian myth in a specifically Irish context.[11] Imagining Judas out drinking with the Church he asks, ' "What have we / In common?" ' ' "Nothing
that I can / See" smiled The Church. "That's where you're wrong" / I
replied. "How so?" inquired The Church. / I smiled "We both betrayed
an innocent man." ' (*Book of Judas*, 141). The reckless, casual force that
energises the language of these poems also animates institutions, objects,
ideas: all emerge in dialogue and in action, so that Kennelly moves further
towards the dramatic in his development of themes. Rather than achieving
inclusiveness of form, all his epics strive, in some measure, towards what is
inevitably outside their boundaries, towards the rough sensual risk of real
experience. In this sense the distinction between performance *of* the poem
and performance *in* the poem can no longer be clearly drawn: Kennelly attempts to replicate the directness of his encounter with an audience even in
the printed text.

Paul Durcan: 'relentless moralist'

Paul Durcan shares with Kennelly a strong emphasis on the performance of
his work and uses this to extend the interpretative reach of poetic texts that
are simultaneously personal and public. The ritual quality of his readings

creates an almost hypnotic effect and accentuates the paradoxical role of forms of exposure in the preservation of the intimacy of his work. Edna Longley distinguishes between what she calls the 'priestly' roles of Durcan and Kennelly, characterising the former as visionary and the latter secular.[12] Certainly the openness of Kennelly's performances can be contrasted with the incantatory and often self-mocking stance adopted by Durcan. Thus the exploration of identity in which both poets participate is integral, in Durcan's case especially, to the ambiguity of physical presence.

Within Durcan's texts themselves the fusion of the topical and the fantastical has prompted critics to term his work surreal. While the poems prove resistant to rational approaches, Derek Mahon has convincingly rejected the surrealist reading in favour of the cubist, arguing that Durcan is 'transfixed by the simultaneity of disparate experience, all sides of the question'.[13] This simultaneity of representation accounts for the prevalence of visual keys to the work, both in critical approaches and explicitly in the later books *Crazy About Women* (1991) and *Give Me Your Hand* (1994) both of which are inspired by collections of paintings.[14] This openness to all possibilities is also a rejection of the singular perspective or fixed standpoint, and itself constitutes a dissenting position in its unwillingness to accept the unifocal stance demanded by society. Public performance also stakes a claim for multiplicity within the single poem: on each occasion different interpretations may be suggested. Yet in Durcan's case the visual emphasis could suggest containment – a drawing inward of the writing, a formal and thematic telescoping of the reckless abandon with which Kennelly addresses similar topics. A personal note can often be caught in Durcan's work, most explicitly in poems concerning his wife and later his father. Yet to read these as detailed revelations is itself an illusion: instead we glimpse the shadow of the suffering speaker, at times pathetic and self-pitying, yet transcending these through near-heroic endurance.

Catholicism is an important target for Durcan's satire but, like Kennelly, he is an insider to the extremes of belief and Durcan allows the linguistic aspects of litany and invocation to permeate the form and style of his work, most notably in his use of repetitive sentence structures. In this way he undermines the pieties of Irish society through a bizarre mimicry of their effects, an aspect of his work that places it closer to Clarke in the astringency of his satire than to any of Durcan's own contemporaries. His aim is perhaps to unsettle rather than to shock, but he not only tackles issues of private morality, of marriage and the family, of social and national pretensions directly, he also defamiliarises them for both narrator and reader by inserting the perspective of a distant observer. In this double context of familiarity and strangeness Durcan addresses the question of what it is to be Irish, with particular awareness of the split perspective between North and South. However, he is more concerned with capturing the difficult negotiations of the moment than with mapping the labyrinths of history. The atrocity commemorated in 'The Minibus Massacre: The Eve of the Epiphany' (1975) is reprised in 'Poem Not Beginning with a Line from Pindar' (1990).[15] Ordinary images – 'Sandwich boxes and flasks, / Decks of playing cards' – reappear but his father's response to the killing is moved to the centre of the poem with shocking effect. ' "Teach the Protestants a lesson" ', he says, followed by the professional ' "The law is the law and the law must take its course" '.[16] The private and public roles of the man – at once judge and father – also reflect the interaction between exterior and interior worlds.

Durcan's interweaving of personal and political relationships in his work is used to weigh individual attitudes to actions made in the name of the nation. In addressing the brutality of both sides of the conflict, he often chooses similar events to suggest the relentless uniformity of violence, yet varies his poetic strategies effectively: 'In Memory: The Miami Showband: Massacred 31 July 1975'[17] begins by quoting '*Beautiful are the feet of them that preach the gospel of peace*' and closes with the same image: 'You made music, and that was all: You were realists/And beautiful were your feet',[18] a strange tenderness emerging in the contemplation of the sacred yet vulnerable nature of the human body. 'Margaret Thatcher Joins IRA'[19] expands its headline title whimsically: 'At the navel of the rath/Waltzed Ruairi Ó Brádaigh/His arms round Mrs Thatcher/In a sweet embrace'.[20] Given the tonal range of these works it can at times be difficult to detect whether Durcan is sceptical of or receptive to the easy emotional response to violence and outrage, or whether the setting of differing responses in close proximity to one another is simply a means of creating the startling effects he seeks.

Though Ireland's tangled relationship with its peoples is often seen as central among Durcan's preoccupations, the extent to which he confronts both universal themes and other cultures underscores the need to establish a critique of Ireland within a broader framework. Collections such as *The Berlin Wall Café* (1985) and *Going Home to Russia* (1987) allow both personal and national interaction with ideas of the foreign in addition to foregrounding cultures with significant legacies of historical division and economic disparity, where dissent is essential for political growth. *Going Home to Russia* has four parts, the last devoted entirely to Russia: its history, its writers, the experience of visiting it and meeting its people. The title poem charts the transition between cultures in ways which examine the meaning of belonging.

Goodbye to the penniless, homeless, trouserless politicians;
Goodbye to the pastoral liberals and the chic gombeens;
Goodbye to the gobberloos and the looderamauns;
Goodbye to the wide boys and their wider wives.

. . .

Copenhagen – the Baltic – Riga – Smolensk –
If there be a heaven, then this is what
It must feel like to be going down into heaven –
To be going home to Russia.[21]

The litany of Ireland's socio-political drawbacks enacts a relentless grounding against which the lightness and freedom of the flight can be measured. Throughout the poem geography is feminised but there is a knowing quality in Durcan's use of this familiar trope: 'the pilot sounds like a man/Who has chosen to make love instead of to rape'. Also implicit throughout is the precarious relationship between the speaker and the land to which he travels. The exploration of identities is pursued through different experiences of place and culture and within an overtly personal framework: Russia is expressed in sensual description and apparently through a sexual relationship. These ambiguities displace confusions of identity and belonging that Durcan himself suffers, being intimately bound to, yet bitterly critical of, the country of his birth.

In the poems charting the failure of his marriage, as well as those in the collection *Daddy, Daddy* (1990), Durcan comes closest to articulating a clear sense of self, yet even here his wife and father acquire iconic status as he seeks new perspectives on each relationship. His poems concerning women have always attracted notice but his continual revisiting of his marriage has been seen variously as a genuine attempt to empathise with his wife's feelings and, in Edna Longley's view, as potentially exploitative. Similarly, she argues, '[i]n poems such as 'Theresa's Bar' or 'Fat Molly', a sensuous, generous, permissive mother/lover may simply invert more austere representations of Cathleen Ní Houlihan'.[22] Certainly the self-effacing nature of the poet's persona in many of these works is double-edged: it proclaims the speaker as flawed, even helpless, yet in doing so it potentially undermines the generosity of his perspective as the erasure of the self results in the elimination of plausible subjective judgement. Elsewhere these perceived incongruities mark Durcan's resistance to clearly defined relationships and to the social norms keeping them in place. 'At the Funeral of the Marriage' evokes the life-in-death renewal of sexuality at the very moment that the speaker's wife becomes a stranger to him. Likewise, a poem such as 'Crinkle, near Birr' (1990) begins, 'Daddy and I were lovers/From the beginning, and when I was six/We got married in the church of Crinkle, near Birr'. Though portraying the intimate estrangement of the father-son relationship in a startling way, the poet cannot – and does not seek to – transcend the imbalance of power between them.

Like Kennelly, Durcan uses humour to draw attention to the social realities of Ireland but he is more measured in his approach: many of his poems take an apparently absurd premise and develop it to a telling extreme, a process which contributes to the dream-like quality to be found in much of his work. Representation of the ordinary world is overlaid with shifting, idiosyncratic visions of life, as though the process of writing itself draws the raw material for the poem towards a state of flux. The acute eye for political hypocrisy and social distortion is balanced by an ability to picture the world transformed by a belief in the possibility of goodness amid the shortfalls of self and society. Eamon Grennan writes: 'Although he has been called a great comedian, he is in fact a relentless – and relentlessly buoyant – moralist: weird as its projections are, the map he makes of the world is a moral map, his tendencies as a poet instinctively utopian'.[23] The utopian drive of Durcan's poetry is in fact its most subversive quality, since it adds complex aspiration to the comic deflation of both private emotion and shared experience. The apparent ease with which this amusement is generated belies the studied centrality of the speaker's voice, on paper and in performance, yet it is this unifying feature that both attunes us to the nature of Durcan's humour and draws attention to its darker elements.

Rita Ann Higgins: 'the one with the fancy words'

The subversive nature of Durcan's poetic achievement emerges in another writer of growing significance, Rita Ann Higgins. Higgins chooses a particular stratum of society for her focus: working-class, more specifically female working-class, experience is her chief concern. Yet she also allows the mores of society at large to inflect her work. The relationship between the individual and the community here can be read on two levels. The poet herself speaks out of the situation she depicts and seeks to align her form and language with the characters and situations in her poems. Thus the act of writing itself becomes entangled with more obvious social themes. The troubling power dynamic between the working-class woman and the system within which she must operate is mediated through language that often exemplifies the pressures brought to bear on the individual 'Away from/ tenants' associations/rent man's/ poor man's/light bills/heavy bills'.[24] Women battle against bureaucracy in Higgins's poems as she refuses to grant them a symbolic role, ruthlessly grounding them instead in the mechanics of living itself.

Yet just as Durcan situates himself as the mock-heroic poet, suffering the vagaries of emotional and social upheaval, so Higgins too must acknowledge the role of poet within her own creations. If language is power then the place of poetic language in this human struggle demands analysis. 'Poetry Doesn't Pay' from *Goddess on the Mervue Bus* (1986) sets ideas of aesthetic worth – 'Your poems, you know,/you've really got something there' – against basic monetary need when the rent man appears. The refusal to accept poetry as an item of worth is not only the act of the man, but of society at large which simultaneously affirms and denies the special power of words – 'After all/you're the poet/girlie missus/the one with/the fancy words' ('Space Invader', *Sunny Side Plucked*, 103).[25] In 'Poetry Doesn't Pay' this slippage between material and aesthetic worlds is a complex one:

> 'I'm from the Corporation,
> what do we know or care about poesy,
> much less grand amnostic dead aunts.'
>
> 'But people keep telling me.'
>
> 'They lie.'
> 'If you don't have fourteen pounds
> and ten pence, you have nothing
> but the light of the penurious moon.'

It is the man from the Corporation who uses the archaism 'poesy' and who consigns the defaulting speaker to live by 'the light of the penurious moon' and he has the last word. Poetic language is here used to render poetry powerless in the material world yet simultaneously, by a cruel irony, to impose its own expression as reality. The worlds of poetry and of utility seem unbridgeable, except that they have both been transformed into the text we read: the poem itself, now safe in respectable and commodified book form, can be seen as an index of the poet's success, a sign that, at some level, poetry does pay.

Here, as elsewhere, the demotic vein of Higgins's work opens itself out to a world of improbabilities, as the 'fancy words' articulate the imagined in place of the actual. Somewhat in the manner of Durcan, language itself becomes a means of revealing and transcending material and emotional poverty. These liberating acts of imagination occur for the speaker rather than for her characters and this inevitably restates the circumscribed role of the verbal – the butcher in 'The German for Stomach': 'wanted to shout/Lapis Lazuli, Lapis Lazuli,//but instead he said,//'You wouldn't put a dog out in it'(*Sunny Side Plucked*, 25). Language becomes both a transformative and disruptive force, yet so often its power is never seized. Often the constraints of personal and social relationships are to blame for these missed opportunities. In 'The Sentence' Chatterina's husband is condemned to the vocal margins: 'his phrases had short back and sides,/his verbs were anorexic/his nouns were Hail Holy Queens/He mouthed the tight-rope of caution'.[26] Only when his wife is rendered inarticulate can he finish either sentence.

This knowing position is one that Higgins often explores. At times it is situated within a self-consciously literary frame – participation in the world of poetry readings and academic conferences generates its own humour and permits the disparity between the world of the poem and of its reception to be highlighted. Public readings often find Higgins addressing the issue of performance itself and in doing so both intensifying the comic possibilities of her work and hinting at the potential duplicity of words. In 'Remapping the Borders' the relationship between language and intention is subtly probed. Revelation is simultaneously denied and affirmed when the poet is asked, after the dance:

> 'Could you see my stocking belt
> as I did the swing?' – 'Me, thigh, knee, no
> I saw nothing
> I saw no knee
> no luscious thigh
> no slither belt,
> with lace embroidered border
> that was hardly a border at all.'

That this description is further embellished when the speaker dwells on it later raises the potential of language, of the act of representation itself, to shape perception. The reader is exposed to the private awareness of the speaker that is never made public within the limits of the poem itself. This sensibility is separated from that of the dancing woman in a way which highlights the power of language to limit, rather than to reinforce, connection.

Both Durcan and Kennelly have produced sustained portrayals of women throughout their poetry. Higgins creates her female figures with an acutely observant eye yet withholds enough to allow uncertainty concerning the relation between the particular and the general, thus her individual women can appear to be at once representative of their environment and standing alone within it. The foregrounding of the woman is similar to Higgins's poetic technique as a whole, the way in which she draws the particular into sharp relief while rendering the complex matrix of interrelationships vital to an understanding of her poetic world – 'Tommy's Wife', depleted from youth and freedom to anger and bitterness in the space of twenty-two lines; 'Mona' in the poem of the same name and Philomena from 'Philomena's

Revenge' locked inside private worlds of fear and anger. In this confrontation with the surfaces of marital and social life Higgins releases the individual to direct expression and it is the vigour and humour of her form and language that expresses her dissent from social appearances most directly. Durcan has commented on 'the unique colour of humour and [. . .] unique clarity' of her work and it is this clarity, this outspokenness, that makes her position as a woman poet especially important.

Debates concerning the role of the woman poet are lengthy and ongoing but the difficulties of moving towards a subject position in language inevitably raise questions relating to the woman poet and her self-representation in art. Catriona Clutterbuck, in 'Gender and Self-Representation in Irish Poetry: The Critical Debate'[27] rightly points out that the issue of self-representation is one which must move beyond the specifically personal to analyse more critically the intersection between private and public realms. This negotiation has proved central to any examination of the dissenting position of the poet in contemporary Irish society, as it prioritises the relationship between the individual creative act and the social structures within which it is articulated. Just as the issue of performance draws attention to the role of author, it also highlights the process of writing (and that of reading) as a potentially disruptive one.

Remapping the borders? Nuala Ní Dhomhnaill

Tensions between margin and centre assert themselves even more vigorously in the debate on the role of the Irish language in contemporary literature in Ireland. Nuala Ní Dhomhnaill's energetic poems are not only among the most important in the Irish language this century but contribute significantly to the discourse surrounding writing in that tradition. The issue of language here moves beyond formal and tonal variety into the realm of cultural politics. The mediation between English and Gaelic literary forms not only reflects the complex diversity of these two positions but often explicitly examines the linguistic and formal negotiations central to their co-existence in contemporary Ireland. In spite of its potential for the unification of cultures, translation is a process suggestive of loss; everywhere in the newly created text is the spectre of missing language; in the words of Louis de Paor, 'From the beginning [. . .] translation from Irish to English is as much an act of obliteration and annihilation as it is one of discovery and exchange'.[28]

Ní Dhomhnaill herself has commented on both the benefits and difficulties of her native language often in connection with the role of the woman poet in contemporary (and ancient) Ireland. She sees the Irish language as a way of recovering the female voice from a poetic tradition which is largely male, and her position has contributed to the accelerated interest in contemporary women's poetry in Ireland: 'Lots of women's poetry has so much to reclaim; there's so much psychic land, a whole continent, a whole Atlantis under the water to reclaim'.[29] Unsurprisingly this act is important for a poet like Ní Dhomhnaill, who is aware that there is both daring and attentiveness required to sustain Gaelic poetic forms. Yet her willingness to allow her work to be freely translated by other poets has disturbed those who argue that this subverts the original act of linguistic independence asserted by the decision to write in Irish. Nevertheless, Ní Dhomhnaill insists on 'the need for Irish to exist *in its own right*, and if you don't understand it, well tough'.[30] The ambiguous role of the translated poet is often reflected in Ní Dhomhnaill's own attitude:

> I am so constantly plagued by the seeming arbitrariness of so much that finally finds its way onto the page, and the compromises and accommodations necessary in even getting it that far, that I suppose it does cause me to have a pretty "laissez-faire" attitude to subsequent translations of it. Mind you, ... I have always put my foot down when it was a question of absolute mistranslation . . .[31]

Caught, it seems, in a matrix of conflicts and tensions, Ní Dhomhnaill views issues of language and of translation as an extension of the essential struggle to create. The sense of precursors – both in terms of tradition and in relation to the changes in an individual text – is a strong one for her and she paradoxically draws attention to her linguistic heritage through the very originality of her art. The important continuities which her work emphasises never imply stasis though: Ní Dhomhnaill's poetic form mutates in the act of translation and takes on the structure of the new language as stanzas reshape and line-lengths accommodate new speech rhythms. Much of this originality lies in the positioning of her work on the border between Irish and English and between ancient and modern. It is the versatility and deftness of her negotiation of these boundaries that makes her work both transformative of cultural norms and challenging for the individual reader.

The resistance that Ní Dhomhnaill mounts to those with fixed views of history, language and social roles is concerted and she recognises these as powerful forces, resisting easy containment: 'Seo radachur núicléach na Staire/ní foláir' ('It's the radioactive rain /Of History') she writes in 'Plútóiniam' ('Plutonium'), 'Éiríonn sé aníos I gcónaí/is de shíor/ón nduibheagán do-aitheanta/atá istigh ionainn' ('It rises up always/Out of the ground/From underworld caves/Within us:') (trans. Eiléan Ní Chuilleanáin, 1999).[32] Radioactivity, potentially both damaging and curative, is incorporated in the cyclical processes of nature: for Ní Dhomhnaill it is the organic limitations and prejudices of both individual and nation that most need challenging.

Ní Dhomhnaill frequently engages with mythic material in her desire to disrupt received versions of Ireland's past and to rethink the relationship between ancient and contemporary values. It also allows her to acknowledge the emotional power and human resonances of mythic story and character. This kind of rewriting is of course a subversive act, especially in the context of mythology as a vehicle for the perpetuation of national ideals and gender imbalances. If the revolution of woman's position in Irish society has placed male certainties under considerable strain, it has also necessitated a re-examination of the nature and emphasis of mythic representation. Ní Dhomhnaill readily uses myth in dialogic form, exploring a range of voices and positions through dramatic presentation. This performative aspect within her work is framed in many readings by the interweaving of original Irish and translated text rarely presenting a single voice or subject position. Ní Dhomhnaill's performances allow listeners to absorb both languages, though they may understand only one of them, and to consider the significance of the shape and sound of the poems, as well as of their meaning. The emphasis on the voice in this poet's work both connects to and examines the place of the oral tradition in Irish letters, and her readings likewise reinforce the energy of this tradition while also tracing significant changes within it. These alterations occur on several levels: for the audience fluctuating attitudes towards the use of the Irish language may impede the fullest engagement with the work presented; in the case of individual poems, Ní Dhomhnaill often specifically addresses the vigorous, if incongruous, encounter between ancient and contemporary worlds – she allows modern vocabulary and cadence to enter her poems naturally, enlivening her subject matter with witty and irreverent touches.

In this poetry we observe not only the discrepancies between male-authored tradition and its female articulation but also the gaps between what woman speaks and what she instinctively feels, between her outward behaviour and inward convictions. Where Higgins uses the wry humour and blunt statement of social observation, Ní Dhomhnaill chooses to explore the female psyche and challenges simplified interpretations of power, both individual and cultural. By introducing these complexities Ní Dhomhnaill places particular demands on the reader and encourages an interrogation of established mythic representations. Her women are strong and the mythic precursors that she draws upon – The Great Queen, Mór and Badb are among them – emphasise this dimension. Yet even these figures are reflective as well as assertive and are often confused by their own power. The acts of self-transformation or shapechanging exemplify the power and uncertainty of their role: one of these powerful females, the Morrigan, when rejected as a young woman by Cuchulainn, turned herself into an eel, a wolf, a heifer, attacking him with each shape change.[33] Ní Dhomhnaill's Great Queen, from the poem 'Agallamh na Mór-Riona le Cu Chulainn' ('The Great Queen Speaks Cu Chulainn Listens'), articulates a similar intention:

Tiocfad aniar aduaidh ort.	I will creep up on you
Bead ag feitheamh ag an áth leat.	will await you at the ford
Raghad i riocht faolchon glaise	I'll be a grey wolf
i ndiaidh na dtáinte	who'll drive the herds
is tiomáinseadh ort iad.	to stampede you
Raghad i riocht eascon	I'll be an eel
faoi do chosa	to trip you
is bainfidh métruip asat.	I will be a polly cow
Raghad i riocht samhaisce maoile	at the herd's head –
i gceann na mbeithíoch	hard for God even
chun gur diachair Dia dhuit	to save you from our hooves.[34]
teacht slán ónár gcosaibh.	

The creaturely transformations which we may observe in Ní Dhomhnaill's work draw attention to the power that surrounds the body in mythological representation. This power can also be traced in the erotic dimension of Ní Dhomhnaill's art which is especially resonant in its creation of new freedoms of expression for women. Her 'Feis' ('Carnival') sets love for a married man within forms of language resonant of mythic narrative: 'Leagaim síos trí bhrat id fhianaise:/brat deora,/brat allais,/brat fola.' ('I lay down three robes before you:/a mantle of tears,/a coat of sweat,/a gown of blood.')[35] Elsewhere she permits her speakers direct expression of sexual desire: 'Ach nuair a chuimhním/ar do phógsa/critheann mo chromáin/is imíonn/a bhfuil eatarthu/ina lacht.' ('when I recall/your kiss/I shake, and all/that lies/between my hips/liquifies/to milk') (*Rogha Dánta*, 39) as Higgins also does, though with less sensual immediacy – 'I yearn/for the fullness/of your tongue' (*Sunny Side Plucked*, 109). That Ní Dhomhnaill also depicts the happy contemplation of adultery and the joys of casual pleasure ensures that she removes her women from the limitations of social laws and stakes a claim not only for individual verbal expression but for a freedom of the body that transcends particular social conditions. Pleasure is to be found both in the moment of sexual fulfilment and the act of personal liberation and it is through the combination of these forces that the poet seizes her power. Absent is the fumbling eroticism of Kennelly's work, where the sexual encounter so often falls short of both pleasure and meaning, and while Higgins usually positions the erotic as at best a form of alleviation, at worst a kind of entrapment, for Ní Dhomhnaill it is a form of articulation akin to words and therefore finds easy expression within her creative ambit.

The undeniable presence of the body within this sexual dynamic has an impact on the relationship between private and public which is significantly mediated through the act of performance. To present the private act for public appraisal is at once to transgress this boundary and to remind the listener of its existence. For these poets sexuality also asserts the primacy of individual experience over social control thus expressing thematically the spirit of liberation so prominent in the formal strategies of many of the poems. While remaining conscious of the power of tradition, all four poets recognise the need to break new ground through questioning the injustices and hypocrisies of public life and they continue to enliven the Irish poetry scene with witty and surprising work. All thrive by adopting an oppositional stance, by asserting a marginal perspective – their own and that of others – at the expense of a safe, accepted position and by taking creative risks to achieve the most direct engagement with reader and listener.

NOTES

1 Seán O'Faolain, quoted in Augustine Martin, *Bearing Witness: Essays on Anglo-Irish Literature* Anthony Roche (ed.), (Dublin: UCD Press, 1996), p. 94.
2 Quoted in Henry Sayre, 'Performance' in F. Lentricchia and T. McLaughlin (eds.), *Critical Terms for Literary Study* (University of Chicago Press, 1990), p. 98.
3 A number of poets whose readings are especially acclaimed have expressed unease concerning the distinction between the terms 'poet' and 'performance poet' as they see the writing processes of each as essentially the same, even if some poems may be enhanced in the performance context. See Stephen Wade and Paul Munden (eds.), *Reading the Applause: Reflections on Performance Poetry by Various Artists* (York: Talking Shop, 1999).
4 Paul Beasley, 'Performance Poetry or Sub Verse' in *Reading the Applause*, p. 49.
5 Ake Persson, *Betraying the Age: Social and Artistic Process in Brendan Kennelly's Work* (Gothenburg: Acta Universitatis Gothoburgensis, 2000).
6 In April 1984 a twenty-four-year-old woman from Kerry, Joanne Hayes, concealed the birth and death of her baby, the result of her relationship with a married man. After the discovery of the stabbed remains of a baby in Cahirciveen on April 14th, Hayes confessed to murder. When her own baby's body was discovered in May (assumed to have died from deliberate neglect) the police suggested that she had given birth to twins by two different fathers but the scientific impossibility of this caused the murder charge to be dropped. A public tribunal into the way in which the police had conducted the case did not lead to any action being taken against them. See Nell McCafferty, *A Woman to Blame: The Kerry Babies Case* (Dublin: Attic Press, 1985).
7 Brendan Kennelly, *Selected Poems* (Dublin: Kerrymount, 1985), p. 215.
8 Brendan Kennelly, 'Voices' in *Strong Words: Modern Poets on Modern Poetry* W.N. Herbert and M. Hollis (eds.), (Newcastle: Bloodaxe Books, 2000), p. 213.
9 Brendan Kennelly, 'Measures' in *Cromwell* (Dublin: Beaver Row Press, 1983), vii.

10 *The Book of Judas* has been criticised by reviewers for its unwieldy length. In April 2002, Bloodaxe Books published *The Little Book of Judas*, a much-reduced selection of the original poems.

11 Brendan Kennelly, *The Book of Judas* (Newcastle: Bloodaxe Books, 1991), p. 11.

12 Edna Longley, *The Living Stream: Literature and Revisionism in Ireland* (Newcastle: Bloodaxe Books, 1994), p. 218.

13 Derek Mahon, *Journalism* (Meath: Gallery Press, 1996), p. 116.

14 *Crazy about Women* (Dublin: National Gallery of Ireland, 1991) is a collection of poems written to coincide with an exhibition of the same name in the National Gallery of Ireland. Durcan followed this with *Give Me Your Hand* (London: Macmillan, 1994), which selects work from the National Gallery of Great Britain.

15 On January 5, 1976 at Kingsmills, Co. Armagh the Republican Action Force stopped a minibus bringing workers home. Ten Protestants were killed; all were civilians.

16 Paul Durcan, *Daddy Daddy* (Belfast: Blackstaff, 1990), p. 140.

17 In 1975 the UVF, a Protestant terrorist group, staged a fake roadblock to ambush an Irish showband returning home from a concert in Belfast. The terrorists planned to load a bomb onto the minibus, so that it would appear to have been transported by the band themselves, but the bomb exploded prematurely killing two UVF men. The others panicked and shot dead three band members.

18 Paul Durcan, *A Snail in My Prime: New and Selected Poems* (London: Harvill, 1993).

19 *The Selected Paul Durcan*, ed. Edna Longley (Belfast: Blackstaff, 1982).

20 Ruairi Ó Brádaigh, one of the founders of the Provisional IRA and President of Provisional Sinn Féin was replaced in that role by Gerry Adams shortly after Sinn Féin declared a cessation of hostilities against Crown forces in February 1975. In 1986 he was to leave to form Republican Sinn Féin, fearing that Adams would abandon claims to a 32-county Ireland in favour of constitutional politics.

21 Paul Durcan, *Going Home to Russia* (Belfast: Blackstaff Press, 1987), pp. 66–7.

22 Longley, *The Living Stream*, p. 216.

23 Eamon Grennan, *Facing the Music: Irish Poetry in the Twentieth Century* (Nebraska: Creighton University Press, 1999), p. 316.

24 Rita Ann Higgins, *Sunny Side Plucked: New and Selected Poems* (Newcastle: Bloodaxe Books, 1996), p. 34.

25 Moynagh Sullivan explores the complex relationship between symbolic and political power through the issues of poetic authority raised in Higgins's poetry in 'Assertive Subversions: Comedy in the Work of Julie O'Callaghan and Rita Ann Higgins' in *Verse* 16, 2, pp. 83–6.

26 Rita Ann Higgins, *An Awful Racket* (Newcastle: Bloodaxe Books, 2001), p. 51.

27 Catriona Clutterbuck, 'Gender and Self-Representation in Irish Poetry: The Critical Debate', *Bullán* 4, 1 (Autumn 1998), pp. 43–58.

28 Louis De Paor, 'Disappearing Language: translations from the Irish', *Poetry Ireland Review* 51 (Autumn 1996), p. 61.

29 Nuala Ní Dhomhnaill, 'The Hidden Ireland: Women's Inheritance' in Theo Dorgan (ed.), *Irish Poetry Since Kavanagh* (Dublin: Four Courts Press, 1996), p. 115.

30 Nuala Ní Dhomhnaill, 'Traductio ad Absurdum', *Krino* 14 (Winter, 1993), p. 50.

31 Kaarina Hollo. 'Acts of Translation: An Interview with Nuala Ní Dhomhnaill', *Edinburgh Review* 99 (Spring 1998), pp. 106–7.

32 Nuala Ní Dhomhnaill, *The Water Horse*, Medbh McGuckian and Eiléan Ní Chuilleanáin (trans.) (Meath: Gallery Press, 1999), pp. 66–7.

33 'On one occasion, when Cú Chulainn was preparing himself for battle she [the Morrigan] appeared to him as a beautiful young seductress. He spurned her impatiently [. . .] and, in her fury, she pitted herself against him in the form of an eel, a wolf and a hornless heifer'. Miranda Green, *Celtic Goddesses* (London: British Museum Press, 1995), p. 44.

34 Nuala Ní Dhomhnaill, *Selected Poems/Rogha Dánta*, with translations by Michael Hartnett (Dublin: Raven Arts Press, 1988), pp. 117–19.

35 Nuala Ní Dhomhnaill, *The Astrakhan Cloak*, Paul Muldoon (trans.) (Loughcrew: Gallery Press, 1992), pp. 14–15.

13

ROBERT FAGGEN

Irish poets and the world

The global reputation of the Irish poetry world can be attributed to many things including, at the risk of sounding too uncritical, its great variety and quality. The sociology and politics of the reception of Irish poetry, particularly in the United States, has been the subject of various levels of critical speculation. Critics have mapped the influences of the literatures of many nations on a range of contemporary Irish poets.[1] This chapter will explore the ways some contemporary Irish poets have reached beyond Ireland to imagine and define their poetic practice. Irish poets have been greatly interested in the achievements of American, Eastern European, French and Greek poets, from Dickinson, Whitman, Williams, Frost and Lowell to Herbert, Milosz and Mandelstam, to Nerval, Cavafy and Seferis. The hold these writers and others have for a number of contemporary Irish poets – Boland, Heaney, Mahon, Kinsella, Muldoon – springs from a desire to establish human identity out of the tensions, debates and violence about national traditions and national identity.

Irish poets have had a particularly strong reception in the United States. There is, of course, the basic fact of sharing something like a common language as well as the moderate success of such anthologisers as Thomas Kinsella and Patrick Crotty in making Irish-language poetry available in English. But Irish literature holds a special place in the American imagination – and not only. For Americans, the Irish poet represents an ideal of bardic authenticity: rustic, romantic, mystical, embattled and vatic. Poetry *is* Irish. For Americans, divided and troubled Ireland itself is an antidote to its own unbearable lightness of prosperity and power (despite recent horrors). Christ-haunted with a deep and mysterious history, Ireland is an exotic but unthreatening presence for Americans. But it is also true that Ireland's struggle for self-definition against colonial power still resonates with America's own historical struggles for self-definition, despite the irony of its current position as reigning global super-power.

All of these factors may have contributed to the strong presence in recent decades in the history of Irish poets at American universities. During the 1980s and 1990s, Seamus Heaney maintained a teaching position at Harvard, one he inherited from Robert Lowell. Thomas Kinsella taught at the University of Southern Illinois and Temple University before his relatively recent return to Ireland. Paul Muldoon is now a fixture in the writing programme at Princeton University and Eavan Boland is professor at Stanford University. Derek Mahon has also been in residence at New York University and Yaddo. There may be, of course, a simple explanation for this presence: the United States has the jobs and the money and has become something of an economic brass ring for distinguished Irish writers. Vincent Buckley once described this phenomenon with a sharp and, perhaps, cynical eye:

> What do Irish poets hope for? To be thought number one. America. What do they fear? To fall down the competition table. Never to be thought number one. To be denied America . . . Irish poets in general are like ambitious youngsters trying to escape from the working class. America is the upper-middle class. Their vertu, however, their source of their energy and appeal, is in the Irishness which they are trying to escape; they have therefore to emphasize this or some version of it. Their destiny, their complex fate, is not become Americans, but to be Irish in relation to America.[2]

It is too easy to reduce the Irish presence in America to competition and economics. And it is also unfair to see Irish poets as merely playing Irish to please the American mob, though no doubt Muldoon, among others, is highly conscious of the way members of a tribe can be transformed from savages to cigar-store Indians and into tricksters depending on the audience. The elusive nature of Irishness and the way America serves as place to escape its traps may be a theme for poets as diverse as Heaney, Kinsella and Muldoon. The chaotic politics of contemporary Ireland, particularly in the North, has obviously contributed to the richness of its poetry and the United States has become something of testing ground for the trials and pleasures of exile and displacement, the liberating experience of confrontation with moderate and welcoming otherness.

Kinsella's relationship to America is an interesting case of a man going away only to return to himself. Many have remarked on the influence of Williams and Pound, for example, on the style and technique of Kinsella. In one short lyric entitled 'Wyncote, Pennsylvania: A Gloss', Kinsella calls attention to the sensuous intensity, desire, delicacy, fear and ephemerality of his experience of the nature of things presented with particularly imagistic technique: a mocking-bird gulping a red berry which flies away into a storm. Being a continent away from Dublin, in a tiny American town, only seems to intensify the sense of being everywhere in a changing world and producing the joy and fear essential to the intensification of the writer's art:

> Another storm coming.
> Under that copper light
> my papers seem luminous.
> And over them I will take
> ever more painstaking care.[3]

This gloss becomes somewhat ironic in that Wyncote was the childhood home of Ezra Pound, expatriate to be and a godfather of international modernism. Here Kinsella, a Dubliner teaching at Temple University, imagines a *locus amoenus* in the home town that Pound rejected. One man's provincial prison becomes another's inspiration.

Despite Kinsella's efforts to bring poetry in Irish to national and global attention, he has not enjoyed quite the same reputation in the United States as some of his peers. His own modernist techniques may go against the expectations that some may have for Irish poets to be the last unembarrassed practitioners of romanticism's passion for nature, the lost past, and the oppressed. In 2002, a front-page article in *The Los Angeles Times* on *The Field Day Anthology of Irish Writing: Irish Women's Writing and Traditions* described the book as an attempt to redress the exclusion of Irish women writers from the canon, an oppression within historical oppression: 'Throughout Irish history, a vibrant and vital culture has fought to have its voice heard against a louder and stronger neighbour. But while colonial ruler Britain tried to ignore or silence the demands of Irish nationalism, a growing international literary reputation helped cement its cause. And now Irish female writers have engaged in a similar struggle with the country's male-dominated literary tradition'.[4] This simplification of matters nevertheless attests to the power and image of Irish literature and poetry in the world. And it does reflect some of the questions and problems that have made contemporary Irish poetry so interesting: the problem of whether there is a monolithic tradition of Irish literature or, at least, a dual tradition: one trying to build on a fractured Anglo-Irish past or one that reinvents the language.

Eavan Boland, whose photograph was featured prominently in the *Los Angeles Times* article, has insisted on a distinction between history and the past. For her, history is an imposition and projection on the silences and sufferings of excluded voices that actually existed in the past. Some sang of heroes while others were tortured or suffered in silence. Boland has challenged (or, interrogated) the attempts to use woman as the figure of Ireland, as she does in 'Mise Eire' (1986; with a pun on 'ire'), rejecting a nationalist poem by Easter Rising poet Patrick Pearse:

> I won't go back to it –
> my nation displaced
> into old dactyls,
> oaths made
> by the animal tallows
> of the candle –[5]

However much she displaces herself from the imagined past, she remains in dialogue with it in ways similar to a number of her contemporaries. Boland also adds to the complex and ironic reinvention of the pastoral (or antipastoral) that has been found in Kavanagh, Montague and Heaney. Proclaiming to start afresh in 'The New Pastoral', (1982) the woman is no longer a romanticised 'shepherdess' but only 'lost':

> I'm a lost, last inhabitant
> displaced person
> in a pastoral chaos.
>
> All day I listen to
> the loud distress, the switch and tick of
> new herds.
>
> But I am no shepherdess.

Boland is not alone among her contemporaries – and not women only – in rethinking the feminine myths of Irish identity or of its pastoral traditions, though probably few could claim such simplicity and directness.[6]

Yeats remains the great meteor not only of Irish poetry but of poetry in the last hundred years. The variety, mystical vision, and sonic power of his work have made him as close as anyone has come for a name for poetry. As much as his name stands alone, it is almost always now shadowed by the words 'after' and 'since'. Yeats's efforts at establishing an Irish national consciousness and, later, at Nietzschean transcendence from a tower of mysticism and art have raised endless questions about the traps of attempting either. His reception in America was complex: from Robinson Jeffers's embracing of the Yeatsian 'tower beyond tragedy' to Robert Frost's view of him as a talented but 'false soul'. To be the successor to Yeats is to assume the highest position in the realm of poetry and yet to become something of a tyrant, if not embarrassment.

W.H. Auden's elegy 'In Memory of W.B. Yeats' has contributed significantly to the world's imagination of what any successor to Yeats might achieve. From the pen of a British émigré who settled in America came a vision of Yeats as figure of universal force whose gift survived history, politics and personal silliness and could be seen as an inspiration for freedom and for praise. Yeats's own late advice from 'Under Ben Bulben' was,

> Irish poets, learn your trade,
> Sing whatever is well made,
> Scorn the sort now growing up
> All out of shape from toe to top,
> Their unremembering hearts and heads
> Base-born products of base beds.
> . . .
> Cast your mind on other days
> That we in coming days may be
> Still the indomitable Irishry.[7]

This is echoed and transformed in the trochees of Auden's elegy which diminish the concerns of national identity and character and stress the need of the poet to inspire individual and universal human dignity:

> Follow, poet, follow right
> To the bottom of the night,
> With your unconstraining voice
> Still persuade us to rejoice;[8]

The Yeats who strove to create a 'special Anglo-Irish culture from the main unwashed body' has been fading somewhat in contemporary Irish poetry before the Joycean impulse for immersion in the 'filthy modern tide',[9] as Yeats called it in 'The Statues', of global modernity.

After Yeats, Patrick Kavanagh took a peculiar and influential anti-modernist step, engaging the Irish peasantry but in an ironic and most un-Yeatsian way. In 'Epic', Kavanagh asserts confidence in the local and the parochial as the sufficient landscape for the ragged heroes. (Kavanagh distinguished between the parochial and provincial, arguing against the latter because of its secondary relation to the urban). The world becomes de-capitalised and local matters can take on prominence and even closeness, paradoxically, to the universal. In particular, the attitude toward matters of alleged global importance and vatic rhetoric become diminished before the integrity of the local, dramatised in the sonnet 'Epic' (1951) in the colloquial vocal posture that dares to contrast Britain's selling out of Czechoslovakia to Hitler in the 1938 'Munich bother' with the deciding of great events, 'who owned / That half a rood of rock, a no-man's land / Surrounded by our pitchfork-armed claims'. He asks the question about 'Which / Was more important?'

> I inclined
> To lose my faith in Ballyrush and Gortin
> Till Homer's ghost came whispering to my mind
> He said: I made the Iliad from such
> A local row. Gods make their own importance.[10]

Kavanagh uses the pastoral ironically: the parochial and the world of the farm in *The Great Hunger* (1942) harbours neither peace nor happiness but – stripped of traditional mythology and attuned to local tenor – reveals the longings and frustrations of the human heart and continually mocks the tourist mythology of Irish peasantry that had been perpetrated by Yeats. This placed Kavanagh in a line with a set of problems associated with pastoral thought in American culture and society – the Jeffersonian love of the rural and the pastoral and the land over and against not only the urban but national consciousness. The premier American poet investigating these problems of pastoral utopia and dystopia was Robert Frost, and his work would in its efforts have a significant influence on contemporary Irish poets, particularly Heaney and Muldoon. Kavanagh seemed less interested in Irish national identity or provincial realism than in a parochial approach to human longing.

Heaney, who grew up on a farm, returns often in his poetry to his rural beginnings, though he focuses on what the experienced imagination brings to its landscapes of unlettered youth as a way to uncover the source of being. And that source often finds itself expressed in the sensuous joys of speech and language. Heaney has found in America a liberating distance from his own original sense of self,[11] and he owes much to American poets and their fascination with landscape imagined into line and sound. The pleasure Frost took in luxuriating in voice as an expression of the primordial self became attractive to Heaney who had also found in Hopkins and Burns the reanimation of the marginal sonorities. Frost proposed the view that sentences were sounds upon which words were strung and asserted that those sentence-sounds exist first in the vernacular and in talk: 'A sentence is a sound in itself on which other sounds called words may be strung . . . [Sentence sounds] are apprehended by the ear. They are gathered by the ear from the vernacular and brought into books. Many of them are already familiar to us in books. I think no writer invents them. The most original writer only catches them fresh from talk, where they grow spontaneously'.[12] When Yeats toured the United States in 1911 with the Abbey Players, Frost was impressed by the Irish poet's emphasis on redeeming the idiom of the language by attention to the vernacular of the peasant. Though Frost eventually became contemptuous of Yeats's poses, his notes at the time indicate his own iconoclastic desire to establish an American idiom by purging the language of British literary idiom: 'I must have registered the pious wish I wished in 1915 when the Germans were being execrated for having destroyed Reims Cathedral. I wished they could with one shell blow Shakespeare out of the English language. The past overawes us too much in art. If America has any advantage of Europe it is in being less clogged with the products of art'.[13]

In his tribute to Frost, 'Above the Brim', Heaney follows him in arguing that the cadences of speech 'reestablish a connection with the original springs of our human being'.[14] Heaney's artesial metaphor is important in this context, for it underscores the imaginative and intellectual force behind such figures in Heaney's poems, notably in an early keynote poem, 'Personal Helicon' (1966).[15] Against the mythic Helicon, we have the re-imagined wells that populated the landscapes of Heaney's youth. Heaney regards as particularly important the power of the poet to transform these fluid sources into poetry, to quicken them into verb, and to set the landscape echoing. He follows Frost's achievements in 'For Once, Then, Something' and numerous other poems in which the primordial well of the past becomes a place for the poet's soundings, not merely narcissism but clarification of identity and selfhood, the voice with 'a clean new music in it'. Heaney's preoccupations are not with nostalgia *per se* but with a longing for the source, for a centre of integrity against the confusions and violence of the present:

> Others had echoes, gave back your own call
> With a clean new music in it. And one
> Was scaresome, for there, out of ferns and tall
> Foxgloves, a rat slapped across my reflection.
>
> Now, to pry into roots, to finger slime,
> To stare, big-eyed Narcissus, into some spring
> Is beneath all adult dignity. I rhyme
> To see myself, to set the darkness echoing.[16]

In fact, Heaney takes delight in something 'beneath all adult dignity', as though the child's play is a way out of the seriousness and conflict of an adult world but still aware of 'darkness'. The poem moves from the personal to the mythic, the local to the global to a kind of celebration not of an imprisoning past but a liberating one. 'Bogland', (1972) also regarded as a signature Heaney poem, mythologises the quest for a grounding centre that holds. It does so consciously against the imagined vast American prairie, what Frost called 'the land vaguely realizing westward', and celebrates the poet's vocation as 'digging', an archaelogical quest for the deep source that lies beneath the palimpsest of history. The bog may yield the skeletons of the past, but beyond them, deeper still, is the oceanic water that carries influences out and into America through oceanic 'seepage':

> Our pioneers keep striking
> Inwards and downwards,
>
> Every layer they strip
> Seems camped on before.
> The bogholes might be Atlantic seepage.
> The wet centre is bottomless.

Heaney achieves a happy-sad recognition of this 'bottomless' centre as well as the levelling lack of originality, however fresh, of each new generation contributing to the endless cycles of history that build an elusive and shifting groundwork.

Frost's emphasis on the power of the colloquial and provincial has complex political force, with playful rebuke of the falsity and weakness of gentrified posturing. When Heaney praises Frost's embodiment of colloquial speech, he focuses on this integrity: 'The curves and grains of the first two lines of 'Desert Places' are correspondingly native to the living speech, without any tone of falsity'. Heaney deliberately echoes one of Frost's own metaphors for good art, the ax-helves hand-made by French-Canadian woodchoppers: 'You know the Canadian woodchoppers whittle their axe-handles following the curve of the grain, and they're strong and beautiful. Art should follow the same lines in nature, like the grain of an axe-handle. False art puts curves on things that haven't any curves'.[17] Frost dramatised this view of art in his complex eclogue 'The Ax-Helve' that features an encounter between a Yankee and a French-Canadian woodchopper named Baptiste. No doubt Heaney recognised the complexity of Frost's allegiances, not only to the Yankee narrator of the poem but to the outcast Catholic, Baptiste. Many of Frost's most interesting and subversive characters and those most associated with the curves and grain of nature are French-Canadians. No doubt Irish writers would recognise, even more than most contemporary American audiences, the ethnic and racial tension in such poems, though even as astute a reader as Tom Paulin can be limited in his perception of Frost's complex allegiances.[18] Frost's comment that, 'We think the word 'provincial' is a shameful word here in America . . . You can't be universal without being provincial, can you? It's like trying to embrace the wind',[19] found a receptive audience in Irish poets locating themselves against the authority of standard English and embracing 'the undersound of [their] own non-standard speech'. Praising Frost, Heaney has asserted that 'his notion of poetry being dependent upon "the sound of sense" is probably under-regarded as "poetics" because of its huge simplicity, but it has been deeply relevant to that historically important shift in English language poetry in this century which saw (and heard) the entry of specific local intonations – Irish, Scottish, Caribbean, Australian – into the central English line'.[20]

Tom Paulin, despite his objections to what he sometimes interprets as Frost's imperial politics, also finds the American bard's emphasis on the 'sound of sense' and on the discovery of origins in the play of the vocal imagination. Frost and the idea of wild and aboriginal in language comes strongly to the fore in the title poem of Paulin's 1999 collection 'The Wind Dog'. Against Biblical and Virgilian epic vatic authority, Paulin invokes Frost's pastoral faith in the rhythms of ordinary speech.

> not to role out the Logos
> –at least at the start
> or say in the beginning was the Word
> –not to start with a lingo
> with the lingo jingo of beginnings
> unsheathed like a sword
> stiff and blunt like a phallus
> or Masonic like a thumb
> –not to begin the *arma virumque*
> –plush Virgil
> but to start with the sound
> the plumque sound of sense . . .
> –Farmer Frost that is
> used to call sentence sound
> because a sentence he said
> was a sound in itself
> on which other sounds called words may be strung[21]

Paulin's evocation of 'Farmer Frost' may be somewhat facetious because he probably knows that Frost hated farming. But Paulin still recognises that his pastoral and georgic poetry (itself a self-conscious literary tradition) as well as his emphasis on the evocation of less literary and polished sounds of the rural and marginal voice form an important guide to a powerful form of imaginative experience.

Heaney's emphasis on local intonations and local settings reaches beyond the provincial, and the violence and ruins of the present are made more poignant in the excavations of the ancient past. Heaney draws connections he finds in Tacitus between sacrifice to a fertility goddess and the sacrifice one might make in the name of Republicanism to the eternal feminine embodiment of nationalist identities. In 'The Tollund Man' (1972), one of several of his extraordinary bog-people poems, the past becomes another country inspired by P.V. Glob's *The Bog People* and its photographs of an ancient sacrificial victim excavated from the Netherlands. The deep past could be used, and indeed has been used, to justify the present. Heaney refuses such justification, and finds only the possibility of imagining 'the sad freedom' of the Tollund man as he rode to his execution as well as alienation from the pointing 'country people'. As Heaney imagines himself journeying to another land, he imaginatively feels the freedom of impending death, at once an exile from the world's cruelty and a victim of violence. The imaginative excavation only intensifies the alienation Heaney feels in the present, as he imagines driving through the Jutland landscape: 'In the old man-killing parishes / I will feel lost, / Unhappy, and at home'. Heaney meditates in later poems on the lives of the sacrificed, outcast and submerged, even meditating upon the transubstantiated crustaceans of 'Oysters' or of 'Away from It All', poems which raise the question of how far one can ever be suffering even in the midst of transforming pleasures. The pleasures of the purely aesthetic are an assertion of freedom against, among other things, the pressures of the politics of identity and oppression:[22]

> To locate the roots of one's identity in the ethnic and liturgical habits of one's group might be all very well, but for the group to confine the range of one's growth, to have one's sympathies determined and one's responses programmed by it was patently another form of entrapment. The only reliable release for the poet was the appeasement of the achieved poem.[23]

Often, the aesthetic wholeness with which Heaney's poems seem to conclude is mitigated by a sense of the limits of transforming suffering and torture into art.

Despite the desire to allow the deep past to teach and heal present suffering, it often seems to leave the contemporary poet with a sense of doubt about the value of his craft and a challenge to the imaginative vocation. The line between the human and the aesthetic blurs in Heaney's bog poems as these urns of human history tease us out of our sense of permanence and complacency. If one looks into the deep past, what can be gleaned from it other than ruins? This is the kind of question that haunts the romantic and modern mind. It also enables one to envision the relation between modern Greek and Irish poets, particularly Seferis and Cavafy. Of course both Joyce and Kazantzakis drew on Homer's *Odyssey* to ground their own search for paternity. Other parallels have been duly noted by scholars of Hellenistic culture:

Both nations still had a peasant tradition at the beginning of the century. Both Ireland and Greece have had a disaspora; both were occupied for centuries by a foreign power; both were were dominated by a single Christian church; intellectuals in both felt on the fringe of things . . . ; both needed to deal with a 'language question'; both reached back to a glorious past in order to feel distinguished yet at the same time suffered constrictions owing to ancestor-worship; both exalted the 'folk' as repositories of virtue and wisdom; both were mightly influenced by the American Revolution and by the phenomenon of a 'national bard'; both experienced grave internal discord that undermined the national purpose; and both experienced civil wars.[24]

Seferis's 'King of Asini' (1938) is an example of a poem of Greek modernity that has been clearly influential on such contemporary Irish poets as Mahon and Heaney for the way it focuses on an individual mentioned but once in Homer, a figure of ancient history, and turns him imaginatively into 'a mud image', for all that might still be recovered from the ruins of both the past and the present:

And the poet lingers, looking at the stones, and asks himself
does there really exist
among these ruined lines, edges, points, hollows and curves
does there really exist
here where one meets the path of rain, wind and ruin
does there exist the movement of the face, the shape of the tenderness
of those who've waned so strangely in our lives,
those who remained the shadow of waves and thoughts with the
sea's boundlessness
or perhaps no, nothing is left but the weight
the nostalgia for the weight of a living existence
there where we now remain insubstantial, bending
like the branches of a terrible willow tree heaped in unremitting despair
while the yellow current slowly carries down rushes uprooted in the mud
image of a form that the sentence to everlasting bitterness has turned to stone:
the poet a void.[25]

The real presence of the human spirit in the ruins may be no more than the isolated projections and acts of the poet's mind and uncertain ground upon which to imagine any personal or collective identity.

Some of Derek Mahon's meditations on the anthropological consciousness and the passage of history would seem to be in dialogue with such a poem. In Mahon's world, the silent rebuke the living, and the line between civilisation and barbarism becomes blurred. As Seamus Deane has noted, 'Mahon does not seek to have a sense of community with the kind of Ireland which is so dominant in Irish poetry. All his versions of community depend on the notion of a disengagement from history achieved by those whose maverick individuality resisted absorption into the official discourses and decencies. Beckett, Villon, Cavafy, Rimbaud, de Nerval, Munch, Malcolm Lowry got to form that miscellany of outsiders whom he transforms into his own specific community, members of an artistic rather than an historical continuum, rebels haunted by a metaphysical dread'.[26] Historical consciousness leaves those in the present adrift in their own diminished world from which no conquest can comfortably proceed. Mahon seeks even more than Heaney to escape history, and he allows the inanimate and the inarticulate to resist and mock being trodden upon. In 'Lives' (1972), a poem dedicated to Heaney, the speaker parodies the attempt to empathise with those swallowed by history and warns against the 'insolent ontology' of romantic consciousness:

> I know too much
> To be anything any more;
> And if in the distant
> Future someone
> Thinks he has once been me
> As I am today,
>
> Let him revise
> His insolent ontology
> Or teach himself to pray.[27]

'A Disused Shed in Co. Wexford' (1975), finds Mahon speaking not only of the neglected of the Irish countryside but through the figure of mushrooms responding to the light of tourists, speaking of all those forgotten and perished through centuries of cataclysm – human and inhuman – from the terrors of ancient Vesuvius or the Nazi genocide. In Auden's poem, 'Musée des Beaux Arts', there is some irony because the narrator who proclaims that suffering occurs while others are casually walking along is himself casually strolling through a gallery of art interpreting (in the tradition of ecphrasis, or verbal descriptons of visual works of art or mute phenomena) suffering through the paintings of 'the old Masters', mostly Breughel. In Mahon's poem, instead of a great Belgian museum and great paintings, we have a disused shed and fungi, and those mute and seemingly unimpressive phenomena ignored by the casual observer or countryside tourist are given great presence and voice:

> They are begging us, you see, in their wordless way,
> To do something, to speak on their behalf
> Or at least not to close the door again.
> Lost people of Treblinka and Pompeii!

'Save us, save us,' they seem to say,
'Let the god not abandon us
Who have come so far in the darkness and in pain.
We too had our lives to live.
You with your light meter and relaxed itinerary,
Let not our naïve labors have been in vain!'

The mushrooms, to paraphrase Mahon, are everything that can be heard imaginatively, the human and the non-human, everything that cries out to be noticed and remembered, as he suggests in 'Heraclitus on Rivers' (1979), in a world of relentless flux:

You will tell me that you have executed
A monument more lasting than bronze;
But even bronze is perishable.
Your best poem, you know the one I mean,
The very language in which the poem
Was written, and the idea of language,
All these things will pass away in time.

The willingness to question the value and power of art in relation to the atrocities and demands of reality has been part of the rhetoric of poetry for centuries but has come into renewed focus in the twentieth century primarily as a result of its war and genocide. The poets of Eastern Europe have become models for those attempting to navigate the terrible waters of irreconcilable political conflicts and maintain a place for art amidst incomprehensible barbarity and human suffering. For Heaney, the work of Zbigniew Herbert, Osip Mandelstam, and particularly Czeslaw Milosz have been instructive in defining the path of exile – from national allegiance and from history – as the essential mode of poetic consciousness.[28] Heaney was born in Co Derry in Northern Ireland but his experience of the extreme sectarian violence drove him to the Republic. A Catholic and Nationalist, Heaney was appalled by violence on both sides of the conflict. The focus of his poetry on the rural aspects of his youth reflects a conscience in flight, astray from the warfare of sectarian politics but unable to escape the pain of displacement and the guilt of a non-participant. Milosz, a Polish Catholic born and raised in Lithuania also lived a life of continued flight from coercions. Eventually he left Poland, unable to accept the advent of the communist regime but remained racked by guilt because of his decision to leave his homeland. Heaney recognised in Milosz an ability to recover human dignity, however, poignantly by returning to the pastoral dreams of his youth, imagining heaven in the midst of hell on earth. The beginning of one of Milosz's great tapestries 'From the Rising

of the Sun' (1974) begins and remains true to the experiences of his youth –
and mankind's youth – in the provinces before the march of knowledge, experience and history. The voice of the individual poet encompasses within
himself his own growth and sophistication as well as that of mankind:

> Whatever I hold in my hand, a stylus, reed, quill, or ballpoint.
> Wherever I may be, on the tiles of an atrium, in a cloister cell, in the hall
>   before the portrait of a king,
> I attend to matters I have been charged with in the provinces.
> And I begin, though nobody can explain why and wherefore.
> Just as I do now, under a dark-blue cloud with a glint of the red horse.
> Retainers are busy, I know, in underground chambers,
> Rustling rolls of parchment, preparing coloured ink and sealing wax.[29]

The double conscience that haunts Milosz as he moves back to the provinces
and finds it as a source of integrity against the experiences of the world also
haunts Heaney most poignantly in the poems of his 1987 volume *The Haw
Lantern* (a book which owes much not only to Milosz but the more austere
parabolic poems of Zbigniew Herbert), particularly 'From the Republic of
Conscience', and 'Alphabets'. The republic of conscience has the qualities of
the provinces, the old country of youth:

> At immigration, the clerk was an old man
> who produced a wallet from his homespun coat
> and showed me a photograph of my grandfather.
>
> The woman in customs asked me to declare
> the words of our traditional cures and charms
> to heal dumbness and avert the evil eye.

In a discussion of his attraction to Milosz's world of provincial Lithuania,
Heaney underscores the mystical and mysterious: 'what attracted me in
Milosz was a sense of a pre-Reformation world, a stirring of the Catholic
unconscious. What happened to the English language after Shakespeare was
that it was kind of swept clean of a lot of pre-reformation association and
melody . . . So what is in the poetry of Milosz for an Irish person from
my kind of background is largely cultural ratification, a Dantesque corrob-
oration that says, yeah, the universe is much bigger than the Thirty-Nine
articles. The language leads you into the eternal . . . '[30]

Yet this eternal world exists only in relation to the temporal, and the fact
that one must travel between these worlds gives poignancy to the imagined one. Heaney was moved by the poignant irony of Milosz's 'The World'
(1943), a sequence reconstructing a child's world – not unlike Blake's *Songs*

of Innocence – in the midst of the second World War. Such a bi-focal vision appeals to Heaney and gives tremendous poignancy to his poems that establish an equilibrium between past and present and loss and redemption. In an early sonnet, 'The Forge' (1969), Heaney meditates through 'a door into the dark', on a vanishing way of life and an image of labour that becomes transformed into an altar of Hephaestan art:

> Inside, the hammered anvil's short-pitched ring,
> The unpredictable fantail of sparks
> Or hiss when a new shoe toughens in water.
> The anvil must be somewhere in the centre,
> Horned as a unicorn, at one end square,
> Set there immovable: an altar
> Where he expands himself in shape and music.

The balance between human and object, creature and creation has some of the innocence and circumscribed knowledge of a child who has not yet given in to noise or waste. Over twenty years later, Milosz, abandoning some of his interest in creating polyphonic tapestries, will begin his book entitled *Provinces* with a Heaney-like meditation entitled 'The Blacksmith Shop' (1991):

> I liked the bellows operated by rope.
> A hand or foot pedal – I don't remember which.
> But that blowing, and the blazing of the fire!
> And a piece of iron in the fire, held there by tongs,
> Red softened for the anvil,
> Beaten with a hammer, bent into a horseshoe,
> Thrown into a bucket of water, sizzle, steam.[31]

Milsoz's attention to that sublime moment when the red-hot metal merges with water to form steam is one of many little reconciliations of tensions and opposites crucial to the celebration of being. His stated object in poetry was 'to find my home in one sentence, as if hammered in metal . . . An unnamed need for order, for rhythm, for form, which three words are opposed to chaos and nothingness'. Both poets find the need through poetry to create a home, a home made more poignant because it has been lost or threatened by time and history. The power of the concise luminous moment containing a world attracted Heaney from the beginning of his career and found a receptive audience in Milosz in the later part of his own. Milosz included Heaney's powerful sonnet from the sequence 'Clearances' – 'When all the others were away at Mass/ I was all hers as we peeled potatoes' – in his 1991 anthology,

A Book of Luminous Things. The restoration in poetic remembrance of a beloved relationship beyond the rituals even of parish and priest unite both poets' sensibilities.

Milosz's theological preoccupations and his distrust of the aesthetic make him, for all his achievement as a poet, more sceptical of art and the pleasures of language than Heaney. One can see the tension between the two sensibilities in Heaney's reading of Milosz's 'Incantation', a poem that Milosz regards as completely ironic in the context of history. Heaney admires the sheer 'above the brim' verbal and rhetorical force of the poem as evidence of its value. In an article in *The New York Times*, Heaney invoked the poem as an example of the moral force of art when it dares to envision or to enchant us into seeing what otherwise would seem impossible:

> It is thrilling to hear the ideal possibilities of human life stated so unambiguously and unrepentantly. For a moment, the dirty slate of history seems to have been wiped clean. The lines return us to the bliss of beginnings. They tempt us to credit all over again the liberations promised by the Enlightenment and harmonies envisaged by the scholastics, to believe that the deep well of religious and humanist value may still be unpolluted . . . And yet there is something problematic about what is being said. While the lines do have original force, the evidence of the ages is stacked against them . . . Mr. Milosz's irony saves him and his poem from illusion and sentimentality; the tragic understanding that coexists with the apparent innocence of his claims only makes those claims all the more unyielding and indispensable.[32]

Yet both poets feel the tension between history and contemplation, a desire to escape the world of action in which all forces seem coercive or worse. Echoing a favourite passage from Milosz's autobiographical *Native Realm*, Heaney suggests why the tortured consciences of some Northern Irish writers find the move to a distant plane of regard liberating:

> The poet is stretched between politics and transcendence and is often displaced from a confidence in a single position by his disposition to be affected by all positions, negatively rather than positively capable. This, and the complexity of the present conditions may go in some way towards explaining the large number of poems in which the Northern Irish writer views the world from a great spatial or temporal distance, the number of poems imagined from beyond the grave, from the perspective of mythological or historically remote characters.[33]

Spatial and temporal distance gives Heaney's 'Alphabets' particular power as he sounds the development of his own experience. Heaney places great value on the recovery of a preternatural, almost Adamic language (his own 'soundings' reminiscent of Thoreau's in *Walden*) though he seems alternately to rejoice in and suffer from the alienation that has come from the process of education. In 'Alphabets', Heaney's own education recapitulates the development of modern man – from the farm and its simple technology to the sophistication that would send us into space and provide us a new view of our planet. The alienation from the source created by education and travel can also bring us back to an astonished sense of the miracle and strangeness of growth and of life, from beginning to end, from alpha to omega. Heaney rejoices in the sonority of the Greek letter 'omega', as it resonates with another ancient Greek word he loves for its sensuous and sensual sonorities, the 'omphalos', the naval and origin and its relation to the Latin 'ovum', and the primal, vernacular utterance of wonder, 'agog':

> . . . As from his small window
> The astronaut sees all that he has sprung from,
> The risen, aqueous, singular, lucent O
> Like a magnified and buoyant ovum –
>
> Or like my own wide pre-reflective stare
> All agog at the plasterer on his ladder
> Skimming our gable and writing our name there
> With his trowel point, letter by strange letter.

At the end, Heaney's work chooses to remain parochially 'agog' to the mystery of existence, going with, as well as behind, the sophistications and pleasures of language to exalt the primordial consciousness. Heaney, the dolorous Dantean pilgrim of *Station Island* (1984), confronts the spectre of Joyce exhorting him to the joy and sensual play of language:

> '. . . The main thing is to write
> for the joy of it. Cultivate a work-lust
> that imagines its haven like your hands at night
> dreaming the sun in the sunspot of the breasts.'

The impulse to this Joycean play in exile and cunning and the joy of language in contrast to the elegiac dwelling on history and earnest spiritual pilgrimage finds a master in Paul Muldoon, particularly in his longer poems of journey, 'Immram', 'The More a Man Has the More He Wants', and 'Madoc'. In each of these poems, mythic figures become caught in quests for paternity and origins, an aboriginal self connected to a dream of an American utopia, the prairie that Heaney set himself against in 'Bogland'. Carol Tell has observed that 'despite Muldoon's fascination with Americana, his rendering of Utopia does not necessarily coincide with the New World paradigm: the journey itself is desirable, the destination elusive'.[34] The New World paradigm is hardly monolithic and more often than not ironic. Against the background of Frost's mysterious idea of the 'unstoried, artless, and uncolonized American landscape' comes an ironic search that seems to lead only to endless uncertainty and a sense of self susceptible and open to all sources and all influences, mocking conclusions and utopias. Colonials and revolutionaries can readily become colonisers and all deeds of gift combine deeds of war. Most notable among such poems are 'The More a Man Has the More He Wants', and the book-length poem 'Madoc'. These poems read as Ovidian studies in change and contingency, with oneiric transformations of identity and conditions that end always in uncertainty. The self remains groundless and susceptible to all the waves of global influence that one finds in and out of books, newspapers, advertising, radio and television. In his prefatory note to *Poems: 1968–1998*, Muldoon deprecates his eventual claim on his own poems, a self-denying authorial ordinance, viewing the poet rather as the ventriloquist through whom the language speaks and shifts: 'I have made scarcely any changes in the texts of the poems, since I'm fairly certain that, after a shortish time, the person through whom the poem was written is no more entitled to make revisions than the reader'.[35]

The character Gallogly could suggest 'gael' or 'gaul logos' – language. In fact the name does suggests 'Golightly', the Gallowglass warriors of Gaelic Ulster, and the Sioux braves of the Oglala tribe. In other words, this is a litany of romantic fantasies of origin that upbraid the claims of identity politics. The main character has made an abortive trip to the United States to buy arms and imagines that he has killed a girl. He is pursued by the phantom of a vengeful American Indian, Mangan Jones, who becomes a trickster doppleganger. One irony, of course, is that a freedom fighter has himself engaged in the taking of innocent life and assumed the role of colonising ravager. He exists in a kind of limbo, between worlds. Muldoon draws several times on the mythology of Frost's world – the mysterious pastoral New England, 'North of Boston', – recognising, as Frost did, that his own landscape was one of mythic uncertainty. A sly allusion to the ambiguous conclusion of Frost's 'For Once, Then, Something', coruscates through the poem. What does one have after looking into a well at one's own reflection – 'A pebble of quartz, truth?'

Fluidity, symbolised in Frost by water rebuking the clear reflection is the only order of the day. Of course, Muldoon's poem is a kaleidoscope of dream-like associations and transformations raising the question of what-if anything – remains stable in the island of the self. At the same moment, we have an allusion to Frost's 'I Could Give All to Time', in which the speaker refers to global geologic change, turning islands to water, and something mysterious he refuses to declare in 'customs'. Is Gallogly being pursued by an

Apache, a 'Mescadoro' travelling in a hallucinogenic dreamland of nativist fantasies that now seek revenge on his own violence? The poem concludes with a broken off allusion both to 'For Once, Then, Something', and another strange pastoral, 'The Mountain', in which the narrator hears a ploughman in 'Lunenberg' (an actual place but one that also seems 'looney') begin to describe the alleged growth of a local mountain when it was 'no bigger than a . . . ' Muldoon's conclusion is a resoundingly inconclusive 'Huh?' recognising the inscrutability of those natural men whom Wordsworth's leech gatherer had once idealised as having a bond to nature instead of being tricksters and jokers, subverting the expectations of everyone around them.

'Madoc' picks up where Robert Southey's epic of the same title left off. Muldoon imagines Coleridge and Southey themselves travelling to America in quest of the Utopian pantisocracy discussed by the two poets. What Muldoon gives us is a multi-vocal spoof of universality framed in short poems attributed or connected to an historical panorama of great philosophers, from Thales to Stephen Hawking. The poem gives the expectation of encompassing the world but ultimately seems a spoof of utopian dreams as mere projections from the vast, global well-spring of the self in endless play. In Muldoon, the carefully crafted structure of poetic consciousness flows in a river running around the world of language and thought.

NOTES

1 See Dennis O'Driscoll, 'Foreign Relations: Irish and International Poetry', in *Poetry in Contemporary Irish Literature*, edited by Michael Kenneally (Gerrards Cross: Colin Smythe, 1995), pp. 48–60.

2 Vincent Buckley, *Memory Ireland: Insights into the Contemporary Irish Condition* (New York: Penguin Books, 1985), p. 213.

3 Thomas Kinsella, *Collected Poems* (Manchester: Carcanet, 2001). It is interesting to note that this was one of only four of his own poems that Kinsella included in his edition of *The New Oxford Book of Irish Verse* (Oxford University Press, 1989), p. 373.

4 Kevin Donegan, 'Women Step Out of Ireland's Literary Shadows', *The Los Angeles Times*, April 23, 2002, section E, p. 1.

5 Eavan Boland, *Collected Poems* (Manchester: Carcanet, 1995).

6 See Edna Longley, 'Irish Bards and American Audiences', *The Southern Review*, 31.1 (July 1995), p. 764: Longley is critical of Boland for having 'been too easily allowed to set the terms of her own reception . . . The terms set forth by Boland include insertion of the woman into 'the national tradition' or the 'Irish poem' (this presumes that both have clear boundaries); a claim to speak for women silenced by 'the wrath and grief' of Irish history – another somewhat sweeping proposal; and subversion of female images propagated by Irish male poets'.

7 *The Collected Poems of W.B. Yeats* (London: Macmillan, 1950).

8 *The English Auden: Poems Essays and Dramatic Writings, 1927–1939*, ed. Edward Mendelson (London: Faber and Faber, 1977).

9 Thomas Kinsella, *The Dual Tradition* (Manchester: Carcanet, 1995), p. 90.

10 Patrick Kavanagh, *The Complete Poems* (Dublin: Goldsmith, 1972).

11 See Michael Allen, 'The Parish and the Dream: Heaney and America, 1969–1987', *The Southern Review* 31.3 (July, 1995), pp. 726–38.

12 Robert Frost to John Bartlett, 1914 in *Selected Letters of Robert Frost*, ed. Thompson (New York: Holt, Rinehart & Winston, 1964), pp. 110–11.

13 *Prose Jottings of Robert Frost*, ed., Lathem and Cox (Vermont: Northeast-Kingdom, 1982), pp. 102–3.

14 Joseph Brodsky, Seamus Heaney and Derek Walcott, *Homage to Robert Frost* (New York: Farrar, Straus & Giroux, 1995), p. 72.

15 See also David Mason, 'Robert Frost, Seamus Heaney, and the Wellsprings of Poetry', *Sewanee Review* 108.1 (Winter 2000), pp. 41–57 and Stephen James, 'Diving Lines: Robert Frost and Seamus Heaney', *Symbiosis* 3.1 (April, 1999), pp. 63–76, and Jacqueline McCurry, ' "But all the fun's in how you say a thing": Robert Frost and Paul Muldoon', *Robert Frost Review* 8 (Fall 1998), pp. 79–92.

16 Seamus Heaney, 'Personal Helicon', in *Opened Ground: Poems, 1966–1996* (London: Faber and Faber, 1998).

17 Robert Frost, *Interviews with Robert Frost*, edited by Edward Connery Lathem (New York: Holt, Rinehart and Winston, 1966), p. 19.

18 See Paulin's discussion of Frost's 'The Vanishing Red' in *Minotaur: Poetry and the Nation State* (Cambridge: Harvard University Press, 1992), p. 172.

19 Frost, *Interviews*, p. 19.

20 Seamus Heaney, 'Voices Behind a Door: Robert Frost', *Poetry Review* 83:4 (Winter 1993–94), p. 31.

21 Tom Paulin, *The Wind Dog* (London: Faber and Faber, 1999).

22 See Stan Smith, 'The Language of Displacement in Contemporary Irish Poetry', in *Poetry in Contemporary Irish Literature* (Gerrards Cross: Colin Smythe, 1995), p. 75.

23 Seamus Heaney, 'Place and Displacement: Recent Poetry from Northern Ireland', in *Finders Keepers* (New York: Farrar, Straus & Giroux, 2002), p. 128.

24 Peter Bien, 'The Nicholas E. Christopher Memorial Lecture', G.P. Savidis Memorial Colloquium: 'Modern Greek Literature Today: Across Europe and Beyond', November 14, 1997.

25 George Seferis, *Collected Poems*, tr. Edmund Keeley and Philip Sherrard (Princeton University Press, 1995), p. 134.

26 Seamus Deane, *Celtic Revivals* (London: Faber and Faber, 1985), p. 160.

27 Derek Mahon, *Collected Poems* (Loughcrew: Gallery, 1999).

28 See Clare Cavanagh, 'From the Republic of Conscience: Seamus Heaney and Eastern European Poetry', *Harvard Review* 6 (Spring 1994), pp. 105–12.

29 Czeslaw Milosz, 'From the Rising of the Sun', in *New and Collected Poems*, tr. Czeslaw Milosz and Lillian Vallee (New York: Ecco Press, 2001), p. 278.

30 Seamus Heaney, Edward Hirsch, Adam Zagajewski and Tomas Venclova, *et al.*, 'Milosz and World Poetry', proceedings of the International Milosz Festival in *Partisan Review* (Winter, 1999), p. 37.

31 Milosz, 'Provinces', *New and Collected Poems*, trans. Czeslaw Milosz and Robert Hass (Harmondsworth: Penguin, 2001), p. 503.

32 Seamus Heaney, 'Poetry's Power Against Intolerance', *The New York Times*, Sunday, August 26, 2001, p. 13.
33 Seamus Heaney, *Finders Keepers*, p. 129.
34 Carol Tell, 'Utopia in the New World: Paul Muldoon's America', Bullan 2.2 (1996), p. 67.
35 Paul Muldoon, *Poems: 1968–1998* (New York: Farrar, Straus & Giroux, 2001).

DAVID WHEATLEY

Irish poetry into the twenty-first century

In a short, early lyric Michael Longley proposes a certain obstinacy, reticence and awkwardness as among the defining characteristics of his subject, 'Irish Poetry'. For Longley, Irish poetry issues forth not in glorious blossoms but 'tuberous clottings', 'a muddy /Accumulation' to be found in 'specializations of light', or, in Joycean style, 'dialects of silence' rather than the spoken word.[1] When he imagines these elements combining in the poem's last lines, it is to form images of suffering: 'the bent spines, /The angular limbs of creatures'. The poem ends by conjuring 'the initial letter, the stance', but even this moment of self-assertion is coloured in 'lost minerals'. If Irish poetry in 2000 had fewer reasons for awkward introspection than it did in 1973, when Longley's poem appeared, its achievements in the intervening years had done much to foster a mood of buoyant well-being.

Already in 1973 Longley had been recognised as part of an outstanding generation of writers that also included James Simmons, Derek Mahon and Seamus Heaney. Among the usual contributory factors to such group identification are a shared regional or educational background and publishing history, early critical reception and journalistic labelling. Whether or not the different writers' work has anything real in common beyond these externals is another question entirely. For the younger poet the question of group identity can never be entirely risk-free: for every Philip Larkin or Thom Gunn who transcends the movement to which he is recruited there will be a John Wain or John Holloway who does not. 'The danger is in the neatness of identifications', as Samuel Beckett warned in 1929,[2] five years before launching a literary movement of his own (or attempting to) in 'Recent Irish Poetry'. With all these warnings in mind, the five poets I have chosen to discuss are Peter McDonald, Peter Sirr, Justin Quinn, Vona Groarke and Conor O'Callaghan. Born between 1960 and 1968, they form a chronological generation but are as different from one another as they are from their elders, form no school and adhere to no shared orthodoxies. They are adventurously cosmopolitan in outlook but attentively rooted in their local habitations. They are formalist or experimental as the mood takes them, writing small, exquisite lyrics, and long, loose free verse sequences, and offer in their variousness compelling examples of the range and scope of Irish poetry as it enters the twenty-first century.

While Michael Longley's 'dialects of silence' suggest a personal and secretive utterance, Irish poetry has its public institutions too, whose context it is essential to understand before considering the individual poets. An obvious institution with which to begin is Irish poetry publishing, or rather the publishing of Irish poetry, since the two are not always the same thing. In his 1995 study *The Dual Tradition* Thomas Kinsella observes of publishing that 'the post-colonial impulse is the deciding consideration: primary publication in England is regarded as the desirable norm by most Irish writers and by the commentators'.[3] In confirmation of this *The Dual Tradition* is itself published by an English press, but in the 1990s the Irish publishing scene found itself in cautiously good commercial health. Kinsella continued to publish his work from Dublin in pamphlet form with the Peppercanister Press, in the intervals between larger volumes from Oxford University Press and latterly Carcanet. With its high production standards, Peter Fallon's Gallery Press could legitimately claim to have succeeded the defunct Dolmen Press as Ireland's premier publishers of poetry. John F. Deane's Dedalus Press continued its commitment to poetry in translation, as well as publishing important editions of Denis Devlin and Brian Coffey. In the west the rise of Salmon Press (founded in Galway but now based in Co Clare) coincided with the coming to prominence of a new generation of women writers including Rita Ann Higgins, Mary O'Malley and Moya Cannon. After the explosive energies of its beginnings, Dermot Bolger's Raven Arts Press wound down its activities, evolving into New Island Books. In Northern Ireland, Blackstaff was joined by Lagan Press, who did much to restore the reputation of older writers overtaken by the 1960s generation, such as Roy McFadden and Padraic Fiacc. Among English presses, Carcanet, Bloodaxe, Cape and Anvil maintained significant Irish presences on their lists, while in London Faber and Faber saw his Nobel Prize victory turn Seamus Heaney into a poetry best-seller matched only by Ted Hughes. Further afield, in the US, Dillon Johnston's Wake Forest University Press remained a crucial conduit.

More so than by individual slim volumes, perceptions of contemporary Irish poetry in recent decades have tended to be shaped by anthologies. The Greek root of 'anthology' translates as 'a gathering of flowers', but in practice Irish anthologists gather as many thorns as they do flowers in a climate where anthologies are never less than highly contentious cultural interventions. The indignation that greeted *The Field Day Anthology* in 1991 is merely the best-known example of the almost constant crossfire generated by the question of canons and canon-formation. With striking editorial hubris Paul Muldoon's 1986 *Faber Book of Contemporary Irish Poetry* contained the work of a mere ten writers, all but two from Ulster. In the same year, Thomas Kinsella chose the preface of his *New Oxford Book of Irish Verse* to dismiss the 'Northern Ireland Renaissance' (Kinsella's quotation marks) as a 'journalistic entity'.[4] Reviewing the anthology *Other Voices: Irish Poetry Now* in 1994, Patrick Ramsey seconded his fellow Northerner John Hughes's description of Southern Irish poetry as 'self-indulgent, lifeless, lazy, turgid, sentimental and unimaginative', adding, as his own contribution, 'boring', 'incompetent', 'crude', 'rhythmically inert' and 'prosaic'.[5] The possibilities for programmatic mutual incomprehension and cultural trench warfare seem inexhaustible. As Peter Sirr has commented: 'Anthology-making is a branch of poetry criticism, though in Ireland, increasingly, it seems to be the whole tree'.[6] Not all such volumes conform to the pattern of intervention and standoff however: Patrick Crotty's *Modern Irish Poetry* (1995) is a judicious and catholic survey of its period, free of overt polemical intent, with Peter Sirr and Peter McDonald as its final two inclusions.

Critical sensitivities are no less acute when Irish poetry is anthologised from abroad. Blake Morrison and Andrew Motion's inclusion of Seamus Heaney in *The Penguin Book of Contemporary British Poetry* (1982) is a celebrated instance, prompting a friendly verse letter rebuke from Heaney denying his eligibility. Since then British anthologists have trodden more carefully, usually taking refuge in what Harry Clifton has mordantly diagnosed as the 'And Ireland' syndrome,[7] though here too subtle crowd-control tactics can be seen (e.g. the one-woman embodiment of Irish-language poetry in Nuala Ní Dhomhnaill, the near-invisibility of Irish poets whose work has been published not in England but the Irish Republic, the United States or even Northern Ireland, and the eclipse of older figures such as Padraic Fallon or Richard Murphy who have not attracted critical sponsorship on the same level as their juniors).

Selective though it may be, critical sponsorship has not been in short supply. The 1990s saw the publication of Irish-themed special issues of prestigious journals such as *The Southern Review*, *Poetry* and *Princeton University Library Chronicle*, and the publication of monographs, edited collections of essays or special issues of journals devoted to poets still in their forties and fifties such as Boland, Durcan and Muldoon. Writers yet to attain this level of canonisation must depend on the more rough and tumble attentions of a lively newspaper reviewing scene. If anthology-style faction fighting besets Irish poetry reviewing, so too do the obverse threats of cosy protectiveness and critical insider dealing. Writing in the Irish special issue of *Poetry*, Dennis O'Driscoll observed how in Ireland 'collections appear which even an American vanity press might blanch at – and they are not only printed but publicised and praised as well'.[8] The worse effects of this syndrome are palliated by the presence of conscientious reviewers such as O'Driscoll himself; but the fact that Irish poetry critics (O'Driscoll among them) are almost without exception also poets is surely significant, suggesting a high and even ominous degree of self-reflexivity in the whole process.[9]

Another apparently uniform trend in Irish poetry is its frequently remarked-on resistance to experiment. In the 1970s the *Lace Curtain* and New Writers Press group had proposed a modernist revision of the Irish canon, with Brian Coffey, Denis Devlin and Thomas MacGreevy as alternative avatars to Kavanagh and Clarke. Another wave of interest in these writers in the 1990s testified to the continuing vitality of this tradition, alongside the publishing activities of Randolph Healy, Billy Mills and Catherine Walsh, and the annual hosting in Cork since 1997 of a conference devoted to alternative poetries. The profile of writing in Irish, too, underwent significant changes in the 1990s. The many translators attracted to the work of Nuala Ní Dhomhnaill created new audiences (bilingual or not) for poetry in Irish, as did the striking new talent of Cathal Ó Searcaigh. While many older Irish poets have been deeply marked by the Irish language, the same cannot be said in truth of Quinn, Groarke and O'Callaghan. Applied to them, Thomas Kinsella's claim for a 'divided tradition' scarred by the loss of the Irish language seems almost nostalgic. Irish-language influences have far from disappeared from the work of younger writers, however, as the examples of Moya Cannon, Peter Sirr, James McCabe, Tom French and Frankie Sewell all show.

The 1980s and 1990s were decades of unprecedented and traumatic social change in both the Republic and Northern Ireland. The obvious model for younger poets drawn to political or satirical themes is Paul Durcan, who marked the Church-State tussles of these years with swingeingly uproarious attacks on the paternalism of Irish life. In its very madcap hilarity however, Durcan's satire charts the loosening clerical grip on public mores since the time of Austin Clarke's late satires in the 1960s and 1970s. By the 1990s, with the removal of legal sanctions on contraception, homosexuality and divorce (though not abortion), the collapse of Church authority had gathered startling momentum, a process abetted by a series of high-profile clerical sexual abuse cases. The depiction of three rural priests in the Irish-written but British-broadcast television comedy *Father Ted* as harmless simpletons was a telling symptom of a society which scarcely related to its clergy as authority figures any more, even for satirical purposes. Anti-clerical feeling is as notably absent from the work of Sirr, Quinn, Groarke and O'Callaghan as traditional devoutness.[10]

One event more than any other symbolises the scale of political movement during these years: the Belfast Agreement of 1998. South of the border, the endorsement of the agreement by an overwhelming majority represented an unprecedented change in the Republic's self-image, involving as it did the dropping of the territorial claim on Northern Ireland under articles 2 and 3 of the 1937 Constitution (Bunracht na hÉireann). Previously the disjunction between constitutional theory and political fact had served to obscure the question of whether writing from the South constituted a separate entity or not. If simply ignoring partition was the easiest option for the nationalist Southern state, attempts to come to terms with it were not without their pitfalls either. The distinctness of Northern Irish poetry had long had its champion in Edna Longley, but when Sebastian Barry argued for a specifically Southern aesthetic in his anthology *The Inherited Boundaries* (1986) he did so in curiously diffident terms. What his seven poets (Sebastian Barry, Dermot Bolger, Harry Clifton, Thomas McCarthy, Aidan Carl Mathews, Michael O'Loughlin and Matthew Sweeney) had in common, for Barry, was a non-identity, abetted by the economic slump of the 1980s and its emigration crisis – so reminiscent of the decade when the *Inherited Boundaries* poets were born. 'To be born in the fifties in the Republic of Ireland', Barry writes, 'was to be born, with no great ceremony, nowhere'.[11] Nowhere, like somewhere, can be located anywhere, to misquote Philip Larkin, and an examination of place in younger Irish poets' work turns up a more sophisticated relationship than the traditional opposition of exile and home. Justin Quinn grafts American influences onto Irish verse in the newly created Czech Republic. Conor O'Callaghan explores neglected sites of Irish poetry, neither the east-coast metropolis nor the Atlantic west, and writes villanelles about an imagined American Pacific seacoast. 'All poets live abroad, don't they?' Peter Sirr humorously asks in a contribution to a *Metre* symposium on diasporic Irish writing.[12]

Another aspect of the 'nowhere' of Southern Irish identity in Barry's anthology is the place it assigns writing by women – precisely nowhere, placing the book at a somewhat coy angle to the explosive sexual politics of the 1980s, with its constitutional referendums on divorce and abortion. By the time of Peggy O'Brien's *Wake Forest Book of Irish Women's Poetry 1967–2000*, fourteen years later, the Southern or Southern-based Nuala Ní Dhomhnaill, Rita Ann Higgins, Paula Meehan, Moya Cannon, Mary O'Malley and Kerry Hardie, all born in the 1950s, had established themselves as contemporary equals of their male *Inherited Boundaries* counterparts. But a sense of doubt and unease about Southern literary identity persisted. Writing almost a decade and a half after Barry, John Goodby struggles to find a unifying identity in the work of writers from the Republic: 'The situation . . . while interestingly fluid, still suffers from the lack of the focus which continues to bind together and give cohesion to the work of the best Northern Irish poets. No single historical moment has galvanised poetry in the Republic'.[13]

Even in 2000 then, the sense of a North-South divide remained strong, without exhausting the range of powerful binaries at work. The reflex assignment of Irish writers into the broadly defined camps of unionist or nationalist, Protestant or Catholic, or, in the case of critics, theorist or liberal humanist, continues to possess a baleful tenacity in Irish debate. Belfast-born poet and critic Peter McDonald politely demurs at contemporary post-colonial anxieties ('being from Belfast, I don't think of myself as having, or wanting, a stake in the "Irishness" debate'),[14] but an *Irish Times* reviewer of his *Mistaken Identities: Poetry and Northern Ireland* can make the remarkable statement, even if intended as a piece of desperate irony: 'Pity, though, a Presbyterian had to write it'.[15] The dismissal is of a piece with the common Southern belief that, in so far as there is a Northern Protestant imagination it must be English in provenance: in *The Field Day Anthology* Declan Kiberd aligns Michael Longley rather improbably with 'British post-modernism', and identifies Longley and Derek Mahon as representing 'a strand of Ulster that identifies itself as British and asserts its rights to the English lyric'.[16] The slippage from 'British' to 'English' is characteristic, ghosted though it is by the allusion to Heaney's *North*.[17] Very large doses of special pleading would be required to argue that the formal qualities of a younger Ulster poet such as Conor O'Callaghan represent cleavings to the 'English lyric', with all the political baggage that phrase carries (though, as we shall see, reactions have not been wanting which attempt to do just that). With writers of Protestant background, however, the identification is easily and unthinkingly made.

Consequently, Peter McDonald's poetry speaks from a position that for many in the Republic simply does not exist. Born in Belfast in 1962, he published his first collection, *Biting the Wax*, in 1989, and a critical study, *Louis MacNeice: The Poet in his Contexts*, two years later. The centrepiece of *Biting the Wax* is 'Sunday in Great Tew', whose dateline alone ('8th November 1987') hints at the atrocity it elegises, in the absence of a place-name or any further details (the place is Enniskillen, where an IRA bombing of the Memorial Day parade had killed eleven people). Memorials and remembrance parades play a major (and highly politicised) role in Northern Irish public life, but the thought of 'Sunday at Great Tew' adding to the culture of official commemoration is one from which the poem draws back: as McDonald has said, 'the sequence includes a kind of anger which resists absolutely the impulse to remembrance as such'.[18] As the media pack descends on Enniskillen, McDonald notes how perpetrators and victims merge in soundbite invocations of age-old hatreds, in which 'the Irish slaughter one another like wogs'.[19] Questions of cultural misunderstanding and non-communication are a frequent theme in *Biting the Wax*, producing a tone of exhaustion in which 'that country' (unnamed) is 'washed-up, written-off, a place for dead people' (*Biting the Wax*, 53). However bad 'that country' may be, getting away from it all poses its own problems: in 'The South' a couple wishing to get as far from danger as possible make the unfortunate choice of the Falkland Islands just before what the poem calls 'that episode' in 1982. The influence of Derek Mahon informs the prevailing dialectic of violence and order, as well as the vision of hypothetical catastrophe we find in 'Short Story', where 'the last /astronaut alive' is left 'wondering /how to make his way back to the moon'. Another long poem is 'Silent Night', spoken by a concentration camp survivor. Its title blackly conflates the horrors of the camps and the carols to which the inmates are treated on Christmas Day, the absurdity of music in such a setting rendering the normal business of the camp all the more grotesque.

McDonald's second collection is *Adam's Dream* (1996), whose title refers not to the Book of Genesis but (by way of Keats's letters) the eighteenth-century Scottish architect Robert Adam. Questions of building and destruction are among its central concerns. In 'About Lisbon', a poem on the great Lisbon earthquake of 1755, McDonald addresses the artful scruple behind Heaney's 'Viking Dublin: Trial Pieces', whose speaker found himself 'coming to consciousness /by jumping in graves'.[20] Its streets deserted, McDonald's destroyed city has nothing to offer the hawker of eyewitness accounts. The speaker cannot even make up his mind if the disaster has taken place yet or not:

> Is it perhaps because
> that morning has yet to come, or because
> the catastrophe has been too long forgotten
> that nobody speaks, that there is nobody to speak,
> that I must wander for hours an unknown city
> and there is nobody here to ask the time?[21]

Of the five poets under consideration here, McDonald comes closest to being neo-classical in his characteristic tone of restraint and distrust of gaudiness; as he has said in interview, 'I think all good poetry exercises decorum in deep and important ways'.[22] Although containing some skilfully musical verse, *Adam's Dream* insists on its strong anti-lyrical drive. Its opening poem, 'Flat sonnet: the situation', answers the demand that a writer from Northern Ireland write about 'the situation', in the media euphemism, by dealing with it in exactly those abstract terms: 'the demand is that you deal with the situation [. . .] / there is no choice but to deal with the situation'. Apparent urgency and anxious detachment combine unnervingly; the poem seems to fidget before our eyes. 'Meissen' begins: 'Everything he touched, it fell to pieces', before going on to describe the 'militant fragility' of porcelain and the fate of a man who has been 'not ruined quite or hurt, but somehow /reduced, and better that way'. Glimpses of the natural world, too, point to vulnerability and threat: in 'The creatures' the animals go 'one by one' rather than 'two by two' into 'the peaceable kingdom', since there is no longer a 'Noah to save them', while in 'From the porch' the poet watches the animals troop past 'like lost things'. In the title poem, Adam sees in the destruction of Lisbon a perfect opportunity for his own creations to rise from the ruins, but by the time we reach the volume's last poem ('Lines on the demolition of the *Adelphi*, 1937') it is Adam's work that is being destroyed:

> Yet I can see, beneath the sooty dust,
> Nothing of lasting worth, no second Rome,
> Merely an English place, mean, gone to rust,
> Not, after all, the imagination's home,
>
> And built on little more than unpaid debts,
> Its future mortgaged and its past resigned,
> No better than where Piranesi sweats
> Beside me in the prison he designed.

Adam's reaction is surprisingly calm, upholding the power of the imagination even as its tangible monuments crumble and fall.

Born in Waterford in 1960, Peter Sirr began to publish early: *Marginal Zones* appeared in 1984, followed three years later by *Talk, Talk*. 'You say /there is a language in which the word for family //is also the word for departure', he writes in 'Home Ballads'[23] (1995): Sirr is a travel poet not just in his descriptions of life in Italy and Holland but in the studied displacement to be found in all his work, whether he writes of home or abroad. Although his mood of relaxed urbanity allies him to the New York School, continental European influences also play their part, as in the poems on and in reply to Fernando Pessoa, Francis Ponge and Leopardi in *Bring Everything*. A linguistic defamiliarisation or *Verfremdungseffekt* is another recurring feature: 'Translations' opens with 'strange fruit for which we have no name', while flocks of birds 'make the noise our language knows'.[24] This tone serves Sirr well in one of the best-known poems from *Marginal Zones*, 'The Collector's Marginalia', in which he adopts an anthropological persona to describe the encounter of modernity and a disappearing native culture. As in Mahon's 'A Disused Shed in Co. Wexford', the scholarly interest in the lost or disappearing tribe cannot but strike the reader as confirmation of its doom:

In three dialects the old people die
And the lights come on in local halls.
A volleyball team is making major strides.

Despite the bathos of the final line, Sirr refuses to engage in facile ide-
alisations of the past at the expense of debased modernity. The texture of
his verse defies nostalgia: his aversion to the jewelled line and fondness for
ending poems with a quizzical ellipsis adds to the lightness of touch he shows
in his frequent changes of scene and jumpcut narrative style. As he writes
in the title poem of *Talk, Talk*, 'I have thrown //everything to the wind but
caution'.[25] By the last poem in the book, 'Vigils', it is clear that Sirr wants
something more than the hasty or provisional statements in which these
early poems excel. He strikes an Eliotian note: '*Listen to me now. Why do
you never listen?*' *Ways of Falling* (1991) is a transitional volume, inquiring at every turn for a way out, or a newer way out than those of his first
two books. 'Escape Manual' begins 'There is always a way, surprisingly',
even if it turns out to be only 'a way of falling / [. . .] always some way
down'.[26] 'Death of a Travel Writer' is preoccupied with failure and endings,
but marks the beginning of an engagement with longer sequences that is a
feature of *The Ledger of Fruitful Exchange* (1995) and *Bring Everything*
(2000).

A highlight of *The Ledger* is 'Pages Ripped from July', which is thematically an Elizabeth-Bishopesque pondering of 'Questions of Travel'. The
poem's first section-title ('Rough Guide to July 18') borrows the name of
a tourist guide to mix touristy chit-chat with deceptively casual references
to its Italian town's bloody history ('seven thousand slaughtered /heads'). In
the final section, 'Worlds', the violent past and blasé present come together
unexpectedly:

Carelessly you would be taken
without any particular excitement,
and bundled onto the stone,
your blood, wholly unremarkable,
pouring into the sun
its brief stain.

'Trade Songs' goes further again in its quasi-epic style, with overtones of
the *Anabase* or *Exils* of St-John Perse. In *Bring Everything*, by contrast, Sirr's
focus returns to Dublin. *Bring Everything* marks an adventurous departure in
representations of the capital city in Irish poetry: Sirr exults in the palimpsests
of history, moving from the Viking city to the multicultural buzz of the Celtic
Tiger with a greedy eye for historical bric-a-brac and commodity detritus.
There is a witty enjoyment, too, of the multiple misunderstandings of which

history is made. In 'Sráid na gCaorach' he reminds us of the comedy of errors that often surrounds bilingual Irish street signs. Its title translates as 'Sheep Street', but through whatever slip of the cartographer's pen the actual street name is Ship Street. When a seagull screeches over nearby Dublin Castle, 'Ship Street startled //rubs the wool from its eyes /and casts off . . .'[27] Another mistaken identity lies behind 'The Beautiful Engines'. Sirr works at the Irish Writers' Centre (IWC) in Dublin, where for a time he found himself in receipt of daily e-mails intended for the Irish Wildbird Conservancy, with tales such as that of 'Des and Margaret, flown home from Cyprus /to wagtails on the north slob, /announcing their engagement en route'. According to Justin Quinn, Sirr 'has seemed a poet without a defining context', but with *Bring Everything* he has 'created a context all by himself'.[28]

Justin Quinn was born in Dublin in 1968 and now lives in Prague. He has published two collections, *The 'O'o'a'a' Bird* and *Privacy*, and is also a widely-published and outspoken reviewer. After the predominantly free verse ethic of the *Inherited Boundaries* group, his work could be interpreted as a return to conservative, formalist order. But this would be to oversimplify grossly: he is as interested in Allen Ginsberg as in James Merrill, and delights in anarchic gestures like that of 'Non-Enclave', exploding the well-made lyric across the page in a typographical *tour de force*. Quinn revels in the technological hum of contemporary life, and likes to describe his field of vision in photographic or cinematic terms. Typically he finds his urban environment in a state of panicked hyperactivity: 'We drive /To get ahead, to stay alive', he writes in 'On Speed'.[29] Exploiting a wide variety of forms from the sonnet and villanelle to the more quirkily original patterns of '6.55 a.m.' and 'Weekend Away', Quinn's work is suavely, even swaggeringly sure of its formal prowess.

The central influence on Quinn is Wallace Stevens, an influence he considers marginalised within Irish writing.[30] The 'o'o'a'a' bird of Quinn's title is a Hawaiian fellow victim of the dodo's to human-induced extinction. In the volume's title poem, the 'o'o'a'a' harangues humanity for its daytripper's view of nature and preference for the music of 'drills at road-works, or asthmatic /Engines under bonnets' over its own modest chirping. The fate of contemporary endangered species is the ersatz ecosystem of the zoo or nature preserve, and in the next poem, 'Minuet', Quinn produces a camp and florid version of pastoral where the 'o'o'a'a' might roam free. The 'views and topiaries' of the speaker's 'cinct demesne' convince him of the perfect balance he has struck between man and nature. Inviting his love to dance with the affectionate nickname 'My Little Dodo!' he reintroduces the theme of threat and extinction while also conjuring the comic escapism of a poem like Lear's 'The Owl and the Pussycat'. Predictably, the idyll breaks down and the speaker is left cursing the birds, and brusquely silencing his partner: 'Your questioning /Is also ill-advised, my dear, and done'. Nationalism and nation-building are repeatedly scrutinised in Quinn's work. The 'O'o'a'a' Bird contains a poem titled 'Patrick Pearse', which, though beginning in the voice of the 1916 poet-rebel, asserts its differences with him by mutating into a third-person narrative. 'Patrick Pearse' is followed by 'Revolutionary' and 'For Robinson Jeffers', in which Quinn ponders the transformative potential of poetry. In the second of these, on the 'inhumanist' Jeffers, the failure of art to change lives produces an epiphany of thwarted utopianism (note the Stevensian neologism 'incended'):

> And trees were still a black coulisse
>
> And lives still not the lives they might still lead
> And water-coloured skies incended nothing
> And there were roads but there was no way out.

In 'Ur-Aisling', a red-haired aisling figure, or visionary embodiment of Ireland, appears and invites the poet to 'Make me a nation as you will'. After he has laid out an infrastructure of 'nostalgias' and 'mythologies /Like slabs across the open land' in obedient patriotism, the nation-builder is treated to a second visit from his muse. This time her mood has changed: ' "You have usurped my power and name – /Your work misjudged, these people pitiful" '. With disarming insouciance, he resigns his commission: 'I shrugged. "So usurp it back again" '.[31] The thought that her male servitors might have so little interest in defending the privilege and authority with which she credits them comes as a startling reversal to the national goddess.

Quinn's interest in politics goes beyond the Irish variety: The 'O'o'a'a' Bird ends with an ambitious sequence in twenty parts, 'Days of the New Republic', chronicling the rebirth of Czech democracy after 1989. But for Quinn the political poem means much more than one devoted to the grand gestures of nation-building. Where Irish migrants have traditionally been the subject of disdain as providers of cheap manual labour, in 'Ukrainian Construction Workers' it is Quinn who is in the privileged role, watching as the Czechs direct these feelings towards a more impoverished immigrant group, and one with uncomfortable affinities to the former Soviet occupiers ('At least this time /they're not in tanks'). Yet even as the builders appear 'transparent men', in their transience and unreality to the Czechs, so too the buildings they raise are 'Transparent things' (in Quinn's Nabokovian phrasing) against 'the whim of Moscow'. While 'Moscow' harks back to Communist days, it also provides a witty rhyme on the Capitalist threat encroaching on the Czech Republic from the West:

Transparent things
Like these estates of towerblocks, civic buildings,
The new life promised everyone by Tesco,

Are what transparent men construct and tear
Straight down tomorrow.
What's left is less a capital and more a
Million people moving in the air.[32]

Sam Leith comments: 'Against a constant implicit desire to see panoptically is posed a recognition of the impossibility of such a view'.[33] Quinn is too shrewd a writer to equate control and technique alone with wisdom. In '6.55 a.m.' he stages the entropic shutdown of a poem from the opening section 5 to a numerical pun on the final section's 'zer- //o'. Emerging blinking from the realm of 'pastiche' and 'text' he bathes in the sunlight, receptively unsure 'as to what /Will happen next'.

One of the stylistic cruxes for Eavan Boland and other Irish women poets in the 1960s and 1970s was how to recuperate subject matter traditionally relegated as feminine without perpetuating assumptions of women's poetry as inescapably domestic or maternal in orientation. Largely thanks to the efforts of Boland, Eiléan Ní Chuilleanáin, Medbh McGuckian and others, Vona Groarke and her contemporaries can afford to be more relaxed in their roles. 'There is no convergence of subject-matter, no orthodoxy of theme or tone, no received notions of what is appropriate or what is beyond our reach', she writes in the introduction to her *Verse* special issue on Irish women poets.[34]

At a first glance, the poems of Groarke's *Shale* (1994) could not be further removed in spirit from Quinn's. The volume's elementally fresh and simple imagery recalls the American poet Louise Glück. In 'What Becomes the River?' a few key terms (river, stone, sea) are repeated with incantatory force, as Groarke's syntax creates a musical balance between movement and pause, transformation and sameness. Even something as solid as rock has its origins in another element, but as the final line reminds us, what underlies all these transformations is the 'clean air of death'. Yet by isolating 'the river' beyond this finality, Groarke suggests that flux wins out after all:

The aftermath

of stone is nothing but a proof that this is always
something else. That everything becomes itself
to breathe the clean air of death. The river.[35]

But *Shale* is not all elemental chant. Spoken by Isaac Newton's telescope, 'Reflections' is a metaphysical poem on the relationship between the scientist

and his implements, knowledge and its tools. History is an important theme
for Groarke, and in one of the finest poems in *Shale*, 'Patronage', she considers her relationship to the Anglo-Irish novelist Maria Edgeworth. Born in
the former Edgeworth family home, now converted to a hospital, Groarke
overlays the novelist's family history with hers, but in a way that disclaims
any direct parallels. 'I have never returned to Maria Edgeworth's house', she
writes in the final stanza; instead she passes by in a train from whose window
the faces of the people sitting out on the lawn 'are lost in the shadow of the
house'. In the introduction to her *Wake Forest Book of Irish Women's Poetry
1967–2000*, Peggy O'Brien notes how many of Medbh McGuckian's poems
'occur within confined spaces, rooms, her house, her walled garden'.[36] The
same is true of Groarke's second collection, *Other People's Houses*, written
against the backdrop of the economic upturn of the late 1990s and its spi-
ralling property prices, and which takes for its epigraph Emily Dickinson's
'One need not be a chamber to be haunted, /one need not be a house'.
'Domestic Arrangements' takes a tour of a large house, but with an eye
to the 'Big House' past, while less exalted structures are explored in 'The
Slaughterhouse' and 'Workhouses'. Groarke's depiction of rural decline is a
reminder that, as a midlander, she is intimately familiar with the landscape
of Oliver Goldsmith's *The Deserted Village*, a resource she puts to use in the
ambitious long poem in her 2002 collection, *Flight*, 'Or to Come'.[37]

New to *Other People's Houses* is a vein of sexual and social comedy, as
in the sharply-drawn bore of 'Home Guest' and 'Folderol', whose narrator
writes 'twenty-four //words for nonsense' on her lover's body when he comes
home late with a 'cock- /and- bull story' of where he has been:

> Including, for the record: blather, drivel, trash,
> prattle, palaver, waffle, balderdash, gibberish, shit.
> Thinking I had made a point of sorts, but not
> so sure when I woke up to find my own flesh
>
> covered with your smudged disgrace
> while you, of course, had vanished without trace.[38]

As in Quinn's 'Ur-Aisling', the reprimand rebounds on the woman from its
slippery male object. The fact that his condemnation rubs off, literally, on
the speaker leaves the poem 'written on the body' in an unexpected way.
Groarke has described her impatience with her first book for being 'too
unrigorous [. . .] too soft-centred',[39] and the profusion of contemporary
references and satirical barbs in *Other People's Houses* shows how keen she
is to take the pulse of her *Zeitgeist*. The fact that she combines this with
a commitment in her most recent poems to further revisionary looks at the

Irish past marks her out as a poet of rare historical scope. But just as Quinn's historical perspectives hold out against panoptical delusions, Groarke too keeps her interaction with her subject matter quizzical and unself-important; as she writes in *Flight*, the last line of 'The End of the Line', a poem about using a library catalogue, '*Your entry*, last name, first name, *should be here*'. History and experience are not mastered, but glance against each other in a spirit of curiosity and adventure.

Born in Newry, Co Down, in 1968, O'Callaghan grew up south of the border in Dundalk and has spoken in interview of feeling a part of Southern rather than Northern publishing culture. The strongest influence on O'Callaghan's early work is Derek Mahon. The opening poem of *The History of Rain* (1993), 'September', strikes a note of exhaustion from the outset ('It's a view that seems too familiar'),[40] and throughout the volume O'Callaghan is at pains to dampen the mood and foreclose horizons, deflecting happiness somewhere else in place and time. A trapped bird flapping to death in 'A Bird in the House' seems less than immediately real, receding instead down one of O'Callaghan's characteristic historical vistas: 'we couldn't distinguish /if what we heard was just imagined /or something remembered becoming still more distant'. Real escape comes in poems about artists and art ('The Dream of Edward Elgar', 'A Large Diver', based on a David Hockney painting), though his exotic elsewheres contain a more sinister side too, as in 'Mengele's House' ('He was the old misery /who had strange kids, /a swimming pool, /and a history').

The 'emotional coolness' of the poems, John Redmond wrote, 'is symptomatic of their lack of personality'.[41] The sound of poachers at night is 'laughter that /can't be helped' (*History of Rain*, 37). In 'Postcard', a poem of leave-taking, O'Callaghan writes 'So I've written some rhetorical questions, /said the weather's bad and nothing's changed. //I'm tired of that'. But in truth making a break with home is something the poems of *The History of Rain* find extremely difficult to do, to the point where tiredness with the weather and a sense of inescapable sameness become invested with a deliberate anti-glamour. O'Callaghan returns to these tropes in his second collection, *Seatown*, a probing re-examination of the Irish pastoral tradition. The Seatown of his title is a suburb of Dundalk, an unremarkable large town as alien in spirit to Dublin as to the Atlantic West. O'Callaghan seizes on its neither/nor status in the jokily polemical 'East':

> I know it's not playing Gaelic, it's simply not good enough,
> to dismiss as someone else's all that elemental Atlantic guff.
> And to suggest everything's foreign beyond the proverbial pale
> would amount to a classic case of hitting the head on the nail.

> But give me a dreary eastern town that isn't vaguely romantic,
> where moon and stars are lost in the lights of the greyhound track
> and cheering comes to nothing and a flurry of misplaced bets
> blanketing the stands at dawn is about as spiritual as it gets.[42]

As the author of an essay on his love of cricket, O'Callaghan knows all about 'not playing Gaelic'.[43] His highlighting of Bury and Blackburn rather than New York or Boston as sites of exile (an over-emotive word, perhaps, for the speaker's Lancashire aunt) accords with the poem's anti-rhetorical bias.[44] 'Landscape with Canal' remakes another 'all-too-well-known' locale by organising itself around a series of hypothetical alternatives to the reader ('The choice is yours', though typically 'it will scarcely matter'). As the interpellated 'you' returns along the towpath 'none the wiser', 'there must always be some faceless other /[. . .] who'll call in the murk ahead, "Who goes there?" /and call once more when you don't quite answer'. Not 'quite' answering rather than staying silent skilfully brings out the mixed feelings O'Callaghan draws on. At moments, particularly when he writes of the sea, he allows his reserve to drop. The first of the volume's two title poems concludes:

> May its name be said for as long it could matter.
> Or, failing that, for as long as it takes the pilot
> to negotiate the eight kilometres from this to open water.

When sex is at issue, as it often is in his work, O'Callaghan can be sarcastic, querulous, lusty and blunt. In interview he notes the absence of the erotic from much Irish love poetry in English, and speaks of handling sex in a tone of 'cold detachment' as a countermeasure.[45] In 'The Oral Tradition' he borrows a title from Eavan Boland, exploiting, as the older poet does not, its sexual innuendo. Like Groarke, he is keenly aware of the ways in which emotions are shaped by domestic spaces: in 'Coventry' he brilliantly harnesses the accidental bombing of Dundalk by the Luftwaffe to the apparently incommensurate occasion of a domestic row, which has condemned the speaker to the spare bedroom.[46] If a spare bedroom is a quintessential O'Callaghan setting, the lodger of 'Sublet' is his quintessential persona, disappearing as abruptly as he arrived and leaving a small but pregnant silence in his wake: 'a half-minute lull /as the house holds its breath, a rustle in the hall, /the front door slamming onto mid-morning rain'.

It is in the nature of contemporary publishing, especially where anthologies are concerned, for the 'new' to equal the young, but the reality of poetic generations is a more complex affair: one of the most original Irish poets to emerge in the 1990s was Fergus Allen, who published his first collection

The Brown Parrots of Providencia at the age of 72.[47] Nevertheless, the 1990s undeniably witnessed a proliferation of younger writers emerging into print. Alongside younger poets with several collections to their names such as John Hughes (b. 1962), Pat Boran (b. 1963), Martin Mooney (b. 1964), Enda Wyley (b. 1966), Sara Berkeley (b. 1967), David Wheatley (b.1970) and Sinéad Morrissey (b. 1972), other writers have registered promising debuts in this period. They include Tom French (b. 1965), Aidan Rooney-Céspedes (b. 1965), Bill Tinley (b. 1965), John Redmond (b. 1967), James McCabe (b. 1968), Colette Bryce (b. 1970) and Caitríona O'Reilly (b. 1973). Other figures again cluster round magazines such as *The Big Spoon, Force 10, Flaming Arrows, The Burning Bush, The Stinging Fly, Incognito* and *College Green*.[48] Amid the O'Callaghanesque fly-by-nights and temporary lodgers, some at least of the rich generation of younger Irish poets are here to stay.

NOTES

1 Michael Longley, *Poems 1963–1983* (London: Secker and Warburg), 1991, p. 92.
2 Samuel Beckett, 'Dante . . . Bruno. Vico . . Joyce', *Disjecta: Miscellaneous Writings and a Dramatic Fragment* (London: John Calder), 1983, p. 19.
3 Thomas Kinsella, *The Dual Tradition* (Manchester: Carcanet Press, 1995), p. 108.
4 Kinsella, *The New Oxford Book of Irish Verse* (Oxford University Press), 1986, p. xxx.
5 Patrick Ramsey, 'Fragrant Necrophilia', *The Irish Review* 15 (Spring 1994), pp. 148–54 (148).
6 Quoted in Tony Curtis (ed.), *As the Poet Said: Poetry Pickings and Choosings* (Dublin: Poetry Ireland, 1997), p. 21.
7 Harry Clifton, 'Big-Endians and Little Endians', review of Simon Armitage and Robert Crawford, *The Penguin Book of Poetry from Britain and Ireland since 1945*, *Poetry Review* vol. 88 no. 3 (Autumn 1998), pp. 43–6.
8 Dennis O'Driscoll, 'A Map of Contemporary Irish Poetry', *Poetry* vol. CLXVII no. 1–2 (October-November 1995), p. 99.
9 For O'Driscoll's criticism, cf. *Troubled Thoughts, Majestic Dreams: Selected Prose* (Loughcrew: Gallery Press, 2001).
10 One significant exception to the secular drift is Aidan Mathews (b. 1956), whose work is baroquely pre-conciliar in its Catholicism: cf. *Windfalls* (1977), *Minding Ruth* (1983) and *According to the Small Hours* (1998).
11 Sebastian Barry, 'Introduction', *The Inherited Boundaries: Younger Poets of the Republic of Ireland* (Dublin: Dolmen Press), 1986, p. 18. Further comments on the national identity-base of Barry's anthology can be found in Ray Ryan, 'The Republic and Ireland: Pluralism, Politics and Narrative Form', in Ray Ryan (ed.), *Writing in the Irish Republic: Literature, Culture, Politics 1949–1999* (London: Macmillan, 2000), pp. 83–92.
12 Peter Sirr, 'Irish Poetry and the Diaspora', *Metre* 3 (Autumn 1997), p. 21.
13 John Goodby, *Irish Poetry since 1950: From Stillness into History* (Manchester University Press, 2000), p. 319.
14 Peter McDonald, 'Irish Poetry and the Diaspora', *Metre* 3 (Autumn 1997), p. 17.

15 Brian Lynch, 'Poetry's Province', review of Peter McDonald, *Mistaken Identities*, *The Irish Times* (24 January 1998), *Weekend*, p. 8.

16 Declan Kiberd (ed.), 'Contemporary Irish Poetry', in Seamus Deane (ed.), *The Field Day Anthology of Irish Writing Volume III* (Derry: Field Day Publications, 1991), p. 375.

17 See Heaney: 'Ulster was British, but with no rights on /The English lyric', in *North* (London: Faber and Faber), p. 65.

18 'A Writer for His Kind: Carol Rumens Talks to Peter McDonald', *Brangle* 2, 1997, p. 40. Cf. also his long poem 'The Victory Weekend, May 1945/May 1995', *Metre* 6 (Summer 1999), pp. 58–65) for another Irish perspective on an English commemoration.

19 McDonald, *Biting the Wax* (Newcastle: Bloodaxe, 1989), p. 60.

20 Heaney, *North*, p. 23.

21 McDonald, *Adam's Dream* (Newcastle: Bloodaxe, 1996), p. 37.

22 'A Writer for His Kind', p. 37.

23 Peter Sirr, *The Ledger of Fruitful Exchange* (Loughcrew: Gallery Press, 1995), p. 33.

24 Sirr, *Marginal Zones* (Loughcrew: Gallery Press, 1984), p. 15.

25 Sirr, *Talk, Talk* (Loughcrew: Gallery Press, 1987), p. 64.

26 Sirr, *Ways of Falling* (Loughcrew: Gallery Press, 1991), p. 28.

27 Sirr, *Bring Everything* (Loughcrew: Gallery Press, 2000), p. 11.

28 Justin Quinn, 'O Seasons, O Cities', review of *Bring Everything*, *Metre* 10 (Autumn 2001), p. 101.

29 Justin Quinn, *The 'O'o'a'a' Bird* (Manchester: Carcanet Press, 1995), p. 14.

30 Cf. Quinn, 'His damned hooba-hoobla-hoobla how', *Poetry Review* vol. 90 no. 2 (Summer 2000), pp. 52–3.

31 Sirr and McDonald both have anti-*aisling* poems of their own: 'Visitor' (in *Marginal Zones*) and 'A Volume of Memoirs is Forthcoming' (in *Biting the Wax*).

32 Justin Quinn, *Privacy* (Manchester: Carcanet, 1999), p. 55.

33 Sam Leith, 'Pshhh', review of *The 'O'o'a'a' Bird*, *Oxford Poetry* vol. VIII, no. 3 (Spring 1995), p. 130.

34 Vona Groarke, 'Editorial', *Verse* vol. 16 no. 2, n. d. [1999], p. 8. For a useful survey of recent Irish women poets, cf. Fionnuala Dillane, 'Changing the Map: Contemporary Irish Women's Poetry' in the same issue, pp. 9–27.

35 Vona Groarke, *Shale* (Loughcrew: Gallery Press, 1994), p. 13.

36 Peggy O'Brien, 'Editor's Preface', *Wake Forest Book of Irish Women's Poetry 1967–2000* (Winston Salem: Wake Forest University Press, 2000), p. xxx.

37 Vona Groarke, *Flight* (Loughcrew: Gallery Press, 2002).

38 *Other People's Houses* (Loughcrew: Gallery Press, 1999).

39 Interview with Fionnuala Dillane and John McAuliffe, *Review of Postgraduate Studies* (Galway), no. 5 (1997), pp. 57–61 (60).

40 O'Callaghan, *The History of Rain* (Loughcrew: Gallery Press, 1993), p. 9.

41 John Redmond, review of *The History of Rain*, *Oxford Poetry* vol. VIII, no. 1 (Summer 1994), p. 37.

42 *Seatown* (Loughcrew: Gallery Press, 1999), p. 42.

43 O'Callaghan, 'Jolly Good Shot Old Boy', in George O'Brien (ed.), *Playing the Field: Irish Writers on Sport* (Dublin: New Island Books, 2000), pp. 50–61.

44 The sensitive nature of O'Callaghan's stance, even in the context of 1990s Ireland, can be seen in Mary O'Malley's parodic riposte to 'East', 'The Loose Alexandrines' (in her *Asylum Road* (Cliffs of Moher: Salmon Publishing, 2001), p. 57). Its speaker sarcastically calls for 'No mad women' and 'more Larkin, less Yeats, no Plath', interpreting O'Callaghan's poem as a cocktail of anglophile cultural cringe, anti-Irishness and misogyny.

45 David Wheatley, 'Interview with Conor O'Callaghan', *Verse* vol. 18 no. 2 (2001), p. 101.

46 O'Callaghan, 'Coventry', *Times Literary Supplement*, 20 October 2000, p. 4.

47 Fergus Allen's three collections are *The Brown Parrots of Providencia, Who Goes There?* and *Mrs Power Looks Over the Bay* (London: Faber and Faber, 1993, 1996, 1999).

48 John Hughes, *The Something in Particular, Negotiations with the Chill Wind, The Devil Himself* (Loughcrew: Gallery Press, 1986, 1991, 1996), Pat Boran, *The Unwound Clock* (Dublin: Dedalus Press, 1990), *History and Promise* (IUP, 1990), *Familiar Things, The Shape of Water, As the Hand, the Glove* (Dublin: Dedalus Press, 1993, 1996, 2001), Martin Mooney, *Grub* (Belfast: Blackstaff, 1993), *Rasputin and his Children* (Blackwater Press, 2000), Enda Wyley, *Eating Baby Jesus, Socrates in the Garden* (Dedalus Press, 1994, 1998), Sara Berkeley, *Penn, Home Movie Nights* (Raven Arts Press, 1986, 1989), *Facts About Water* (Newcastle: Bloodaxe, 1994), David Wheatley, *Thirst, Misery Hill* (Loughcrew: Gallery Press, 1997, 2000), Sinéad Morrissey, *There Was Fire in Vancouver, Between Here and There* (Manchester: Carcanet, 1996, 2002), Tom French, *Touching the Bones* (Loughcrew: Gallery Press, 2001), Aidan Rooney-Céspedes, *Day Release* (Loughcrew: Gallery Press, 2000), Bill Tinley, *Grace* (Dublin: New Island Books, 2001), James McCabe, *The White Battlefields of Silence* (Dublin: Dedalus Press, 1999), John Redmond, *Thumb's Width* (Manchester: Carcanet, 2001), Colette Bryce, *The Heel of Bernadette* (Picador, 2000), Caitríona O'Reilly, *The Nowhere Birds* (Newcastle: Bloodaxe, 2001).

FURTHER READING

Contemporary Irish Poets

(Poets' names are printed in bold with relevant critics listed in roman typeface underneath if relevant.)

Allen, Fergus. *The Brown Parrots of Providencia.* London: Faber, 1993.
  Mrs Power Looks Over the Bay. London: Faber, 1999.
  Who Goes There? London: Faber, 1996.
Barry, Sebastian. *Fanny Hawke Goes to the Mainland Forever.* Dublin: Raven Arts, 1987.
  The Rhetorical Town. Dublin: Dolmen, 1985.
  The Water Colourist. Dublin: Dolmen, 1983.
Beckett, Samuel. *Collected Poems 1930–1978.* London: John Calder, 1984.
  Disjecta: Miscellaneous Writings and a Dramatic Fragment, ed. Ruby Cohn. London: John Calder, 1983.
Harvey, Laurence. *Samuel Beckett: Poet and Critic.* Princeton University Press, 1970.
Berkeley, Sara. *Facts About Water.* Newcastle: Bloodaxe, 1994.
  Home Movie Nights. Dublin: Raven Arts, 1989.
  Penn. Dublin: Raven Arts, 1986.
Boland, Eavan. *Against Love Poetry: Poems.* New York: Norton, 2001.
  Code. Manchester: Carcanet, 2001.
  Collected Poems. Manchester: Carcanet & New York: Norton, 1995.
  The Lost Land. Manchester: Carcanet, 1998; New York: Norton, 1999.
  'Moving Statues'. *The Writer and Religion.* Ed. William Gass and Loren Cuoco. International Writer's Center Series. Carbondale and Edwardsville, Il.: Southern Illinois University Press, 2000. 13–21.
  Object Lessons: The Life of the Woman and the Poet in Our Time. London: Vintage; New York: Norton, 1996.
Clutterbuck, Catriona. 'Irish Critical Responses to Self-Representation in Eavan Boland, 1987–1995'. *Colby Quarterly* 35.4 (Dec 1999).
  'Irish Women's Poetry and the Republic of Ireland: Formalism as Form'. Ray Ryan (ed.). *Writing in the Irish Republic: Literature, Culture, Politics.* London and New York: Macmillan and St. Martin's, 2000.
  Irish University Review: Eavan Boland Special Issue, 23, 1 (1993).
Bolger, Dermot. *Taking My Letters Back, New and Selected Poems.* Dublin: New Island Books, 1998.

Boran, Pat. *As the Hand, the Glove.* Dublin: Dedalus, 2001.
  Familiar Things. Dublin: Dedalus, 1993.
  The Shape of Water. Dublin: Dedalus, 1996.
  The Unwound Clock. Dublin: Dedalus, 1990.
Bryce, Colette. *The Heel of Bernadette.* London: Picador, 2000.
Cannon, Moya. *Oar.* Galway: Salmon, 1990.
  The Parchment Boat. Loughcrew: Gallery Press, 1997.
Carson, Ciaran. *The Ballad of HMS Belfast.* Loughcrew: Gallery Press, 1999.
  Belfast Confetti. Meath: Gallery Press, 1989.
  'Escaped from the Massacre?' *Honest Ulsterman*, 50 (Winter, 1975), 183–6.
  First Language. Loughcrew: Gallery Press, 1993.
  The Inferno of Dante Aligheri. London: Granta, 2002.
  The Irish for No. Newcastle: Bloodaxe, 1987.
  Last Night's Fun: A Book about Irish Traditional Music. London: Jonathan Cape,
    1996.
  The New Estate. Belfast: Blackstaff, 1976.
  Opera Et Cetera. Loughcrew: Gallery Press, 1996.
  Selected Poems. Winston Salem NC: Wake Forest University Press, 2001.
  The Star Factory. London: Granta, 1997.
  The Twelfth of Never. Loughcrew: Gallery Press, 1998.
Brearton, Fran. 'Mapping the Trenches: Gyres, Switchbacks and Zig-zag Circles
  in W.B. Yeats and Ciaran Carson'. *Irish Studies Review*, 9. 3 (Dec. 2001),
  373–86.
Houen Alex. 'Re-placing Terror: Poetic Mappings of the Northern Ireland
  "Troubles" ', *Terrorism and Modern Literature from Joseph Conrad to Ciaran
  Carson.* OUP, 2002.
Interview by Rand Brandes. *Irish Review*, 8 (Spring, 1990).
Interview by Frank Ormsby. *Linen Hall Review* (April, 1991).
Clarke, Austin. *A Penny in the Clouds.* Dublin: Moytura, 1990.
  Collected Poems, ed. Liam Miller. Dublin: Dolmen, 1974.
  'Love in Irish Poetry and Drama', *Motley*, 1: 5 (October 1932), 3–4.
  Poetry in Modern Ireland. Cork: Mercier, 1951.
  Reviews and Essays of Austin Clarke, ed. Gregory A. Schirmer. Gerrards Cross:
    Colin Smythe, 1995.
  Selected Poems, ed. Hugh Maxton. Dublin: Lilliput, 1991.
  Twice Round the Black Church. Dublin: Moytura, 1990.
Brown, Terence. 'Austin Clarke: Satirist', in *Ireland's Literature.* Gigginstown:
  Lilliput, 1988.
Corcoran, Neil. 'The Blessings of Onan: Austin Clarke's *Mnemosyne Lay in Dust*',
  Irish University Review, 13: 1 (Spring 1983).
Davie, Donald: 'Austin Clarke and Padraic Fallon', in Douglas Dunn (ed.), *Two
  Decades of Irish Writing: A Critical Survey.* Manchester: Carcanet, 1975.
Denman, Peter. 'Austin Clarke: Tradition, Memory and Our Lot', in Terence Brown
  and Nicholas Grene (eds.). *Tradition and Influence in Anglo-Irish Poetry.*
  London: Macmillan, 1989.
Goodby, John. ' "The Prouder Counsel of Her Throat": Towards a Feminist Reading
  of Austin Clarke', *Irish University Review*, 29: 2 (Autumn/Winter 1999).
Halpern, Susan. *Austin Clarke, His Life and Works.* Dublin: Dolmen, 1974.

Harmon, Maurice. *Austin Clarke: A Critical Introduction*. Dublin: Wolfhound, 1989.

Harmon, Maurice (ed.). *Irish University Review: Austin Clarke Special Issue*, 4: 1 (1974).

Kinsella, Thomas. 'The Poetic Career of Austin Clarke', *Irish University Review*, 4: 1 (1974).

McCormack, W.J. 'Austin Clarke: The Poets as Scapegoat of Modernism', in Patricia Coughlan and Alex Davis (eds.). *Modernism and Ireland: The Poetry of the 1930s*. Cork University Press, 1995.

Poetry Ireland Review: Special Austin Clarke Supplement, 22, 3 (1988).

Schirmer, Gregory A. *The Poetry of Austin Clarke*. Gerrards Cross: Colin Smythe, 1983.

Tapping, Craig. *Austin Clarke: A Study of his Writings*. Dublin: Dolmen, 1981.

Clifton, Harry. *The Desert Route: Selected Poems*. Loughcrew: Gallery Press, 1992.

Night Train Through the Brenner. Loughcrew: Gallery Press, 1994.

Coffey, Brian. *Poems and Versions, 1929–1990*. Dublin: Dedalus, 1991.

Moriarty, Dónal. *The Art of Brian Coffey*. Dublin: University College Dublin, 2000.

Cronin, Anthony. *New and Selected Poems*. Manchester: Carcanet, 1982.

Minotaur. Dublin: New Island Books, 1999.

Delanty, Greg. *American Wake*. Belfast: Blackstaff, 1995.

The Blind Stitch. Manchester: Carcanet, 2001.

Cast in the Fire. Dublin: Dolmen, 1986.

Southward. Dublin: Dedalus, 1992.

The Hellbox. Oxford University Press, 1998.

de Paor, Louis. *Próca Solais is Luatha*. Dublin: Coiscéim, 1988.

30 Dán. Dublin: Coiscéim, 1992.

Seo, Siúd agus Uile. Dublin: Coiscéim, 1996.

Corcach, agus dánta eile. Dublin: Coiscéim, 1999.

Devlin, Denis. *Collected Poems of Denis Devlin*, ed. J.C.C. Mays. Dublin: Dedalus, 1989.

Davis, Alex. *A Broken Line: Denis Devlin and Irish Poetic Modernism*. University College Dublin, 2000.

Durcan, Paul. *Crazy about Women*. Dublin: National Gallery of Ireland, 1991.

Cries of an Irish Caveman. London: Harvill, 2002.

Daddy, Daddy. Belfast: Blackstaff, 1990.

Give Me Your Hand. London: Macmillan, 1994.

A Snail in My Prime: New and Selected Poems. London: Harvill, 1993.

McCracken, Kathleen. *Radical Vision: Paul Durcan*. Newcastle: Bloodaxe, 2003.

Toibin, Colm (ed.). *The Kilfenora Teaboy: A Study of Paul Durcan*. London: Dufour, 1996.

Egan, Desmond. *Selected Poems*, ed. Hugh Kenner. Omaha: Creighton University Press, 1992.

Fallon, Padraic. *Collected Poems*. Manchester: Carcanet, 1990.

Fiacc, Padraic. *Missa Terriblis*. Belfast: Blackstaff, 1986.

Ruined Pages. Belfast: Blackstaff, 1994.

The Selected Padraic Fiacc. Belfast: Blackstaff, 1979.

Semper vacare. Belfast: Lagan, 1999.

Fitzmaurice, Gabriel. *Ag Síobshiúl chun an Rince*. Dublin: Coiscéim 1995.

Giolla na Amhrán. Dublin: Coiscéim 1998.

The Village Sings. Indreabhán: Cló Iar-Chonnachta.

A Wren-boy's Carnival: Poems 1980–2000. Dublin: Wolfhound. 2001.

French, Tom. *Touching the Bones*. Loughcrew: Gallery Press, 2001.

Grennan, Eamon. *Facing the Music: Irish Poetry in the Twentieth Century*. Omaha: Creighton University Press, 2000.

Relations: New and Selected Poems. St Paul, MN: Graywolf, 1998.

Selected and New Poems. Loughcrew: Gallery Press, 2000.

Still Life with Waterfall. Loughcrew: Gallery Press and St Paul MN: Graywolf, 2002.

Groarke, Vona. *Shale*. Loughcrew: Gallery Press, 1994.

Other People's Houses. Loughcrew: Gallery Press, 1999.

Flight. Loughcrew: Gallery Press, 2002.

Hardie, Kerry. *A Furious Place*. Loughcrew: Gallery Press, 1996.

Hartnett, Michael. *Adharca Broic*. Dublin: Gallery Press, 1978.

A Farewell to English. Dublin: Gallery Press, 1975.

Selected and New Poems. Loughcrew: Gallery Press, 1994.

Heaney, Seamus. 'An Open Letter', A Field Day Pamphlet, 2 (Derry: Field Day, 1983).

Beowulf (trans.) London: Faber; New York: Norton, 1999.

Death of A Naturalist. London: Faber, 1966.

Door into the Dark. London: Faber, 1969.

Electric Light. London: Faber, 2001.

Finders Keepers: Selected Prose, 1971–2001. London: Faber; New York: Farrar, Straus & Giroux, 2002.

North. London: Faber, 1975.

The Government of the Tongue. London: Faber, 1988.

The Haw Lantern. London: Faber, 1987.

Opened Ground: Poems, 1966–1996. London: Faber; New York: Farrar, Straus & Giroux, 1998.

Preoccupations: Selected Prose 1968–1978. London: Faber, 1980.

Seeing Things. London: Faber, 1991.

Station Island. London: Faber, 1984.

(trans.) *Sweeney Astray*. London: Faber, 1984.

The Redress of Poetry. London: Faber, 1995.

The Spirit Level. London: Faber, 1996.

'Voices Behind a Door: Robert Frost', *Poetry Review* 83:4 (Winter 1993–94).

Wintering Out. London: Faber, 1972.

Allen, Michael. 'The Parish and the Dream: Heaney and America, 1969–1987'. *The Southern Review* 31.3 (July, 1995).

Allen, Michael. ed. *Seamus Heaney: A Collection of Critical Essays*. London: Macmillan, 1997.

Brandes, Rand. 'Seamus Heaney: An Interview', *Salmagundi*, No. 80 (Fall 1988).

Carson, Ciaran. 'Escaped from the Massacre?' (review of North) *Honest Ulsterman*, 50 (Winter, 1975).

Cavanagh, Clare. 'From the Republic of Conscience: Seamus Heaney and Eastern European Poetry', *Harvard Review* 6 (Spring 1994).

Corcoran, Neil. *The Poetry of Seamus Heaney*. London: Faber, 1998.

Deane, Seamus. 'Unhappy and at Home: Interview with Seamus Heaney', *The Crane Bag*, vol. 1, no. 1 (Spring, 1977).

Hart, Henry. *Seamus Heaney: Poet of Contrary Progressions*. Syracuse University
 Press, 1992, p. 31.
Kinahan, Frank. Interview with Seamus Heaney, *Critical Inquiry* 8.3 (Spring 1982).
Lloyd, David. ' "Pap for the dispossessed": Seamus Heaney and the Poetics of Iden-
 tity', in *Anomalous States: Irish Writing and the Post-Colonial Moment*. Dublin:
 Lilliput, 1993.
Morrison, Blake. *Seamus Heaney*. London: Methuen, 1982.
O'Donoghue, Bernard. *Seamus Heaney and the Language of Poetry*. Brighton:
 Harvester, 1994.
Parker, Michael. *Seamus Heaney: The Making of the Poet*. University of Iowa, 1993.
Tobin, Daniel. *Passage to the Center: Imagination and the Sacred in the Poetry of
 Seamus Heaney*. Lexington: University of Kentucky, 1999.
Vendler, Helen. *Seamus Heaney*. Cambridge: Harvard University, 1998.
Hewitt, John. *Ancestral Voices: the Selected Prose of John Hewitt*, ed. Tom Clyde.
 Belfast: Blackstaff, 1987.
 The Collected Poems of John Hewitt, ed. Frank Ormsby. Belfast: Blackstaff, 1991.
Higgins, Rita Ann. *An Awful Racket*. Newcastle: Bloodaxe Books, 2001.
 Goddess on the Mervue Bus. Galway: Salmon, 1986.
 Philomena's Revenge. Galway: Salmon, 1992.
 Sunny Side Plucked: New and Selected Poems. Newcastle: Bloodaxe Books, 1996.
 Witch in the Bushes. Galway: Salmon, 1988.
Sullivan, Moynagh. 'Assertive Subversions: Comedy in the Work of Julie O'Callaghan
 and Rita Ann Higgins'. *Verse* 16, 2.
Hughes, John. *The Devil Himself*. Loughcrew: Gallery Press, 1996.
 Negotiations with the Chill Wind, Loughcrew: Gallery Press, 1991.
 The Something in Particular. Loughcrew: Gallery Press, 1986.
Hutchinson, Pierce. *Collected Poems*. Loughcrew: Gallery Press, 2002.
Iremonger, Valentin. *Sandymount, Dublin: New and Selected Poems*. Dublin:
 Dedalus, 1988.
Jenkinson, Biddy. *Amhras Neimhe*. Dublin: Coiscéim, 1997.
 Baisteadh Gintlí. Dublin: Coiscéim, 1986.
 Dán na hUidhre. Dublin: Coiscéim, 1991.
 An Grá Riabhach. Dublin: Coiscéim, 2000.
 Rogha Dánta. Cork University Press, 1999.
 'A View from the Whale's Back', *Poetry Ireland Review*, 52 (Spring, 1993), 61–9.
Joyce, Trevor. *with the first dream of fire they hunt the cold: a body of work
 1966/2000*. Dublin: New Writers' Press/Cullompton: Shearsman, 2001.
 'The Point of Innovation in Poetry', in Harry Gilonis (ed.), *For the Birds: Pro-
 ceedings of the First Cork Conference on New and Experimental Irish Poetry*.
 Sutton: Mainstream Poetry/Dublin: hardPressed Poetry, 1998.
Kavanagh, Patrick. *Collected Poems*. London: MacGibbon & Kee, 1964.
 Collected Pruse. London: MacGibbon & Kee, 1967.
 The Green Fool. London: Michael Joseph, 1938.
 Kavanagh's Weekly. Dublin, 12 April–15 July, 1952.
 Selected Poems, ed. Antoinette Quinn. Harmondsworth: Penguin, 1996, 2000.
 Tarry Flynn. London: Pilot, 1948.
Agnew, Una. *The Mystical Imagination of Patrick Kavanagh*. Dublin: Columba,
 1991.

Allison, Jonathan. *Patrick Kavanagh: A Reference Guide*. New York: G.K. Hall, 1996.

Gifford, Terry. 'The Anti-Pastoral Tradition'. *Pastoral*. London and New York: Routledge, 1999.

Grennan, Eamon. 'From Simplicity to Simplicity: Pastoral Design in Kavanagh'. *Facing the Music: Irish Poetry in the Twentieth Century*. Creighton University Press, 1999.

Heaney, Seamus. 'From Monaghan to the Grand Canal'. *Preoccupations: Selected Prose 1968–1978*, London: Faber, 1980.

'The Placeless Heaven: Another Look at Kavanagh'. *Finders Keepers*. London: Faber, 2001.

Kavanagh, Peter. *Patrick Kavanagh: Man and Poet*. The Curragh: Goldsmith, 1987.

Kennelly, Brendan. 'Patrick Kavanagh's Comic Vision'. *Ariel* (July, 1970).

Kiberd, Declan. 'Underdeveloped Comedy: Patrick Kavanagh'. *Irish Classics*. Cambridge: Harvard University Press, 2000.

Longley, Edna. 'Pastoral Theologies'. *Poetry and Posterity*. Newcastle: Bloodaxe, 2000.

'Poetic Forms and Social Malformations'. *The Living Stream: Literature & Revisionism in Ireland*. Newcastle: Bloodaxe, 1994.

Montague, John. 'A Speech from the Dock'. *The Figure in the Cave and Other Essays*, ed. Antoinette Quinn. New York: Syracuse University Press, 1989.

Nemo, John. *Patrick Kavanagh*. Boston: Twayne, 1979.

O'Loughlin, Michael. *After Kavanagh*. Dublin: Raven Arts, 1985.

Quinn, Antoinette. *Patrick Kavanagh: A Biography*. Dublin: Gill & Macmillan, 2001.

Patrick Kavanagh: Born-Again Romantic. Dublin: Gill & Macmillan, 1991.

Warner, Alan. *Clay is the Word: Patrick Kavanagh, 1904–67*. Dublin: Dolmen, 1973.

Kennelly, Brendan. *Cromwell*. Dublin: Beaver Row, 1983.

Selected Poems. Dublin: Kerrymount, 1985.

The Book of Judas. Newcastle: Bloodaxe Books, 1991.

Persson, Ake. *Betraying the Age: Social and Artistic Process in Brendan Kennelly's Work*. Gothenburg: Acta Universitatis Gothoburgensis, 2000.

Kinsella, Thomas. *Collected Poems 1956–2001*. Manchester: Carcanet, 2001.

The Dual Tradition: An Essay on Poetry and Politics in Ireland. Manchester: Carcanet, 1995.

(trans.) with Sean Ó Tuama. *An Duanaire: Poems of the Dispossessed*. Dublin: Dolmen, 1981.

'The Irish Writer', in *Davis Mangan Ferguson: Tradition and the Irish Writer*. Dublin: Dolmen, 1970.

(ed.). *The New Oxford Book of Irish Verse*. Oxford University Press, 1986.

Brian, John. *Reading the Ground: The Poetry of Thomas Kinsella*. Washington: CUA Press, 1996.

Harmon, Maurice. *The Poetry of Thomas Kinsella*. Atlantic Highlands, NJ: Humanities Press, 1975.

Irish University Review Special Issue: Thomas Kinsella. 31, 1 (Spring / Summer, 2001).

Jackson, Thomas H. *The Whole Matter: The Poetic Evolution of Thomas Kinsella*. Dublin: Lilliput, 1995.

McCormack, W.J. 'Politics or Community: Crux of Thomas Kinsella's Aesthetic Development', *Tracks* 7 (1987).

Longley, Michael. *An Exploded View.* London: Gollanz, 1973.

 Gorse Fires, London: Jonathan Cape, 1991.

 No Continuing City. London: Macmillan, 1969.

 The Ghost Orchid. London: Jonathan Cape, 1995.

 Poems 1963–1983, Harmondsworth: Penguin, 1986.

 The Weather in Japan. London: Jonathan Cape, 2000.

 Tuppenny Stung: Autobiographical Chapters. Belfast: Lagan, 1995.

Johnstone Robert. 'The Longley Tapes', (interview), *Honest Ulsterman*, 78 (Summer 1985).

McDonald, Peter. 'Micheal Longley's Homes', *Mistaken Identities: Poetry and Northern Ireland.* Oxford: Clarendon, 1997.

Peacock, Alan J., and Kathleen Devine (eds.). *The Poetry of Michael Longley.* Gerrards Cross: Colin Smythe, 2000.

MacGreevy, Thomas. *Collected Poems of Thomas MacGreevy*, ed. Susan Schreibman. Dublin: Anna Livia, 1991.

Mac Lochlainn, Gearóid. *Sruth Teangacha / Stream of Tongues* (Indreabhán: Cló Iar-Chonnachta, 2002).

MacNeice, Louis. *Collected Poems.* ed. E.R. Dodds. London: Faber, 1966.

 Selected Literary Criticism. ed. Alan Heuser. Oxford: Clarendon, 1987.

 Selected Prose. ed. Alan Heuser. Oxford: Clarendon, 1990.

 Selected Plays eds. Alan Heuser and Peter McDonald. Oxford: Clarendon, 1993.

Brearton, Fran. 'Louis MacNeice Between Two Wars', in *The Great War in Irish Poetry.* Oxford University Press, 2000.

Brown, Terence. *Louis MacNeice: Sceptical Vision.* Dublin: Gill and Macmillan, 1975.

Devine, Kathleen and Alan Peacock (eds.). *Louis MacNeice and his Influence.* Gerrards Cross: Colin Smythe, 1998.

Longley, Edna. *Louis MacNeice: A Study.* London: Faber, 1988.

McDonald, Peter. *Louis MacNeice: The Poet in His Contexts.* Oxford: Clarendon, 1991.

McKinnon, William T. *Apollo's Blended Dream: A Study of the Poetry of Louis MacNeice.* London: Oxford University Press, 1971.

Marsack, Robyn. *The Cave of Making: The Poetry of Louis MacNeice.* Oxford: Clarendon, 1982.

Stallworthy, Jon. *Louis MacNeice.* London: Faber, 1995.

Mahon, Derek. *Antarctica.* Dublin: Gallery Press, 1985.

 Collected Poems, Loughcrew: Gallery Press, 1999 and Chester Springs: Dufour, 2000.

 Lives. Oxford University Press, 1972.

 (trans.). Jaccottet, Philippe, *Selected Poems.* Harmondsworth: Penguin, 1988.

 Journalism: Selected Prose, 1970–1995. Loughcrew: Gallery Press, 1995.

 Night-Crossing. Oxford University Press, 1968.

 Poems 1962–1978. Oxford University Press, 1979.

 'Poetry in Northern Ireland'. *Twentieth Century Studies*, 4 (Nov. 1970).

 The Hudson Letter. Loughcrew: Gallery Press, 1995.

The Hunt By Night. Oxford University Press, 1982.

The Snow Party. Oxford University Press, 1975.

The Yellow Book. Loughcrew: Gallery Press, 1997.

Haugton, Hugh. 'On Sitting Down to Read "A Disused Shed in County Wexford" Once Again'. *Cambridge Quarterly*, 31, 2 (2002).

Irish University Review: Derek Mahon Special Issue. 24, 1 (1994).

Kelly, Willie. 'Each Poem for me is a New Beginning', interview with Derek Mahon, *The Cork Review* 2.3 (June 1981).

Kennedy-Andrews, Elmer (ed.). *The Poetry of Derek Mahon*. Gerrards Cross: Colin Smythe, 2002.

'An interview by Terence Brown'. *Poetry Ireland Review* 14 (Autumn 1985).

'Q & A with Derek Mahon'. *Irish Literary Supplement* (Fall 1991).

Scammell, William, interview with Derek Mahon. *Poetry Review*. 81.2 (Summer, 1991).

Mathews, Aidan. *According to the Small Hours*. London: Jonathan Cape, 1998.

Exit/Entrance. Loughcrew: Gallery Press, 1990.

Minding Ruth. Loughcrew: Gallery Press, 1983.

Windfalls. Dublin: Dolmen, 1977.

Maxton, Hugh (see also W.J. McCormack). *Gubu Roi: Poems & Satires, 1991–1999*. Belfast: Lagan, 2000.

Jubilee for Renegades: Poems 1976–1980. Dublin: Dolmen, 1982.

Passage (with surviving poems). Bradford on Avon, 1985.

The Puzzle-Tree Ascendant. Dublin: Dedalus, 1988.

Waking: An Irish Protestant Upbringing. Belfast: Lagan, 1997.

McCabe, James. *The White Battlefields of Silence*. Dublin: Dedalus, 1999.

McCarthy, Thomas. *Mr Dineen's Careful Parade: New & Selected Poems*. London: Anvil Press Poetry, 1999.

McDonald, Peter. *Adam's Dream*. Newcastle: Bloodaxe, 1996.

As If. Oxford: Thumbscrew, 2001.

Biting the Wax. Newcastle: Bloodaxe, 1989.

Mistaken Identities: Poetry and Northern Ireland. Oxford: Clarendon, 1997.

Serious Poetry: Form and Authority from Yeats to Hill. Oxford University Press, 2002.

McGuckian, Medbh. *Captain Lavender*. Loughcrew: Winston Salem: Wake Forest University Press, 1994.

Drawing Ballerinas. Loughcrew: Gallery Press, 2001.

The Flower Master. Oxford University Press, 1981.

Marconi's Cottage. Winston Salem: Wake Forest University Press and Loughcrew: Gallery Press, 1991.

On Ballycastle Beach. Oxford University Press, 1987.

'Rescuers and White Cloaks: Diary 1968–69', *My Self, My Muse: Irish Women Poets Reflect on Life and Art*. Ed. Patricia Boyle Haberstroh. New York: Syracuse University Press, 2001.

Selected Poems, 1978–1994. Winston-Salem: Wake Forest University Press and Loughcrew: Gallery Press, 1997.

Shelmalier. Winston-Salem: Wake Forest University Press and Loughcrew: Gallery Press, 1998.

Soldiers of Year Two. Winston-Salem: Wake Forest University Press, 2002.

Venus and the Rain. Oxford University Press, 1984.

Brandes, Rand. 'Interview with Medbh McGuckians', *Chattahoochee Review*. 16.3 (Spring, 1996).

Hobbs, John. '"My Words Are Traps": An Interview with Medbh McGuckian'. *New Hibernia Review*, 2.1 (Spring, 1998).

Murphy, Shane. 'Obliquity in the Poetry of Paul Muldoon and Medbh McGuckian'. *Éire-Ireland*, 31.3–4 (1996).

Meehan, Paula. *Mysteries of the Home: Selected Poems*. Newcastle: Bloodaxe, 1996.

Mhac an tSaoi, Máire. *An Cion go dtí Seo*. Dublin: Sáirséal – Ó Marcaigh, 1987, repr. 1988.

Trasládáil. Belfast: Lagan, 1997.

Montague, John. *A Chosen Life*. London: Duckworth, 2001.

Collected Poems. Loughcrew: Gallery Press, 1995.

The Figure in the Cave and Other Essays, ed. Antoinette Quinn. Dublin: Lilliput & New York: Syracuse University Press, 1989.

The Rough Field, Dublin: Dolmen, 1972.

Smashing the Piano. Loughcrew: Gallery Press, 1999.

Irish University Review: John Montague Special Issue. 19, 1 (1989).

Mooney, Martin. *Grub*. Belfast: Blackstaff, 1993.

Rasputin and his Children. Blackwater, 2000.

Morrissey, Sinéad. *Between Here and There*. Manchester: Carcanet, 2002.

There Was Fire in Vancouver. Manchester: Carcanet, 1996.

Muldoon, Paul. *Collected Poems: 1968–1998*. London: Faber and Farrar, Straus & Giroux, 2001.

'Getting Round: Notes Towards an *Ars Poetica*.' *Essays in Criticism*, 48, 2 (April, 1998).

New Weather, 2nd edn. London: Faber, 1994.

The Prince of the Quotidian. Loughcrew: Gallery Press, 1994.

To Ireland, I. Oxford University Press, 2000.

Batten, Guinn. ' "He Could Barely Tell One from the Other": The Borderline Disorders of Paul Muldoon's Poetry'. *South Atlantic Quarterly*, 95, 1 (Winter, 1996).

Keller, Lynn. 'An Interview with Paul Muldoon'. *Contemporary Poetry*, 35.1 (Spring, 1994).

Kendall, Tim. *Paul Muldoon*. Bridgend: Seren, 1996.

and Peter McDonald (eds.). *Paul Muldoon: Critical Essays*. Liverpool University Press, 2003.

Murphy, Shane. 'Obliquity in the Poetry of Paul Muldoon and Medbh McGuckian'. *Éire-Ireland* 31, 3–4 (1996).

' "The Eye that Scanned It": The Picture Poems of Heaney, Muldoon, and McGuckian'. *New Hibernia Review*, 4.4 (Winter, 2000).

Smith, Kevin. 'Lunch with Pancho Villa'. (interview) *Rhinoceros* 4 (1990).

Tell, Carol. 'Utopia in the New World: Paul Muldoon's America'. *Bullan* 2.2 (1996).

Wills, Clair. *Reading Paul Muldoon*, Newcastle: Bloodaxe, 1998.

Murphy, Richard. *Collected Poems*. Loughcrew: Gallery Press, 1999.

The Kick: A Memoir. London: Granta, 2002.

Harmon, Maurice (ed.). *Richard Murphy: Poet in Two Traditions*. Dublin: Wolfhound Press, 1978.

Ní Chuilleanáin, Eiléan. *Acts and Monuments*. Loughcrew: Gallery Press, 1972.

The Brazen Serpent. Winston Salem, NC: Wake Forest University Press and Loughcrew: Gallery Press, 1991.

The Girl Who Married the Reindeer. Loughcrew: Gallery Press, 2002.

The Magdalene Sermon. Loughcrew: Gallery Press, 1989 and Winston Salem, NC: Wake Forest University Press, 1991.

'Nuns: A Subject for a Woman Writer'. *My Self, My Muse: Irish Women Poets Reflect on Life and Art*. Ed. Patricia Boyle Haberstroh. Syracuse University Press, 2001.

The Rose Geranium. Loughcrew: Gallery Press, 1981.

The Second Voyage. Winston Salem, NC: Wake Forest University Press and Loughcrew: Gallery Press, 1977.

Site of Ambush. Loughcrew: Gallery Press, 1975.

Kerrigan, John. 'Hidden Ireland: Eiléan Ní Chuilleanáin and Munster Poetry'. *Critical Quarterly* 40.4 (Winter 1998).

Johnston, Dillon. ' "Our Bodies' Eyes and Writing Hands": Secrecy and Sensuality in Ní Chuilleanáin's Baroque Art'. *Gender and Sexuality in Modern Ireland*, Anthony Bradley and Maryann Gialanella Valiulis (eds.). Amherst, MA.: University of Massachusetts, 1997.

Ní Dhomhnaill, Nuala and Paul Muldoon (trans.). *The Astrakhan Cloak*. Winston Salem, NC: Wake Forest University Press and Loughcrew: Gallery Press, 1992.

Cead Aighnis. An Daingean: An Sagart, 1998.

Feis. Maynooth: An Sagart, 1991.

'The Hidden Ireland: Women's Inheritance', in Theo Dorgan (ed.). *Irish Poetry Since Kavanagh*. Dublin: Four Courts, 1996.

Pharaoh's Daughter. Winston Salem: Wake Forest University Press and Loughcrew: Gallery Press, 1990.

Selected Poems/Rogha Dánta. Michael Hartnett (trans). Dublin: Raven Arts, 1988.

The Water Horse. Medbh McGuckian and Eiléan Ní Chuilleanáin (trans.). Loughcrew: Gallery Press, 1999 and Winston Salem: Wake Forest University Press, 2000.

'Why I Choose to Write in Irish'. *The New York Times Book Review*, January 8 1995.

Hollo, Kaarina. 'Acts of Translation: An Interview with Nuala Ní Dhomhnaill'. *Edinburgh Review* 99 (Spring 1998).

McDiarmid, Lucy and M. Durkan. 'Question and Answer: Nuala Ní Dhomhnaill'. *Irish Literary Supplement* (Fall 1987).

Sewell, Frank. *Modern Irish Poetry: A New Alhambra*. Oxford University Press, 2001.

O'Callaghan, Conor. *The History of Rain*. Loughcrew: Gallery Press, 1993.

Seatown. Loughcrew: Gallery Press, 1999.

O'Callaghan, Julie. *Edible Anecdotes*. Dublin: Dolmen, 1983.

No Can Do. Newcastle: Bloodaxe, 2000.

What's What. Newcastle: Bloodaxe, 1991.

Ó Direáin, Máirtín. *Béasa an Túir*. Dublin: An Clóchomhar, 1984.
Craobhóg Dán. Dublin: An Clóchomhar, 1986.
Dánta 1939–1979. Dublin: An Clóchomhar, 1980.
Mac Giolla Léith, Caoimhín (ed.), *Cime Mar Chách: Aistí ar Mháirtín Ó Direáin*. Dublin: Coiscéim, 1993.
O'Donoghue, Bernard. *Gunpowder*. London: Chatto, 1995.
Here nor There. London: Chatto, 1999.
The Weakness. London: Chatto, 1991.
O'Driscoll, Denis. *The Bottom Line*. Dublin: Dedalus, 1994.
Hidden Extras. Dublin: Dedalus, 1987.
Kist. Dublin: Dolmen, 1982.
Long Short Story. Dublin: Dedalus, 1993.
Quality Time. London: Anvil, 1997.
Troubled Thoughts, Majestic Dreams: Selected Prose. Loughcrew: Gallery Press, 2001.
Weather Permitting. London: Anvil, 1999.
O'Grady, Desmond. *The Headgear of the Tribe: Selected Poems*. Ed. Peter Fallon. Loughcrew: Gallery Press, 1979.
The Road Taken: Poems 1956–96. University of Salzburg Press, 1996.
O'Loughlin, Michael. *Another Nation: New and Selected Poems*. Dublin: New Island Books, 1996.
O'Malley, Mary. *A Consideration of Silk*. Galway: Salmon, 1990.
The Knife in the Wave. Galway: Salmon, 1993.
Where the Rocks Float. Galway: Salmon, 1997.
Ó Muirthile, Liam. *Tine Chnámh*. Dublin: Sáirséal Ó Marcaigh, 1984.
An Peann Coitianta. Dublin: Comhar, 1991.
Dialann Bóthair. Loughcrew: Gallery Press, 1992.
An Peann Coitianta 2: 1992–1997. Dublin: Cois Life Tta, 1997.
Walking Time: agus dánta eile. Indreabhán: Cló Iar-Chonnachta, 2000.
O'Reilly, Caitriona. *The Nowhere Birds*. Newcastle: Bloodaxe, 2001.
Ó Ríordáin, Seán. *Eireaball Spideoige*. 1952. Dublin: Sáirséal and Dill, 1986.
Brosna 1964. Dublin: Sáirséal and Dill, 1987.
Tar Éis Mo Bháis 1978. Dublin: Sáirséal and Dill, 1986.
Ó Coileáin, Seán. *Seán Ó Ríordáin: Beatha agus Saothar*. Dublin: An Clóchomhar, 1982, repr. 1985.
Sewell, Frank. 'Seán Ó Ríordáin: Joycery-Corkery-Sorcery', in *The Irish Review*, 23 (Winter 1998).
Ormsby, Frank. *The Ghost Train*. Loughcrew: Gallery Press, 1995.
A Northern Spring. London: Secker and Warburg, 1986.
A Store of Candles. Oxford University Press, 1977.
Ó Searcaigh, Cathal. *An Bealach 'na Bhaile / Homecoming*. Indreabhán: Cló Iar-Chonnachta, 1993).
Na Buachaillí Bána. Indreabhán: Cló Iar-Chonnachta, 1996.
Out in the Open. (trans. Frank Sewell), Indreabhán: Cló Iar-Chonnachta, 1997.
An Tnúth leis an tSolas. Indreabhán: Cló Iar-Chonnachta, 2001.
Longley, Michael. 'A Going Back to Sources'. *Poetry Ireland Review* 39 (Autumn, 1993).

Sealy, Dúghlas. Untitled review of Ó Searcaigh. *Homecoming / An Bealach 'na Bhaile*, in *Comhar* (July 1993).

Sewell, Frank. *Modern Irish Poetry: A New Alhambra*. Oxford University Press, 2001.

O'Siadhail, Michael. *Poems: 1975–1995*. Newcastle: Bloodaxe, 1999.

Ó Tuairisc, Eoghan / Eugene Watters. *Lux Aeterna*. Dublin: Allen Figgis, 1964.

The Week-End of Dermot and Grace. Dublin: Allen Figgis, 1964.

Poetry Ireland Review: Eugene Watters Special Issue, No. 13 (Spring 1985).

Paulin, Tom. *The Day-Star of Liberty: William Hazlitt's Radical Style*. London: Faber, 1998.

Fivemiletown. London: Faber, 1987.

The Invasion Handbook. London: Faber, 2002.

Liberty Tree. London: Faber, 1983.

The Strange Museum. London: Faber, 1980.

Walking a Line. London: Faber, 1994.

The Wind Dog. London: Faber, 1999.

Writing to the Moment: Selected Critical Essays, 1980–1996. London: Faber, 1996.

Flint, Kate, 'Face to Face'. (interview), *The English Review* 4.1 (September, 1993).

Hardy, Jane. 'The Dust over a Battlefield'. (interview), *Poetry Review* 87.1 (Spring, 1997).

Hughes, Eamonn. 'Q&A with Tom Paulin'. *Irish Literary Supplement* 7.2 (1991).

Raphael, Tom. "The Promised Land". (interview), *Oxford Poetry* 7.1 (1983).

Powerscourt, Sheila. *Sun Too Fast*. London: Geoffrey Bles, 1974.

Quinn, Justin. *Fuselage*. Loughcrew: Gallery Press, 2002.

'The Irish Efflorescence'. *Poetry Review* vol. 91 no. 3 (Autumn 2001).

The 'O'o'a'a' Bird. Manchester: Carcanet, 1995.

Privacy. Manchester: Carcanet, 1999.

Redmond, John. *Thumb's Width*. Manchester: Carcanet, 2001.

Rooney-Céspedes, Aidan. *Day Release*. Loughcrew: Gallery Press, 2000.

Rosenstock, Gabriel. *Conlán: dánta le Seamus Heaney*. Dublin: Coiscéim, 1989.

Rogha Rosenstock. Indreabhán: Cló Iar-Chonnacta, 1994.

Sheerin, Joe. *A Crack in the Ice*. Gerrards Cross: Colin Smythe, 1995.

Elves in the Wainscotting. Manchester: Carcanet, 2002.

Simmons, James. *Poems 1956–1986*. Loughcrew: Gallery Press, 1986.

Sirr, Peter. *Bring Everything*. Loughcrew: Gallery Press, 2000.

The Ledger of Fruitful Exchange. Loughcrew: Gallery Press, 1995.

Marginal Zones. Loughcrew: Gallery Press, 1984.

Talk, Talk. Loughcrew: Gallery Press, 1987.

Ways of Falling. Loughcrew: Gallery Press, 1991.

Sweeney, Matthew. *Selected Poems*. London: Jonathan Cape, 2002.

Tinley, Bill. *Grace*. Dublin: New Island Books, 2001.

Wheatley, David. *Misery Hill*. Loughcrew: Gallery Press, 2000.

Thirst. Loughcrew: Gallery Press, 1997.

Wingfield, Sheila. *Collected Poems 1938–1983*. London: Enitharmon, 1983.

Wyley, Enda. *Eating Baby Jesus*. Dublin: Dedalus, 1994.

Socrates in the Garden. Dublin: Dedalus, 1998.

Anthologies

Barry, Sebastian (ed.). *The Inherited Boundaries: Younger Poets of the Republic of Ireland*. Dublin: Dolmen, 1986.

Bolger, Dermot (ed.). *The Bright Wave / An Tonn Gheal*. Dublin: Raven Arts, 1991.

Crotty, Patrick (ed.). *Modern Irish Poetry: An Anthology*. Belfast: Blackstaff, 1995.

Dawe, Gerald (ed.). *The Younger Irish Poets*. Belfast: Blackstaff, 1982.

Dawe, Gerald (ed.). *The New Younger Irish Poets*. Belfast: Blackstaff, 1991.

Deane, Seamus (gen. ed.). *The Field Day Anthology of Irish Writing*, 3 vols. Derry: Field Day Publications, 1991.

Delanty, Greg and Nuala Ní Dhomhnaill (eds.). *Jumping off Shadows: Selected Contemporary Irish Poets*. Cork University Press, 1995.

Denvir, Gearóid (ed.). *Duanaire an Chéid*. Indreabhán: Cló Iar-Chonnachta, 2000.

Duffy, Noel and T. Dorgan (eds.). *Watching the River Flow: A Century in Irish Poetry*. Dublin: Poetry Ireland, 1999.

Fallon, Peter and Derek Mahon (eds.). *The Penguin Book of Contemporary Irish Poetry*. Harmondsworth: Penguin, 1990.

Fitzmaurice, Gabriel (ed.). *Irish Poetry Now: Other Voices*. Dublin: Wolfhound, 1993.

Kennelly, Brendan (ed.). *The Penguin Book of Irish Verse*. Harmondsworth: Penguin, 1979.

Kiberd, Declan (ed.). 'Contemporary Irish Poetry', in Deane (ed.), *The Field Day Anthology of Irish Writing*, Volume III. Derry: Field Day Publications, 1991.

Kiberd, Declan and Gabriel Fitzmaurice (eds.). *An Crann faoi Bhláth / The Flowering Tree*. Dublin: Wolfhound, 1991.

Kinsella, Thomas (ed.). *The New Oxford Book of Irish Verse*. Oxford University Press, 1986.

Longley, Edna (ed.). *The Bloodaxe Book of 20th Century Poetry from Britain and Ireland*. Newcastle: Bloodaxe, 2001.

Longley, Michael (ed.). *20th Century Irish Poems*. London: Faber, 2002.

Mahon, Derek (ed.). *The Sphere Book of Modern Irish Poetry*. London: Sphere Books, 1972.

Montague, John (ed.). *Bitter Harvest: An Anthology of Contemporary Irish Verse*. New York: Scribner, 1989.

Montague, John (ed.). *The Faber Book of Irish Verse*. London: Faber, 1974.

Muldoon, Paul (ed.). *The Faber Book of Contemporary Irish Poetry*. London: Faber, 1986.

O'Brien, Peggy (ed.). *The Wake Forest Book of Irish Women's Poetry 1967–2000*. Wake Forest University Press, 2000.

Ormsby, Frank (ed.). *Poets of the North of Ireland*, 2nd edn. Belfast: Blackstaff, 1990.

Ormsby, Frank (ed.). *A Rage for Order: Poetry of the Northern Ireland Troubles*. Belfast: Blackstaff, 1992.

Various editors. *The Field Day Anthology of Irish Writing, Vols IV & V: Woman's Writing and Traditions*. Cork University Press, 2002.

Irish Poetry: Criticism

Andrews, Elmer (ed.). *Contemporary Irish Poetry*. Basingstoke: Macmillan, 1992.

Andrews, Elmer (ed.). 'The Belfast Group: A Symposium'. *Honest Ulsterman* 54 (Nov/Dec 1976).

Brearton, Fran. *The Great War in Irish Poetry: W.B. Yeats to Michael Longley*. Oxford University Press, 2000.

Brown, John. *In the Chair: Interviews with Poets from the North of Ireland*. Clare: Salmon, 2002.

Brown, Terence. *Northern Voices: Poets from Ulster*. Dublin: Gill and Macmillan, 1975.

Brown, Terence and Nicholas Grene (eds.). *Tradition and Influence in Anglo-Irish Poetry*. London: Macmillan, 1989.

Clutterbuck, Catriona. 'Gender and Self-Representation in Irish Poetry: The Critical Debate'. *Bullán* 4, 1 (Autumn 1998).

Coughlan, Patricia and Alex Davis (eds.). *Modernism and Ireland: The Poetry of the 1930s*. Cork University Press, 1995.

Corcoran, Neil. *After Yeats and Joyce: Reading Modern Irish Literature*. Oxford University Press, 1997.

Corcoran, Neil (ed.). *The Chosen Ground: Essays on the Contemporary Poetry of Northern Ireland*. Bridgend: Seren Books, 1992.

Poets of Modern Ireland. Cardiff: University of Wales, 1999.

Dawe, Gerald. *Against Piety: Essays in Irish Poetry*. Belfast: Lagan, 1995.

Dillane Fionnuala. 'Changing the Map: Contemporary Irish Women's Poetry'. *Verse* vol. 16 no. 2, n. d. [1999].

Dorgan, Theo (ed.). *Irish Poetry Since Kavanagh*. Dublin: Four Courts, 1996.

Duffy, Noel and Theo Dorgan (eds). *Watching the River Flow: A Century in Irish Poetry*. Dublin: Poetry Ireland, 1999.

Garratt, Robert F. *Modern Irish Poetry: Tradition and Continuity from Yeats to Heaney*. Berkeley & London: University of California, 1986.

Gonzalez, Alexander. *Contemporary Irish Women Poets: Some Male Perspectives*. Westport, CN: Greenwood, 1999.

Goodby, John. *Irish Poetry Since 1950: From Stillness Into History*. Manchester University Press, 2000.

Gregson, Ian. *The Male Image: Representations of Masculinity in Postwar Poetry*. Basingstoke: Macmillan, 1999.

Grennan, Eamon. *Facing the Music: Irish Poetry in the Twentieth Century*. Omaha: Creighton University Press, 1999.

Haberstroh, Patricia Boyle (ed.). *My Self, My Muse: Irish Women Poets Reflect on Life and Art*. New York: Syracuse University Press, 2001.

Haberstroh, Patricia Boyle (ed.). *Women Creating Women: Contemporary Irish Women Poets*. New York: Syracuse University Press, 1996.

Haffenden, John. *Viewpoints: Poets in Conversation*. London: Faber, 1981.

Herbert, W.N. and Matthew Hollis (eds.). *Strong Words: Modern Poets on Modern Poetry*. Newcastle: Bloodaxe, 2000.

Johnston, Dillon. *Irish Poetry after Joyce*. 2nd edn. New York: Syracuse University Press, 1996.

The Poetic Economies of England and Ireland, 1912–2000. London: Macmillan, 2001.

Kelly, Aaron (ed.). *Critical Ireland: New Essays in Literature and Culture*. Dublin: Four Courts, 2001.

Kenneally, Michael (ed.). *Poetry in Contemporary Irish Literature*. Gerrards Cross: Colin Smythe, 1995.

Kennedy, David. *New Relations: The Refashioning of British Poetry, 1980–1992*. Bridgend: Seren, 1996.

Longley, Edna. *The Living Stream: Literature and Revisionism in Ireland*. Newcastle: Bloodaxe, 1994.

Poetry and Posterity. Newcastle: Bloodaxe, 2000.

Poetry in the Wars. Newcastle: Bloodaxe, 1986.

Mahon, Derek. 'Poetry in Northern Ireland', *Twentieth Century Studies*, 4 (November 1970).

Matthews, Stephen. *Irish Poetry: Politics, History, Negotiation*. London: Macmillan, 1997.

McCormack, W.J. *From Burke to Beckett: Ascendancy, Tradition and Betrayal in Literary History*. Cork University Press, 1994.

MacDonagh, Thomas. *Literature in Ireland: Studies Irish and Anglo-Irish* (1916) Dublin: Relay, 1996.

McDonald, Peter. *Mistaken Identities: Poetry and Northern Ireland*. Oxford: Clarendon, 1997.

Serious Poetry: Form and Authority from Yeats to Hill. Oxford University Press, 2002.

Metre 3 (Autumn 1997 – Symposium on Irish Diasporic Writing).

Montague, John. *The Figure in the Cave and Other Essays*, ed. Antoinette Quinn. Syracuse University Press, 1989.

Murphy, Mike. *Reading the Future: Irish Writers in Conversation with Mike Murphy*. Dublin: Lilliput, 2000.

O'Brien, Sean. *The Deregulated Muse: Essays on Contemporary British and Irish Poetry*. Newcastle: Bloodaxe, 1998.

O'Driscoll, Denis. *Troubled Thoughts, Majestic Dreams: Selected Prose*. Loughcrew: Gallery, 2001.

Ó Dúill, Gréagóir (ed.). *Fearann Pinn: Filíocht 1900 go 1999*. Dublin: Coiscéim, 2000.

Paulin Tom. *Minotaur: Poetry and the Nation State* (London: Faber, 1992).

Princeton University Library Chronicle (Special Issue on Irish Poetry), 59, 3 (1998).

Schirmer, Gregory A. *Out of What Began: A History of Irish Poetry in English*. Ithaca: Cornell University Press.

Scully, James (ed.). *Modern Poets on Poetry*. London: Collins, 1966.

Sewell, Frank. *Modern Irish Poetry: A New Alhambra*. Oxford University Press, 2000.

Smith, Michael. 'Irish Poetry Since Yeats: Notes Towards a Corrected History'. *Denver Quarterly*, 5 (1971).

Smith, Michael (ed.). *The Lace Curtain* (1969–78).

Storey, Mark (ed.). *Poetry and Ireland Since 1800: A Source Book*. London: Routledge, 1988.

General criticism and history

Bradley, Anthony and Maryann Gialanella Valiulis (eds). *Gender and Sexuality in Modern Ireland*. University of Massachusetts Press, 1997.

Brown, Terence. *Ireland's Literature*. Gigginstown: Lilliput, 1988.

Ireland: a Social and Cultural History 1922–1985. London: Fontana Books, 1985.

Buckley, Vincent. *Memory Ireland: Insights into the Contemporary Irish Condition*. New York: Penguin Books, 1985.

Cairns, David and Shaun Richards. *Writing Ireland: Colonialism, Nationalism and Culture*. Manchester University Press, 1988.

Carlson, Julia (ed.). *Banned in Ireland: Censorship & the Irish Writer*. London: Routledge, 1990.

Corkery, Daniel. *The Hidden Ireland: a Study of Gaelic Munster in the Eighteenth Century* (1924). Dublin: Gill and Macmillan, 1970.

Synge and Anglo-Irish Literature. Cork University Press, 1931.

Cronin, Anthony. *Dead as Doornails*. Dublin: Dolmen, 1976.

Cronin, Michael. *Translating Ireland: Translations, Languages, Cultures*. Cork University Press, 1996.

Deane Seamus. *Celtic Revivals: Essays in Modern Irish Literature, 1880–1980*. London: Faber, 1985.

Dunn, Douglas (ed.). *Two Decades of Irish Writing: A Critical Survey*. Manchester: Carcanet, 1975.

Foster, Hal. *The Return of the Real: The Avant-Garde at the End of the Century*. Cambridge, MA: MIT, 1996.

Foster, John Wilson. *Colonial Consequences: Essays in Irish Literature and Culture*. Dublin: Lilliput, 1991.

Foster, R.F. *Modern Ireland 1600–1972*. Harmondsworth: Penguin, 1988.

The Irish Story: Telling Tales and Making it Up in Ireland. Harmondsworth: Penguin, 2001.

Gibbons, Luke. *Transformations in Irish Culture*. Cork University Press, 1996.

Graham, Colin. *Deconstructing Ireland: Identity, Theory, Culture*. Edinburgh University Press, 2001.

Graham, Colin and Richard Kirkland (eds.). *Ireland and Cultural Theory*. London: Macmillan, 1999.

Greene, Miranda. *A Dictionary of Celtic Myth and Legend*. London: Thames and Hudson, 1992.

Houen, Alex. *Terrorism and Modern Literature from Joseph Conrad to Ciaran Carson*. Oxford University Press, 2002.

Kearney, Richard. *Transitions: Narrative in Modern Irish Culture*. Dublin: Wolfhound, 1988.

and Mark Patrick Hederman (eds.). *The Crane Bag Book of Irish Studies*. Gerrards Cross: Colin Smythe, 1983.

Kiberd, Declan. *Idir Dhá Chultúr*. Dublin: Coiscéim, 1993.

Inventing Ireland: The Literature of the Modern Nation. London: Jonathan Cape, 1995.

Irish Classics. Cambridge: Harvard University Press, 2000.

Kirkland, Richard. *Literature and Culture in Northern Ireland Since 1965: Moments of Danger*. London: Longman, 1996.

Lee, J.J. *Ireland 1912–1985: Politics and Society*. Cambridge University Press, 1989.

Lloyd, David. *Anomalous States: Irish Writing and the Post-Colonial Moment*. Dublin: Lilliput, 1993.

Nationalism and Minor Literature: James Clarence Mangan and the Emergence of Irish Cultural Nationalism. Berkeley and London: University of California, 1987.

Mahony, Christina Hunt. *Contemporary Irish Literature: Transforming Tradition*. New York: St Martin's, 1998.

Martin, Augustine. *Bearing Witness: Essays on Anglo-Irish Literature*. ed. Anthony Roche. University College Dublin, 1996.

McCarthy, Conor. *Modernisation: Crisis and Culture in Ireland, 1969–1992*. Dublin: Four Courts, 2000.

O'Brien Johnson, Toni and Shaun Richards. *Gender in Irish Writing*. Milton Keynes: Open University Press, 1991.

Ó Tuama, Sean. *Repossessions: Selected Essays on the Irish Literary Heritage*. Cork University Press, 1995.

Roberts, Neil. *Narrative and Voice in Postwar Poetry*. London: Longman, 1999.

Robinson, Alan. *Instabilities in Contemporary British Poetry*. London: Macmillan, 1988.

Ryan, Ray ed. *Writing in the Irish Republic: Literature, Culture, Politics 1949–1999*. London: Macmillan, 2000.

Sheppard, Robert. *Far Language: Poetics and Linguistically Innovative Poetry*. Exeter: Stride, 1999.

Sloan, Barry. *Writers and Protestantism in the North of Ireland: Heirs to Damnation*. Dublin: Irish Academic Press, 2000.

Smyth, Gerry. *Decolonisation and Criticism: The Construction of Irish Literature*. London: Pluto, 1998.

South Atlantic Quarterly: Special Issue on Irish Cultural Studies (ed. John Paul Waters). 95, 1 (Winter, 1996).

Stewart, A.T.Q. *The Narrow Ground*. (1977). London: Faber, 1989.

Walshe, Éibhear (ed.). *Sex, Nation and Dissent in Irish Writing*. Cork University Press, 1997.

Welch, Robert (ed.). *The Oxford Companion to Irish Literature*. Oxford: Clarendon, 1996.

Welch, Robert (ed.). *Irish Writers and Religion*. Gerrards Cross: Colin Smythe, 1992.

Williams, John, Ellis Caerwyn and Máirín Ní Mhuiríosa. *Traidisiún Liteartha na nGael*. Dublin: An Clóchomhar, 1979.

Wills, Clair. *Improprieties: Politics and Sexuality in Northern Irish Poetry*. Oxford: Clarendon, 1993.

Wilson, R. and Somerville-Arjat, G. *Sleeping with Monsters: Conversations with Scottish and Irish Women Poets*. Dublin: Wolfhound, 1990.

INDEX

CAMBRIDGE COMPANIONS TO LITERATURE

CAMBRIDGE COMPANIONS TO CULTURE